THE MEXICAN REVOLUTION

an annotated guide

to recent scholarship

*Reference
Publications
in
Latin American
Studies*

William V. Jackson
Editor

THE MEXICAN REVOLUTION

*an annotated guide
to recent scholarship*

W. DIRK RAAT

G.K.HALL&CO.

70 LINCOLN STREET, BOSTON, MASS.

Library of Congress Cataloging in Publication Data

Raat, W. Dirk (William Dirk), 1939-
  The Mexican Revolution.

  Includes indexes.
  1. Mexico—History—1910-1946—Bibliography.
  2. Mexico—History—1910-1946—Historiography. I. Title.
  Z1426.5.R15 1982 [F1234]   016.97208'2   82-11783
  ISBN 0-8161-8352-X

This publication is printed on permanent/durable acid-free paper
MANUFACTURED IN THE UNITED STATES OF AMERICA

to Kelly and Michael

Contents

Contents

Contents

The Author

W. Dirk Raat is Director of International Education
and professor of history at the State University of
New York at Fredonia. He is past president
of the New York State Latin Americanists (NYSLA) and
author of several articles on Mexican history that have
appeared in major journals in English, Spanish, and
Japanese. One of these articles received the James A.
Robertson Award from the Conference on Latin American
History. His published books include El positivismo
durante el porfiriato; Revoltosos: Mexico's Rebels
in the United States, 1903-1923; and Mexico: From
Independence to Revolution, 1810-1910.

Preface

The last two decades, 1960–1980, have witnessed an important change in the quality and quantity of Mexican revolutionary studies. The subject matter of the history of the Mexican Revolution, sometimes writ large to be synonymous with twentieth-century Mexico, has become a topic of interest to Mexicans and non-Mexicans alike. The Tlatelolco massacre of 1968 naturally led many thinking Mexicans to question the achievements of the Revolutionary Party and tradition. Fidel Castro's revolution in Cuba prompted many Europeans, especially French and Soviet writers, to compare the Mexican and Cuban revolutionary experiences. Since 1970 Asiatic scholars and other "third world" students have considered Mexico to be an important case study in revolution, development, and modernization. And, of course, the North American universities have been most prolific in their production of competent Mexicanists interested in dissecting the Mexican experience. Yet fascination with the topic has not led to comprehensive historiographies and bibliographies of the work produced since 1960. The present work is one attempt to fill the bibliographical gap. This is the only volume in English of recent publication that attempts both an in-depth historiographical analysis and an annotated bibliography of Mexican revolutionary studies.

The aim of this work is to assist the serious student, researcher, or professor to locate adequate materials on the topic of the Mexican Revolution. Although directed primarily at historians, this book should be of assistance to Mexicanists of various disciplines as well as the interested layman. Political scientists interested in the evolution of the modern bureaucratic state can certainly profit by studying the Mexican example. Economists and sociologists seeking information on social change, revolution (actual and theoretical), and modernization can gain much by observing the historical developments in Mexico. Educators, theologians, and philosophers might want to study educational, cultural, religious, and intellectual history. Businessmen and lawyers will find herein materials relating to economic, business, legal, and international history. The invitation is an open one.

Preface

Scope

This bibliography is designed to serve as a guide to books, monographs, and journal articles, published between 1960 and July 1980, on the subject of the history of the Mexican Revolution, 1900-1940. Delimiting the chronology of the Revolution to the years 1900-1940 is in agreement with conventional concepts of periodization. Comprehensive and theoretical works that treat the Revolution and related themes before 1900 and after 1940 are listed in chapter 3 under "General Works."

Limited to published books and articles, this bibliography is not comprehensive. Pamphlets and newspapers, for example, have been excluded. A truly comprehensive work would have been beyond the energies and resources of a single compiler. Whatever the book lacks in comprehensiveness should be more than compensated for by a unity of purpose and meaning that one person can bring to a bibliographical task such as this. In any case, an effort has been made to select books and articles that represent the major "traditional" and "revisionist" trends in recent revolutionary historiography. To make the bibliography representative, several works of limited accessibility have been included, especially biographical and regional studies published in provincial parts of Mexico and general and theoretical works published in Eastern Europe. The bibliography includes works published in the Americas and Europe, with emphasis upon Mexico, the United States, the United Kingdom, France, the Netherlands, the Federal Republic of Germany, and the Soviet Union.

This guide complements, but does not supplant, what is currently the best bibliographical guide to Mexican revolutionary history, the multivolume Fuentes de la historia contemporánea de México by Luis González and Stanley R. Ross (published between 1961 and 1967). Scholars interested in works published before 1960, including newspapers and pamphlets, are directed to that guide (see entries 13 and 24).

Methodology

The compiler used several bibliographical aids and guides in attempting to locate and describe relevant books and articles. All of these are described in chapter 1 under "Bibliographies, Guides, and Aids to Research." Of these the more useful were the Handbook of Latin American Studies, Veinticinco años de investigación histórica en México, Bibliografía Histórica Mexicana, and Historical Abstracts.

For three years, between 1977 and 1980, the compiler attempted to review physically each item through examining local library collections. While liberal use was made of the State University of New York interlibrary loan system, most research took place at the Nettie Lee Benson Latin American Collection at the University of Texas at Austin. In addition, the compiler worked in the following centers to examine the works of European authors: for British publications, the Institute of Latin American Studies at the University of London; for European books and articles, the Centro de Estudios y Documentación Latinoamericanos in Amsterdam, and the Ibero-Amerikanisches Institut Stiftung Preussischer Kulturbesitz in Berlin.

When materials could not be obtained for "in-hand" review, as was the case for many of the publications from provincial Mexico, an effort was made to locate at least two separate entries from bibliographies, indexes, or union lists.

Form of Entry

Each entry contains the usual bibliographical information for books and articles as suggested in A Manual of Style, 12th edition, revised (1969), published by the University of Chicago Press. For books this includes author, title, place of publication, publisher, and date. Where appropriate, names of compilers, editors, and translators have been noted. New or revised editions are also noted. References to journal articles consist of author, title of article, name of journal, volume number, date, and pagination. In a few cases it was not possible to complete a citation with volume numbers, dates, or the actual pagination. These instances are rare and are restricted to articles from the more obscure Mexican or European journals. Abbreviations have been limited to "key" journals as noted in the "Abbreviations" following the introductory discussion.

Spanish titles follow Spanish rules of capitalization as outlined in the MLA Style Sheet; that is, in titles of books only the first word and names of persons and places are capitalized, while in journal titles the predominant usage is to capitalize all major words. For purposes of consistency the words Revolución and Revolución Mexicana have been capitalized.

Most of the more than twelve hundred entries have descriptive annotations. In a few instances, where the work was considered to be especially significant, a lengthy critical annotation has been included. A work of this nature might be important because of innovative research techniques and methodology, creative use of sources, an imaginative interpretation, literary quality, or the place of the work in the historiography of the Mexican Revolution. Those entries that have very brief or no annotations were considered important titles to be included even though the compiler was unable to obtain the actual work for "in-hand" review. An exception to this are the many works in the biography section (chapter 7). Individually many are insignificant, yet collectively they testify to important popular and political trends in recent Mexico that will interest the historiographer of the Revolution.

Arrangement

Preceding the bibliography proper is an introductory discussion of recent trends in the historiography of the Mexican Revolution. This essay surveys the variety and type of historical works--books and articles--that have characterized the field during the last two decades, 1960-1980. Topics discussed include a description of new archival holdings, printed documents, bibliographical tools, historical criticism and methodology, and traditional and revisionist interpretations. This essay concludes with several examples of revisionist work and suggestions concerning future research needs. This historiographical essay is a brief review of the historical literature of the Mexican Revolution, and as such it should not be considered a detailed guide to the annotated bibliography that follows. If the reader so chooses, the essay can be used in conjunction with the bibliography. Several cross-references have been included so that works cited can be found in the annotated bibliography. Scholars not interested in historiography should consult the bibliography directly, using as aids the table of contents and indexes.

Organization of the bibliography is both topical and chronological, with cross-references included at the end of each section and subsection. The first chapter relates to bibliographical guides and aids to research. The compiler has attempted to make this chapter comprehensive so that the serious scholar and researcher can find works published before 1960, which are not included in the bibliography. This chapter describes bibliographies, indexes, aids and guides to research, archival guides, guides to theses and dissertations, geographical reference works, book reviews, specialized dictionaries and encyclopedias, and supplementary reference materials. As a complement to this discussion, the second chapter contains a description of works on historiography and methodology.

From chapter 3 on the work proceeds from the general to the specific. Chapter 3 treats of general works, many of which cover periods beginning before 1900 and ending after 1940. Several of these are either comprehensive or theoretical histories and could not be organized under a chronological heading. Chapters 4 through 7 deal with regional and state history, documentary sources (printed documents), memoirs, and biographies.

Chapters 8 through 11 treat successive periods of Mexican history. For example, chapter 8 covers the Porfiriato; that is, the old regime, especially the last decade of the Porfiriato, from 1900 to 1910, when the underlying causes of revolution developed. The remaining chapters refer to the Epic Revolution (1910-1920), the Northern Dynasty (1920-1934), and the Cárdenas Era (1934-1940). Within these chapters the reader can find subject matter headings for political, legal, and military history; diplomatic history and international affairs; economic and social history; religious and Church history; the history of education; and cultural and intellectual history.

The work concludes with a subject index and name index. The names of important places, events, and concepts have been included in the

subject index. These are ideas that derive from both titles and
annotations. The name index only includes the names of persons who
are authors, translators, editors, or compilers. All index references, as well as cross-references, refer to item number (not page
number).

Acknowledgments

In preparing this book I was fortunate to have the kind assistance of
very many associates and colleagues, as well as some institutional
funding. Of special importance was Stanley R. Ross of the University
of Texas at Austin, who inspired the work, suggested the European
dimension, and aided me in obtaining funds. I am also particularly
indebted to individuals associated with the Mexican Studies Committee
of the Conference on Latin American History, especially William H.
Beezley, G. Michael Riley, and Richard E. Greenleaf. Other colleagues
who aided me include Nettie Lee Benson, of the University of Texas at
Austin; Magnus B. Mörner, of the University of Pittsburgh and Latin-
Amerika-Institutet, Stockholm; and Marvin D. Bernstein, of the State
University of New York at Buffalo. The staff of the New York Public
Library was also helpful.

In Europe I was assisted by the following: Harold Blakemore,
Secretary, and Alan Biggins, Assistant Librarian, Institute of Latin
American Studies, London; Raymond Th. J. Buve, University of Leiden;
Rudolf de Jong, Director, Hispanic Materials, International Instituut
voor sociale geschiedenis, Amsterdam; Fred Jongkind and Anneke M.C.
Roos, Centro de Estudios y Documentación Latinoamericanos (CEDLA),
Amsterdam; Reinhard Liehr, University of Bielefeld; and Wilhelm
Stegmann and Wolfgang Ulland, Ibero-Amerikanisches Institut Stiftung
Preussischer Kulturbesitz, Berlin. Of my friends in Mexico, I
especially acknowledge the assistance of Lucila Flamand, of the
Archivo de la Secretaría de Relaciones Exteriores. Editorial assis-
tance was provided by Professor William V. Jackson, Janice Meagher,
and Karin Kiewra.

Finally, a special thanks to colleagues and students at the State
University of New York at Fredonia, in particular Gary D. Barber,
Robert H. Deming, Marvin Lunenfeld, Dennis R. Preston, Robert C.
Schweik, Jon W. Weekly, Clark M. Zlotchew, Ed Fraser, Suzanne Gawron,
and Shirley Pruitt. Mary Notaro typed the bibliography. The Research
Foundation of the State University of New York provided a grant-in-
aid for summer travel and study in Europe. The Mexican Studies
Committee of the Conference on Latin American History assisted with
a modest travel allowance for work at the University of Texas at
Austin, as did the Office of the Vice President for Academic Affairs,
SUNY, Fredonia.

Prefacio

Durante las dos últimas décadas (1960-1980), se ha efectuado un cambio importante en la calidad y en la cantidad de estudios sobre la Revolución Mexicana. El estudio de la historia de la Revolución Mexicana, historia a veces concebida en términos que la equiparan con el México del siglo XX, ha captado el interés tanto de no=mexicanos como de mexicanos. Naturalmente, la matanza de Tlatelolco de 1968 resultó en que muchos mexicanos pensantes pusieran en tela de juicio los logros del Partido Revolucionario y de la tradición. La revolución de Fidel Castro en Cuba hizo que muchos europeos, sobre todo escritores franceses y soviéticos, comparasen las experiencias revolucionarias mexicana y cubana. Desde 1970, los eruditos asiáticos y otros estudiosos del "Tercer Mundo" han considerado a México como un importante caso clínico del proceso revolucionario, del desarrollo, y de la modernización. Y, desde luego, las universidades norteamericanas han sido abundantemente prolíficas en la producción de mexicanistas competentes que se interesan por disecar la experiencia mexicana. No obstante, la fascinación que suscita este tema no nos ha llevado a la producción de historiografías y bibliografías comprensivas que abarquen todas las obras aparecidas desde 1960. Esta obra es una tentativa de llenar la laguna bibliográfica que existe. Éste es el único volumen en lengua inglesa de publicación reciente que intenta tanto un análisis historiográfico profundo como una bibliografía comentada de estudios acerca de la Revolución Mexicana.

Aunque dirigido principalmente a historiadores, este libro será útil tanto a mexicanistas de diversas disciplinas como a los no profesionales que tienen interés en la materia. Los estudiosos de la ciencia política que se interesan por la evolución del estado burocrático moderno podrían, sin lugar a dudas, sacar provecho de un estudio del ejemplo mexicano. Los economistas y sociólogos deseosos de información sobre los cambios sociales, la revolución (concreta y teórica), y la modernización, pueden aprender mucho al observar su evolución histórica en México. Los educadores, teólogos y filósofos posiblemente quisieran estudiar la historia educacional, religiosa, e intelectual. Los hombres de negocios y abogados encontrarán, en estas páginas, materias relacionadas a la historia económica, comercial, legal, e internacional. Todos pueden aprovecharse.

Prefacio

Alcance del Libro

Esta bibliografía tiene como objeto servir de guía a los libros, monografías, y artículos de revistas eruditas publicados entre 1960 y julio de 1980 acerca de la historia de la Revolución Mexicana, 1900-1940. El delimitar la cronología de la Revolución a los años 1900-1940 concuerda con los conceptos convencionales de la periodización. Las obras comprensivas y teóricas que tratan de la Revolución y de temas afines y que son anteriores a 1900 y posteriores a 1940 quedan registradas en el capítulo 3 bajo la rúbrica "General Works" (Obras Generales).

Ya que se limita a libros y artículos publicados, ésta no es una bibliografía comprensiva. Se han excluido, por ejemplo, panfletos y diarios. Una obra realmente comprensiva habría sido superior a las energías y los recursos de un solo compilador. Lo que le puede faltar a este libro en cuanto a comprensividad debe compensarse con la unidad del propósito y del significado que una persona, trabajando solo, puede aportar a una tarea bibliográfica de esta índole. Sea como fuere, se ha hecho lo posible por seleccionar los libros y artículos que representan las principales tendencias "tradicionalistas" y "revisionistas" de la historiografía revolucionaria reciente. Para que la bibliografía sea representativa, se han incluido varias obras de accesibilidad limitada, especialmente los estudios biográficos y regionales publicados en las provincias mexicanas y las obras generales y teóricas publicadas en la Europa Oriental. Esta bibliografía incluye libros publicados en las Américas y en Europa, concentrándose en México, los Estados Unidos, el Reino Unido, Francia, los Países Bajos, la República Federal de Alemania, y la Unión Soviética.

Esta guía tiene como propósito complementar, y no suplantar, lo que actualmente es la mejor guía bibliográfica a la historia de la Revolución Mexicana, los múltiples tomos de Fuentes de la historia contemporánea de México por Luis González y Stanley R. Ross (publicados entre 1961 y 1967). Los estudiosos interesados en las obras publicadas antes de 1960, sin excluir diarios y panfletos, debieran dirigirse a esa guía (véanse artículos 13 y 24).

Metodología

El compilador ha usado varias ayudas y guías bibliográficas al procurar localizar y describir los libros y artículos pertinentes. Estas todas se hallan descritas en el capítulo 1 bajo la rúbrica "Bibliographies, Guides, and Aids to Research" ("Bibliografías, Guías, y Ayudas a la Investigación"). Entre éstas, las más útiles han sido el Handbook of Latin American Studies, Veinticinco años de investigación histórica en México, Bibliografía Histórica Mexicana, y Historical Abstracts.

Prefacio

Durante tres años, es decir entre 1977 y 1980, el compilador intentaba repasar físicamente cada obra examinando las colecciones de bibliotecas locales. Aunque se ha utilizado liberalmente el sistema de préstamos interbibliotecarios de la State University of New York, la mayor parte de la investigación se llevó a cabo en la Colección Latinoamericana Nettie Lee Benson de la University of Texas at Austin. Adicionalmente, el compilador ha trabajado en los siguientes centros para examinar las obras de autores europeos: para publicaciones británicas, el Instituto de Estudios Latinamericanos de la University of London; para libros y artículos europeos, el Centro de Estudios y Documentación Latinoamericanos de Amsterdam, y el Ibero-Amerikanisches Institut Stiftung Preussischer Kulturbesitz de Berlín.

Cuando ciertas obras no pudieron obtenerse para examen personal, como resultó con muchas de la publicaciones procedentes de las provincias mexicanas, se esforzaba por hallar por lo menos dos citas bibliográficas distintas en las bibliografías, índices, u otras listas.

Forma de la Cita Bibliográfica

Cada asiento contiene la información bibliográfica regular en cuanto a libros y artículos que sugiere A Manual of Style, duodécima edición revisada (1969), publicado por la University of Chicago Press. Tratándose de libros, esta información incluye el nombre del autor, título, lugar de publicación, casa editorial, y fecha. Se han apuntado los nombres de compiladores, anotadores y traductores cuando han venido al caso. Las ediciones nuevas o revisadas también han sido notadas. Las referencias a artículos de revistas eruditas constan del nombre del autor, título del artículo, nombre de la revista, número, fecha, y paginación. En unos pocos casos no fue posible completar la citación con las fechas o la paginación verdadera. Estos casos son escasos y se limitan a artículos procedentes de revistas mexicanas o europeas bastante desconocidas. Las abreviaturas se han limitado a las referencias a las revistas principales, como aclara la lista de abreviaturas ("Abbreviations") que sigue a la discusión introductoria.

Los títulos en castellano se atienen a las reglas referentes a la impresión de mayúsculas en español según la MLA Style Sheet, es decir, en los títulos de libros, únicamente la primara palabra y los nombres de personas y de lugares llevan mayúscula, mientras que la usanza predominante en los títulos de revistas se refleja en el empleo de mayúscula para todas las palabras principales. Para prestar cierta uniformidad, los términos Revolución y Revolución Mexicana siempre llevan mayúscula.

La mayoría de los artículos—hay más de mil doscientos—llevan anotaciones descriptivas. En algunos casos, donde se ha considerado que la obra tiene importancia extraordinaria, se han incluído unos comentarios críticos muy largos. Una obra de esta índole pudiera ser importante por las técnicas innovadoras de investigación y de metodología, la ultilización creativa de fuentes, la interpretación imaginativa, la calidad literaria, o la posición de la obra en la historio-

grafía de la Revolución Mexicana. Aquellos artículos que llevan anotaciones muy breves o que no tienen anotación alguna, el compilador
los incluyó por considerarlos suficientemente importantes aunque éste
no logró conseguir la obra misma para una reseña física. Las excep-
ciones son las muchas obras contenidas en la sección bibliográfica
(capítulo 7). Consideradas individualmente, muchas de éstas son poco
sustanciales; sin embargo, tomadas como un todo indican importantes
tendencias populares y políticas del México contemporáneo que intere-
sarán al historiógrafo de la Revolución Mexicana.

Formato

Una discusión introductoria de las tendencias recientes en la historiografía de la Revolución Mexicana precede a la bibliografía propia-
mente dicha. Este ensayo estudia la variedad y los tipos de las obras
históricas--tanto libros como artículos--que han caracterizado este
campo durante los dos últimas décadas, 1960-1980. Varios asuntos
quedan esbozados y discutidos, incluso una descripción de las nuevas
adquisiciones en los archivos, documentos impresos, instrumentos bi-
bliográficos, crítica histórica y metodología, e interpretaciones tradicionalistas y revisionistas. Este ensayo concluye con varios ejem-
plos de la obra revisionista y con indicaciones de lo que hace falta
a la investigación del futuro. Este ensayo historiográfico es una
breve reseña de los escritos sobre la Revolución Mexicana y por con-
siguiente no debiera considerarse como una guía detallada a la bibliografía anotada que lo sigue. Si el lector lo desea, el ensayo puede
emplearse en combinación con la bibliografía. Se han incluído varias
referencias ("see" y "see also" véase y véase también) de manera que
se puedan encontrar las obras referidas en la bibliografía anotada.
Los eruditos que no se interesan por la historiografía deberían con-
sultar la bibliografía directamente, empleando como ayudas el índice
general y los otros índices.

La organización de la bibliografía es temática y cronológica al
mismo tiempo; también hay contrarreferencias al final de cada división y subdivisión. El capítulo primero trata de guías bibliográficas y ayudas a la investigación. El compilador ha procurado hacer
que este capítulo sea comprensivo de modo que el estudioso y el inves-
tigador puedan encontrar obras publicadas antes de 1960, las cuales
no están incluídas en esta bibliografía. Este capítulo trata de bibliografías, índices, ayudas, y guías a la investigación, guías a los
archivos, guías a las tesis y disertaciones doctorales, obras geográ-
ficas de consulta, reseñas de libros, diccionarios y enciclopedias es-
pecializados, y materiales suplementarios de consulta. Como comple-
mento a esta discusión, el capítulo segundo contiene una descripción
de obras sobre historiografía y metodología.

Desde el capítulo 3 en adelante, la obra procede desde lo general
hasta lo particular. El capítulo 3 trata de obras generales, muchas
de las cuales tratan de períodos que comienzan antes de 1900 y que
terminan después de 1940. Varios de éstos son historias o comprensivas

o teóricas y no pudieron organizarse bajo un título cronológico. Los capítulos 4 a 7 tratan de historia regional y estatal, fuentes documentarias (documentos impresos), memorias, y biografías. Los capítulos 8 a 11 se refieren a períodos sucesivos de la historia mexicana. Por ejemplo, el capítulo 8 trata del Porfiriato; es decir, el antiguo régimen, sobre todo la última década del Porfiriato desde 1900 hasta 1910 cuando evolucionaron las causas subyacentes de la Revolución. Los capítulos restantes tratan de la Revolución Epica (1910-1920), la Dinastía del Norte (1920-1934), y la Epoca de Cárdenas (1934-1940). Dentro de estos capítulos el lector puede hallar títulos temáticos para la historia política, legal y militar; historia religiosa ye eclesiástica; historia de la educación;. e historia cultural e intelectual.

La obra termina con un índice de temas (subject index) y otro de nombres (name index). Los numbres de lugares, acontecimientos, y conceptos importantes han sido incluídos en el índice de temas. Estas som ideas que se derivan tanto de los títulos como de las anotaciones. El índice de nombres incluye únicamente los nombres de autores, traductores, anotadores o compiladores. Todas las referencias de los índices, como las contrarreferencias, se refieren al número del artículo (no al número de página).

Agradecimiento

Al preparar el libro tuve la buena suerte de recibir la generosa ayuda de muchísimos asociados y colegas además de cierta medida de apoyo económico institucional. Stanley R. Ross, de la University of Texas at Austin, fue sumamente importante; fue él quien inspiró la obra, sugirió la dimensión europea, y me ayudó a obtener fondos. También debo mucho a ciertos individuos asociados al Mexican Studies Committee del Conference on Latin American History, especialmente William H. Beezley, G. Michael Riley, y Richard E. Greenleaf. Otros colegas que me ayudaron son Nettie Lee Benson, de la University of Texas at Austin; Magnus B. Mörner, de la University of Pittsburgh y Latin-Amerika-Institut, Estocolmo; y Marvin D. Bernstein, de la State University of New York at Buffalo. Los empleados de la New York Public Library también fueron muy serviciales.

En Europe me auxiliaron las siguientes personas: Harold Blakemore, Secretario, y Alan Biggins, Ayudante de Bibliotecario, del Institute of Latin American Studies, University of London; Raymond Th. J. Buve, Universität Leiden; Rudolf de Jong, Director, Materiales Hispánicos del International Instituut voor sociale geschiendenis, Amsterdam; Fred Jongkind y Anneke M.C. Roos, Centro de Estudios y Documentación Latinoamericanos (CEDLA), Amsterdam; Reinhard Liehr, Universität Bielefeld; y Wilhelm Stegmann y Wolfgang Ulland, Ibero-Amerikanisches Institut Stiftung Preussischer Kulturbesitz, Berlín. Entre mis amigos mexicanos, reconozco especialmente el auxilio de Lucila Flamand, del Archivo de la Secretaría de Relaciones Exteriores. El profesor William V. Jackson, Janice Meagher, y Karin Kiewra ayudaron a corregir el texto para la imprenta.

Prefacio

Por último, doy gracias especiales a los colegas y estudiantes de la State University of New York at Fredonia, particularmente a Gary D. Barber, Robert H. Deming, Marvin Lunenfeld, Dennis R. Preston, Robert Schweik, Jon W. Weekly, Clark M. Zlotchew, Ed Fraser, Suzanne Gawron, y Shirley Pruitt. Mary Notaro escribió la bibliografía a máquina. La Research Foundation de la State University of New York me proporcionó una beca para que vo viajara durante el verano y estudiara en Europa. El Mexican Studies Committee del Conference on Latin American History participó con una modesta asignación para el viaje a la University of Texas at Austin, como hizo también la Oficina del Vice-Presidente para Asuntos Académicos de la State University of New York at Fredonia.

Translated by Clark M. Zlotchew

Introduction

Recent Trends in the Historiography of the Mexican Revolution

There has been a dramatic change in the course of scholarship during
the last two decades, 1960-1980; a historiographical trend which is,
to quote historian David C. Bailey, "almost as complex as the Revolution itself" (180*, p. 62). This change can be illustrated by com-
paring the words of Robert A. Naylor in 1962 with those of Bailey
sixteen years later. Naylor, commenting upon the consensus of professional opinion among scholars in the field of modern Mexican history, noted that "the residue [of historical literature] reveals few
studies which meet even modest historical standards.... In very general terms all social history, all economic history, and most of the
political and intellectual history remain to be written on nineteenth
and twentieth century Mexico" (224, pp. 353-54). In 1978, Bailey,
after noting the diversity and profusion of works on the Mexican
Revolution, concluded that "the salient characteristic of recent
revolutionary scholarship is its sophistication. There have been
imaginative advances in methodology, and historians now regularly
apply techniques and accept insights from other disciplines. Social
and economic history have overtaken the 'great man' approach that
prevailed in previous decades" (180, p. 63).

Most conspicuous today is the professional quality of the work.
The standards of craftmanship are generally high with most monographs
and articles reflecting the writers' attempt to realize the ideals of
objectivity and completeness while adhering to the logical demands of
historical thinking. These works are the products of intensive archival research in Mexico and elsewhere, the happy result of progress
in library science, increasing accessibility to sources, and an ever-
growing availability of adequate bibliographical tools. Because of
developments in historiographical studies, these writings are often
critical, revealing the authors' awareness of problems in conceptualization and methodology.

---

*Numbers in parentheses refer to bibliographical entries.

Introduction

The methodology has become increasingly varied and sophisticated, due in part to the influence of the social sciences upon history and the computer "revolution" in America and Europe. Fortunately this has not led to the total abandonment of narrative and descriptive techniques in favor of analytical approaches. Traditional categories of thought have been modified so that distinctions between economic, social, intellectual, political, and diplomatic history are simply a matter of scope, emphasis, whim, and convenience. Thus we speak, for example, of "cultural caudillos," "political economy" (an older usage undergoing resurgence), "the politics of global capitalism," "political education," "modernization and patronage," "the political careers of socioeconomic elites," "caudillos and peasants," etc.

The recent publications can also be called cosmopolitan.[1] Mexican revolutionary studies, almost a Mexican and North American monopoly at one time, are now being researched, written, and published in Mexico, parts of Latin America, Europe (especially the United Kingdom, France, the Netherlands, the Federal Republic of Germany, and the Soviet Union), Japan, Canada, Australia, and the United States. This international dimension, reflected in the utilization of new national (and regional) archives, has given the study of Mexico a global perspective and "polish" often lacking in studies of other parts of Latin America. Indeed, the products of Mexican historians are easily comparable to the best works coming out of Argentina, Chile, Cuba, and Brazil today. Equally important, Mexicanists outside of Mexico have shown an increased awareness of their obligation to share the results of their research with their Mexican counterparts. All of this has been facilitated by the recent growth of Mexico City as an international publishing center.

Coinciding with these developments in recent revolutionary scholarship are the changes in scholarly interpretation of the Revolution, changes usually referred to as the "new revisionism." The revisionists have seriously challenged the traditional interpretation of the Revolution as a populist, antifeudalistic break with the Porfirian past. This so-called "pro-Revolutionary" interpretation was developed by distinguished North Americans like Frank Tannenbaum, Ernest Gruening, Wilfrid Hardy Callcott, and others writing in the late 1930s and early 1940s. The transition from traditional to revisionist began in the 1950s with studies by José C. Valadés, Stanley R. Ross, and Daniel Cosío Villegas. Since 1960 the tendency has been to challenge the traditional periodization of the Revolution, to argue for the continuity of the present with the Porfirian past, and to see the Revolution as ultimately an antipopulist, bourgeois movement that shaped reform from above through an increasingly capitalistic modern state.

Although, as Barry Carr recently suggested, "we are rapidly reaching a point where it can be said 'We are all revisionists now'" (190, p. 7), it would appear that we are not there yet. Even though Catholic dissidents and neo-Marxist thinkers tend to share similar

revisionist assumptions about what the Revolution was not, they, like
other revisionists, are not in total agreement about what the Revolution was and what it means today. In fact it would appear that
the situation remains in flux today with a new generation of younger
historians already arguing for an eventual synthesis of the traditional and revisionist interpretations.[2]

Archives and Printed Documents

Whatever the disputes concerning interpretation, there can be no
doubting that the decades of the sixties and seventies witnessed a
steady infusion of research into monographic literature, the result
of increasing accessibility of scholars to archival and library
sources. A major impetus to background studies of the Revolution
came with the transfer of the Porfirio Díaz collection from the
Universidad Nacional Autónoma de México (UNAM) to the Universidad
de las Américas and the subsequent microfilming of major portions of
the collection. Another impetus came in the 1960s with the inaug-
uration of the Centro de Estudios de Historia de México at the
Fundación Cultura de Condumex in the industrial section of the
Vallejo area of Mexico City. The Center's holdings include the
archives of Venustiano Carranza and Francisco León de la Barra.
Another recently completed microfilm collection is the 60,000 papers
of the Archivo del Presidente Francisco I. Madero. Composed of
twenty-two reels, the Madero archive was filmed by the Museum of
National Anthropology in Mexico City.

In the 1970s the staff of the Archivo de la Secretaría de
Relaciones Exteriores de México completed their move into the ground
floor of the convent next to the Iglesia de Santiago Tlatelolco in
Mexico City's "Plaza of Three Cultures" section. Here can be found
the valuable documents of the "Revolución Mexicana Durante los Años
de 1910 a 1920," which can be used in the ample work space of the
Biblioteca José Malafragua above the archive. Recently Alejandra
Moreno Toscano has been directing the reorganization of the Archivo
General de la Nación (AGN) and in the process new resources have
been uncovered.

Research into regional history has been facilitated by the
decision of the directors of the Instituto Nacional de Antropología
e Historia to establish local centers in Oaxaca, Guanajuato, Puebla,
Guadalajara, and Hermosillo. Other state and municipal archives
are beginning to be used in Chihuahua, Baja California, Veracruz,
Coahuila, Querétaro, Yucatán, and Michoacán. The AGN is also lo-
cating and cataloguing state and municipal archives. In addition,
the Church of Jesus Christ of Latter Day Saints has been active in
filming Mexican parish and civil registers, and as of 1977 had made
105,548 rolls of microfilm available to the researcher through the
Genealogical Society of Utah (81).

Introduction

Admittance to the military files of the Archivo Histórico de la Defensa Nacional remains restricted, unfortunately, but an alternative source for military history is the National Archives in Washington, D.C. The records of the Adjutant General's Office (War Department), as well as materials from the Military Intelligence Division and the Office of Naval Intelligence, have been available since the late 1960s. The records of the U.S. Department of State (Record Group 59) are open through 1950. Thanks to the efforts of Charles Harris and Louis Sadler one can now review the archives of the Bureau of Investigation (after 1922, the FBI) for the epic revolutionary period. For papers not readily available in the National Archives, action under the Freedom of Information Act can be initiated. Finally, foreign archives are starting to get more use for the history of the Mexican Revolution, especially Britain's Public Record Office and Germany's Foreign Ministry.

Although much work remains to be done, there are several archival guides to revolutionary collections. Richard E. Greenleaf and Michael C. Meyer have prepared a field research guide to archival collections in Mexico (58). One of the better descriptive guides is Berta Ulloa's index and analysis of the Archivo de Relaciones Exteriores (118-19). Several guides exist for the U.S. National Archives (89, 91, 117). Laurens B. Perry has done the profession a genuine service with the preparation of his guide to the Porfirio Díaz Collection (109). Brief descriptions of lesser-known collections are beginning to appear in professional journals and newsletters, especially The Americas (95, 110, 120), Historia Mexicana (82, 102, 115), Hispanic American Historical Review (112), and the University of Perpignan publication, L'Ordinaire des Mexicanistes (64). Information on regional archives is scarce, but does exist for Saltillo (73), Puebla (98), and Sonora (110). Subject catalogues to the major Latin American collections have been published by G.K. Hall of Boston, including the Biblioteca Nacional (76), the University of Texas (77), the University of Florida (78), Tulane (79), and the Ibero–Amerikanisches Institut in Berlin (69, 114). Guides to European archives and libraries are readily available (61-62, 74), especially for the British Isles (107, 121), Spain (86, 105), France (61-62, 102, 105), West and East Germany (61-62, 69, 105, 115), and the Netherlands (96, 105).

Easily the most important collection of printed documents is the twenty-seven-volume Documentos históricos de la Revolución Mexicana (515), edited by Isidro and Josefina Fabela. This is an indispensible source for the magonista, maderista, villista, zapatista, and carrancista phases of the Revolution—especially for political and diplomatic history. Also worth noting is Manuel González Ramírez's four-volume Fuentes para la historia de la Revolución Mexicana (524). Compiled with an introduction to each volume, volume 3 remains the authoritative work on the Cananea strike of 1906. Other important "precursor" sources include the variety of magonista documentary collections which have been published recently in Mexico (509-10,

517-23, 538-39). Obviously magonismo is undergoing a resurgence in today's Mexico.

Bibliographical Tools

A host of new bibliographical tools have appeared since 1960. The five-volume Fuentes de la historia contemporánea de México (13, 24), edited by Luis González and Stanley R. Ross, is a basic guide to books, pamphlets, newspapers, and periodicals. That work, published by El Colegio de México between 1961 and 1967, provided the base for the preparation of a multi-volume history of Mexico called Historia de la Revolución Mexicana, 1911-1960 (278). The Historia, produced by the staff of El Colegio de México, is an excellent example of the professionalization of Mexican historiography that has developed in the post-World War II era. Also published under the auspices of El Colegio de México is the annual guide to books, articles, and theses in Mexican history entitled Bibliografía histórica mexicana (30, 35), and an annotated bibliography of twenty-five years of · historical research and writing, 1940-1965, called Veinticinco años de investigación histórica (31).

Latin American bibliographies for individual European countries include Leo Okinshevich's compilation on writings in the Soviet Union (20) and, for Germany, the publication of the German Study Group for Research on Latin America headquartered in Hamburg (18; see also entry 29). Other important bibliographies include, on diplomatic history, Daniel Cosío Villegas (147) and David Trask et al. (148); on intellectual history, David Maciel (153); and, on economic history, the Mexican history section of Roberto Cortés Conde et al. (149). An extensive current guide to books and articles remains the multivolume Handbook of Latin American Studies (38), to be published in the future by the University of Texas Press. Another current guide is the Hispanic American Periodicals Index (49), a subject-author index to approximately 250 important scholarly journals of Latin American interest, many from Mexico.

Historical Criticism and Methodology

Historiographical analysis and criticism are finally being given serious treatment by historians in Mexico, North America, and Europe. The Third International Congress of Mexican Studies, meeting in Oaxtepec in November of 1969, featured several sessions on the historiography of revolutionary scholarship (208). Stephen R. Niblo and Laurens B. Perry have published a study on "Recent Additions to Nineteenth-Century Mexican Historiography" (226). Regional historiography and methodology have received competent treatment by Luis González (199, 201) and Barry Carr (190). John Womack, Jr., has written a challenging, in-depth historiographical analysis of the literature of the Mexican economy during the 1910-1920 period (251). European writers who have published on the topic of revolutionary historiography include the Soviet writers M.S. Alperovich

Introduction

(178) and Nikolái M. Lavrov (209), the German scholar Manfred Mols, and the Swiss historian Hans Werner Tobler (221). Several pieces that describe new trends in revolutionary writing include works by David C. Bailey (180), Charles W. Bergquist (183), Charles A. Hale and Michael C. Meyer (206, 220), and Eugenia Meyer (214).

As with the work in historical criticism, scholars have shown great innovation in their methodological approaches to the study of the Revolution. Historian James W. Wilkie received the Herbert Eugene Bolton Memorial Prize for The Mexican Revolution: Federal Expenditure and Social Change Since 1910 (311-12). Through analysis of statistical data Wilkie succeeded in delimiting Mexico's revolutionary history into four ideological periods reflecting policies and priorities of the revolutionary governments. He also constructed an ingenious "poverty index" designed to measure the extent of social change in Mexico's contemporary history. Although his style of quantitative history stirred controversy and scholarly debate (see entries 181, 183, 245, 248-49), very few individuals will deny the contribution Wilkie has made through accumulating data from sources seldom tapped by previous historians.

In other applications of computer and quantitative methods historians have developed the techniques of prosopography (also called collective biography or multiple career analysis) to develop Mexican sociopolitical history. Peter H. Smith analyzed career information on more than six thousand individuals who held high office in Mexico since 1900 to determine the relationship between political careers, economic class, and elite composition (375-77). Of a lesser magnitude is John Conklin's elite study of the Mexican presidency (359). Similarly, Roderic A. Camp drew on original data from more than one hundred political figures to weigh the impact of education on career mobility (354, 357), and John H. Coatsworth used econometric techniques to study the Porfiriato (728).

Because prosopography usually involves the study of elites, it is encouraging to see quantitative studies as well of lower social strata in the form of historical demography and settlement patterns. Moisés González Navarro authored a two-volume work on population and society in Mexico (395), a major work in demographic history. In urban studies, Richard W. Wilkie has published an essay on "Urban Growth and the Transformation of the Settlement Landscape of Mexico, 1910-1970" (426). In another study that adopts a multidisciplinary approach, Raymond Th. J. Buve borrowed G.E. Black's theory on the dynamics of modernization as a model for his study on patronage in rural Mexico (352).

Another significant methodological development for recent history is oral history, in particular the interviewing of survivors of the Revolution. This technique was used by James Wilkie in his aforementioned study on federal expenditures and was further developed by him and Edna Monzón de Wilkie in México visto en el siglo XX (585), a collection of transcribed interviews with seven important aging figures of the Revolution, including Manuel Gómez Morín (founder of the Partido Acción Nacional), Vicente Lombardo Toledano, labor leader of the Confederación de Trabajadores de México (CTM), and ex-president Emilio Portes Gil. A more extensive effort is the Programa de Historia Oral of the Departamento de Etnología y Antropología del Instituto Nacional de Antropoligía e Historia, a project which includes interviews with lesser-known figures of the revolutionary era. Although most historians have restricted their use of oral history to elite participants, such as Donald J. Mabry's interviews with Partido Acción Nacional (PAN) leaders (1229), some, following the lead of anthropologists Robert Redfield and Oscar Lewis (see entry 194), have sought to reconstruct popular history. Of this genre are labor studies by John M. Hart (1008) and Barry Carr (999, 1120), David Ronfeldt's investigation of the ejiditarios of Atencingo (499), and Luis González's interviews with the inhabitants of San José de Gracia (487).

Traditional and Revisionist Interpretations

In sum, the last two decades have seen extraordinary progress in professional revolutionary studies. These improvements in craftsmanship have paralleled, and contributed to, changes in historical interpretation. A contemporary generation of revisionist historians no longer depicts everything that happened in Mexico's twentieth century as one long revolution. Regional history reveals a variety of revolutionary, nonrevolutionary, and counterrevolutionary situations. The revisionists understand Mexico's contemporary history in gradual "evolutionary" as well as abrupt "revolutionary" terms; they see failure as well as success, continuity as well as catastrophe. Although beginning only in the 1950s, this revisionism expanded rapidly in the wake of the horrors of the Tlatelolco massacre of 1968. We now see a new direction in Mexican historiography that has challenged, reinterpreted, and discarded much of the traditionalism and mythology produced between 1910 and 1950 by the so-called "pro-Revolutionary school of Mexican history."

This "pro-Revolutionary school" had its beginnings, according to historian Michael C. Meyer, between 1910-1920 with the "historian-as-participant" who wrote about the revolutionary experience in very personal terms; in fact in terms of an "exaggerated" personalismo-- a blind commitment, not to ideology or program but to the image of individual "revolutionary" caudillos. This generation produced a historical literature colored by villismo, zapatismo, carrancismo, or obregonismo. In the late 1920s and 1930s, as the uprising of 1910 appeared to mushroom into social upheaval, the Revolution (now spelled with a capital "R") begain to be viewed as the essence of the Mexican state. In the 1930s and 1940s the "lo mexicano" school of Samuel Ramos, José Gaos, and Leopoldo Zea fostered this identity between history and mexicanidad.

Introduction

At the same time, United States academics, imbued with their own
notions of secular progress à la New Deal, started their own love
affairs with "Good Neighborism," Lázaros Cárdenas, and the Mexican
Revolution--beginning with Herbert Priestly and Charles Hackett in
the 1920s, who were later joined by Frank Tannenbaum, Henry Bamford
Parkes, Wilfred Hardy Callcott, Eyler Simpson, and Ernest Gruening.
With the emergence of a modern, bourgeois state in Mexico in the
later 1930s and early 1940s, "Revolution" became synonymous with
modernization and industrial progress, and history became one of
many vehicles for the glorification of the state, its bureaucracy,
and its political elites. As Bailey notes, "the views of the pro-
Revolution school harmonized with the history of the Revolution
propagated by the political elite that emerged to govern Mexico"
(180, p. 69).

Political biographies and histories circulated that glorified
Madero and Carranza as apostles of "Democracy" and heroes of
"Revolution," with Díaz, Huerta, and their allies branded as
reactionaries and villains. The "pro-Revolutionary school" affirmed
that the Revolution had been a continuous process from 1910 to the
present. Mexico, viewed as a national entity, was moving, albeit
at times violently and abruptly, in a unified, purposive, and
progressive direction away from dictatorship and feudalism, towards
liberal democracy, social justice, and economic equality. In
addition, by the 1950s, Mexico was considered to be the model for
modern Latin American revolutions, and for some traditionalists after
Fidel Castro, the "preferred revolution" for Latin America. This,
then, was the traditional view challenged by the revisionists.

Although much revisionism is simply the natural product of the
historiographical process and the result of increasing professionalization, and even though revisionism is not identical with anti-
Revolution literature (which has a longer history)[3], nevertheless,
historians, like everyone, share in the "climate of opinion" of the
times and are motivated and have their views shaped by political
and moral concerns. In this respect, as Octavio Paz has noted (455),
1968 was a pivotal year, with protests and disturbances in Prague,
Belgrade, Rome, Paris, Tokyo, Santiago, Chicago, and especially
Mexico City, where government granaderos killed, injured, and
arrested hundreds of demonstrators at Tlatelolco.

Disenchantment with government continued in the aftermath of
Tlatelolco as the debacle of Vietnam was followed by the Watergate
scandals in the United States and the "Corpus Christi massacre" of
1971 in Mexico. The failure of president Luis Echeverría's populist
and nationalist programs, his retreat in the face of opposition from
both the Right and the Left, and the continuation of the familiar
pattern of government cooptation and repression after 1973, led
to disillusionment with the reformist policies of "institutionalized
revolutionaries" and a critique by scholars, thinkers, and historians
of the "pro-Revolution" construct.

Introduction

Popular writers also reflected this mood and attitude. Throughout the 1960s and 1970s there was a proliferation of biographies and
documentary collections of Zapata and zapatismo, Villa and villismo,
and Flores Magón and magonismo (see chapters 4 and 7). Most of
these were, to use John Womack's words, "slices of sweet puff." Yet
collectively they reflected a nostalgia for the unrealized promises
of the Revolution and indicated an awareness that the Revolution
had not been a victory for the campesino or urban worker. In the
instance of the magonista literary resurgence, it would appear that
nostalgia and criticism were of the antistatist, antigovernment,
proanarchist variety. Not wanting to be excluded from the populism
of the hour, the Mexican government moved, first in 1966 through
the Cámara de Diputados, and again in 1978, to declare Villa a hero-
patriot and to name 1978 the "Year of Francisco Villa," thus
assuring book publishers of continued commercial success in the 1980s.

By 1970 several writers reflected skepticism and even hostility
toward the claims of the Revolution. In 1960 the English edition of
Carlos Fuentes's novel, La región mas transparente (Where the air is
clear), appeared (448). It was more than a Marxist critique of the
Revolution; it was a condemnation of capitalism and the degenerate
bourgeois values of Mexico and the western world. Beginning in
1965, Pablo González Casanova argued against the completeness of
the Revolution. He was especially critical of the complacency
surrounding the economic "miracle of Mexican development" and
Mexico's "quasi-democracy" (361). One year later Moisés González
Navarro spoke of an "unbalanced revolution" ("la revolución
desequilibrada"), a situation in which the costs of the Revolution
were paid for by the workers while the benefits went to the fortunate
few (325). Writing in 1969, Octavio Paz critiqued the "pyramid" of
the Mexican Revolution. Through the use of literary metaphors and
historical images he criticized the Revolutionary government, Party,
and tradition (455). His comments were not well received by either
the Mexican intelligensia or the president of Mexico, Gustavo Díaz
Ordaz, who went on public television to speak against Paz and for
the nation. Obviously the critiques of the sixties were thought
threatening by those whom Carlos Fuentes called the "keepers of
the Cactus Curtain."

After 1970 other voices, including those of historians, were
added to the clamor. Many of these were from the political Left.
In 1971 James D. Cockcroft caused a small uproar when he dedicated
the Mexican edition of Intellectual Precursors of the Mexican
Revolution to "los presos políticos" of Tlatelolco (731). Adolfo
Gilly, writing from Lecumberri Prison, talked of "la revolución
interrumpida"--a Revolution which was interrupted two times on its
way to socialism because of the repression of popular groups by
the emerging bourgeoisie. His work was published in 1972 (275).
At the same time Marxist historian Arnoldo Córdova argued per-
suasively that the Revolution was a political movement designed
to promote capitalism, and that social reforms were instituted only

to manipulate the masses. As a result, the Mexican Revolution was a logical continuation of the Porfiriato (321, 441).

The mood and content of revisionism was continued with the 1976 publication of Contemporary Mexico (266), the published proceedings of the Fourth International Congress. Curiously, only one photograph was selected to illustrate that work--James Wilkie's photo of the "Plaza de Tlatelolco" in 1967, a silent protest and reminder of Mexico's past wrongs. By 1980 the angry impressions schematically sketched by Gilly, Paz, and others were given empirical content with the professional findings of quantitative historians. Roderic Camp's Mexico's Leaders (354) illustrated the elite role of Mexican education in preparing the middle class for government service. Similarly, Peter Smith, in his Labyrinths of Power (375), a work based on career information of several thousand individuals, demonstrated that the Revolution was important in creating and institutionalizing a system of elite circulation that promised greater political mobility to the same stratum (i.e., the privileged middle class) of the population from which prerevolutionary elites were chosen. Octavio Paz intuited this development in The Labyrinth of Solitude (456), and Smith measured it in Labyrinths of Power. At decade's end the humanist and social scientist had joined ranks in asking questions about human nature and history.

Revisionism: The Revolution, 1900-1940

While generalizing about the Revolution in its entirety has pre-occupied many writers, most historians prefer a limited approach that isolates individuals and events and delimits time. A recent problem in conceptualization is that of the periodization of the Revolution. As Eugenia Meyer notes, concepts of periodization can be correlated to ideology and group interests, so that bourgeois historians usually speak of a continuous revolution from 1910 to the institutionalized Revolution of today, while Marxists and others on the Left see the historical process in Mexico as an incomplete or interrupted revolution (327). The hallowed date for the tradi-tionalist has been 1910, a year that is no longer considered a cosmic divide. Taking their cues from the periodization of Daniel Cosío Villegas's Historia moderna (734), Albert Michaels and Marvin Bernstein organize Mexican history around the emergence and development of the Mexican national bourgeoisie, a process which began in the 1870s, underwent gestation during the Porfiriato, and triumphed between 1946 and 1958 (328).

Armed with a new concept of periodization, and having been encouraged to drop from their vocabulary the idea of "precursorism," most students of the Porfiriato can now be considered "revolutionary" historians who study the Porfiriato for its own sake, not for its relation to events after 1910. Obviously, if earlier interpretations of the Revolution must be revised, so too the history of the "not-so-Old Regime." If such revision seems ambiguous and less than consistent, it at least has the virtue of not being, in Emerson's words, "a foolish consistency."

Reflecting the new directions, many revisionist studies of the Porfiriato, 1876-1911, concentrate on socioeconomic history. Many would agree with John Womack (251) that capitalist production became dominant during the 1890s (not, as the traditionalists argue, after 1917) and that Mexican economic history is a function of United States economic history. Neo-Marxist Juan Felipe Leal concluded that the Mexican state after 1867 reflected the capitalist interests of a developing industrial bourgeoisie and was the representative of foreign enclaves in Mexico; as such it became a semi-colonial state by 1914 (763-64). José Luis Ceceña collected useful data concerning foreign ownership of Mexican properties to demonstrate the impact of global capitalism on the Porfirian and later revolutionary economies (378). These generalizations about the relationship between foreign and domestic elites were substantiated by Mark Wasserman's case study of the Terrazas clan in Chihuahua (807, 505-506). In a similar manner the impact of imported capital on the economy (especially the railroads), and the resulting labor conditions in the countryside were studied by the Chicago school of John Coatsworth (728) and Friedrich Katz (756).

Political and intellectual history of the Porfiriato also has undergone revision in the past few years. James Cockcroft, in a well-documented study of the "precursors" (732), argued that radical *magonistas* initiated a populist revolution after 1900 that ultimately failed because of bourgeois repression and schisms within radical ranks. W. Dirk Raat has shown that domestic and foreign elites in Mexico and North America created a binational police and espionage system, which, through harassment and repression, effectively [4] curtailed populist and radical elements between 1903 and 1923 (778). John Hart's work on anarchism in Mexico complements the Cockcroft and Raat studies, with Hart arguing for ideological continuity between the Porfiriato and the early Revolution (747). Disagreeing with the thrust of these works is Rodney Anderson, who believes that the Partido Liberal Mexicano (PLM) and the ideology of anarchism had little influence upon the Mexican working class (707). Finally, two other revisionist studies deserve mention: Paul Vanderwood's demythologizing of the rurales (802-805), and Raat's work on positivism and scientism in Díaz's Mexico (779-780), in which it is argued that, contrary to the traditional view, positivism was not the official, or even most dominant, intellectual current of the Porfiriato.

Probably the most promising revisionist trend is the development in regional history. By focusing upon specific individuals and particular events in a regional context, historians have amply demonstrated the concept of "many revolutions" (perhaps an idea not too far removed from the thesis of Lesley Byrd Simpson's classic Many Mexicos), especially for the 1910-1934 period. Biography,

prospography, and regional studies have given us a radically
different view of the Epic Revolution, 1910–1920, and the era of
the so-called Northern Dynasty, 1920–1934.

Michael Meyer took a new look at Victoriano Huerta and concluded
that, in the context of 1913–1914 and compared to Francisco Madero
before him and Venustiano Carranza after him, the Huerta regime was
not counterrevolutionary (866). Douglas Richmond recently published
a synthesis of the Carranza years and concluded that Carranza was
more of an "authoritarian populist" than a political moderate (887).
John Womack produced an impressive narrative history, Zapata and
the Mexican Revolution (1042), which placed Emiliano Zapata back
in the context of Morelos and revealed the essentially conservative
goals of the zapatistas. Well-received by the profession, within
three years after the appearance of the English edition the book
had been published in Spanish and German (1040–41, 1043). Since then
Ronald Waterbury has compared the revolution of peasants in Morelos
with the inertia of Oaxaca Indians, revealing once again the limited
appeal of the zapatista movement (1039). The future holds great
promise, as Friedrich Katz is working on a biography of Francisco
Villa that will show that Villa was neither a single-minded bandit,
not the single-minded agrarian reformer other historians have called
him (854), and Linda B. Hall has recently published a biography of
Alvaro Obregón.[5]

The general picture that emerges of the Epic Revolution is one
in which violence deepened regional disparities and increased the
economy's rate of accumulation (in effect building a capacity for
later expansion). In short, the Epic Revolution is the history
of a floundering bourgeoisie that resorted to a tyrannical state to
institute capitalist reforms and curtail the gains of radical
labor (see Womack, entry 251). This general thesis is sustained
by a number of labor histories, including those by Ramón Ruiz (1032),
John Hart (1008), and Barry Carr (998–99).

Between 1910 and 1934 powerful regional caudillos were either
coopted or coerced into submission as Mexico's new rulers evolved
a party system that mobilized the peasants and workers from above.
The system sanctioned presidential (patrón) rule throughout the
country. The Obregón–Callas period, beginning in the 1920's, is
now recognized as a time when the central government systematically
eliminated regional caudillos.

Raymond Buve has described the phenomenom of "controlled
mobilization" among caudillo Domingo Arenas and the peasantry of
Tlaxcala (475, 995–96). Linda Hall has described the way Obregón
manipulated agrarian reform for purposes of political consolidation
and centralization (1083). One radical caudillo who lost power
and then his life to the Obregón machine was Felipe Carrillo Puerto
in Yucatán. Carrillo's career has been analyzed and described in
convincing detail by Gilbert M. Joseph (489–490).[6] Other radical

Introduction

populist caudillos who suffered what Heather Fowler Salamini calls "political marginality" were Primo Tapia in Michoacán (discussed by Paul Friedrich, entry 482), and Adalberto Tejeda in Veracruz (studied by Salamini, entries 1133-34).

A variety of other regional studies reflect these and related themes. For example, William H. Beezley's monograph on Abraham González (471) reveals that Chihuahua's rebels were not oppressed peasants but cowboys, muleteers, clerks, and miners who were frustrated by rural domestic and foreign elites. Katz has made similar discoveries for the Revolution in Chihuahua (1013). Political strife in Puebla, Coahuila, and Sonora are the respective topics of David Ronfeldt (499), Douglas Richmond (496), and Susan Deeds (836).

Luis González describes three revolutions in his native town of San José de Gracia in Michoacán, the greatest changes occurring during the Cristero rebellion of 1925-1932 (487). Contrary to traditional liberal and Marxist accounts, Jean A. Meyer depicts the Cristero revolt as an authentic peasant resistance movement against an authoritarian, capitalist state (1148). Also arguing against the traditional view of the church as a reactionary body, David C. Bailey traces the history of the Cristeros from 1913 through the 1920s (1140).

Unlike traditional accounts of the Lázaro Cárdenas era, 1934-1940, which usually interpret cardenismo as a radical and corrective phase of the ongoing Revolution, revisionists generally emphasize the moderate ideological nature of the Cárdenas government. This is the position of Tzvi Medín (1186), David Raby (1191), and Josefina Vázquez (1238). Both Vázquez and Jorge Mora Forero argue that socialist education was not implemented during the Cárdenas period and that a majority of teachers were either indifferent or hostile to socialism (1237-38). It would also appear that under Cárdenas the process of centralization and mobilization reached maturity with corporatism finally being consolidated. Both Arnaldo Córdova (1178-79) and Lyle C. Brown (1211) have described Cárdenas's organization of the peasants into the Confederación Nacional Campesina (CNC) and urban labor into the CTM, and how he made these sectors tools for promoting state and corporate capitalist interests. In the final analysis the kind of state capitalism that emerged under Cárdenas was closer to national socialism than Marxian socialism.

Future Research Needs

There are other examples of revisionism, but those cited above are fairly representative of recent trends. In spite of the achievements of the last two decades, additional work remains. There are no good biographies of important secondary figures such as Gildardo Magaña, Antonio Villarreal, and Joaquín Amaro; for that matter, the

profession is still awaiting a prize-winning biography of Porfirio
Díaz. More biographies are needed of Mexican and foreign empresarios,
such as C.L. Sonnichsen's study of Colonel Greene (694) and Desmond
Young's Weetman Pearson (704). In local studies, someone should do
for Enrique Creel what William Beezley has done for Abraham González
and Friedrich Katz is likely to do for Francisco Villa.

Intellectual historians should rescue their subject matter from
the philosophers and move away from the philosophy and history of
ideas toward a sociology of knowledge. Specifically, for the post-
1911 period they should abandon their preoccupation with mexicanidad
to study other concepts, ideas, and attitudes. We know about the
ideologies of protest, but what about philosophies and concepts that
rationalize the status quo such as positivism (alive and well after
1911), pragmatism, scientism, and other "isms" of modernization and
capitalist development. A prosopography that compared the ideas
of elite groups would be most rewarding; for example, a comparative
study of the científicos with the carrancistas (would there be any
differences in values and world-view?). Intellectual historians
should avail themselves of oral history techniques and write the
history of popular beliefs and values, not just the history of
literate intellectuals.

Regional history needs further development, especially for
bibliographical tools. For balance, the focus should be on the
South and West and on the period before 1910 or after 1920. New
concepts should be used to delimit and define regional boundaries.
Instead of political categories, some local history should be
defined in terms of historical and cultural geography; for example,
instead of the Revolution in Chihuahua, why not the Revolution
in the Sierra Madre or even the Gran Chichemeca? The latter fits
the historical and economic realities of the northern frontier
and the American Southwest and reminds us that there was a Mexican
Revolution in the continental United States. Again, instead of
the Oaxaca Indians, why not the Revolution in the Mixteca? As one
can see, the examples are endless.

Thanks to Berta Ulloa, Friedrich Katz, Robert Freeman Smith,
Peter Calvert, Lorenzo Meyer, and others, diplomatic history has
been integrated with economic history, and their research reflects
the utilization of both domestic and foreign archives. The next
generation of diplomatic scholars would do well to follow their
examples. Concerning political history, given the present concern
of revisionist historians with cooption and repression, it is
surprising that no one has written the history of Mexico's servicio
secreto from the Porfiriato to as far as the authorities will allow.

In spite of several new works in socioeconomic history, much
remains to be done. Labor historians need to study working-class
consciousness and develop an awareness of ethnic and family history.
Economic historians need to study corporations like El Aguila

or umbrella organizations like the National Conference of Chambers of Commerce and do for the popular sector of the Partido de la Revolución Mexicana (the Confederación Nacional de Organizaciones Populares) what Arnaldo Córdova has done for the CTM and CNC. Social historians, some of whom write as if they believe, to quote Kurt Vonnegut, "it is no disgrace to be poor, but it might as well be," should study the great unwashed in the cities. Middle-class historians should stop expecting the poor to be preoccupied with poverty and write the history of something other than the "culture of poverty." We know about the workers in the Confederación Regional de Obreros Mexicanos (CROM), the CTM, and the Casa, but what about the lumpen, the unorganized, the outcast, the prostitute, the Saturday night bandido, and the rest of the crowd at Garibaldi Square?

Religious history can be explored, especially for the Epic Revolution where studies are practically nonexistent. We know that anticlericalism was a powerful emotion in the late Porfiriato and the early Revolution, but what were the clerics doing? Were there no revolutionary priests before the cristeros? Concerning education, what is the relationship between the schools and technology, technology and "Revolutionary" politics? A final peculiarity worthy of note is that in spite of the influence of Adlerian psychoanalysis at the University of Mexico in the 1930s (reflected in the "lo mexicano" tradition), Mexico's Mexicanists have been unwilling to experiment in the field of psychohistory.

Conclusion

Having surveyed the literature, one is tempted to sum it all up with the words of the Muse Unanimous: "Every man her own Revisionist." But to do so would be misleading. In the final analysis "revisionist" and "pro-Revolution school" are simply labels that should not obscure understanding. Mexican historiography has a long and proud history, and the foundations of our knowledge come from the traditionalists on both the Right and Left. None of us have ultimate answers, at least as historians. Hopefully, the recent literature should help us to understand contemporary Mexico better and ourselves a little more intimately.

Notes

1. For Japanese and European historiography of the Mexican Revolution see W. Dirk Raat, "Mexico's Global Revolution: Recent Trends in Mexican Revolutionary Studies in Japan, the United Kingdom, and Europe" (Paper read at the Fourth Conference of Mexican and United States Historians, Chicago, Illinois, 8 September 1981).

2. Gilbert M. Joseph, "Mexico's 'Popular Revolution': Mobilization and Myth in Yucatán, 1910-1940" (Paper delivered at the American Historical Association meeting, San Francisco, California, December 1978), pp. 4-5.

3. It is obvious that not all traditional writers approved
of the Revolution. The ex-Huertista Jorge Vera Estañol reflected an
antirevolutionary bias in his Historia de la Revolución Mexicana:
Orígenes y Resultados, first published in Mexico in 1957 (see entry
310). For a good bibliographical essay of the literature to the
early 1960s, see Charles C. Cumberland, Mexico: The Struggle for
Modernity (New York and Oxford: Oxford University Press, 1968),
pp. 352-65.

4. W. Dirk Raat, Revoltosos: Mexico's Rebels in the United
States, 1903-1923 (College Station: Texas A&M University Press,
1981).

5. Linda B. Hall, Alvaro Obregón and the Mexican Revolution
1912-1920 (College Station: Texas A&M University Press, 1981).

6. See also Gilbert M. Joseph, Revolution from Without: The
Mexican Revolution in Yucatán, 1915-1924 (Cambridge: Cambridge
University Press, 1981).

Abbreviations

HAHR	Hispanic American Historical Review
HM	Historia Mexicana
JISWA	Journal of Interamerican Studies and World Affairs
NMHR	New Mexico Historical Review
UNAM	Universidad Nacional Autónoma de México

I. Bibliographies, Guides, and Aids to Research

BIBLIOGRAPHIES OF BIBLIOGRAPHY

1 BARNARD, JOSEPH D., and RASMUSSEN, RANDALL. "A Bibliography
   of Bibliographies for the History of Mexico." Latin
   American Research Review 13, no. 2 (1978): 229-35.
       A list of 155 reference guides for the history of
   Mexico--bibliographies, research aids, archival guides,
   periodical indexes, biographical dictionaries, etc. Not
   comprehensive; for example, it is not complete in the
   coverage of bibliographies concerned with local history.
   Some citation errors.

2 GROPP, ARTHUR E., comp. A Bibliography of Latin American
   Bibliographies Published in Periodicals. 2 vols.
   Metuchen, N.J.: Scarecrow Press, 1976.
       Extensive compilation of bibliographies referring to
   Latin America published in Latin American periodicals and
   elsewhere. Over 9,700 references drawn from more than
   1,000 periodicals published prior to and through 1965.
   Subject-author index facilitates its use. Materials on
   Revolution organized under "Mexico-History-Revolution,
   1910-." Serves as a companion guide to the author's
   A Bibliography of Latin American Bibliographies (see
   entry 3).

3 _____. A Bibliography of Latin American Bibliographies.
   Metuchen, N.J.: Scarecrow Press, 1968.
   _____. _____. Supplement, 1971.
       An updated and expanded version of Cecil Knight Jones's
   Bibliography of Latin American Bibliographies, published
   by the Library of Congress in 1942 (reprint by Greenwood
   Press, 1969). Unlike Jones's edition, this compilation
   arranges items by subject rather than by country (e.g.,
   "History-Mexico").

1

Bibliographies of Bibliography

CORDEIRO, DANIEL RAPOSO, ed. A Bibliography of Latin American
Bibliographies: Social Sciences and Humanities. Vol. 1.
Metuchen, N.J.: Scarecrow Press, 1979.
    Supplements for the years 1969 through 1974 the original
Scarecrow bibliographies prepared by Arthur E. Gropp.
During the period surveyed, some 1750 bibliographies on
Latin American subjects have been published.

4 MEYER, EUGENIA W. de and BONFIL, ALICIA O. de. "A Bibliography of Bibliographies and Other Guides." In Research
in Mexican History, edited by Richard E. Greenleaf and
Michael C. Meyer, pp. 181-87. Lincoln: University of
Nebraska Press, 1973.
    A scholar's bibliography for research in Mexican history;
lists 105 items, primarily bibliographies, historiographical essays, and guides to archives.

BIBLIOGRAPHIES AND INDEXES

BIBLIOGRAPHIES

Retrospective

5 Agrarian Reform in Latin America: An Annotated Bibliography.
Compiled by the staff of the Land Tenure Center Library.
Madison: University of Wisconsin, 1974.
    Includes 323 items on Mexico, primarily of an histor-
ical nature, on the Revolution, the ejido, caciquismo,
campesinos, land and economic development, Article 27 of
the Constitution of 1917, and federal reform programs
(pp. 368-434). All items annotated; personal author
index, corporate author index, and subject index.

6 ARROYO, LUIS LEOBARDO. A Bibliography of Recent Chicano
History Writings, 1970-1975. Los Angeles: Chicano
Studies Center, University of California, 1975.
    Includes bibliography for 1900-1941 period. Booklet
introduction is a concise historiography of the development of Chicano history.

7 BARRETT, ELLEN C. Baja California II, 1536-1964: A Bibliography of Historical, Geographical, and Scientific Literature Relating to the Peninsula of Baja California and to
the Adjacent Islands in the Gulf of California and the
Pacific Ocean. Los Angeles: Westernlore Press, 1967.
    Includes a chronological index to Books I and II. Some
items on the Baja Revolution.

Bibliographies and Indexes

8   BAYITCH, S.A. Latin America and the Caribbean: A Biblio-
    graphical Guide to Works in English. Coral Gables, Fla.:
    University of Miami Press, 1967.
       Expands author's 1961 bibliography with less emphasis
    on law and more on international relations.

9   BERROA, JOSEFINA, comp. México bibliográfico, 1957-1960:
    Catálogo general de libros impresos en México. Mexico:
    J. Berroa: 1961.
       An author list of approximately 4,000 titles, followed
    by a subject index. Gives full information, including
    prices.

10 CARR, BARRY. "The Mexican Revolution Revisited." In
    Latin American Review of Books, Vol. 1, edited by Colin
    Harding and Christopher Roper, pp. 136-41. Palo Alto,
    Calif.: Ramparts Press, 1973.
       A review essay of political studies of the Mexican
    Revolution published between 1971 and 1972, and a list
    of thirty-five works of interest on Mexican Revolutionary
    history published between 1970 and 1972.

11 CHILCOTE, RONALD H. Revolution and Structural Change in
    Latin America: A Bibliography on Ideology, Development,
    and the Radical Left (1930-1965). 2 vols. Stanford,
    Calif.: Hoover Institution on War, Revolution and Peace,
    1970.
       A country-by-country listing of books, pamphlets, and
    periodical articles. Most references are in English,
    Spanish, Portuguese, and French, but some German and
    Russian materials are listed. Volume 2 (pp. 219-94) con-
    tains a short introductory essay outlining the political
    themes of the Mexican Revolution and a list of 695 books,
    pamphlets, and articles (some of which have one-sentence
    annotations). Author index provided.

12 CUMBERLAND, CHARLES C. "The United States-Mexican Border:
    A Selective Guide to the Literature of the Region."
    Supplement to Rural Sociology 25 (1960): 1-236.
       An inclusive guide, in bibliographical essay form, to
    the literature of the border region. Includes books,
    articles, theses, monographs, government publications,
    and unpublished works. Topics include guides, diplomatic
    relations, travel and geography, immigration history,
    education, land use, economic activity, culture, government
    and politics, Indians, and the Spanish-speaking population
    of the United States. Mexican Revolution section focuses
    upon Villa and Pershing expedition. Author index.

Bibliographies and Indexes

13 GONZALEZ y GONZALEZ, LUIS; MONROY, GUADALUPE; and URIBE,
    SUSANA. Fuentes de la historia contemporánea de México:
    Libros y folletos. 3 vols. Mexico: El Colegio de México,
    1961-62.
        Complete and well-organized guide to books and pamphlets
    on Mexico, 1910-1940.
        Contents: vol. 1, "Generalidades," "Territorio,"
    "Sociedad;" vol. 2, "Economía," "Política," "Religión;"
    vol. 3, "Education." "Filosofía y ciencias," "Letras y
    artes." Vol. 3 also contains general and title indexes.

14 GRIFFIN, CHARLES CARROLL, ed. Latin America: A Guide to the
    Historical Literature. Austin: Published by the Conference
    on Latin American History by University of Texas Press, 1971.
        A cooperative work sponsored jointly by the Conference
    on Latin American History and the Hispanic Foundation
    (Library of Congress). A selective scholarly bibliography
    with critical annotations covering the whole field of
    Latin American history. More than 7,000 items; cutoff
    date for publications included is 1966. Mexican section
    (pp. 376-403) includes a short historiographical-biblio-
    graphical essay by Stanley R. Ross and annotated entries
    to general works, printed documents, government and
    politics, foreign relations, literature, and biographies
    of the Revolutionary and post-Revolutionary eras of
    Mexican history. Author index; detailed table of contents.

15 IGUÍNIZ, JUAN BAUTISTA. Bibliografía biográfica mexicana.
    Mexico: UNAM, Instituto de Investigaciones Históricas,
    1969.
        An annotated bibliography of biographical and historical
    studies of Mexico. Section on books and articles arranged
    alphabetically by author's last name, while section on
    newspapers and journals is arranged alphabetically by
    newspaper and periodical name. A revision and enlargement
    of the 1930 edition. 1314 items; index.

16 JOHNSON, CHARLES W., comp. México en el siglo XX: Biblio-
    grafía política y social de publicaciones extranjeras.
    Mexico: UNAM, Instituto de Investigaciones Sociales, 1969.
        An unannotated bibliography of 2644 entries of foreign
    publications from 1900 to 1969 on political, socioeconomic,
    and cultural themes. Included are books, articles, govern-
    ment publications, pamphlets, theses, and an appended list
    of serial publications and reference sources used. See
    especially section 12, pages 285-319, on "La revolución
    mexicana."

17 LAMBERT, MICHAEL. Bibliographie latino-américaniste:
    France 1959-1972. Mexico: Institut Français d'Amérique
    Latine, 1973.
        A bibliography of books published in French in France
    between 1959 and 1972 relating to Latin America. The year
    of Castro's revolution was chosen since it was that event
    which stimulated interest in Latin America in France.
    1550 titles listed without annotation; arranged alpha-
    betically by author's last name. Subject index.

18 Lateinamerikaforschung: Neuere Veröffentlichungen in der
    Bundesrepublik Deutschland. Hamburg: Arbeitsgemeinschaft
    Deutsche Lateinamerikaforschung, 1976.
        A guide to recent (since mid-1960s) publications on
    Latin America in the Republic of Germany. Compiled by
    the staff of the Iberoamerika Kunde, Dokumentations-
    Leitstelle in Hamburg on the occasion of the 1976 Frankfurt
    book fair. A publication of ADLAF (German Study Group for
    Research on Latin America), headquartered in Hamburg.
    Books and pamphlets listed under institutions and authors.
    Author index. Addendum containing information about
    ADLAF.

19 NACLA's Bibliography on Latin America. New York: North
    American Congress on Latin America, 1973.
        A listing with brief descriptive annotations of articles
    and books on the history, economics, and politics of
    Latin America. The focus is on antiimperialism and pref-
    erence is given to writers on the Left. Items organized
    by topic and country, with Mexican section containing
    nineteen items on the Revolution. Cross-referenced
    index.

20 OKINSHEVICH, LEO, comp., and CARLTON, ROBERT G., ed. Latin
    America in Soviet Writings: A Bibliography. 2 vols.
    Baltimore: Johns Hopkins Press, 1966.
        Annotated bibliography of books and articles in the
    Russian language about Latin America. Included also are
    Soviet translations of works by Latin American authors.
    Vol. 1 covers work published between 1917-1958; vol. 2 is
    for the 1959-1964 period. Coverage of earlier items
    (before 1926) is less comprehensive than later period.
    Materials on the Mexican Revolution organized under
    "History-Mexico." 8,688 entries, topically arranged.
    Supersedes 1959 edition of the same title.

Bibliographies and Indexes

21 PLUMB, WALTER J. "A British Bibliography of Mexico." Inter-
cambio Organo de la Cámara de comercio Británica, no. 43
(July 1964): 63-71.
A brief list of works by Britons on Mexico, 1555-1964,
arranged chronologically by date of first publication.
Compiler is past director of the Instituto Anglo-Mexicano
de Cultura.

22 RAMOS, ROBERTO: Bibliografía de la historia de México. 2d ed.
Mexico: Instituto Mexicano de Investigaciones Económicas,
1965.
5,164 items (mainly books) in alphabetical sequence
by author; no index.

23 _____. Bibliografía de la Revolución Mexicana. 2d ed.
3 vols. Mexico: Biblioteca del Instituto Nacional de
Estudios Históricos de la Revolución Mexicana, 1959-1960.
Originally published between 1931 and 1940 with over
5,000 titles. No useful index.

24 ROSS, STANLEY R. Fuentes de la historia contemporánea de
México: Periódicos y revistas. 2 vols. Mexico: El
Colegio de México, 1967.
Guide to Mexican newspapers and periodicals, especially
the Hemeroteca Nacional collection in Mexico City. More
than 27,000 items from more than 200 Spanish-language
magazines, newspapers, and journals published in Mexico
and the United States between 1908 and 1958. Brief
annotations; no author index.

25 SABLE, MARTIN HOWARD. Latin-American Studies in the Non-
Western World and Eastern Europe: A Bibliography on
Latin America in the Languages of Africa, Asia, the Middle
East, and Eastern Europe, with Transliterations and
Translations in English. Metuchen, N.J.: Scarecrow
Press, 1970.
More than 2,900 items; author and subject indexes.

26 _____. A Guide to Latin American Studies. 2 vols. Los
Angeles: Latin American Center, University of California,
1967.
An annotated bibliography of 5,024 items covering the
entire range of Latin American civilization, emphasizing
publications since 1955. Author and subject indexes.

27 SÁENZ CIRLOS, VICENTE JAVIER. Guía de obras de consulta
    sobre México en el campo de las ciencias sociales.
    ' :errey: Instituto Tecnológico y de Estudios Superiores
    ae Monterrey, 1974.
        An annotated bibliography of reference works related to
    the social sciences, broadly defined, in Mexico.

28 SARNACKI, JOHN. Latin American Literature and History in
    Polish Translation: A Bibliography. Port Huron,
    Michigan: John Sarnacki, 1973.
        A bibliography of more than 800 items derived from
    bibliographies previously published in Poland and on
    the compiler's own investigations in North American
    archives. Includes literature, literary criticism,
    historical studies, socioeconomic works, and religious
    publications. An additional chapter speaks of the role of
    Polish immigrants in Latin America.

29 STEGER, HANNS-ALBERT; SCHRADER, ACHIM; and GRAEBNER, JURGEN.
    Latinamerikaforschung in der Bundesrepublic Deutschland
    und in Berlin West . Arbeitsunterlage zur Lateinamerika-
    forschung series, no. 10. Dortmund: COSAL, 1966.
        A guide to Latin American publications in the Republic
    of Germany and West Berlin.

30 URIBE de FERNÁNDEZ de CÓRDOBA, SUSANA."Bibliografía histórica
    mexicana." HM 16 (July-Sept. 1966): 93-153.
        Contains 972 items on works and articles published on
    Mexican history in Mexico and other countries. Forty-one
    items on Porfiriato and Revolution, pp. 120-22.

31 Veinticinco años de investigación histórica en México.
    Mexico: El Colegio de México, 1966. Originally appeared
    in two issues of Historia Mexicana 15, nos. 59-60 (Oct.-
    Mar. 1965-66 and Apr.-June 1966): 155-445, 447-782.
        An annotated bibliography of twenty-five years of his-
    torical research and writing, 1940-1965. Of special
    interest are the forty-nine annotated items compiled by
    Stanley R. Ross on the political history of the
    Revolution. Ross's list includes bibliographies and
    guides, biographies and memoirs, specialized monographs,
    and general studies.

32 ZIMMERMAN, IRENE. A Guide to Current Latin American
    Periodicals: Humanities and Social Sciences. Gainesville,
    Fla.: Kallman Publishing Co., 1961.
        A guide to periodicals with descriptive and evaluative
    annotations. Organized by country, subject (e.g., history,

Bibliographies and Indexes

folklore, international relations, etc.), and chronology
(from 1831 to 1960). Ninety-six items listed under
Mexico (pp. 132-63).
A kind of bibliography is the Harvard University shelflist,
see entry 99. For additional bibliography see entries
192, 206, 209, and 213.

Current

33 America, History and Life: A Guide to Periodical Literature.
    Santa Barbara, Calif.: Clio Press, 1964-.
        Quarterly; abstracts of articles on the history of the
    United States and Canada, including the Mexican Revolution
    in the borderlands and the American Southwest. Annual
    index.

34 Anuario bibliográfico. Mexico: Biblioteca Nacional, 1967-.
        Official Mexican national bibliography.

35 Bibliografía histórica mexicana. Mexico: El Colegio de
    México, 1967-.
        Annual publication of the Centro de Estudios
    Históricos of El Colegio de México. Contains a large
    number of items, some briefly annotated, of books,
    articles, and theses on Mexican history. Later issues
    (1975-) contain no annotations. Topical organization
    includes sections on bibliography, historiography,
    political history, regional history, social history,
    economic history, legal history, diplomatic history,
    literary history, art history, history of science,
    history of education, personal testimonies, and folklore.
    Political history section subdivided into chronological
    periods, including the Porfiriato and the Revolution.
    Analytical index.

36 Boletín bibliográfico mexicano. Mexico: Librería de Porrúa
    Hnos. 1940-.
        The only continuous record of Mexican publishing since
    1940. A bimonthly listing, description, and review of
    up-to-date books and pamphlets; includes news notes and
    advertisements. Some notes contain evaluative comments
    designating books of research value. Lists include books
    published outside of Mexico, especially in Spain and
    Buenos Aires. Inadequate indexing; no author indexes.

37 British Bulletin of Publications on Latin America, the
    Caribbean,Portugal and Spain. London: Canning House,
    The Hispanic and Luso-Brazilian Council, 1949-.

Canning House Library compilation of books, essays, and articles published in English on Latin America, the West Indies, Portugal, and Spain. Done in collaboration with bibliographer Dr. A.J. Walford. Listed by geographical area. Issued twice a year in April and October.

38 Handbook of Latin American Studies, 1935–. Cambridge, Mass.: Harvard University Press, 1938–1955; Gainesville: University of Florida Press, 1956–.

An annotated and selective, yet extensive, guide to recent publications on Latin America in anthropology, economics, art, education, geography, government, politics, international relations, sociology, folklore, history, language, literature, music, and philosophy. Covers principal historical reviews published in the Americas, most archival bulletins, many regional historical bulletins from Latin America, outstanding articles appearing in Spanish or other European historical reviews, and books on Latin American history. Not comprehensive; seldom devotes space to new editions and impressions of books previously listed.

With 1964 issue, divided into two sections, social sciences and humanities, now published in alternate years. Humanities volumes include history (e.g., "History-Mexico, Revolution and Post-Revolution"). Subject indexing begins with no. 16; author index exists to nos. 1–28, 1936–1966, compiled by Francisco José and María Elena Cardona, Gainesville, University of Florida Press, 1968, 421 pp. Beginning with no. 41, issues are prepared by the Hispanic Division of the Library of Congress and published by the University of Texas Press.

39 Historical Abstracts: Bibliography of the World's Periodical Literature. Santa Barbara, Calif.: Clio Press with the International Social Science Institute, 1955–.

An abstract journal, published quarterly, with signed abstracts contributed by scholars mainly from the United States. To 1964 Abstracts covers the world's periodical literature from 1775 to 1945. After 1964 the United States and Canada are excluded. Beginning with the 1971 volume (vol. 17) it has been published in two parts. Since 1973 Part A covers modern history, 1450–1914, with Part B containing twentieth-century abstracts. Currently indexes some 2,200 periodicals; annual author, biographical, geographical, and subject index.

Bibliographies and Indexes

40 Staff Research in Progress or Recently Completed in the Human-
    ities and the Social Sciences (Latin American Studies in
    the Universities of the United Kingdom). London: Institute
    of Latin American Studies, University of London, 1968-.
        An inventory of research on Latin America by members of
    the academic staff of the Institute of Latin American
    Studies, University of London. Annual compilation; nos.
    1-10 run from 1968 through 1978. Names of persons are
    listed alphabetically under subjects, and there is an
    alphabetical index of authors.

INDEXES

Retrospective

41 BALLESTEROS, VICENTE. Revista de la historia de América:
    índice General, 1963-1972. Mexico: Instituto Pano-
    americano de Geografía e Historia, 1973.
        Continuation of the General Index of the same publica-
    tion, which appeared in 1967 and which included numbers
    1-54, corresponding to the years 1938-1962.

42 Combined Retrospective Index Set to Journals in History,
    1838-1974. 11 vols. Vol. 4, World History: Mexico
    through West Indies. Arlington, Va.: Carrollton Press,
    1977.
        CRIS/History is a comprehensive guide to articles on
    world history from 1838 to 1974 in 243 English-language
    periodicals. First nine volumes arranged by subject
    category and keyword; last two volumes organized by
    author. Vol. 4 (pp. 1-37) includes Mexican history,
    with over sixty items on the Mexican Revolution.

43 FORSTER, MERLIN H. An Index to Mexican Literary Periodicals.
    New York and London: Scarecrow Press, 1966.
        Indexes sixteen literary journals published in Mexico
    between 1920 (e.g., México Moderno) and 1960 (e.g.,
    Estaciones). Contains summaries with data on each journal;
    a list of authors; an index to authors; and an index to
    subject matter treated by the journals.

44 "Guía del Boletín, vols. 27-30, 1956-1959." Boletín del
    Archivo General de la Nación 30 (1959): 667-96.
        A consecutive list of contents with indexes of personal
    and place names for volumes 27-30 of the Boletín del
    Archivo General de la Nación. The Boletín is devoted
    exclusively to the publication of National Archives
    (Mexico) documents and inventories.

45 Índice general de publicaciones periódicas latino-americanas:
    Humanidades y ciencias sociales, 1961-1970. Vols. 1-2,
    Boston: G.K. Hall, 1963-64; Vols. 3-10, Metuchen, N.J.:
    Scarecrow Press, 1965-71.
       Quarterly, later annual, guide to articles. Originally
    an author and subject index; changed with volume 3 to an
    alphabetical listing by subject. Ceased with vol. 10, no.
    2, and no cumulation of vol. 10 was published. For addi-
    tional coverage see item 46.

46 Index to Latin American Periodical Literature, 1961-1965.
    2 vols. Boston: G.K. Hall, 1968.
       First supplement to the eight volume compilation of the
    Index to Latin American Periodical Literature, 1929-1960
    (G.K. Hall, 1962). Compiled in the Columbus Memorial
    Library of the Pan American Union from the Library card
    catalog; entries by authors and subjects. Only twenty-six
    items listed for Mexican revolutionary period.

    _____, 1966-1970. 2 vols. 1979.
       Second supplement to the Index, 1929-1960. Prepared
    by the Columbus Memorial Library of the Pan American Union.
    Lists articles by author and title from 3,000 periodicals,
    including the national official gazettes of the Latin
    American countries. Articles containing information about
    Latin Americans are included in the listings.
       For a current index to Hispanic American periodicals
    see the Hispanic American Periodicals Index, entry 49.

47 MEYER, EUGENIA W. de. "Índice bibliográfico de libros
    norteamericanos sobre la Revolución Mexicana." Anales
    del INAH [Instituto Nacional de Antropología e Historia]
    19 (1966): 265-78.

48 MURO, LUIS. Historia Mexicana: Índice (Julio 1951-Junio
    1976). Mexico: El Colegio de México, 1977.
       A guide to articles and reviews that were published in
    the Historia Mexicana between July 1951 and June 1976
    (vols. 1-25). Arranged by subject headings within chrono-
    logical divisions. Most items are annotated. Includes
    87 items on bibliography; 88 on historiography and related
    topics; 121 on the Mexican Revolution--economy, society,
    politics, and culture (pp. 109-19).

Current

49 Hispanic American Periodicals Index. Tempe: Arizona State
    University Press, 1974; Los Angeles: UCLA Latin American

Bibliographies and Indexes

Center, University of California, 1975-.
A systematic subject-author index (plus cross references)
to approximately 250 important scholarly journals of Latin
American interest. Covers all major disciplines in the
social sciences and the humanities. Published annually.
Journals indexed of special interest to Mexicanists in-
clude: Américas; The Americas; Anuario de Letras; Artes
de México; Boletín del Archivo General de la Nación;
Boletín del Instituto de Investigaciones Bibliográficas;
Cuadernos Americanos; Diálogos; Estudios de Historia
Moderna y Contemporánea de México; HAHR; HM; Journal of
Latin American Studies; Latin American Research Review;
JISWA; Inter-American Economic Affairs; Logos; Revista
de la Universidad de México; Revista Mexicana de Ciencias
Políticas y Sociales; and Revista Mexicana de Sociología.

RESEARCH AIDS AND GUIDES TO RESEARCH

50 American Historical Association's Guide to Historical Lit-
    erature. New York: Macmillan Co., 1961.
       Section Z on Latin America, including Mexico, compiled
    under the direction of Howard F. Cline. All items
    annotated; index. An important first aid for students
    and librarians.

51 BEEZLEY, WILLIAM H. "Research Possibilities in the Mexican
    Revolution: The Governorship." Americas 29 (Jan. 1973):
    308-13.
       Calls for a research effort at the subnational level.

52 BENSON, NETTIE LEE. "Latin American Books and Periodicals."
    In Bibliography: Current State and Future Trends, edited
    by Robert B. Downs and Frances B. Jenkins, pp. 253-62.
    Urbana, Chicago, and London: University of Illinois
    Press, 1967.
       An explanation of enumerative or systematic bibliography
    and analytical or critical bibliography.

53 BIRKOS, ALEXANDER S., and TAMBS, LEWIS A. Academic Writer's
    Guide to Periodicals. Vol. 1, Latin American Studies.
    Kent, Ohio: Kent State University Press, 1971.
       First of a projected seven-volume area study series
    covering periodicals devoted to the disciplines within
    the social sciences and the humanities. Entries include
    periodical titles, editorial personnel, sponsors, number
    of paid subscribers, subject areas, scope, and editorial
    policies. Analytical, topical, and chronological indexes.

Research Aids and Guides to Research

54 BRYAN, ANTHONY T. The Politics of the Porfiriato: A Research
    Review. Bloomington: Indiana University Press, 1973.
      Pamphlet-size guide to research on the Porfiriato after
    1955. Includes archival collections, books, articles,
    and recent dissertations.

55 "CEISAL (Consejo Europeo de Investigaciones Sociales sobre
    América Latina)." Boletín de Estudios Latinoamericanos
    y del Caribe 22 (June 1977): 122-26.
      A list of European addresses of committees, groups and
    institutes affiliated with CEISAL.

56 FERNO, RENATE, and GRENZ, WOLFGANG, comps. Handbuch der
    Deutschen Lateinamerika-Forschung. Hamburg: Institute
    für Iberoamerika Kunde; Bonn: Akadeinischer Austausch-
    dienst, 1980.
      An index of institutions, investigators and experts in
    Germany dealing with Latin America. Contains three sep-
    arate lists of institutions, individuals, and periodicals.
    Data on these three lists is cross-indexed by field,
    geographical area of interest, and topics of concern.
    Index categories are translated into Spanish and
    Portuguese.

57 GEOGHEGAN, ABEL RODOLFO. Obras de referencia de América
    Latina: Repertorio selectivo y anotado de enciclopedias,
    diccionarios, bibliografías, repertorios biograficos,
    catálogos, guías, anuarios, índices, etc. Buenos Aires:
    1965.
      Includes all types of reference works that refer to
    Latin America, regardless of subject matter and place of
    publication. Lists 2,694 items arranged by Universal
    Decimal Classification, with analytical index. Many
    annotations.

58 GREENLEAF, RICHARD E., and MEYER, MICHAEL C., comps. and eds.
    Research in Mexican History. Lincoln: University of
    Nebraska Press, 1973.
      A comprehensive guide with practical information about
    research topics, problems, and methodology. Includes a
    bibliography of bibliographies, a field research guide,
    archival descriptions, a guide to archival collections,
    and an appended "scholar's map" of Mexico City. William
    H. Beezley, Michael C. Meyer, Lyle C. Brown, and Albert
    L. Michaels have authored articles on research on
    Revolutionary Mexico, 1910-1940. William D. Raat has
    compiled "Two Decades of Unpublished Doctoral Dissertations
    on Mexico, 1950-70."

Research Aids and Guides to Research

59 HARO, ROBERT P. Latin Americana Research in the United
    States: A Guide and Directory. Chicago: American Library
    Association, 1971.
        Provides information on Latin American library collec-
    tions and research centers in Canada and the United States.
    Includes names of bibliographers and an annotated list of
    book catalogues.

60 Latin American Studies in the Universities of the United
    Kingdom. London: Institute of Latin American Studies,
    University of London, 1966–.
        Annual list of teachers and guide to syllabuses. Twelve
    issues between 1966 and 1978. Names of persons are listed
    alphabetically within the grades of professor, reader,
    lecturer, etc., and for purposes of convenience, a
    distinction is made, under categories A and B, between
    those persons who are directly engaged in the teaching of
    Latin American courses and those who are not.

61 MESA–LAGO, CARMELO. Latin American Studies in Europe.
    Pittsburgh: Center for Latin American Studies, University
    of Pittsburgh, 1980.
        A comprehensive and standardized guide on Latin American
    studies programs in Europe and an analysis and comparison
    of such programs. The first part provides a guide to, or
    country reports on, close to 100 Latin American studies
    programs in Europe. Thirteen European countries are
    given full coverage. They are Austria, Czechoslovakia,
    Federal Republic of Germany, France, German Democratic
    Republic, Italy, the Netherlands, Poland, Portugal, Spain,
    Sweden, the Union of Soviet Socialist Republics, and the
    United Kingdom. The second part of this report is an
    analysis and comparison of the programs, the timing of
    their inception, the motivations for their creation, and
    the principal initiator of such programs. This is followed
    by an evaluation and ranking of the programs, including
    library collections and publications.

62 MÖRNER, MAGNUS B., and CAMPA, RICCARDO. Investigación en
    ciencias sociales e históricas sobre América Latina:
    Enfoque preliminar para una guía. Rome: Consejo Europeo
    de Investigaciones en Ciencias Sociales sobre América
    Latina (CEISAL), 1975.
        A guide to bibliographies and research aids for
    historical and social science work on Latin America.
    Especially valuable for its listing of Latin American
    research centers in Europe (the Germanys, Austria,
    Belgium, Czechoslovakia, Scandinavia, Spain, France,

14

Great Britain, Hungary, Italy, Holland, Portugal, Switzerland, and the Soviet Union) and European professional groups.

63 National Directory of Latin Americanists. 2d ed. Hispanic Foundation Bibliographical Series, no. 12. Washington, D.C.: Library of Congress, 1972.
  Biographies of 2,695 specialists in the social sciences and humanities. Includes "area" and "non-area" specialists, including physical scientists, diplomats, and businessmen. Supplants 1966 edition.

64 L'Ordinaire des Mexicanistes. Perpignan, France: Institut d'Etudes Mexicaines, Université de Perpignan, 1974-.
  Newsletter (mimeographed) of the Institute of Mexican Studies, University of Perpignan. Translated title: The Mexican Approach. Printed eight times a year. Contents: news; bibliography; documents; guides to Mexican archives and libraries; research; etc.

65 OSS, ADRIAAN van, comp. Latinoamericanistas en Europa: Registro Bio-Bibliográfico de 1976. Amsterdam: Centro de Estudios Documentación Latinoamericanos, 1976.
  Bio-bibliographies of 518 European scholars specializing in Latin America as of 1975-1976. An alphabetical listing of authors includes information on their publications, institutional affiliation, language facility, date and place of birth, and home and office addresses. Two appendixes include a place listing of individuals and a list of persons by discipline.

66 Revista de Historia de América. Mexico: Commission on History of the Pan American Institute of Geography and History (PAIGH), 1938-.
  Provides extensive quarterly bibliographies of books, pamphlets, and articles on hemispheric history. The Revista, a semiannual, contains bibliographical articles, documents, and reviews. The PAIGH Commission is composed of outstanding historians from all nations of the western hemisphere. An extensive annual index (separately printed) and a detailed table of contents enhances its usefulness.

67 ROSS, STANLEY R. "Bibliography of Sources for Contemporary Mexican History." HAHR 39 (May 1959): 234-38.
  Description of the bibliographical project of the El Colegio de México seminar group (which eventually led to the publication of the multivolume Fuentes de la historia contemporánea de México).

Research Aids and Guides to Research

68 SHEEHY, EUGENE P., comp. Guide to Reference Books. 9th ed.
    Chicago: American Library Association, 1976.
    _____. Supplement, 1980.
         Annotated descriptions of general bibliographies, library
    catalogs, guides to dissertations, record guides, serial
    publications, historiographical works, atlases, directories,
    and encyclopedias. Latin American section (pp. 622-30)
    subdivided by country. Mexican section includes
    specialized bibliographies, guides to records, and
    dictionaries and encyclopedias.

69 STEGMANN, WILHELM. "The Latin American Institute in Berlin
    and Latin American Studies in West Germany." Working Paper,
    no. B-14, read at the 23rd Seminar on the Acquisition of
    Latin American Library Materials, University of London,
    16-21 July, 1978, at Austin, Texas. Mimeographed.
         Speech delivered by the Director of the Latin American
    Institute in Berlin. Topic is the Latin American Institute
    of Berlin within the framework of Latin American research
    and library resources in West Germany. Includes a ground
    plan of the main floor of the Ibero-Amerikanisches Institut.

70 ULLOA ORTÍZ, BERTA. "Diplomacy in the Borderlands: An
    Analysis of Some Research Material and Opportunities in the
    Archivo de la Secretaría de Relaciones Exteriores de
    México, 1910-1920." Paper read at the Conference on the
    Borderlands, 26 October 1973, at San Antonio, Texas.
    Mimeographed.

71 WALFORD, A.J. Guide to Reference Material. 2d ed. 3 vols.
    London: Library Association, 1975.
         Guide to reference books and bibliographies, with
    emphasis on items published in Britain. Vol. 2 covers
    social and historical sciences, philosophy and religion.
    Mexico section, pp. 574-75.

72 WERLICH, DAVID P. Research Tools for Latin American Histo-
    rians: A Select Annotated Bibliography. New York:
    Garland, 1979.
         First section devoted to various classes of reference
    works. A final section includes reference works for each
    of the twenty Latin American republics. Entries give facts
    of publication, number of pages, and Library of Congress
    catalog card numbers. Bibliography cross-referenced;
    author and subject indexes.

For a guide to research in the United Kingdom see entry 17. For an
inventory of research by the staff of the Institute of Latin American

Guides to Libraries and Archives

Studies at the University of London, <u>see</u> entry 40. For Latin
American research centers in the U.S. <u>see</u> entry 97. For research
opportunities in Mexican history <u>see</u> entry 224.

GUIDES TO LIBRARIES AND ARCHIVES

CATALOGUES AND OTHER GUIDES TO ARCHIVES, INSTITUTES, LIBRARIES AND
SPECIAL COLLECTIONS

73 BAILEY, DAVID C., and BEEZLEY, WILLIAM H. <u>A Guide to
    Historical Sources in Saltillo, Coahuila</u>. Latin American
    Studies Center, Monograph Series, no. 13. East Lansing:
    Michigan State University, 1975.
        A guide (descriptive listing) to the public, private,
    and ecclesiastical archives of Coahuila, located in
    Saltillo. Introduction argues in favor of Mexican micro-
    history. Several materials listed and described for the
    Porfiriato and the Revolution, especially for the Archivo
    General del Estado de Coahuila. Concludes with a biblio-
    graphy of local and regional history, including guides.

74 BARTLEY, RUSSELL H., and WAGNER, STUART L. <u>Latin America in
    Basic Historical Collections: A Working Guide</u>. Hoover
    Institution Bibliographical Series, no. 51. Stanford,
    Calif.: Stanford University, 1972.
        A concise description and bibliography of major archives,
    libraries, and special collections germane to the study
    of Latin American history. Describes holdings of major
    archives and repositories (public and private, national
    and local) in Anglo-America, Latin America, Europe, Iberia,
    and elsewhere. Most important national archives of
    Mexico included, as well as the major research centers
    of the United States and Europe.

75 CASTANEDA, CARMEN. "Los archivos de Guadalajara." HM 25
    (July-Sept. 1975): 143-62.
        This article brings together information about archives
    for the history of Mexico in general and the north and
    west in particular. Listed is information about nine
    archives, seven civil and two religious. Included are
    the main archives for the state of Jalisco, including the
    Cultural Archive of the State of Jalisco and the Histor-
    ical Archive of the State of Jalisco, and the municipal
    archive of Guadalajara. Information listed includes histor-
    ical period covered by the archive materials, branch
    libraries, contents, current director, address, and
    business hours. Bibliography.

Guides to Libraries and Archives

76 Catálogo de la Biblioteca Nacional de Antropología e Historia.
    10 vols. Boston: G.K. Hall, 1972.
        A catalog of the library holdings of the library of the
    National Museum of Anthropology and History. Indispensable
    to researchers in the historical and anthropological sci-
    ences. Author, title, subject, and added entries are
    arranged in one alphabetical sequence, and the catalog
    contains many analytics for journal articles. Mexican
    Revolution section (vol. 7, pp. 454-68) lists 288 sources.

77 Catalog of the Latin American Collection of the University
    of Texas Library Austin . 31 vols. Boston: G.K. Hall,
    1969.
    _____. Supplement 1. 5 vols., 1971.
    _____. Supplement 2. 3 vols., 1973.
    _____. Supplement 3. 8 vols., 1975.
    _____. [Supplement 4.] Catalog of the Nettie Lee Benson
    Latin American Collection. 3 vols., 1977.
        A dictionary catalog of authors, titles, and subjects
    for books, pamphlets, periodicals, newspapers, and micro-
    film. The library's collection exceeds 160,000 volumes.
    Updated by Bibliographic Guide to Latin American Studies
    (G.K. Hall, 1979-). See entry 122.

78 Catalog of the Latin American Collection, University of
    Florida Libraries. 13 vols. Boston: G.K. Hall, 1973.
        Catalog of 120,000 volumes of books, pamphlets,
    periodicals, and government documents. Strongest discipline
    represented is history. Mexican Revolution section (vol.
    9, pp. 134-58) contains 509 items on history, politics
    and government, and intellectual life.

79 Catalog of the Latin American Library of the Tulane University
    Library [New Orleans]. 9 vols. Boston: G.K. Hall,
    1970.
    _____. Supplement, 2 vols., 1973.
    _____. Supplement, 2 vols., 1975.
    _____. Supplement, 2 vols., 1978.
    Dictionary catalog; does not include entries for news-
    papers, maps, or manuscripts. Collection strong in Mexico
    and Central America.

80 Catalogue of the Library of the Hispanic Society of America
    [New York]. 10 vols. Boston: G.K. Hall, 1962.
    _____. First Supplement, 4 vols., 1970.
        Card catalog of over 100,000 items; primarily books on
    Spain, Portugal, and Hispanic America.

81 COTTLER, SUSAN M.; HAIGH, ROGER M.; and WEATHERS, SHIRLEY A.
    Preliminary Survey of the Mexican Collection. Number 1,
    Finding Aids to the Microfilmed Manuscript Collection of
    the Genealogical Society of Utah, edited by Roger M. Haigh.
    Salt Lake City: University of Utah Press, 1978.
    _____. Supplement, 1979.
        Finding aid to the 105,584 rolls of Mexican microfilm
    filmed and owned by the Genealogical Society of Utah. This
    survey report lists all filmed Mexican parish and civil
    registers held by the Society as of September 1977. List-
    ings are arranged alphabetically, by province and then
    by municipality within each province. Each listing in-
    dicates the location of the repository, the type of record,
    the number of rolls, and the roll numbers of "other
    material," i.e., microfilm material of little or no
    genealogical significance, containing few vital statistics,
    but of possible scholarly use. Twelve states not included
    in the present catalog include Baja California (and Baja
    Sur), Sonora, Sinaloa, Chihuahua, Durango, Nayaít, Querétaro,
    Colima, Guerrero, Chiapas, and Tabasco. Especially strong
    are Jalisco, Michoacán, and the Federal District. Time
    span is from the late seventeenth century into the twentieth
    century, with some material as recent as 1970. Most civil
    records stop in the 1920s or 1930s. Parish and civil
    registers include records on births, baptisms, marriages,
    deaths, wills, divorces, guardianships, adoptions, church
    affairs, and criminal cases. An obvious source for studies
    on Church-State relations and church infrastructure.

82 EVANS, G. EDWARD, and MORALES, FRANK J. "Fuentes de la
    historia de México en archivos norteamericanos." HM 18
    (Jan.-Mar. 1969): 432-62.
        A guide to depositories in the United States and their
    documentary holdings for the history of Mexico.

83 FRANCO, J.L. Documentos para la historia de México.
    Havana: 1961.
        Materials on Mexican history in the Cuban National
    Archives.

84 GARCÍA y GARCÍA, J. JESUS. Guía de archivos. Mexico:
    Instituto de Investigaciones Sociales, UNAM, 1972.
        A directory of Mexican archives. Organized into two
    sections: Archives-Mexico, and Archives-Federal District.
    Emphasis on materials dealing with the socioeconomic
    development of Mexico. Index.

Guides to Libraries and Archives

85 GARNER, JANE. Sources of Information on the Manuscript and
   Archival Collections in the Nettie Lee Benson Latin
   American Collection. Austin: University of Texas,
   General Libraries, 1980.
     A bibliography to the finding aids (guides, lists, and
   calendars) that exist for manuscript and archival collections (both in the original and on microfilm) held by
   the Nettie Lee Benson Latin American Collection at the
   University of Texas at Austin. Of special interest are
   two unpublished finding aids listed on page 4: the
   Lázaro de la Garza Archive (northern Mexico, 1913-1936,
   including Francisco Villa correspondence) and the Mexican
   Papers of John W.F. Dulles (1,600 items relating to
   politics in twentieth-century Mexico).

86 GÓMEZ CANEDO, LINO. "Archivos y bibliotecas de Espana que
   interesan a la historia de México." Anuario de Biblio-
   teconomía y Archivonomía 3 (1963): 9-42.
     A survey of Mexican materials in the major archives of
   Spain--Archivo General de Indias (Sevilla); Archivo General
   de Simancas y Archivo Histórico Nacional; Archivos de los
   Ministerios (Militar, Marino, Asuntos Exteriores, Hacienda);
   the three great Madrid libraries (Nacional, Palacio, and
   Academia de la Historia); special institutions (Museo
   Naval; Servicio Histórico Militar; Biblioteca del Escorial;
   Biblioteca Colombina); archivos notariales, municipales,
   eclesiásticos, universitarios, y familares; and others.
   Most materials are for the colonial and prerevolutionary
   era, although the Órdenes Militares section of the Archivo
   Histórico Nacional in Madrid has data on the Porfiriato.

87 GONZALEZ CICERO, STELLA MARÍA. "Fondos documentales mexicanos
   en bibliotecas del extranjero." Boletín del Archivo
   General de la Nación 1 (1977): 35.
     A list of documents concerning Mexico in foreign
   depositories that are now available on microfilm at the
   Archivo General de la Nación.

88 GORMLY, MARY. Resources for Latin American Studies. Los
   Angeles: Latin American Studies Center, California State
   University, 1977.
     A bibliography of reference sources available in the
   John F. Kennedy Memorial Library of the California State
   University at Los Angeles. Includes biographies, book
   reviews, dictionaries, encyclopedias, newspapers, and
   journals. Also lists United States National Archive
   materials for revolutionary Mexico.

89 Guide to the National Archives of the United States.
    Washington, D.C.: National Archives and Records Service,
    General Services Administration, 1974.
        In addition to being a guide to all of the Record Groups
    in the National Archives, the annotations and Record Group
    introductions provide basic data on the origin and develop-
    ment of government agencies and bureaus.

90 Guide to the Sources of the History of the Nations. A,
    Latin America. The Hague: Government Pub. Office, 1966-69.
        Vol. 3, a guide to the sources in the Netherlands for
    the history of Latin America, by M.P.H. Roessingh; vol. 4,
    a guide (in Spanish) to sources for the history of Latin
    America in Spain.

91 GUSTAFSON, MILTON O., ed. The National Archives and Foreign
    Relations Research. Athens: Ohio University Press, 1974.
        Research guide to the National Archives in Washington,
    D.C. Describes the Record Groups of several governmental
    departments. In addition, an article by Robert Freeman
    Smith deals with research problems and resources peculiar
    to the topic of United States-Latin American relations
    in the twentieth century.

92 HALE, RICHARD W., Jr., Guide to Photocopied Historical
    Materials in the United States and Canada. Ithaca:
    Cornell University Press, 1961. Published for the American
    Historical Association.

93 HAMER, PHILIP M., ed. A Guide to Archives and Manuscripts in
    the United States. New Haven: Yale University Press,
    1961.
        Compiled for the National Historical Publications
    Commission. Contents organized alphabetically by state.

94 HAMMOND, GEORGE P., ed. A Guide to the Manuscript Collections
    of the Bancroft Library. Berkeley and Los Angeles: Univ-
    ersity of California Press, 1972.
        A guide to a collection of manuscripts on the history
    of Mexico. Contains documents by José María Andrade,
    José Fernando Ramírez and others. Twentieth-century
    holdings include the Silvestre Terrazas archive--an
    excellent resource for the late Porfiriato and early
    Revolution.

95 HENDERSON, PETER V. N. "The Archivo del Presidente Francisco
    I. Madero." Americas 36 (April 1980): 527-35.

Guides to Libraries and Archives

A description of the 60,000 pages of the Alfredo Álvarez Archive recently microfilmed by the Museum of National Anthropology (renamed the Archivo del Presidente Francisco I. Madero). A microfilm duplicate of the papers is available at the University of Nebraska. The archive is composed of twenty-two reels, most of which are divided into Madero's outgoing correspondence and stenographers' notebooks of the presidential years and letters addressed to Madero or his close associates. Most materials are in chronological order and run from 1891 to 1913.

96   Latijns America [CEDLA]. Amsterdam. CEDLA, 1978.
        A guide to and description of the activities of the
        A guide to and description of the activities of the
Institute of Latin American Studies in Amsterdam. Describes CEDLA's organization, the contents of the library (CEDLA-bibliotheek), publications and contents of the CEDLA periodical (Boletín de Estudios Latinoamericanos y del Caribe; published twice yearly in June and December, from April 1965 to present). Includes Mexican studies.

97 KOSLOW, LAWRENCE E. Facilities for Research on Mexico at Latin American Centers in the United States. Tempe. Center for Latin American Studies, Arizona State University, 1971.
        Describes the focus of thirty-eight Latin American Research Centers in the United States, with information on publications, interested faculty, periodicals received, and special library services.

98 LaFRANCE, DAVID G.; LOBDELL, FRED; and SABBAH, MAURICE LESLIE. "Fuentes históricas para el estudio de Puebla en el siglo XX." HM 27 (Oct.-Dec. 1977): 260-72.
        Review of the sources available for the study of twentieth-century Puebla. In the city of Puebla the best sources of documents are the Archive of the Municipal Secretariat of Puebla, General Archive of the Notaries, Archive of the State Congress, and the Autonomous University of Puebla. In Mexico City, documents relating to Puebla are available in the National Newspaper Library, the Miguel Lerdo de Tejada Library of the Secretary of the Treasury and Public Credit, and the Library of the National Institute of Anthropology and History.

99 Latin America and Latin American Periodicals. Widener Shelf-list, nos. 5-6. 2 vols. Cambridge, Mass.: Harvard University Press, 1966.

A Harvard University Library shelflist of 27,292 titles;
primarily works on history and civilization.

100 LIAGRE, LEONE, and BAERTEN, JEAN. Guide des sources de
l'histoire d'Amérique Latine Conservées en Belgique.
Brussels: Archives Générales du Royaume, 1967.
Guide to sources on Latin American history in Belgium.
Vol. II/I of the Guide to the Sources of the History of
the Nations series.

101 MENDOZA LÓPEZ, MIGUEL. Catálogo General del Archivo del
Ayuntamiento de la Ciudad de México. Mexico: Instituto
Nacional de Antropología e Historia, Departamento de
Investigaciones Históricas, 1972.
This is a catalog to the 7,490 volumes held in the
Archives del Ayuntamiento.

102 MEYER, JEAN A. "México en los archivos diplomáticos y
consulares de Francia." HM 19 (Oct.-Dec. 1969): 302-308.
A short list, not intended to be exhaustive, of the
diplomatic and consular archives of France. Designed
as an aid for students and researchers of Mexican
diplomatic history.

103 MEYER, MICHAEL C. "Albert Bacon Fall's Mexican Papers: A
Preliminary Investigation." NMHR 40 (April 1965): 165-74.
A general introduction (not a detailed description) to
the Fall Papers located at the Henry E. Huntington Library
with microfilm copies at the University of New Mexico and
the University of Nebraska.

104 MILLARES CARLO, AGUSTÍN. Repertorio bibliográfico de los
archivos mexicanos de interés para la historia de México.
Mexico: Biblioteca Nacional de México, Instituto Bibliográfico Mexicano, 1959.
Lists more than 1,000 published bibliographies, catalogs,
and guides to collections and archives in Europe and
America relating to Mexican history; annotations and subject index. (An enlarged revision of the first section of
the author's 1948 Repertorio.)

105 MORALES PADRÓN, FRANCISCO, ed. Anuario de Estudios Ameri-
canos. Vol. 25, El Americanismo en europa. Seville:
Escuela de Estudios Hispano-Americanos de Sevilla, 1970.
A guide to Latin American research centers, libraries,
and archives in Spain, France, Great Britain, and Holland.
Essays contributed by Francisco Morales Padrón, Frédéric
Mauro, Harold Blakemore, and Harry Hoetink. Entire issue

Guides to Libraries and Archives

of this annual edition devoted to the guide.

106 MORENO, ROBERTO. "La historia mexicana y la Biblioteca
     Nacional." Boletín del Instituto del Investigaciones
     Bibliográficas 1 (1969): 153-63.
         Bibliographic sources and manuscripts in the Biblioteca
     Nacional of Mexico for the study of Mexican history.

107 NAYLOR, BERNARD; HALLEWELL, LAURENCE; and STEELE, COLIN.
     Directory of Libraries and Special Collections on Latin
     America and the West Indies. London: University of
     London, Athlone Press, 1975.
         A listing of 146 libraries throughout the British Isles.
     Entries arranged in alphabetical order of the postal towns
     in which the libraries are situated. Each entry has a
     description of the contents and organization of the collec-
     tion with additional information on admission, inquiries,
     microreading, copying facilities, typewriters, lending
     services, union record, and publications of or about the
     library. An appendix contains a list of other British
     groups concerned with Latin America, and a list of relevant
     serial publications. Index to entry numbers.
         For the study of Mexico in particular, the following
     collections are suggested: Bristol; Cambridge; Institute
     of Latin American Studies, Univ. of Glasgow; British
     Museum Library; Wellcome Institute of the History of
     Medicine (London); Portsmouth Polytechnic Library; and the
     Bodleian Library, University of Oxford (70,000 vols., best
     collection in Great Britain outside the British Museum).

108 NEUBECK, DEBORAH K. Guide to a Microfilm Edition of the
     Mexican Mission Papers of John Lind. St. Paul: Minnesota
     Historical Society, 1971.

109 PERRY, LAURENS B. Inventario y guía de la colección General
     Porfirio Díaz. Mexico: University of the Americas Press,
     1969.
         Gives a summarized history of the collection which has
     been partially utilized in different eras. The thirty
     volumes published by Elede in conjunction with the UNAM,
     make up only a small part of the general archive. The
     archive consists of 371 rolls of microfilm which cover
     the years 1876 to December of 1911. The archive is made
     up of letters, scattered documents, telegrams, codes,
     pamphlets, receipts, etc. The collection was mainly
     controlled by the UNAM but later was taken into the hands
     of the Universidad de las Américas, which has organized
     and published the present guide.

110   RADDING de MURRIETA, CYNTHIA. "Archival Research in Sonora, Mexico." Americas 32 (April 1976): 618-32.
      Survey of five different archives in Sonora at three levels--parish, municipal, and state. Author is a member of the Centro Regional del Noroeste, Instituto Nacional de Antropología e Historia, based in Hermosillo, Sonora.

111   RAMOS, ROBERTO. "Catálogo de obras de la revolución mexicana que se encuentran en servicio en la Biblioteca Nacional de México." Boletín Bibliográfico, no. 355 (Nov. 1966): 18-19.
      First of a continuing series of works on the Mexican Revolution in the National Library of Mexico.

112   RICHMOND, DOUGLAS W. "The Venustiano Carranza Archive." HAHR 56 (May 1976): 290-94.
      Descriptions of 1913-1920 materials recently acquired by the Centro de Estudios de Historia de México. Mostly incoming correspondence; especially strong on social and economic conditions.

113   ROMERO CERVANTES, ARTURO. "Afinidades y diferencias entre los precursores magonistas." Boletín Bibliográfico de la Secretaría de Hacienda y Crédito Público 15 (1969): 412-13.
      A study of the letters found in the Archivo General de la Nación.

114   Schlagwortkatalog des Ibero-Amerikanischen Instituts: Preussischer Kulturbesitz [Subject Catalog of the Ibero-American Institute. Prussian Cultural Foundation]. 30 vols. Boston: G.K. Hall, 1977.
      A subject catalog to the holdings of the Latin American Institute of Berlin, among the largest institutions in Europe collecting Spanish, Portuguese and Latin American library materials (almost a half million titles) on a multidisciplinary basis. The catalog is divided into four parts: (a) a general section (vols. 1-19); (b) a geographical section (vols. 19-23); (c) a section of place names (vols. 23-24); and (d) a biographical section (vols. 24-30). Subject headings in the general and geographical sections are listed directly in alphabetical order. Place names are listed under the respective countries, whereas names of persons in the biographical section are listed by profession. For the Mexican Revolution (see vol. 21, geographical section: "Mexiko-Geschichte, 20. Jh.," pp. 603-35) 449 items are listed. Other materials relevant to the Mexican Revolution can be found in the biographical

Guides to Libraries and Archives

section. Includes indexes to place names and biographical section.

115 SEMO, ENRIQUE. "Documentos mexicanos en archivos de la República Democrática Alemana." HM 19 (Jan.-Mar. 1970): 418-31.
An inventory of Mexican documents in the principal archives of the Democratic Republic of Germany. Materials mostly relate to commercial relations, diplomacy, and politics from the mid-nineteenth century to 1934.

116 TERRAZAS, SILVESTRE. Silvestre Terrazas, 1873-1944: Correspondence and Papers. Berkeley, California: Bancroft Library, n.d.
The collection of manuscripts is important for the period 1910-1915.

117 ULIBARRI, GEORGE S., and HARRISON, JOHN P. Guide to Materials on Latin America in the National Archives of the United States. Washington, D.C.: National Archives and Records Service, General Services Administration, 1974.
A revised and expanded edition of Harrison's earlier Guide to Materials on Latin America in the National Archives (1961).

118 ULLOA ORTÍZ, BERTA. Revolución Mexicana, 1910-1920. Mexico: Secretaría de Relaciones Exteriores, 1963.
A descriptive guide to the 259 bound volumes in the "Mexican Revolution" section of the Foreign Relations Archive in Mexico City. In spite of the title, several materials are described for the 1904-1910 period. Besides the lengthy descriptions, the name index is a helpful tool.

119 _____. La Revolución Mexicana a través del Archivo de la Secretaría de Relaciones Exteriores. Mexico: UNAM, 1963.
Careful analysis of the contents of the Foreign Relations Archive; complementary volume to Revolución Mexicana, 1910-1920.

120 VELÁZQUEZ, MARIA del CARMEN. "Bibliographical Essay: The Colección SepSetentas." Americas 35 (January 1979): 373-89.
A bibliographical essay of the Colección SepSetentas—315 volumes published by the Departamento de Divulgación de la Secretaría de Educación Pública during the Echeverría years (1970-1976). Examines those works which deal with Mexican national history. Includes a list of authors and titles.

Guides to Libraries and Archives

121   WALNE, PETER, ed.   A Guide to Manuscript Sources for the His-
      tory of Latin America and the Caribbean in the British
      Isles.   London: Oxford University Press in collaboration
      with the Institute of Latin American Studies, University
      of London, 1973.
          A comprehensive guide to archival and manuscript sources
      for the history of Latin America, the Caribbean, and the
      Philippine Islands preserved in the British Isles.
      Arrangement of entries is in the alphabetical order of
      English counties, followed by Scotland, Wales, Northern
      Ireland, and the Republic of Ireland. A major exception
      is the placement of business records, found at the end
      of the book. Addenda and index.
          Students of the Mexican Revolution should note the
      records of the British War Office, misc., 1904-1908; the
      antislavery papers in the Rhodes House Library, Oxford
      (e.g., slavery in Yucatán, 1910-1912); and the collection
      of the Royal Botanic Gardens, Richmond, Surrey (Mexico,
      1898-1928).

For a listing of Latin American research centers in Europe see entry
62. For the library of the Ibero-Amerikanisches Institut see entries
69 and 114. For the relationship of documents to archival research
see entry 219.

UNION LISTS

122   Bibliographic Guide to Latin American Studies, 1978. 3 vols.
      Boston: G.K. Hall, 1979-.
          This annual guide is in dictionary format with name and
      subject cross-references supplied. Includes cataloguing
      input by the University of Texas Nettie Lee Benson Latin
      American Collection into the OCLC, Inc., system, a computer-
      ized data base, and items selected from the Library of Con-
      gress's machine-readable cataloguing for Latin American
      materials. First issue includes materials catalogued at
      the University of Texas, Austin, from September 1977
      through August 1978. Serves as current supplement to the
      Catalog of the Latin American Collection of the University
      of Texas Library. See entry 77.

123   CHARNO, STEVEN M. Latin American Newspapers in United States
      Libraries: A Union List. Conference on Latin American
      History publication, no. 2. Austin: University of Texas
      Press, 1969.
          Lists about 5,500 newspapers published in Puerto Rico
      and the twenty Latin American republics. Arrangement by
      place of publication, first by country, then by city.

Guides to Libraries and Archives

124   KOSTER, C.J., ed. Latin American History with Politics:
       A Serials List. Westmead, Farnborough, Hants, England:
       Gregg International Publishers, 1973.
           Second of a three-part series of guides to Latin Amer-
       ican periodicals published under the direction of The
       Committee on Latin America, Canning House. Restricted to
       those periodicals that are housed in over sixty British
       libraries and indexed in the National Union Catalogue of
       Latin Americana. Lists 117 Mexican serials (pp. 87-95)
       alphabetically by title, with dates of publication, and
       name of libraries in British Isles where held. Preface
       by R. A. Humphreys; "Note on Periodical Indexes" by
       A.J. Walford. Title index.

125   MESA, ROSA QUINTERO, comp. Latin American Serial Documents.
       Vol. 4, Mexico. Ann Arbor, Mich.: University Microfilms,
       Xerox Corp., 1970.
           An inclusive bibliography of serial documents published
       in Mexico and available in holdings in the United States
       and Canada. Covers only serials issued by federal govern-
       ment and related agencies. A cooperative effort of six-
       teen U.S. universities. Includes publications of govern-
       mental agencies, national museums, national libraries,
       and national universities. Newspapers and inter-American
       publications excluded. Listed by author and title, with
       beginning date of serial, place of publication, frequency,
       and major holdings in the United States and Canada.

GUIDES TO THESES AND DISSERTATIONS

126   Catalogue des thèses et mémoires sur l'Amérique latine
       soutenues en France de 1954 a 1969. Paris: Université
       Institut des hautes études de l'Amérique latine, Centre
       de documentation, 1969.
           A listing of theses on Latin America completed in French
       institutions of higher studies between 1954 and 1969.
       Mexican section (pp. 150-58) lists works on literature,
       history, geography, economy, politics, society, ethnology,
       and law. Literature section especially good for the
       Mexican Revolution, with several items on women, indig-
       enism, corridos, Octavio Paz, Carlos Fuentes, Martín
       Luis Guzmán, and Mariano Azuela.

127   CHAFFEE, WILBER A., Jr., and GRIFFIN, HONOR M. Dissertations
       on Latin America by U.S. Historians, 1960-1970: A Biblio-
       graphy. Austin: University of Texas Press, 1973.

Entries grouped by countries and arranged alphabetically within each group by author's last name. Each entry is followed by information on the availability of the dissertation on interlibrary loan or microfilm. Includes dissertations (without abstracts) completed or in progress as of April 1971. Mexico subdivided into pre- and post-Independence. Ninety-four items for post-Independence Mexico.

128 DEAL, CARL W., ed. Latin America and the Caribbean: A Dissertation Bibliography. Ann Arbor: University Microfilm International, 1978.
WALTERS, MARIAN G., ed. _____. Supplement, 1980.
Lists 7,200 dissertation titles published by University Microfilms International through 1977 and supersedes UMI's Latin America: A Catalog of Dissertations, published in 1974. Mexican history section (pp. 76-81) lists 378 titles. Supplement brings to 9,168 the number of titles on Latin America.

129 Catálogo de tesis sobre historia de México. Mexico: Comité Mexicano de Ciencias Históricas, 1976.
A listing of 1120 theses and dissertations produced in Mexico, the United States, France, and England, on Mexican history, between 1931-1975. Produced by the Comité Mexicano de Ciencias Históricos, a group which was founded in 1966 at the Biblioteca del Archivo General de la Nación and consists of historians from the Archivo General de la Nación, the Universidad Nacional Autónoma de México, the Colegio de México, and the Universidad Iberoamericana.

130 INSTITUTE OF LATIN AMERICA. Latin American Research and Publications at the University of Texas at Austin, 1893-1969. Austin: University of Texas Press, 1971.
Lists doctoral dissertations and master's theses, together with 304 publications of the Institute and the Texas Press. A short description of each doctoral dissertation makes the publication a useful research tool. Reflects several outstanding research facilities, especially for border relations and Mexican history. Arranged chronologically, with author and subject indexes.

131 List of Doctoral Dissertations in History (Now in Progress or Completed at Universities in the United States).
Washington, D.C.: American Historical Association, 1947-.
Listing arranged by field of history with author and university indexes; up-to-date supplements. Originally published annually, now irregularly.

Guides to Theses and Dissertations

132 RAAT, WILLIAM DIRK. "Two Decades of Unpublished Doctoral
Dissertations on Mexico, 1950-1970." In Research in
Mexican History, edited by Richard E. Greenleaf and Michael
C. Meyer, pp. 197-211. Lincoln: University of Nebraska
Press, 1973.
Lists thirty-five dissertations for the Porfiriato and
fifty for the Revolution.

133 Theses in Latin American Studies at British Universities in
Progress and Completed. London: University of London,
Institute of Latin American Studies, 1966-.
Annual; listing by university with author and subject
indexes. Compiled from information provided by the
correspondents of the Institute in universities of the
United Kingdom. Includes Ph.D. work and theses. Information listed includes approved title, the author, name
of the supervisor, the university, expected date of com-
pletion, and the degree sought or awarded. Revised
annually. Nos. 1-12 run from 1966 through 1978. Author
index; subject index of research theses.

134 ZUBATSKY, DAVID S., comp. Doctoral Dissertations in History
and the Social Sciences on Latin America and the Caribbean
Accepted by Universities in the United Kingdom, 1920-1972.
London: Institute of Latin American Studies, University
of London, 1973.
A comprehensive guide to dissertations in the humanities
and social sciences (language and literature excluded)
submitted for degrees from 1920 to the academic year 1971-
72. Under country or geographical region, all dissertations have been classified on the basis of their contents.
221 entries (some duplicates). Includes a bibliography
of sources. Seventeen dissertations about Mexico, only
two of which deal directly with the Revolution. Most
dissertations are on Jamaica, the West Indies, and
Trinidad and Tobago.

BOOK REVIEWS

135 History: Reviews of New Books. Washington, D.C.: Helen
Dwight Reid Educational Foundation, 1979-.
Reviews of recently published history books. Each
volume contains reviews of over 500 books, each one
reviewed within three to twelve months after publication.
Works on Mexican history reviewed under "Americas" section
towards the back of each issue. Monthly (published ten
times yearly) with annual index.

Specialized Dictionaries and Encyclopedias

136   MATOS, ANTONIO, ed. <u>Guía a las reseñas de libros de y sobre</u>
      <u>Hispanoamérica (1972-1975)</u>. 4 vols. Detroit: Blaine
      Ethridge, 1976-77.
        A guide to reviews of books from and about Hispanic
      America. An index and summary of reviews which appeared
      between 1972-1975 in nearly 350 of the principal review
      media. Text in English or Spanish; summaries prepared
      in the language of the original review. Includes books
      on Mexican-Americans, as well as Mexican history. Listed
      alphabetically by name of author(s) of works reviewed.
      Title index. <u>See also</u> entries 137 and 138.

137   _____. <u>Guía a las reseñas de libros de y sobre Hispano-</u>
      <u>américa</u>. Río Piedras, Puerto Rico: n.p., 1975.
        An author-title list with citations of reviews of Latin
      American books which appeared in periodicals in the General
      Library of the University of Puerto Rico between 1960-
      1964.

138   _____, ed. <u>A Guide to Review of Books from and about</u>
      <u>Hispanic America (Guía a las reseñas de libros de y sobre</u>
      <u>Hispanoamérica)</u>. Detroit: Blaine Ethridge, 1972-.
        Annual guide; includes 25- to 100- word summaries of
      reviews of books in the fields of social science and the
      humanities.

SPECIALIZED DICTIONARIES AND ENCYCLOPEDIAS

139   <u>Diccionario biográfico de México</u>. 3 vols. Monterrey:
      Editorial Revisa, 1968.
        A dictionary of biography for Mexico. Information for
      about 3000 Mexicans prominent in a wide variety of
      activities.

140   <u>Diccionaria Porrúa: Historia, biografía e geografía de</u>
      <u>México</u>. 3d ed., 2 vols. Mexico: Editorial Porrúa, 1971.
        Biographical, historical, and geographical dictionary,
      with appendix. Identifies a wide variety of persons,
      places, and events. Entries range in length from brief
      identifications to short articles which include biblio-
      graphies.

141   <u>Enciclopedia de México</u>. 12 vols. Mexico City: Instituto de
      la Enciclopedia de México, 1966-76.
        An inclusive encyclopedia of Mexico, including some
      signed articles with bibliographies on history, anthro-
      pology, folklore, science, law, economics, society, and
      literature.

Specialized Dictionaries and Encyclopedias

142   OCAMPO de GOMEZ, AURORA, and PRADO VELAZQUEZ, ERNESTO.
      Diccionario de escritores mexicanos. Mexico: UNAM, 1967.
         Gives biographical and bibliographical information
      about authors from pre-Hispanic times to 1967. Although
      it concentrates on authors of fine literature, it does
      include important figures in history and biography. Con-
      tains an index of authors.

143   SANTAMARÍA, FRANCISCO J. Diccionario de mejicanismos.
      Mexico: Editorial Porrúa, 1974.
         A dictionary of Mexican Spanish which gives the meaning
      of the word, the geographical area in which it is used
      in the manner described, examples of usage, and biblio-
      graphical citations for written usage of the word.

For a biographical dictionary of political figures, see entry 611.

GUIDES TO SUPPLEMENTARY REFERENCE MATERIAL

ART

144   FERNANDEZ, JUSTINO. Arte mexicano de sus orígenes a nuestros
      días. Mexico: Editorial Porrúa, 1975.
         Arranged by historical period, this work provides an
      introduction to Mexican art. Last section is on contem-
      porary art (1910 to the present). A bibliography follows
      each chapter. Illustrations; indexes of artists and
      illustrations.

DEMOGRAPHIC HISTORY

145   MORENO TOSCANO, ALEJANDRA. "Fuentes para la demografía
      histórica: Estadísticas vitales, 1906-1910." Boletín
      del Archivo General de la Nación 1 (1977): 44-46.
         Reprint of replies to a Mexican government request
      in 1917 for demographic information concerning the effect
      of the Revolution of 1910 upon marriages, births, deaths,
      and population. Based on documents of the Ramo de Gober-
      nación.

DIPLOMACY

146   CAMARILLO, TERESA. Representantes diplomáticos de México en
      Washington. Mexico: Secretaría de Relaciones Exteriores,
      1974.
         Data on Mexico's diplomatic representatives to Washing-
      ton, D.C., from José Manual Zozaya in 1822 to 1973.

Guides to Supplementary Reference Material

147 COSÍO VILLEGAS, DANIEL. Cuestiones internacionales de
     México: Una bibliografía mexicana. Mexico: Secretaría
     de Relacciones Exteriores, 1966.
        A bibliography of the diplomacy of the Revolution;
     10,766 items; detailed author index. No annotations.
     Divided into eight sections, from general to particular
     headings. Indispensable work for the international rela-
     tions of Mexico.

148 TRASK, DAVID F.; MEYER, MICHAEL C.; and TRASK, ROGER R., comps.
     and eds. A Bibliography of United States-Latin American
     Relations Since 1810: A Selected List of Eleven Thousand
     Published References. Lincoln: University of Nebraska
     Press, 1968.
     _____. Supplement, 1979.
        An extensive listing of books, articles, pamphlets, and
     documents published in several languages (Spanish, Portu-
     guese, French, German, Italian, Russian, and Japanese).
     Descriptive annotations occasionally included. Chapter
     11-H contains the Mexican Revolution, 1910-1940. Detailed
     index. Supplement updates chronology to include Nixon
     and Ford administrations.

ECONOMIC HISTORY

149 CORTÉS CONDE, ROBERTO, and STEIN, STANLEY J., eds. Latin
     America: A Guide to Economic History, 1830-1930.
     Berkeley, Los Angeles, and London: University of Calif-
     ornia Press, 1977.
        A cooperative effort of scholars from six nations of
     the American continent, sponsored by the Joint Committee
     on Latin American Studies (of the American Council of
     Learned Societies), the Social Science Research Council,
     and the Consejo Latinoamericano de Ciencias Sociales.
     "Part Seven: Mexico" (pp. 435-543) was authored and
     compiled by Enrique Florescano with assistance from Jorge
     Ceballos and contains an historiographical essay and an
     annotated bibliography of the social, economic, and demo-
     graphic history of Mexico from 1821 to 1970 (in Spanish).
     Locates copies in Mexican libraries; author index.

150 LEAL, JUAN FELIPE, and WOLDENBERG, JOSÉ. "Orígenes y
     desarrollo del artesanado y del proletariado industrial
     en méxico: 1867-1914 (bibliografía comentada)." Revista
     Mexicana de Ciencia Política 21 (1975): 131-59.
        An annotated bibliography on the artisan class and the
     industrial proletariat in Mexico, including theoretical

Guides to Supplementary Reference Material

> works, statistical resources, bibliography, publications
> by organizations representing these groups, and labor
> legislation.

For a select bibliography on the Mexican economy from 1910 to 1920,
see entry 251. See also entry 35.

FILM

151   CYR, HELEN W. A Filmography of the Third World: An Annotated
      List of 16mm Films. Metuchen, N.J.: Scarecrow Press,
      1976.
          Lists short to feature-length films, fictional and
      non-fictional, of Third World films. A few items on the
      Mexican Revolution. Index of film titles; list of
      directors; cinematographers; film distributors.

GEOGRAPHY

152   Atlas of Mexico. Austin: University of Texas at Austin,
      Bureau of Business Research, 1975.
          Maps related to the physical setting, population,
      history, and economic activities of Mexico. Appendix
      gives tabular summaries of information which is presented
      graphically in the main part of the atlas.

153   GARCÍA de MIRANDA, ENRIQUETA, and FALCÓN de GYVES, ZAIDA.
      Atlas: Nuevo atlas Porrúa de la República Mexicana. Mexico:
      Ed. Porrúa, 1972.
          Includes historic, state, and thematic maps on such
      topics as climate, flora and fauna, population, commun-
      ications, agricultural production, etc. Index of places.

INTELLECTUAL HISTORY

153   MACIEL, DAVID R. "Introducción bibliográfica a la historia
      intelectual de México." Aztlán 3 (Spring 1972): 83-132.
          An annotated bibliographical guide to the intellectual
      history of Mexico, including the Porfiriato and the
      Revolution. Organized by topics with the contemporary
      revolutionary period being divided into general studies,
      the reaction against Positivism, ideology, European
      influences, nationalism, radicalism, and individual
      thinkers (Vasconcelos, Caso, Ramos, Gaos, and Zea).

Guides to Supplementary Reference Material

154 ORTIZ GONZALEZ, LEONCIO. "Fichas para una bibliografía y
     hemerografía de Samuel Ramos." Boletín Bibliográfico de
     la Secretaría de Hacienda y Crédito Público 12 (1966):
     inclusive.
          A bibliography of one hundred index cards to works
     produced by philosopher Samuel Ramos, including trans-
     lations and prefaces.

LAW

155 CLAGETT, HELEN L., and VALDERRAMA, DAVID M. A Revised Guide
     to the Law and Legal Literature of Mexico. Washington,
     D.C.: Library of Congress, 1973.
          A major revision of the 1947 Guide to the Law and Legal
     Literature of the Mexican States. Combines legislative
     history and commentaries on the codified and statutory
     fields of law with exhaustive bibliographical footnotes
     to texts and literature. A product of the Hispanic Law
     Division of the Library of Congress, each chapter contains
     a legislative history from 1821 through the present code
     or basic body of law in force as of 1970. Chapter headings
     include constitutional law; civil law and procedure;
     commercial law; criminal law and procedure; the judicial
     system; administrative law; aliens; land, mining, and
     petroleum laws; finance and taxation; transportation and
     communication; social legislation; international law--
     private and public; general works; legislation; court
     reports and digests; and bibliographies. Appendix--current
     state codes; index of persons.

LITERATURE

156 BRUSHWOOD, JOHN S. Mexico in its Novel: A Nation's Search
     for Identity. Austin: University of Texas Press, 1966.
          Second printing of an encyclopedic reference work on
     the Mexican novel. A chronological dictionary of Mexican
     novelistic prose: lists of authors and titles; commentaries
     in a context of Mexican socioeconomic history; chrono-
     logical list of novels written in Mexico from 1832 to
     1963; selected bibliography. In Spanish as México en
     su Novela. Mexico: Fondo de Cultura Económica, 1974.

157 RUTHERFORD, JOHN. An Annotated Bibliography of the Novels of
     the Mexican Revolution of 1910-1917 in English and Spanish.
     Troy, N.Y.: Whitston Publishing Co., 1972.
          A guide to novels and autobiographies written by
     Mexicans about the historic events of 1910-1917. Annotates
     106 novels published before 1941 and several other new

Guides to Supplementary Reference Material

            novels of the Revolution which appeared since then.
            Supersedes Ernest Moore's <u>Bibliografía de novelistas de</u>
            <u>la Revolución mexicana</u> (Mexico, 1941).

For a current bibliography which includes literary history <u>see</u>
entry 35.

MEXICAN AMERICANS

158   ANZALDUE, MIKE. <u>Mexican American Literature: A Preliminary</u>
       <u>Bibliography of Literary Criticism</u>. Austin: Institute
       of Latin American Studies, 1980.
          A good beginning for those embarking upon a course of
       Chicano history and culture.

159   CABELLO-ARGANDOÑA, ROBERTO; GÓMEZ-QUIÑONES, JUAN; and
       HERRERA DURAN, PATRICIA, comps. <u>The Chicana: A Compre-</u>
       <u>hensive Bibliographic Guide</u>. Los Angeles: Chicano
       Studies Center, UCLA, 1976.
          A collection of bibliographic data of the various
       contributions of the Chicana.

160   MARTÍNEZ, JULIO A. <u>Chicano Scholars and Writers: A Bio-</u>
       <u>Bibliographical Directory</u>. Metuchen, N.J. and London:
       Scarecrow Press, 1979.
          A major reference work presenting biographical and
       bibliographic information on Chicano and non-Chicano
       writers specializing in Chicano-oriented and Latin
       American studies. Representation includes academics and
       professionals in other fields (e.g., psychology, writing,
       social work, etc.).

161   MEIER, MATT S., and RIVERA, FELICIANO. <u>A Selective Biblio-</u>
       <u>graphy for the Study of Mexican American History</u>. San
       Jose, Calif.: Spartan Bookstore, 1972.
          Items (without annotations) arranged chronologically
       with three topical areas--labor and immigration, Mexican
       American culture, and civil rights.

162   MILLER, WAYNE C. et al. <u>A Comprehensive Bibliography for the</u>
       <u>Study of American Minorities</u>. 2 vols. New York: New
       York University Press, 1976.
          Vol. 2, pp. 911-53, is "Mexican Americans: A Guide to
       the Mexican-American Experience." Introductory essay con-
       tains a brief survey of Mexican American history and a
       bibliographical essay on aids, general historical works,
       regional studies, and sociological, educational, and

economic works. Works are listed under the following
headings: Bibliographies, Periodicals, History (general
and Southwest), Sociology, Immigration and Labor, Education,
Psychology and Medicine, Politics, Religion, Biography
and Autobiography, Literary Criticism, Painting, Sculpture
and Architecture, Anthologies of Literature, Drama, Novels,
Short Stories, Poetry, Folklore, and Music. "Spanish
Americans" included in Vol. 1, pp. 349-80. Author-title
index; supplement in progress.

163   NOGALES, LUIS G. The Mexican American: A Selected and
      Annotated Bibliography. 2d ed. Stanford: Stanford
      University and the United States Office of Education, 1971.
            Contains nearly 500 entries. This work represents
      one of the more complete compilations of source material
      on Chicano history and culture. Included are annotations
      of unpublished doctoral dissertations and material found
      in Mexico City libraries. The work also includes works
      unfavorable to the Chicano.

164   TREJO, ARNULFO D. Ethnic Studies Information Guide. Vol. 1,
      Bibliografía Chicana. Detroit, Mich.: Gale Research Co.,
      1975.
            History section includes forty-nine items, all annotated.
      Work also contains a directory of newspapers and period-
      icals; author and title index.

165   WOODS, RICHARD D. Reference Materials on Mexican Americans:
      An Annotated Bibliography. Metuchen, N.J.: Scarecrow
      Press, 1976.
            Bibliography of reference works relating to the Mexican
      American, including monographs and multimedia materials
      (e.g., films, filmstrips, tapes, kits, etc.). Coverage
      limited to continental United States. 387 entries;
      author, title, and subject indexes.

For a bibliography of recent Chicano history see entry 6. See also
entry 12.

MUSIC

166   CHASE, GILBERT. A Guide to the Music of Latin America.
      Washington, D.C.: Pan American Union, 1962.
            An annotated bibliography which contains items on
      contemporary musical activity in Mexico, biography, and
      Mexican folk music (e.g., posadas and corridos). Author
      index.

Guides to Supplementary Reference Material

REGIONAL TOPICS

167   GARCÍA, MORA J.C. "Breve bibliografía sobre el área
       Mazahua." Boletín Bibliográfico de la Secretaría de
       Hacienda y Crédito Público 19 (1973): 14-19.
             An annotated bibliography on works published in the
       twentieth century on this linguistic group in the states
       of México and Michoacán. The entries are arranged alpha-
       betically by author, with the library where they can be
       found indicated.

168   TRUJILLO, G. PEDRO. Bibliografía de Baja California. Tijuana,
       Baja Calif.: Editorial Californidad, 1967-.
             First volume of a projected series of publications on
       Baja California. Several references to books and articles
       on magonismo and the Baja Revolution. 1,160 items listed
       with information as to which of the eighteen libraries
       located in southwestern California and northwestern Baja
       California the item can be found. Author, library, and
       chronological indices.

169   JAMAIL, MILTON H. The United States-Mexico Border: A Guide
       to Institutions, Organizations and Scholars. Tucson:
       University of Arizona, Latin America Area Center, 1980.
             A comprehensive listing of groups involved in border
       affairs. Narrative section discusses the context of the
       border in United States-Mexico relations. Listings include
       federal, regional, state and local organizations, both
       public and private. Includes universities located on the
       border or with a special interest in border affairs. Over
       200 borderland scholars mentioned.

170   ROMERO CERVANTES, ARTURO. "Alberto Fuentes D., primer gober-
       nador revolucionario de Aguascalientes." Boletín Biblio-
       gráfico de la Secretaría de Hacienda y Crédito Público 10
       (1964): 6-10.
             Documents and bibliography about the revolutionary
       governor of Aguascalientes, Alberto Fuentes D. Divided
       into two parts: a) general information reproduced from
       newspapers, editorials, and journals arranged chrono-
       logically according to the citations listed in the second
       part; b) the bibliography.

For a bibliography of over 1000 titles on micro-history, see entry
199. See also entry 477 for bibliography and archives of Nuevo León.

Guides to Supplementary Reference Material

STATISTICS

171   Bibliography of Selected Statistical Sources of the American
      Nations [Bibliografia de fuentes estadisticas escogidas
      de las naciones americanas]. 1947. Reprint. Detroit,
      Mich.. Blaine Ethridge-Books, 1974.
          Reprint of 1947 edition published by the Inter-American
      Statistical Institute in Washington, D.C. Mexican section
      (pp. 188-200) contains census data, demographic sources,
      and economic statistics for late and post-Revolution era.
      In English and Spanish.

THEATRE

172   LAMB, RUTH S. Bibliography of the Mexican Theatre of the
      Twentieth Century. Claremont, Calif.: Ocelot Press, 1975.
          Contains a short essay on the history of Mexican theatre
      from "Emancipation" (1900-1930), through the "Renovation"
      (1928-1950), to the "New Theatre" era (1950-1975), as
      well as a bibliography of the Mexican theatre of the
      twentieth century, a critical bibliography, and a list of
      Mexican magazines and newspapers which contain theatre
      criticism, and bibliography or texts of plays.

TRAVEL LITERATURE

173   COLE, GAROLD L. American Travelers to Mexico, 1821-1972: A
      Descriptive Bibliography of Criticism. Troy, N.Y.:
      Whitston Publishing Co., 1970.

WOMEN'S HISTORY

174   KNASTER, MERI. Women in Spanish America: An Annotated
      Bibliography from pre-Conquest to Contemporary Times.
      Boston: G.K. Hall, 1977.
          Thirty-three items on women in the Mexican Revolution
      included in section on "Politics and Twentieth Century
      Revolutionary Movements."

175   _____. "Women in Latin America: The State of Research,
      1975." Latin American Research Review 11, no. 1 (1976):
      3-74.
          A review of bibliographical efforts and a bibliography
      of women's studies.

176   PESCATELLO, ANN. Female and Male in Latin America.
      Pittsburgh, Pa.: University of Pittsburgh Press, 1973.

Guides to Supplementary Reference Material

        A collection of twelve essays with bibliographical notes accompanying each essay. Includes an extensive, unannotated bibliography (see pp. 293-334).

177   _____. "The Female in Ibero-America: An Essay on Research Bibliography and Research Directions." <u>Latin American Research Review</u> 7, no. 2 (1972): 125-41.
        The pioneering essay on women in Latin America as a field of research. Includes a brief annotated bibliography.

II. Historiography and Methodology

178   AL'PEROVICH, M.S. "El enfoque de algunos problemas de historia moderna y contemporánea de México en la literatura burguesa norteamericana de postguerra." In La Revolución Mexicana: Cuatro estudios soviéticos, by M.S. Al'perovich, B.T. Rudenko, and N.M. Lavrov. Translated by A. Martínez Verdugo and A. Méndez García. Mexico: Ediciones Los Insurgentes, 1960, pp. 157-76.

    An historiographical survey of U.S. writers since World War II by a noted Soviet historian. Writers surveyed include C. Cumberland, N. Whetten, H. Cline, F. Tannenbaum, H.B. Parkes, S.A. Mosk, W. Townsend, and J. Daniels.

179   ARNAIZ y FREG, ARTURO. "Medio siglo de estudios sobre la vida histórica de México." Memorias de la Academia Mexicana de la Historia 28 (1969): 346-54.

180   BAILEY, DAVID C. "Revisionism and the Recent Historiography of the Mexican Revolution." HAHR 58 (Feb. 1978): 62-79.

    A survey of histories written since the early 1960s. The author's focus is on the revisionism of the 1960s and 1970s, a revisionism that challenges the pro-Revolutionary school of North American and Mexican historiography published between the 1930s and the late 1950s. Recent trends tend to challenge the traditional periodization of the Revolution (i.e., 1910-1940), emphasize regional differences, argue for a continuing militarism, consider traditional anticlerical accounts simplistic, and stress the continuity of an emerging bourgeoisie from the Porfiriato to contemporary times.

181   BARKIN, DAVID. "Public Expenditures and Social Change in Mexico: A Methodological Critique." Journal of Latin American Studies 4 (May 1972): 105-12.

    An economist's critique of James Wilkie, The Mexican Revolution: Federal Expenditures and Social Change Since 1910. Concludes that Wilkie's combination of historical

analysis and archival persistence has produced the most
complete set of statistics available about the way in
which the central government has allocated funds in Mexico.
Supports Wilkie's conclusion "that there has been a substantial improvement in living conditions since the
Mexican Revolution. . ." and that political revolution
destroyed the old institutional order without creating
democracy; that the social revolution attacked the social
structure; that economic revolution brought industrialization to a high point but did not create balanced growth
or a large internal market.

182   BEEZLEY, WILLIAM H.   "The Mexican Revolution: A Review."
      Latin American Research Review 13, no. 2 (1978): 299-306.
         A review essay of seven recent studies of the Revolu-
      tion: Michael C. Meyer, Huerta; Edwin Lieuwen, Mexican
      Militarism; Robert E. Quirk, The Mexican Revolution and
      the Catholic Church; David C. Bailey, Viva Cristo Rey!;
      Jean A. Meyer, The Cristero Rebellion; E.V. Niemeyer, Jr.,
      Revolution at Queretaro; and Sinecio López Méndez et al.,
      Los campesinos de la tierra de Zapata.   Author identifies
      four themes from these works: (1) crisis of presidential
      succession, (2) resurgence of the church, (3) growing
      nationalism, and (4) persistent regionalism.

183   BERQUIST, CHARLES W.   "Recent United States Studies in Latin
      American History: Trends Since 1965."   Latin American
      Research Review 9, no. 1 (1974): 3-35.
         Includes an analysis of Mexican historiography.   For
      example, James Wilkie's oral history approach and his
      quantitative techniques; John Womack's ability to fuse
      social science analysis with traditional narration in his
      study on Zapata and the Mexican Revolution; and recent
      trends in intellectual history as illustrated by the works
      of William Dirk Raat, Karl Schmitt, and James Cockcroft.
      Also includes an analysis of HAHR articles.

184   BOBB, BERNARD E., and ROSS, STANLEY R.   "Historiografía
      mexicanista: Estados Unidos, 1959-1960."   HM 11 (Oct.-
      Dec. 1961): 286-313.
         A study of North American writings on Mexico in two
      parts: Part I, "Nueva España," by Bernard E. Bobb; Part
      II, "Mexico independiente," by Stanley R. Ross.   See
      entry 244.

185   BOYD, LOLA E.   "Fact and Opinion: Zapata in the Literature
      of the Mexican Revolution."   Hispania 52 (1969): 903-10.
         Analyzes the existing studies on Zapata and concludes
      that there is nothing definite about him, no complete,
      objective biography.

186   BROWN, LYLE C. "Political and Military History of the State
       of Michoacán, 1910-1940." In El trabajo y los trabajadores
       en la historia de México, compiled by Elsa Cecilia Frost,
       Michael C. Meyer, and Josefina Zoraida Vázquez, pp. 801-
       805. Mexico and Tucson: El Colegio de México and the
       University of Arizona Press, 1979.
           A brief survey of secondary works on the Revolution in
       Michoacán.

187   BRYAN, ANTHONY. "Political Power in Porfirio Díaz's Mexico:
       A Review and Commentary." Historian 38 (August 1976):
       648-68.
           An interim assessment of the status of research on the
       1876-1911 rule of Porfirio Díaz in Mexico. The author
       suggests historians study Díaz's creation and use of
       authoritarian power, and calls for local and regional
       studies on the Porfiriato to obtain a precise picture of
       the causes of the 1910 Revolution.

188   CALVERT, PETER. "The Individual in the 'Cartorial State.'"
       Journal of Latin American Studies 10 (Nov. 1978): 347-56.
           A review essay of historical studies on the emergence
       of the positive state in Mexico, especially "presidential-
       ism" and bureaucracy. Reviews works by A. Córdova, R.
       Díaz-Guerrero, M.S. Grindle, and others.

189   _____. "The Mexican Revolution: Theory or Fact?" Journal
       of Latin American Studies 1 (May 1969): 51-68.
           An analysis and survey of Mexican revolutionary histor-
       iography. Identifies four analytical categories within
       which historical works fall: (a) those sources which
       consider the process of disaffection; (b) those which
       emphasize the events of political change; (c) those which
       stress programs of social renovation (e.g., political
       reform, agrarianism, labor reform, and the Revolution as
       a historical tendency); (d) those devoted to studying the
       myth of revolutionary coherence. Notes the limitations of
       works with close proximity to the events, the lack of
       good biographies (most are participant-observer auto-
       biographies), and the need to analyze the individual
       structures of a Revolution which should no longer be treated
       as unique and indivisible.

190   CARR, BARRY. "Recent Regional Studies of the Mexican Revolu-
       tion." Latin American Research Review 15, no. 1 (1980):
       3-14.
           An analysis of historical literature published in the
       1970s which treats of regional aspects of the Mexican
       Revolution. Notes that the proliferation of regional
       studies is due to a growing awareness among professional
       historians of the methodological limitations of national-

level research, a growing use of state and local archives by both professional and amateur scholars, the publication of a number of guides to local and state archives in the U.S., and the partial "democratization of research" which has involved more ordinary working men and women in "peoples" history. Special emphasis on Mark Wasserman's study on Chihuahua and Gilbert Joseph's work on the Yucatán.

191   CORWIN, ARTHUR F. "Historia de la emigración mexicana, 1900–1970: Literatura e investigación." HM 22 (Oct.-Dec. 1972): 188–200.
       Analyzes historical and sociological studies produced in the U.S. and Mexico relating to Mexican emigration to the U.S., the works dating chiefly from the 1920s. A variety of themes, topics, and source materials have yet to be exploited, including official Mexican attitudes toward the phenomenon, the resistance of emigrants to naturalization processes and procedures, consular records, and the archives of the U.S. Immigration and Naturalization Service. Primary and secondary sources.

192   COSÍO VILLEGAS, DANIEL. Nueva historiografía del México moderno. Mexico: Editorial del Colegio Nacional, 1966.
       An historiographical essay and bibliography of the history of modern Mexico, 1867–1911. An expanded version of the 1953 edition of La historiografía política del México moderno. 1,276 items listed on reference works, general histories, regional histories, biographical works, and narrative histories of the epoch. Author and editor index.

193   _____. Nueva historiografía política del México moderno. Mexico: Editorial del Colegio Nacional, 1966.
       Concerned primarily with books and articles covering the Reforma and Porfiriato.

194   COY, PETER. "A Watershed of Mexican Rural History: Some Thoughts on the Reconciliation of Conflicting Inter-pretations." Journal of Latin American Studies 3 (May 1971): 39–57.
       Studies the controversy in ethnography over the differing interpretations of the Mexican village of Tepoztlán by Robert Redfield and Oscar Lewis. Redfield published in 1926; Lewis in 1943. Their interpretations reflected different historical realities and conditions.

195   ESPINOZA, LYDIA. "Historia regional: El rincón de la fatalidad." Nexos 1 (July 1978): 21.
       Explores questions related to regional history.

196 ESTELA, ROLDAN ROMAN. "Agrární otázka ve Mexicke Revoluci 1910-1917 v soucasné historiografii." Ceskoslovenský Casopis Historický 12 (1964): 80-83.
Surveys current Mexican history writings on the agrarian question with special regard to publications by Ricardo García Granados, Jorge Vera Estañol and Jesús Silva Herzog.

197 FLORESCANO, ENRIQUE. "O razvitii istoricheskoi nauki v Meksike." Novaia i Noveishaia Istoriia 11 (1967): 129-37.
Survey of the growth and development of the study of history in Mexico in the twentieth century.

198 FRANCO, MARÍA TERESA. "El ingeniero Francisco Bulnes y el doctor Jean Meyer--un caso de afinidad sorprendente." HM 28 (July-Sept. 1978): 90-105.
A comparison of words, phrases, and ideas that appear in the last section of Francisco Bulnes's El verdadero Díaz y la Revolución (Mexico: Eusebio Gómez de la Puente, 1920) with those in the first part of Jean Meyer's La Revolución Mejicana (Barcelona: Dopesa, 1973), which appeared in French as La Révolution mexicaine (Paris: Calman Levy, 1973). Argues that Meyer has plagiarized ideas, textual expressions, and complete paragraphs from Bulnes. Concludes that Meyer's work is less a revision that a re-vision of ideas originally developed by Bulnes.

199 GONZALEZ y GONZALEZ, LUIS. Invitación a la microhistoria. Mexico: SepSetentas, 1973.
A series of essays which define and evaluate the characteristics and methods of local (or micro-) history. Final section includes a bibliography of one thousand titles published between 1871 and 1970--all related to Mexican micro-history.

200 _____. "Linaje, miseria y porvenir de la historia local." Humanitas 13 (1972): 301-13.
Analysis of status of local history in Mexico by one of its most distinguished practitioners.

201 _____. "Microhistoria para multiméxico." HM 21 (Oct.-Dec. 1971): 225-41.
Notes that while history on the grand scale treats kings, queens, and masses, or "fictions" such as the state or spirit of a people, microhistory is an "individualized account of humble people." Microhistory demands an appreciation of local geography and literature and requires more flexibility than is characteristic of most historical methodology. After reviewing Mexico's traditions of local history, the author suggests future research possibilities in local history such as regionalism, local economics, and individual haciendas.

202   GONZÁLEZ, PABLO. El centinela fiel del constitucionalismo.
      Saltillo: Textos de Cultura Historiográfica, 1971.
      Biography written by one of General Pablo González's
      sons after having studied over 60,000 documents. He also
      criticizes various histories of the Revolution.

203   GURRÍA LACROIX, JORGE. "Historiografía sobre Emiliano
      Zapata." Memorias de la Academia Mexicana de la Historia
      20 (1973): 246-66.

204   HALE, CHARLES A. "The Liberal Impulse: Daniel Cosío
      Villegas and the Historia moderna de México." HAHR 54
      (August 1974): 479-98.
      Review article and historiographical essay about Mexico's
      remarkable intellectual and historian, Daniel Cosío
      Villegas and the monumental work he directed and partly
      authored, the nine-volume Historia moderna de México.
      Hale notes how the work is organized into three parts--
      political, socioeconomic, and diplomatic--within a two-
      part periodization consisting of the Restored Republic
      (1867-1876) and the Porfiriato (1876-1910). He argues
      that, while Cosío has an obvious liberal constitutionalist
      bias, he was still able to present the Porfiriato in a
      judicious and objective manner; an approach which breaks
      new historiographical ground by abandoning the standard
      Revolutionary perspective. A revised picture of the Por-
      firiato emerges with Díaz the nationalist laying the bases
      of a modern national economy within a society characterized
      by construction as well as exploitation. Hale concludes
      by noting that Cosío and his collaborators "have given
      new life to the professional study of modern and contem-
      porary Mexico."

205   _____. "The History of Ideas: Substantive and Method-
      ological Aspects of the Thought of Leopoldo Zea." Journal
      of Latin American Studies 3 (May 1971): 59-70.
      A study in the problems of method in the history of
      ideas in Mexico. Analysis of the José Gaos tradition in
      general, and Leopoldo Zea in particular.

206   _____, and MEYER, MICHAEL C. "Mexico: The National
      Period." In Latin American Scholarship Since World War II,
      edited by Roberto Esquenazi-Mayo and Michael C. Meyer,
      pp. 115-38. Lincoln: University of Nebraska Press, 1971.
      Bibliographical and historiographical essay of 177
      books and articles on modern Mexican history.

207   HENNESSY, ALISTAIR. "Artists, Intellectuals and Revolution:
      Recent Books on Mexico." Journal of Latin American Studies
      3 (May 1971): 71-88.

Review essay of books treating of artists (muralists), educators, and intellectuals in the Mexican Revolution. Includes analyses of A. Rodríguez, A History of Mexican Mural Painting; Josefina Vázquez de Knauth, Nacionaismo y educación en México; J. Cockcroft, Intellectual Precursors of the Mexican Revolution; J. Womack, Zapata and the Mexican Revolution; P. González Casanova, Democracy in Mexico; L. Graham, Politics in a Mexican Community; and James and Edna Wilkie, México en el siglo XX.

208   Investigaciones contemporáneas sobre historia de México: Memorias de la tercera reunión de historiadores mexicanos y norteamericanos. Mexico: UNAM, El Colegio de México, and the University of Texas at Austin, 1971.
Proceedings of the Third Conference of Historians of Mexico and the United States, meeting in Oaxtepec, Morelos, 4-7 November 1969. Students of the historiography of the Mexican Revolution will be especially interested in the following papers: Luis González, "La historiografía local: aportaciones mexicanas"; Clark W. Reynolds, "The Economic Historiography of Twentieth-Century Mexico"; Jean Meyer, "Historia de la vida social"; Frederick C. Turner, "Historical Sociology and Mexican Social History"; Laurens B. Perry, "Political Historiography of the Porfirian Period of Mexican History"; James W. Wilkie, "New Approaches in Contemporary Mexican Historical Research"; John Womack, Jr., "Mexican Political Historiography, 1959-1969"; and William Dirk Raat, "Ideas and History in Mexico: An Essay on Methodology."

209   LAVROV, NIKOLAI M.   "Ob istoriografii Maksikanskoi Revoliutsii 1910-1917 Godov." Novaia i Noveishaia Istoriia 11, no. 3 (1967): 138-45.
Short bibliographical discussion of Soviet and non-Soviet historical literature concerning the Mexican Revolution of 1910-1917. Emphasis is on the work of contemporary Soviet scholars. The author is Chief of Section, Latin American Section, Institute of World History, USSR Academy of Sciences.

210   _____. "Crítica a la crítica de la Revolución Mexicana." Historia y Sociedad 3 (1967): 46-55.
Critique by a noted Soviet historian.

211   MABRY, DONALD J.   "Mexican Anticlerics, Bishops, Cristeros, and the Devout during the 1920s: A Scholarly Debate." Journal of Church and State 20 (Winter 1978): 81-92.
An analysis of several works on the Catholic Church and the Mexican Revolution, especially the cristero revolt, including those of the Americans Robert Quirk and David

C. Bailey, the Russian Nicolás Larin, the Mexican Alicia
Olivera Sedano, and the French historian Jean Meyer. Concludes that Meyer's work, a multi-volume revisionist study
which argues that the cristeros were an authentic campesino
revolutionary group, is the most important of those surveyed because of its original perspective and thorough
research; one that "did not automatically adopt the
'revolutionary line' on the subject."

212   MATUTE, ALVARO. La teoría de la historia en México, 1940-
      1973. Mexico: Secretaría de Educación Pública, 1974.
         After a precise prologue, there follows a selection
      of excerpts from the writings of many of Mexico's contem-
      porary professional historians--from Edmundo O'Gorman to
      Alfonso Caso; from Ramón Iglesia to Reyes Heroles; from
      José Gaos to Luis González. Analysis is in terms of what
      Matute believes to be the two main historiographical
      traditions of contemporary Mexico: positivism and his-
      toricism, with Silvio Zavala representing the first, and
      O'Gorman the latter.

213   MAURO, FRÉDÉRIC. "Historiografía mexicanista: Francia
      (1959-1960)." HM 11 (July-Sept. 1961): 151-56. "Historio-
      grafía mexicanista: Francia (1961-1963)." HM 14 (July-
      Sept. 1964): 144-47.
         Brief surveys of French contributions to Mexican his-
      tory writing published between 1959 and 1963. Latter
      article includes a brief bibliography with a few items on
      the Revolution.

214   MEYER, EUGENIA W. de. Conciencia histórica norteamericana
      sobre la Revolución de 1910. Mexico: Instituto Nacional
      de Antropología e Historia, 1970.
         A Mexican appraisal of United States contributions to
      Mexican Revolutionary historiography. Analysis of changing
      attitudes toward the Revolution over several decades of
      historical research and writing.

215   _____. Ernest Gruening: Experiencias y comentarios sobre
      el México post-revolucionario. Mexico: Instituto Nacional
      de Antropología e Historia, 1970.
         Gruening's autobiographical account as related to, and
      transcribed by, Eugenia Meyer. An oral history project.
      See also entry 217.

216   _____. "Del ser mexicano y de la historiografía de la
      Revolución." In Conciencia y autenticidad históricas:
      Escritos en homenaje a Edmundo O'Gorman. Edited by
      Juan A. Ortega y Medina. Mexico: UNAM, 1968.
         Testifies to the "internal" nature of Mexican historio-
      graphy and the "self-analysis" involved in the Mexican

historian's reconstruction of the revolutionary past.

217   _____. "La Revolución Mexicana en la historiografía anglosajona." <u>Anuario de Historia</u> 5 (1965): 83-95.
An analysis of the book, <u>Mexico and Its Heritage</u>, by Ernest Gruening.

218   MEYER, MICHAEL C. "Habla por ti mismo Juan: Una propuesta para un método alternativo de investigación." HM 22 (Jan.-Mar. 1973): 396-408.
Using examples from the Madero archive the author demonstrates how documents written by semiliterate persons can be utilized to present a view of reality often distinct from the commonly held views of intellectuals.

219   _____. "A Venture in Documentary Publication: Isidro Fabela's <u>Documentos históricos de la Revolución Mexicana.</u>" HAHR 52 (Feb. 1972): 123-29.
Review essay of the monumental Fabela documentary series. Suggests how it complements archival research.

220   _____. "Perspectives on Mexican Revolutionary Historiography." NMHR 44 (April 1969): 167-80.
A general interpretative survey of Mexican historiography from 1910 to the 1950s. Concludes that history writing before 1945 was the "apotheosis of the Revolution," while the postwar period has been characterized by "professionalization." Professional history has produced important biographies (especially of Madero), inter-disciplinary works, multi-volume studies, regional histories, and new documentary publications. Contends that Mexican historians have not produced major historiographical studies comparable to those produced for Chile, Argentina, Cuba, or Brazil. Implores revolutionary historians to set aside partisanship and permit the narratives or judgments to flow honestly from the facts.

221   MOLS, MANFRED, and TOBLER, HANS WERNER. "Mexiko: Bilanz einer Revolution. Revolution und nachrevolutionäre Entwicklung im Lichte der historischen und sozialwissenschaftlichen Forschung." In <u>Jahrbuch für Geschichte von Staat, Wirtschaft und Gesellschaft Lateinamerikas.</u> Vol. 12, edited by Richard Konetzke and Hermann Kellenbenz, pp. 284-391. Cologne and Vienna: Böhlau Verlag, 1975.
<u>Yearbook for the History of State, Economy, and Society of Latin America</u>, vol. 12, which contains Tobler's essay on Mexican historiography (1910-1940) as well as Mols's social scientific analysis of Mexico since 1940. These are reproduced as chapters 1 and 2 respectively in the authors' <u>Mexiko: Die institutionalisierte</u>

Revolution (1976). Historiographical section notes recent
revisionist trends in historical and social science literature. Authors call for an extensive historiographical
review which is less a detailed scholarly survey and more
a discussion of trends and directions.

222 MONTEJANO y AGUIÑAGA, RAFAEL. La historiografía potosina.
San Luis Potosí, Mex.: Academia de Historia Potosina,
1974.
Discusses regional historiography in Mexico today,
focusing on chronicles and local histories of the state
and city of San Luis Potosí.

223 MOSELEY, EDWARD H. "Myth and Reality in the Novel of the
Mexican Revolution: A Tool for the Historian." Secolas
Annales, no. 6 (1975): 24-41.
Historians ought not to ignore novels dealing with the
Mexican Revolution. Although they must be used with care,
novels offer insights that cannot be obtained elsewhere.
Primary and secondary sources.

224 NAYLOR, ROBERT A. "Research Opportunities in Modern Latin
America: I, Mexico and Central America." Americas 18
(April 1962): 352-65.
As of 1962, the author suggests that the field of Mexican
history writing is wide open; that few studies meet even
modest historical standards, especially for the history of
nineteenth- and twentieth-century Mexico.

225 NEEDLER, MARTIN C. "Daniel Cosío Villegas and the Interpretation of Mexico's Political System." JISWA 18 (May
1976): 245-52.
The Mexican political system is so complex that it is
difficult for Mexicans and non-Mexicans alike to understand it. The view of Mexico in the United States is
that the government is a democracy in which there is no
competition between parties, but among sectors of the
official party. This view tends to ignore the real abuses
of power such as the Tlatelolco Massacre of 1968. The
Mexican view of their government is not very analytical.
Daniel Cosío Villegas has moved in the direction of analysis
but as an historian and not as a social scientist. While
his approach has some shortcomings his work has been
generally praiseworthy. Based on three recently published
books by Daniel Cosío Villegas. Note, bibliography.

226 NIBLO, STEPHEN R., and PERRY, LAURENS B. "Recent Additions
to Nineteenth-Century Mexican Historiography." Latin
American Research Review 13, no. 3 (1978): 3-45.

A revised and expanded version of a paper presented to the American Historical Association in Atlanta on 29 December 1975. Pages 35-45 review works on the Porfiriato, including the general studies of Daniel Cosío Villegas, Ralph Roeder, and José C. Valadés, as well as some two dozen articles and books by historians of the Porfiriato. The authors have been greatly influenced and favorably impressed by José Luis Ceceña, concluding that the "most transcendent topic that we find in the period under consideration is the acute integration of Mexico into the global economy in the second half of the nineteenth century"--that is, dependent capitalism.

227　O'GORMAN, EDMUNDO. "Cincuenta años de historiografía mexicana, 1910-1960." Memorias de la Academia Mexicana de la Historia 26 (1967): 52-63.

228　_____. "La historiografía." In México: cincuenta años de Revolución. Vol. 4, La cultura. México: Fondo de Cultura Económica, 1962, pp. 193-203.
　　　Four short essays on the history of Mexican historical writing, the last of which compares the late Porfirian México su evolución social (1900-02) with the earlier México a través de los siglos (1884-89).

229　OSWALD, J. GREGORY. "Mexico en la historiografía soviética." HM 14 (Apr.-June 1965): 691-706.
　　　A response to Soviet historian L. Iu. Slezkin. A general survey of Soviet writing from the 1930s to the early 1960s. Includes a select bibliography of Soviet monographs and articles, most of which treat of the Revolution.

230　_____. "La Revolución Mexicana en la historiografía soviética." HM 12 (Jan.-Mar. 1963): 340-57.
　　　An analysis of Soviet history writing published in the early 1960s on the Mexican Revolution, especially the 1910-1917 years. Notes the achievements of the UNAM seminar on modern Mexico, in particular the work of Juan A. Ortega y Medina. Concludes that Soviet writing is very dependent upon North American sources, even though the aim of the Soviets is that of discrediting bourgeois falsification of Mexican history. Most prolific Soviet historians are M.S. Al'perovich, B.T. Rudenko, and N.N. Lavrov.

231　PERRY, LAURENS B. "Political Historiography of the Porfirian Period of Mexican History." In Investigaciones contemporáneas sobre historia de México, pp. 458-77. Mexico and Austin: UNAM and University of Texas Press, 1971.

Written in three sections: the works of Daniel Cosío
Villegas, rare documents found in Mexico City dealing
with the Porfiriato, and a list of studies that the author
feels are important in order to fully understand this
period of history.

232   POTASH, ROBERT A. "Historiografía del México independiente."
HM 10 (Jan.-Mar. 1961): 361-412.
Spanish version of "Historiography of Mexico Since
1821."

233   _____. "Historiography of Mexico Since 1821." HAHR 40
(Aug. 1960): 383-424.
A critical guide to the principal writings on Mexican
national history by Mexicans and non-Mexicans. Surveys
interpretations and methods of four decades of historiography and suggests that future research on the Revolution
will be revisionist. Notes that since 1940 the Revolutionary epoch has inspired the greatest number of historical publications, and that these reflect new trends in
economic, social, and intellectual history (unlike the
political and biographical literature prior to 1940).

234   QUIRARTE, MARTÍN. "Ensayos de interpretación histórica
sobre Madero." Revista de la Universidad de México 28
(1973): 11-14.
Commentary on Valadés, Madero, imaginación y realidad.

235   RAAT, WILLIAM DIRK. "Synthesizing the Mexican Experience."
Latin American Research Review 15, no. 3 (1980): 266-72.
Review essay of three works: Michael C. Meyer and
William L. Sherman, The Course of Mexican History; Samuel
H. Mayo, A History of Mexico: From Pre-Columbia to Present;
and Jan Bazant, A Concise History of Mexico: From Hidalgo
to Cárdenas, 1805-1940.

236   _____. "Ideas and History in Mexico: An Essay on Methodology." In Investigaciones contemporáneas sobre historia
de México, pp. 687-99. Mexico and Austin: UNAM and the
University of Texas Press, 1971.
A comparison of "internal" history of ideas with
"external" intellectual history, the first being idealist,
literary, and subjective, while the latter is functional,
practical, and objective. The "internal" tradition has
dominated the history of intellectual life in Mexico, with
philosophers, rather than historians, doing most of the
work. Study concludes with a case study of Leopoldo Zea's
works on positivism in Mexico.

237   _____. "Ideas e historia en México: Un ensayo sobre
metodología." Latinoamerica 3 (1970): 175-88.

Translation of "Ideas and History in Mexico: An Essay
on Methodology" by Ludivina García Arias. Original paper
read at the Third Reunion of Historians of Mexico and the
United States at Oaxtepec, 1969, and published in the
proceedings.

238   _____. "Leopoldo Zea and Mexican Positivism: A Reappraisal."
HAHR 48 (Feb. 1968): 1-18.
Winner of the James A. Robertson Award, in which the
author critiques philosopher Zea's accounts of positivism
in Mexico and concludes with suggestions concerning the
writing of intellectual history.

239   RAMOS, CARMEN. "Myth and Method in Modern Mexican Historiography." Latin American Research Review 13, no. 2 (1978):
296-98.
A critical review of Mexican micro-history as evidenced
in the works of Luis González's Invitación a la microhistoria and Álvaro Matute's La teoría de la historia en
México.

240   ROSS, STANLEY R. "Twentieth-Century Mexican History: An
Overview from the United States." In Contemporary Mexico:
Papers of the Fourth International Congress of Mexican
History, edited by James W. Wilkie, Michael C. Meyer, and
Edna Monzon de Wilkie, pp. 775-87. Los Angeles and Mexico:
University of California Press and El Colegio de México,
1976.
A survey of North American historical research and
writing on twentieth-century Mexico in the 1970s. Notes
the activities of Mexicanists, including publications in
the HAHR, the activities of the Conference on Latin
American History, the development of research aids, the
use of social science techniques (oral history and historical statistics), and innovations in the field of
local and regional history.

241   _____. "Imágenes de la Revolución Mexicana." Latinoamerica 1 (1968): 37-48.
Argues for a nominalistic approach to the study of the
Revolution, suggesting that the Revolution should be
separated into its component elements and studied through
its "images."

242   _____. "El historiador y el periodismo mexicano." HM 14
(Jan.-Mar. 1965): 347-82.
A narrative of the development of newspapers in Mexico
from colonial times to the present. Author notes the
tradition of the opposition press which developed during
the Porfiriato and continued throughout the revolutionary
era (pp. 367-77). As such, newspapers served to develop

a public opinion receptive to the idea of necessary change. Illustrates the historical and political influence of the Mexican press. Concludes that Mexican newspapers are important sources for the historian, especially those newspapers which contain reproductions of primary materials.

243 _____. "Aportación norteamericana de la Revolución Mexicana." HM 10 (July 1960-June 1961): 282-308.
   A general essay which surveys North American historiography of the Revolution (mostly books and monographs) from John Kenneth Turner's Barbarous Mexico (1910) to works in the 1950s by Howard Cline, William Townshend, Oscar Lewis, Charles Cumberland, Robert Quirk, and others.

244 _____. "Historiografía mexicanista. Estados Unidos, 1959-1960. II, México independiente." HM 11 (Oct.-Dec. 1961): 299-313.
   Second section of a two-part study by Bernard E. Bobb and Stanley R. Ross on Mexican historical literature published in English during 1959-1960 by North American writers. Part II surveys articles and books since Independence, with eight books on modern Mexico and the Revolution being discussed—those by Edwin Lieuwen, Oscar Lewis, Richard Hancock, Robert Scott, Elizabeth Ann Rice, E. David Cronon, Robert E. Quirk, and William Sherman (with Richard Greenleaf).

245 SKIDMORE, THOMAS E., and SMITH, PETER H. "Notes on Quantitative History: Federal Expenditure and Social Change in Mexico Since 1910." Latin American Research Review 5, no. 1 (1970): 71-85.
   A critique of James Wilkie's The Mexican Revolution: Federal Expenditure and Social Change Since 1910. Concludes that Wilkie has collected valuable data in two areas previously neglected by historians-actual federal government expenditures, and nonmonetary indices of social welfare. Notes limitations of the study, especially Wilkie's failure to collect data on expenditures of decentralized agencies and mixed public-private enterprises, and his dismissal of the revenue side of federal fiscal policy. Study is further marred by a failure to define critical concepts like "ideology" and by improper correlations. These methodological errors mislead the reader as to possible causal relationships between federal policy and social change.

246 TAVERA ALFARO, XAVIER. "Francisco I. Madero y algunos historiadores extranjeros." Memorias de la Academia Mexicana de la Historia 22 (1963): 135-51.
   Comments on books concerning Madero written by

M. Márquez Sterling, Voltairine de Cleyre, F. Tannenbaum,
S. Ross, N.M. Lavrov, M.S. Alperovich, and B.T. Rudenko.
Favorable review of Ross and the work of Alperovich and
Rudenko.

247   TOBLER, HANS WERNER. "Zur Historiographie der mexikanischen
       Revolution 1910-1940." In Mexiko: Die institutional-
       isierte Revolution, by Manfred Mols and H.W. Tobler,
       pp. 4-48. Cologne and Vienna: Böhlau Verlag, 1976.
          An historiographical essay of the literature of the
       Revolution divided into four parts: the late Porfiriato;
       the 1910-1920 Revolution; the Sonoran period (1920-1935);
       and the Cárdenas era. Emphasis is on the 1910-1920
       period. Most works cited are books, many by North American
       writers.

248   WILKIE, JAMES W. "On Quantitative History: The Poverty
       Index for Mexico." Latin American Research Review 10:
       no. 1 (1975): 63-76.
          Discusses the merits of factor analysis in response to
       a critique of the author's book The Mexican Revolution:
       Federal Expenditure and Social Change Since 1910, 2d ed.
       (Berkeley, 1970), using the example of the poverty index
       in Mexico.

249   _____. "New Hypotheses for Statistical Research in Recent
       Mexican History." Latin American Research Review 6, no. 2
       (1971): 3-17.
          Suggests new areas of research in quantitative history.
       Gives examples of little-examined descriptive statistics
       which might be investigated fruitfully to reveal new
       political, economic, and social aspects. Examples include
       election statistics, expenditures of central government
       income, and unemployment statistics.

250   WOMACK, JOHN, Jr. "The Historiography of Mexican Labor."
       In El trabajo y los trabajadores en la historia de México,
       compiled by Elsa Cecilia Frost, Michael C. Meyer, and
       Josefina Zoraida Vázquez, pp. 739-56. Mexico and Tucson:
       El Colegio de México and University of Arizona Press, 1979.
          A synthesis of labor history presented by John Womack
       to the participants at the Fifth Congress of Historians
       of Mexico and the United States at Pátzcuaro, Michoacán,
       in October 1977. Concludes with a list of new kinds of
       historical problems to be dealt with in the future, in-
       cluding studies of the changes in productive structures,
       studies in the history of technology, studies in the
       history of education and apprenticeship, studies in the
       geographic origins of workers to discover the historical
       function of religious and ethnic factors in the formation
       of the working class, studies in the history of family

structures, studies in the history of unions, studies in
the history of working-class consciousness, studies in
history of other classes.

251   . "The Mexican Economy During the Revolution, 1910-
1920: Historiography & Analysis." Marxist Perspectives 1
(Winter 1978): 80-123.
    An in-depth historiographical analysis of the literature
of the Mexican economy during the 1910-1920 period.
Argues that "positivist" thinking has dominated the views
of "generalist" historians and economists who have
described (not analyzed) the Revolutionary decade economically as nothing more than destruction, disruption, and
devastation. These writers fall into three schools of
thought: (1) Institutionalists, (2) Marxists, and (3)
Neoclassicists. Although differing among themselves on
the quality and timing of the country's "growth" and
"development," they generally agree that between 1910 and
1920 the Revolution destroyed the old economic order,
paving the way for "economic surplus" and "development."
Notable exceptions to this tradition include the works of
Adolfo Gilly, Jean Meyer, and Clark Reynolds, all of whom
argue that the Revolutionary decade was characterized by
"growth" in some sectors and regions during different
phases, changing relations of production, and a redistri-
bution of productive forces.
    During the last ten years historiography has moved in
a "revisionist" direction. The revisionists argue that
Mexican economic history is a function of United States
economic history, that the Mexican Revolution witnessed
the defeat of the first massive popular struggle against
capitalism in Mexico. Revisionists suggest that capitalist
production became dominant during the 1890s (not, like
the traditionalists, after 1917), and the violence of the
Revolutionary decade deepened regional disparities and
increased the economy's rate of accumulation (in effect
building a capacity for later expansion). In short, the
Revolution is the history of a floundering bourgeoisie
that resorted to a tyrannical State to institute capitalist
reforms and curtail the gains of radical labor. Unlike
the traditionalists, revisionists like Meyer argue that
history moves, not through a series of positivist stages,
but dialectically as contradictions working through time.
    Contains useful charts and tables on gross domestic
product, foreign investment, patterns of trade, comparative
growth of U.S. and Mexican economies, production, and land
distribution from 1910-1970; inclusive bibliography.
Available to readers on request is Womack's "A Selected
Bibliography on the Mexican Economy during the Revolution,
1910-1920," which lists over three hundred printed sources.

252 _____. "La Economía en la Revolución (1910-1920):
     Historiografía y análisis." <u>Nexos</u> 1 (Nov. 1978): 3-8.
         Critique of economic analyses of the Mexican Revolution,
     1910-1920.

For related historiographical items <u>see</u> entries 6, 10, 14, 35, 47-48,
149, 289, 316, and 490. For periodization <u>see</u> entries 318, 327, 328,
and 331. Wilkie's work on the Revolution is 311 and 312. For use
of the <u>corrido</u> as an historical source, <u>see</u> entry 460.

III. General Works

253 ALBA, VICTOR. The Mexicans: The Making of a Nation. New
York: Frederick A. Praeger, 1967.
A readable general narrative of Mexico's history with
emphasis on the modern era.

254 Análisis ideológico de la Revolución Mexicana, 1910-1971.
Mexico: PRI, 1972.
Contents: "Revolución y estructura," by Octavio
Hernández; "El estado mexicano y el desarrollo nacional"
and "Revolución y sociedad democrática," by Enrique
González Pedrero; "Revolución y desarrollo político," by
Jesús Reyes Heroles; "Revolución y desarrollo económico,"
by Gilberto Loyo; "Revolución y desarrollo social," by
José Iturriaga; "El ejército de la Revolución." by Miguel
Rivera Becerra; "Dinámica de la reforma agraria," by
Horacio Labastida; "Partido de la Revolución," by Enrique
Ramírez; "Revolución y militancia política," by Rodolfo
Echeverría Ruiz; "Revolución y pluralismo político," by
Luis H. Ducoing; "Revolución, tecnología y cultura," by
Gonzalo Aguirre Beltrán; "La Revolución y los problemas
internacionales del mundo," by José Gallastegui; "Los
orígenes de la Revolución," by Vicente Fuentes Díaz;
"Revolución y federalismo," by Enrique Olivares Santana;
"Clausura," by Manuel Sánchez Vite.

255 ARREDONDO MUÑOZLEDO, BENJAMÍN. Historia de la Revolución
Mexicana. Mexico: Librería de Porrúa, 1971.
A brief history of the Revolution from the "constitutionalist" point of view. Based on secondary sources,
with little analysis.

256 _____. Breve historia de la Revolución Mexicana. 8th
ed., rev. Mexico: Librería de Porrúa, 1970.
Short narrative account of the Revolution; a revision
of A Concise History of the Mexican Revolution.

Comprehensive Studies

257   BARKIN, DAVID. "Education and Class Structure: The Dynamics
       of Social Control in Mexico." Politics and Society 5
       (1975): 185-200.
             Concludes that the educational system has accentuated
       class differences and has not prevented a growing inequality
       in income distribution.

258   BAZANT, JOHN. A Concise History of Mexico: From Hidalgo
       to Cárdenas, 1805-1940. New York and Cambridge: Cambridge
       University Press, 1977.
             A narrative history of national Mexico emphasizing
       political and socioeconomic factors. Narrative ends with
       the traditional year 1940. Central theme of social con-
       flict over land.

259   _____. "Tres revoluciones mexicanas." HM 10 (Oct.-Dec.
       1960): 220-42.
             Examines the character of Mexico's three revolutions:
       Independence, Reform, and the Revolution of 1910.

260   BELLO HIDALGO, LUIS. Antropología de la Revolución: De
       Porfirio Díaz a Gustavo Díaz Ordaz. Mexico: Costa-Amic,
       1966.

261   BLANCO MOHENO, ROBERTO. Crónica de la Revolución Mexicana.
       3 vols. México: Editorial Diana, 1967.
             Volume 1, De la decena trágica a los campos de Celaya;
       volume 2, Querétaro. Tlaxcalantongo. La Bombilla;
       volume 3, Vasconcelos. Cárdenas. Calles.

262   BRANDENBURG, FRANK R. The Making of Modern Mexico. Engle-
       wood Cliffs, N.J.: Prentice-Hall, 1964.
             A study of Mexico, 1910-1964, in terms of the "Mexican
       Proposition," a national, mexicanized form of modernization
       and revolution that has transformed Mexico from a back-
       ward society into a dynamic nation. Written in the days
       of the Alliance for Progress, this is an optimistic treat-
       ment of Mexico's "preferred revolution." Bibliography.

263   BREMAUNTZ, ALBERTO. Panorama social de las revoluciones de
       México. Mexico: Ediciones Jurídico Sociales, 1960.
             Author examines causes, programs, policies, phases,
       and effects of revolutionary and postrevolutionary admin-
       istrations, concluding that the Mexican Revolution had
       a strong socialist tradition.

264 BRENNER, ANITA. The Wind that Swept Mexico: The History of the Mexican Revolution of 1910-1942. Austin and London: University of Texas Press, 1971.
Reprint of 1943 edition. Contains almost twice the number of photograph pages (184) as narrative pages (106). Photos, assembled by George R. Leighton, were remade from exhibit prints provided through the courtesy of the New York Public Library. An excellent pictorial source. The narrative is marred by awkward phrasing and oversimplifications.

265 CLINE, HOWARD FRANCIS. "Mexico: A Matured Latin American Revolution, 1919-1960." Annals of the American Academy of Political and Social Science 334 (1961): 84-94.
Sympathetic account of the achievements of the revolution by a noted Latin Americanist.

266 Contemporary Mexico: Papers of the Fourth International Congress of Mexican History. Edited by James W. Wilkie, Michael C. Meyer, and Edna Monzón de Wilkie. Mexico and Los Angeles: El Colegio de México and the University of California, UCLA Latin American Center, 1976.
Papers delivered at Santa Monica, California, 17-21 October 1973. Theme: Interdisciplinary studies on twentieth-century Mexico. Papers of special interest to students of the Revolution include: Peter H. Smith, "Continuity and Turnover within the Mexican Political Elite, 1900-1971"; Ramón Eduardo Ruiz, "Madero's Administration and Mexican Labor"; Arnaldo Córdova, "La transformación del PNR en PRM: El triunfo del corporativismo en México"; Friedrich Katz, "Agrarian Changes in Northern Mexico in the Period of Villista Rule, 1913-1915"; Heather Fowler Salamini, "Adalberto Tejeda and the Veracruz Peasant Movement"; Alicia Olivera de Bonfil, "La iglesia en México, 1926-1970"; Juan Gómez-Quiñones, "Piedras contra la luna, México en Aztlán y Aztlán en México: Chicano-Mexican Relations and the Mexican Consulates, 1900-1920"; Albert L. Michaels and Marvin Bernstein, "The Modernization of the Old Order: Organization and Periodization of Twentieth-Century Mexican History"; and Eugenia Meyer, "La periodización de la historia...." See entries 327-28, 377, 742, 1013, 1033, 1134, and 1178.

267 CUMBERLAND, CHARLES CURTIS, ed. The Meaning of the Mexican Revolution. Boston, Mass: D.C. Heath, 1967.

Comprehensive Studies

   An anthology of twenty selections treating of various
themes, including the philosophy of the Revolution, the
church-state conflict, agrarian reform, economic
nationalism, industrialization, and the democratic
process.

268 DELGADO MOYA, RUBEN. Perfil histórico de la Revolución
   Mexicana. Mexico: Editorial Diana, 1975.

269 DE VORE, BLANCHE B. Land and Liberty: A History of the
   Mexican Revolution. New York: Pageant Press, 1966.
   Readable narrative of the Revolution.

270 D'HORTA, ARNALDO PEDROSO. México: Uma revoluçao insolúvel.
   Rio de Janeiro: Editora Saga, 1965.
   A general work about the unfinished Mexican Revolution.

271 FEHRENBACH, T.R. Fire and Blood: A History of Mexico.
   New York: Macmillan Co., 1973.
   A popular history of Mexico from Paleolithic times to
   1973. Well-researched, gigantic effort with understandably
   sweeping generalizations.

272 GARCÍA, RUBÉN. Anécdotas y sucedidos de la Revolución.
   Mexico: B. Costa-Amic, 1972.

273 GARCÍA URBIZU, FRANCISCO. Zamora en la Revolución. Centenario
   de la independencia. Porfirio Díaz. Hombres destacados
   en la revolución. Madero. Combates y corridos de la
   revolución. Pancho Villa. Prefectos y presidentes de
   Zamora. Presidentes de México. Exposición universal en
   San Francisco, Cal. Thomas Alva Edison. José Mojica.
   México progresa. Anécdotas páginas amenas. Epopeya
   cristera. Agrarismo. Zamora, Michoacán: Librería de
   Porrúa, 1970.

274 GASTÉLUM, BERNARDO J. La Revolución Mexicana: Interpretación
   de un espíritu. México: Editorial Porrúa, 1966.
   An account of historical events covering the period
   from the Conquest to the government of Cárdenas. More
   than half of the narrative deals with the Revolution.

275 GILLY, ADOLFO. La Revolución interrumpida. Mexico:
   Ediciones El Caballito, 1972.
   Provocative Marxist critique of the Revolution written
   from Lecumberri prison in the period 1966-1970. Although
   Gilly argues that the Revolution was interrupted on its

way to socialism, he still holds out hope that the Revolution will ultimately become a socialist one.

276   GOLDAR, ERNESTO. La Revolución Mexicana. Buenos Aires:
Centro Editor de América Latina, 1972.

277   HELLMAN, JUDITH ADLER. Mexico in Crisis. New York: Holmes &
Meier, 1978.
    Revisionist study of the course of the Mexican Revo-
lution since 1910. Author argues that the Revolution of
1910 resulted in a consolidation of economic and political
power by bourgeois interests that emerged from the chaos
of twenty years of civil strife; that developments since
1940 have benefitted middle- and upper-income groups at
the expense of the workers and peasants; and that political
power has been monopolized by the government and the
official party, the PRI. A comprehensive study of the
victory of Mexico's elites; most readable. Includes a
case study of the student movement of 1968. Derived
mostly from secondary sources.

278   Historia de la Revolución Mexicana 1911-1960. 25 vols.
Mexico: El Colegio de México, 1977-.
    A multivolume monograph series of the history of the
Mexican Revolution. This series is an excellent example
of the professionalization of recent Mexican historiography
that has developed in the post-World War II era. Daniel
Cosío Villegas was the original editor of the series; the
current editor is Luis González. All works in the series
are numbered, contain notes and bibliography, and have been
authored by members of the Colegio de México staff. Works
published (out of sequence) as of 1979 are: La revolución escindida, by Berta Ulloa; La reconstrucción
económica, by Enrique Krauze, Jean Meyer, and Cayetano
Reyes; Estado y sociedad con Calles, by Jean Mayer, Enrique
Krause, and Cayetano Reyes; Los inicios de la institucional-
ización, by L. Meyer, Rafael Segovia, and Alejandra Lajous;
El conflicto social y los gobiernos del maximato, by L.
Meyer; Los artífices del cardenismo, by Luis González;
La educación socialista, by Victoria Lerner; Del cardenismo
al avilacamachismo, by Luis Medina; Civilismo y modernización
del autoritarismo, by Luis Medina; and El entendimento con
los Estados Unidos y la gestión del desarrollo estabilizador,
by Olga Pellicer de Brody and Esteban Mancilla.

279   JOHNSON, WILLIAM WEBER. Heroic Mexico: The Violent Emergence
of a Modern Nation. Garden City, New York: Doubleday, 1968.
    Excellent narrative history of 1910-1940 period. Material
has been drawn from a variety of secondary sources, along

Comprehensive Studies

with published documents and newspapers. Well written, with
anecdotes, vignettes, and picturesque details.

280 Kunst der mexikanischen Revolution: Legende und Wirklichkeit.
     Organisation der Ausstellung Helga Prignitz. Berlin:
     Neue Gesellschaft für Bidlende Kunst, 1974.
     The Mexican Revolution--legend and reality.

281 LANGMAS, I.A. "Mexico To-day: Aspects of Progress Since
     the Revolution." World Today 17 (Apr. 1961): 158-67.
     A brief survey of the Mexican Revolution since 1910.

282 LEVINE, ROBERT M. "The Mexican Revolution: A Retrospective
     View." Current History 66 (May 1974): 195-99.
     Oversimplified synthesis: useful as an introduction
     and guide to themes and issues of the Revolution.

283 MANCISIDOR, JOSE. Historia de la Revolución Mexicana. 22d
     ed. Mexico: Editores Unidos, 1973.
     Interprets the Revolution in terms of the classical
     Marxist class struggle.

284 MARTINEZ DOMINGUEZ, ALFONSO. La Revolución Mexicana está
     en pie. Mexico: Asociación de Profesionistas e
     Intelectuales, 1968.

285 México: Cincuenta años de Revolución. 4 vols. Mexico:
     Fondo de Cultura Económica, 1960-62.
     Official publication to commemorate the 50th anniversary
     of the Mexican Revolution. A compendium of essays by a
     variety of specialists on the economy, social life, politics,
     and culture of the Mexican Revolution. Essays are of un-
     even quality, often overlap, and offer a rather standard
     pro-Revolutionary interpretation. Contents: Vol. 1, La
     economía; vol. 2, La vida social; vol. 3, La política;
     vol. 4, La cultura. A 1963 abridged one-volume edition
     is also available from the publisher.

286 MEYER, JEAN A. La Revolución Mejicana, 1910-1940. Trans-
     lated by Luis Flaquer. Barcelona: DOPESA, 1973.
     See entry 287.

287 _____. La Révolution Mexicaine, 1910-1940. Paris:
     Calmann-Levy, 1972.
     Revisionist synopsis of the Mexican Revolution. Argues
     that the modern Mexican state is the successor of the
     ruling class under the old regime--that is, the continu-
     ation of a Porfirian state explains the post-1910 phenom-
     enon of a "permanent revolution." Organized into two

parts. The first is a chronological section on the end of the Porfiriato, the "Time of Troubles." 1914-1920, the Sonorians, the Cristeros, and from Calles to Cárdenas. The second part is entitled "Analysis" and treats of economic problems, agrarian reform society, political institutions and ideology. Extensive bibliography; chronology.

288 MEYER, MICHAEL C., and SHERMAN, WILLIAM L. The Course of Mexican History. New York: Oxford University Press, 1979.
      A survey history of Mexico containing a balanced and objective analysis of Mexico's past based on traditional and revisionist sources. Narrative of the Revolution is one of the more complete to appear in a survey text to date.

289 MOLS, MANFRED, and TOBLER, HANS WERNER. Mexiko: Die institutionalisierte Revolution. Cologne and Vienna: Böhlau Verlag, 1976.
      A general study of the social, political, and economic dimensions of the Mexican Revolution that includes an historiographical essay on the literature of the Revolution. After a brief introductory essay by both authors on the institutionalized Revolution, historian Tobler analyzes the historiography of the Revolution, 1910-1940. The next two chapters are a social scientific analysis of the "Institutionalized Revolution" since 1940. This is followed by Tobler on peasant revolts and agrarian reform during the Revolution, from the Porfiriato to 1970. A final chapter by political scientist Mols deals with Mexico under Luis Echeverría (1970-1976). Essays are well documented with materials from Mexican, U.S., and European libraries. German-Spanish glossary of terms.

290 MORALES, JOSE IGNACIO. Historia de la Revolución Mexicana. Puebla: Editorial Periodística e Impresora de Puebla, 1970.
      Ends with the government of Díaz Ordaz.

291 NAVARRO BOLANDI, HUGO. La Revolución Mexicana y su proceso evolutivo. Mexico: Empresas Editoriales, 1969.
      Treats in detail the regimes of Madero and Alemán.

292 OTERO SILVA, MIGUEL. México y la Revolución Mexicana: Un escritor venezolano de la Unión Soviética. Caracas: Dirección de Cultura, Universidad Central de Venezuela, 1966.
      Product of a conference which took place in the Salón de la Fundación Mendoza.

Comprehensive Studies

293   PARKES, HENRY BAMFORD. A History of Mexico. Boston:
      Houghton Mifflin Co., 1969.
      Revised survey of Mexico from the Conquest to López
      Mateos.

294   PRIETO, JUAN FRANCISCO. "La Revolución Mexicana ante las
      formas comunitarias." Comunidades (Madrid) 1 (1966): 58-
      72.
      Considers that the Revolution represents a reaction
      against liberalism and individualism.

295   REYES HEROLES, JESUS. La historia y la acción: La Revolu-
      ción y el desarrollo político de México. Madrid:
      Seminarios y Ediciones, 1972.
      Compilation of various works published in different
      eras.

296   RICCIU, FRANCESCO. La Revolución Mexicana. Barcelona:
      Editorial Bruguera, 1970.
      Spanish translation of original Italian study. See
      entry 297.

297   _____. La rivoluzione messicana. Milan: Dall'Oglio,
      1968.
      Part of the "Great Revolutions of the 20th Century"
      series by the author of La rivoluzione spagnola. Narrative
      history from Porfiriato to Cárdenas; influenced by
      Octavio Paz's idea of the Revolution as a regeneration of
      mexicanidad.

298   ROMERO FLORES, JESUS. Historia de la Revolución Mexicana
      (Un siglo en la vida de México). 3d ed. Mexico:
      B. Costa-Amic, 1975.
      Romero Flores, a veteran of the Revolution, recounts in
      narrative form the history of the Revolution from the
      Porfiriato to the presidency of Echeverría.

299   _____. Síntesis histórica de la Revolución Mexicana.
      Mexico: B. Costa-Amic, 1974.

300   _____. Revolución Mexicana: Anales históricos 1910-1974.
      Mexico: Costa-Amic, 1974.

301   SALAZAR, ROSENDO. Esta es nuestra revolución: El mensaje
      vital de la Revolución Mexicana. Mexico: B. Costa-Amic,
      1967.
      Study of the Revolution by a well-known labor radical.

General Works

302   SANCHEZ AZCONA, HECTOR. La Revolución Mexicana. Mexico:
       Editorial del Magisterio, 1966.

303   SILVA HERZOG, JESUS. La Révolution Mexicaine. Translated by
       Raquel Thiercelin. Paris: Françoise Maspero, 1968.
       Translation of Breve historia de la Revolución Mexicana.
       See entry 304.

304   _____ . Breve historia de la Revolución Mexicana. 6th ed.
       Mexico: Fondo de Cultura Económica, 1969.
       Historical synthesis from the time of Santa Anna to the
       contemporary era. Studies the Constitution of 1917 and
       concludes with the assassination of Alvaro Obregón.

305   TARACENA, ALFONSO. Historia extraoficial de la Revolución
       Mexicana: Desde las postrimerías del porfirismo hasta
       sucesos de nuestros díaz. Mexico: Editorial Jus, 1972.
       Journalist-author's synthesis of the Revolution.

306   _____ . La Revolución desvirtuada: Continuación de la
       verdadera Revolución Mexicana. 5 vols. Mexico: B. Costa-
       Amic, 1966-68.
       Suggests that basic principles of the Revolution have
       been forgotten since 1932. These volumes contain almost
       daily entries for the 1933-1937 period and are a continua-
       tion of La verdadera Revolución Mexicana. See entry 307.

307   _____ . La verdadera Revolución Mexicana. 17 vols. Mexico:
       Editorial Jus, 1960-65.
       Expanded version of earlier edition. A chronological
       synthesis, or synthetic memoir, of the Revolution from
       1900 to 1932. In spite of the pretentiousness of the
       author in designating his effort "The True History of the
       Mexican Revolution," scholars should find this journalistic-
       historical work a handy reference.

308   VALADES, JOSE C. Historia general de la Revolución Mexicana.
       5 vols. Mexico: Editores Mexicanos Unidos, 1976.
       New and expanded edition of Valadés's classic narrative
       of the history of the Revolution from 1910 to 1946 (a
       concluding chapter brings the narrative up to the election
       of 1964). Based on primary and secondary works (mostly
       printed) listed at end of text. Well illustrated with
       reproductions of historical photographs. Vol. 1, back-
       ground to Revolution to fall of Madero; vol. 2, rise of
       Huerta to defeat of Villa in 1915; vol. 3, Celaya (1915)
       to Plan de Agua Prieta (1920); vol. 4, death of Carranza

Comprehensive Studies

(1920) to the fall of Ortiz Rubio (1932); vol. 5, Cárdenas
(1932) to the legacy of Alemán after 1946. Index.

309 _____. Historia general de la Revolución Mexicana. 5 vols.
Mexico: Manuel Quesada Brandi Editores, 1963-65.
According to historian Michael Meyer, this is the "best
general history of the Revolution."

310 VERA ESTAÑOL, JORGE. Historia de la Revolución Mexicana:
Orígenes y resultados. Mexico: Editorial Porrúa, 1976.
One of the better conservative accounts of the Revolution. More concerned with social causes and moral issues
than with individuals or factions. Third edition; first
appeared in 1957. Index.

311 WILKIE, JAMES W. La Revolución Mexicana (1910-1976): Gasto
federal y cambio social. Translated by Jorge E. Monzon.
Mexico: Fondo de Cultura Económica, 1978.
Mexican edition in Spanish of 312. See entry 312.

312 _____. The Mexican Revolution: Federal Expenditures and
Social Change Since 1910. Berkeley and Los Angeles:
University of California Press, 1967.
A quantitative study of the Mexican Revolution, 1910 to
the early 1960s, examined from the point of view of federal
expenditure and social change. Through analysis of statistical data, the author identifies four ideological periods
in the history of the Revolution: political revolution
(1910-1930), when the federal expenditures of a passive
state went into military outlays, pensions, public debt
payments, and administrative expenses; social revolution
(1930-1940), which included expenditures on education,
health, welfare, Indian affairs, and potable water and
sewage disposal systems; economic revolution (1940-1960),
that is, expenditures on agriculture, irrigation, credit
systems, communications, public works, investments, and
unclassified and minor economic expenditures; and the
balanced revolution (1960 to the present). The author also
constructs an index of poverty based upon illiteracy,
language use, "ruralness," footware, diet, and availability
of sewage disposal. Concludes by relating federal expenditure to changes in the index of poverty, suggesting that
social change is a slow process that has only developed to
a significant extent since 1950; that Mexico's Revolution
is not dead, but only beginning. Winner of the 1967 Herbert
Eugene Bolton Memorial Prize.

Theoretical Works

313   WOLFSKILL, GEORGE, and RICHMOND, DOUGLAS W. Essays on the
      Mexican Revolution: Revisionist Views of the Leaders.
      Austin and London: University of Texas Press, 1979.
          Lectures given on 16 March 1978 at the University of
      Texas at Arlington; Walter Prescott Webb memorial lectures
      in anthology form. Contents: "Introduction," by Michael
      C. Meyer; "Madero: The 'Unknown' President and His
      Political Failure to Organize Rural Mexico," by William
      H. Beczley; "Villa: Reform Governor of Chihuahua," by
      Friedrich Katz; "Carranza: The Authoritarian Populist as
      Nationalist President," by Douglas W. Richmond; "Obregón:
      Mexico's Accommodating President," by David C. Bailey;
      and "Cardenas: Creating a Campesino Power Base for
      Presidential Policy," by Lyle C. Brown. See entries
      823, 854, 887, 1078, and 1211.

314   ZAMORA, JOSE H. Semblanzas y perfiles de la Revolución
      Mexicana. Mexico: El Libro Español, 1962.

For the debate on James Wilkie's methodology see entries 181, 183,
245, and 248-49. For a review essay of some comprehensive histories
see entry 235.

                        THEORETICAL WORKS

315   AGUILAR MONTEVERDE, ALONSO. "La Revolución Mexicana: 50
      años después." Cuadernos Americanos 149 (Nov.-Dec., 1966):
      55-75.
          Evaluation of the movement of and possible solutions to
      the fundamental problems of the nation.

316   AL'PEROVICH, M.S.; RUDENKO, B.T.; and LAVROV, NIKOLAI M.
      La Revolución Mexicana: Cuatro estudios soviéticos.
      Mexico: Ediciones de Cultura Popular, 1975.
          A collection of four essays by three Soviet scholars on
      various aspects of the Mexican Revolution. Authors utilize
      a dialectical criterion and the assumptions of dialectical
      materialism to revise North American bourgeois history.
      Rudenko and Lavrov treat the revolutionary era from 1910-
      1917. Al'perovich authored two other essays: United
      States-Mexico relations and Mexican historiography since
      1945; problems in North American bourgeois literature on
      modern and contemporary Mexico.

General Works

Theoretical Works

317   BASURTO, JORGE. "Oligarquía, nacionalismo y alianza de clases
      en México." Revista Mexicana de Ciencia Política 21
      (1975): 43-50.
            Compares the relationship between the landowners and
      the oligarchy in early twentieth-century Mexico to the
      current relationship between the middle classes and the
      Mexican government, showing that the same elements which
      made Porfirio Díaz's dictatorship insupportable are
      present to an even greater degree in the political scene
      of today.

318   BORAH, WOODROW. "Discontinuity and Continuity in Mexican
      History." Pacific Historical Review 48 (Feb. 1979): 1-25.
            An examination of periodization in Mexican history
      using the test of continuity and discontinuity. Concludes
      that the true division came not with the Mexican Revolution
      but with the Porfirian accord. Thus in modern Mexican
      history there are two periods, one from 1760 to 1877, the
      other from the Porfiriato to the present.

319   CASTILLO, FAUSTO. "La revolución hizo mucho por los mexicanos,
      pero no consiguió hacerlos 'actuar.'" Solidaridad 10
      (1969): 50-51.

320   CHEVALIER, FRANCOIS. "El modelo mexicano de revolución."
      Cuadernos Americanos 210 (Jan.-Feb. 1977): 172-84.
            Overview of different "models" of revolution in Mexico
      beginning with independence and ending with discussion of
      the Revolution of 1910. Author concentrates on issues
      of land and religion.

321   CORDOVA, ARNOLDO. La formación del poder político en
      México. Mexico: Ediciones Era, 1975.
            A theoretical and historical study of the formulation
      of political power in Mexico, i.e., the positive state
      characterized by "presidentialism" and "class collabora-
      tionism" through the ruling Revolutionary Party. Argues
      that the Mexican Revolution is a political revolution,
      not a social revolution; that is to say, one in which
      private property is not entirely abolished and property
      relations transformed.

322   DAVILA, GERARDO. Como México no hay dos: Porfirismo,
      revolución, neoporfirismo; Reportajes documentales.
      Mexico: Editorial Nuestro Tiempo, 1971.
            Through selected documents and using argument by analogy
      the author characterizes contemporary Mexico as an era of
      neoporfirismo.

323 FRANK, ANDRE GUNDER. "Mexico: The Revolution Revisited."
     In Latin America: Yesterday and Today, edited by John
     Rothchild, pp. 324-32. New York, Toronto, and London:
     Bantam, 1973.
          Interprets the Revolution as an antifeudalist movement
     by an alliance of bourgeois and peasant elements.

324 _____. "Mexico: The Janus Faces of 20th-Century Bourgeois
     Revolution." In Whither Latin America?, edited by Paul M.
     Sweezy and Leo Hubermann, pp. 72-90. New York: Monthly
     Review Press, 1963.
          Describes the Janus faces of the Mexican Revolution:
     progress and poverty; GNP and per capital income; the
     wealth of downtown Mexico City and the poverty of rural
     Tlaxcala. Includes a brief survey of Mexico's history,
     with emphasis upon the Revolutionary decade, the Cárdenas
     era, and the post-1940 period. Considers the initial rev-
     olution to have been an alliance between peasants and the
     bourgeoisie, with only the bourgeoisie having final access
     to power. Describes plight of ejidatarios and the rise of
     a new bourgeoisie. Describes the social structure--
     indigenous Indians; landless rural people; the unemployed;
     lumpenproletariat; ejidatarios; private small holders;
     workers and the "aristocracy of the proletariat"; the petty
     bourgeoisie; and the bourgeois upper class. Notes social
     mobility on an individual-by-individual basis. Argues
     that the United States, the new bourgeoisie, and the PRI
     control Mexico's less-than-radical "revolutionary"
     politics. Based primarily on personal observation and U.S.
     and Mexican newspapers.

325 GONZALEZ NAVARRO, MOISES. "México: La Revolución desequili-
     brada." Revista de la Universidad de Sonora 10 (1966):
     5-24.
          Speaks of an "unbalanced revolution" in which the costs
     of Revolution were paid for by the workers while benefits
     went to the fortunate few.

326 LABASTIDA, HORACIO, and ELIAS, ANTONIO PEREZ. Una evaluación
     de la Revolución. Mexico: Estado de México, 1970.

327 MEYER, EUGENIA [W. de]. "La periodización de la historia
     contemporanea de México." In Contemporary Mexico: Papers
     of the Fourth International Congress of Mexican History,
     edited by James W. Wilkie, Michael C. Meyer, and Edna Monzón
     de Wilkie, pp. 730-46. Los Angeles and Mexico: University
     of California Press and El Colegio de México, 1976.
          Delimits several concepts of periodization of the Mexican
     Revolution and relates them to particular groups. For

Theoretical Works

example, the bourgeois conception of the Revolution is that of a continuous revolution from 1910 to the present; the petite bourgeoisie and moderate socialists adhere to the idea of a 1910 democratic-bourgeois revolution that has only been partially realized; the Marxist conception, reflected in part by the Trotsktite Adolfo Gilly, is that of an interrupted revolution. The revolution was twice diverted from its original direction as an agrarian, anti-imperialistic, anticapitalistic revolution. These two interruptions occurred in 1919-1920 and 1940. The next phase of the revolution should be nationalistic, socialistic, and proletarian.

328   MICHAELS, ALBERT L., and BERNSTEIN, MICHAEL. "The Moderniza-
      tion of the Old Order: Organization and Periodization of
      Twentieth-Century Mexican History." In Contemporary
      Mexico: Papers of the Fourth International Congress of
      Mexican History, edited by James W. Wilkie, Michael C.
      Meyer, and Edna Monzón de Wilkie, pp. 687-710. Los Angeles
      and Mexico: University of California Press and El Colegio
      de México, 1976.
          Organizes Mexican history since 1876 around the emergence
      and development of the Mexican national bourgeoisie. The
      Porfiriato saw the gestation of the national bourgeoisie;
      the 1910-1917 stage marks the establishment by the national
      bourgeoisie of a socially sound legal base; from 1917 to
      1932 the victors of 1917 came to power and began to imple-
      ment their vision of a national capitalistic Mexico; the
      1932-1946 period served as a transition of power in which
      the politicians of the 1920s and 1930s left power in the
      hands of a New Group; 1946 to 1958 was a period in which
      the national bourgeoisie triumphed and restored the Por-
      firiato; and from 1958 to 1973 the national bourgeoisie
      has been in retreat.

329   ROSS, STANLEY R. "Forging a Nation." Revista de Historia de
      América 83 (Jan.-June 1977): 135-51.
          Discussion of the Revolution and its legacy in connec-
      tion with Mexico's struggle to develop a national identity.

330   _____. Is the Mexican Revolution Dead? Rev. ed. Phila-
      delphia: Temple University Press, 1975.
          New English edition of 1966 publication, updated with
      an expanded preface, a new section on the post-1964 period
      (including two excerpts of remarks by presidents of Mexico),
      and an enlarged bibliography. The original group of
      commentators represents some of the best-known revolutionary
      intellectuals. An invaluable tool for undergraduates and
      for teachers wishing to elicit a discussion of the tradi-
      tional interpretation of the Revolution.

331   . "Chronology and Periodization of the Mexican
        Revolution." Texas Quarterly 16 (1973): 7-21.
        Reviews the periodization of Mexican history that
        facilitates management of data and provides hypotheses for
        interpreting the Mexican Revolution. Such divisions are
        artificial; one learns to study transitional periods that
        furnished watersheds for Mexico's self-reorientation, as
        during Manuel Avila Camacho's administration, 1940-46,
        when he linked Cárdenas's agrarian revolution with the
        industrial revolution of Miguel Alemán. Secondary sources.

332   SCHULGOVSKII, A.F. México en un momento crucial de su
        historia. Moscow: n.p., 1967.
        A theoretical work on contemporary Mexico by the chief
        of the Department of Socio-Political Problems of the
        Institute of Latin America, Academy of Sciences.

333   SEOANE CORRALES, EDUARDO. El ejemplo mexicano. Lima, Peru:
        Francisco Moncloa Editores, 1967.
        Author argues that the Mexican Revolution is a model to
        be followed by all of Latin America.

334   SILVA HERZOG, JESUS. "Opinions heterodoxas sobre la Revolución
        Mexicana." Cuadernos Americanos 206 (May-June 1976): 7-24.
        Discusses ideological influences on Mexican Revolution
        and argues that Revolution was made against, rather than
        by, the bourgeoisie. Argues that the Mexican Revolution
        does not follow the European pattern in that there did
        not exist in Mexico institutions similar to European feud-
        alism and nobility; that the Revolution was not a bourgeois
        revolution. It was a revolution directed against the
        national and foreign bourgeoisie by the popular campesino
        and national groups.

335   SLOAN, JOHN W. "United States Policy Responses to the Mexican
        Revolution: A Partial Application of the Bureaucratic
        Politics Model." Journal of Latin American Studies 10
        (Nov. 1978): 283-308.
        A review of United States policy attempts to protect
        United States private investors in Mexico during the
        Mexican Revolution from 1911 to 1941. Evidence provided
        by diplomatic historians and biographers. Seeks to answer
        the question: did the principal players share a common
        concern about the goal and the means of protecting United
        States investors as the dependence theorists would predict,
        or were there differing perspectives as Abraham Lowenthal's
        and Graham Allison's bureaucratic politics model would
        claim? Concludes that to a great extent the diplomatic
        record would support the assumption of the bureaucratic

Theoretical Works

politics model; that, although U.S. policy was influenced
by economic interests, the dependency theory is overly
simplistic, with the investor community speaking with many
voices and the policymakers differing widely concerning
means of action.

336   TANNENBAUM, FRANK. "Spontaneity and Adaptation in the
Mexican Revolution." Journal of World History 9 (1965):
80-90.
        Argues that the Mexican Revolution was spontaneous in
idea, concept, and objective--little influenced by
Marxism, anarchism, and the ideas of the Enlightenment.
The Revolution followed an adaptative path, seeking new,
national solutions to old problems.

337   TOBLER, HANS WERNER. "Die mexikanische Revolution: Einige
Forschungs--und Interpretationsprobleme." Bulletin de la
Société suisse des Américanistes, no. 38 (1974): 81-88.
        The author, a professor of Latin American history at
the University of Zurich, entertains the question of the
correct interpretation of the Mexican Revolution. After
a brief examination of the causes of the Revolution, he
surveys the 1910-20 era, the Cárdenas period, and the postrevolutionary scene. He distinguishes the northern revolution from the southern one, and argues that the Sonoran
dynasty simply substituted a "revolutionary" elite for
the ancient Porfirian oligarchy, and in spite of the
agrarian reforms realized by Cárdenas, the history of
modern Mexico has been more evolutionary than revolutionary,
with political stability and economic growth the indicators
of progess and change. Based on previous works by R.
Scott, F. Katz, J. Womack, G. Magaña, R. Hansen, S. Ross,
and J. Silva Herzog.

338   UNZUETA, GERARDO. "Enseñanzas de El Capital a los revolucionarios mexicanos." Historia y Sociedad 3 (1966): 5-29.
        The impact of Marx's Das Kapital on the Mexican
revolutionaries.

339   WOMACK, JOHN, Jr. "The Spoils of the Mexican Revolution."
Foreign Affairs 48 (July 1970): 677-87.
        A brief essay on the course of the Mexican Revolution
from 1910 to 1970. Traces the growth of authoritarian
government and national capitalism in a Mexico in which
"the business of the Mexican Revolution is now business."
Womack argues that the heritage of revolt is over and the
national capitalists, having confirmed their right to rule,
are now integrating Mexico into the patterns of international capitalism.

General Works

340   YAÑEZ, AGUSTIN. Conciencia de la revolución. Mexico:
       Secretaría de Educación Pública, 1968.

For comparative revolutions and theory see entry 346.

COMPARATIVE STUDIES

341   CESPEDES, AUGUSTO. "México y Bolivia: Dos revoluciones y
       dos destinos." Cuadernos Americanos 149 (Nov.-Dec. 1968):
       1-28.
          Comparative study of the two revolutions of Latin
       America. The author argues that both are authentic and
       original in two underdeveloped countries. Identifies the
       similarities and differences between the indigenous popu-
       lations of both countries. Draws a parallel between the
       pictorial art of the two nations that appeared during the
       revolutions. Mexico's Rivera, Siqueiros and Orozco had
       much influence over the Bolivian artist Alandia Pantoja.
       Lastly, the author affirms that Mexico liquidated the old
       institutions: militarism, the church, the oil companies
       and the influence of the U.S. State Department, but that
       in Bolivia there was a rise in counter-revolutionary
       forces.

342   COATSWORTH, JOHN H. "Obstacles to Economic Growth in Nine-
       teenth-Century Mexico." American Historical Review 83
       (Feb. 1978): 80-100.
          A general interpretative essay of Mexico's economic
       history in the nineteenth century that compares Mexico's
       national income with the industrialized countries of the
       United States and Great Britain. Explains the widening
       gap in productivity between the U.S. and Mexican economies
       as being due to two main obstacles--inadequate transport
       (geography) and inefficient economic organization ("feud-
       alism"). Concludes that the participation of foreign
       capital during the Porfiriato accelerated the discontent
       of dispossessed villagers and those "middle sectors" who
       produced the Revolution of 1910.

343   ECKSTEIN, SUSAN. The Impact of Revolution: A Comparative
       Analysis of Mexico and Bolivia. Beverly Hills and London:
       Sage Publications, 1976.
          A political and economic analysis.

344   KAUTSKY, JOHN H. Patterns of Modernizing Revolutions: Mexico
       and the Soviet Union. In Sage Professional Papers in
       Comparative Politics, vol. 5, series no. 01-056, edited
       by Aristide R. Zolberg and Richard L. Merritt. Beverly

Comparative Studies

Hills and London: Sage Publications, 1976.
Argues for similarities over differences; compares
Díaz and Witte.   Author influenced by the careers of Flores
Magón brothers.   Useful modern bibliography.

345   KOSSOK, MANFRED; KUBLER; JURGEN; and ZEUSKE, MAX.   "Ein Ver-
such zur Dialektik von Revolution und Reform in der historischen Entwicklung Lateinamerikas (1809-1917)."   In Studien
zur Vergleichenden Revolutionsgeschichte, edited by
Manfred Kossok, pp. 160-79.   Berlin: Akademie-Verlag, 1974.
A study in comparative revolutions in Latin America from
1809 to 1917, with coverage on the modern revolutions of
Mexico, Bolivia, and Cuba.   Notes that Mexico led the
revolutionary process in Latin America with an antifeudalistic, anti-imperialistic struggle of a democratic
character led by bourgeois and workers' elements.
Concludes that Mexico is in a transitory stage between
capitalism and socialism, although imperialistic elements
control its productive forces.   Based on previous studies
by Kossok, C. Furtado, M. S. Alperovich, N. M. Lavrov,
V. I. Lenin, and K. Marx.   Kossok is a well-known East
European historian who is Director of the Latin American
History section of the Karl Marx University in Leipzig.

346   LEIDEN, CARL, and SCHMITT, KARL.   The Politics of Violence:
Revolution in the Modern World.   Englewood Cliffs, N.J.:
Prentice Hall, 1968.
Theoretical and comparative study of revolution in the
modern world.   Theoretical section deals with patterns,
violence, terror, causes, stages, leaders, followers, and
ideology.   Case studies of Mexico, Turkey, Egypt, and
Cuba.   Concluding chapter on comparisons and prospects.

347   RAAT, WILLIAM DIRK.   "Ideología y revolución en América Latina:
Un estudio comparativo de las revoluciones mexicana,
boliviana y cubana."   Latinoamerica, no. 8 (1975): 179-89.
A comparative study of the ideologies of revolution in
Mexico, Bolivia, and Castro's Cuba.   Includes a list of
suggested reading consisting of printed primary materials.

POLITICAL, LEGAL, AND MILITARY HISTORY

348   AZCARATE, JUAN F.   Esencia de la Revolución.   Mexico:
B. Costa-Amic, 1966.
A revolutionary general from Nuevo León narrates the
violent phase of the movement from 1910 through 1929.

349   BLANCAS, BENITO R.   Ensayo histórico sobre la Revolución

Mexicana y la Democracia. 2d ed. Mexico: Editorial
Porrúa, 1974.
Author defines the Revolution as a political and armed
movement to destroy the socioeconomic structure.

350   BOILS, GUILLERMO. Los militares y la política en México:
1915-1974. Mexico: El Caballito, 1975.
Study of Mexican military with emphasis on the military's
function as a sociopolitical control mechanism.

351   BRADING, D.A., ed. Caudillo and Peasant in the Mexican
Revolution. Cambridge: Cambridge University Press, 1980.
Consists of case studies and general perspectives, all
based on recent research, which follow the careers of
several caudillos with the aim of analyzing the means by
which these revolutionary chieftains first obtained power
and then promoted or opposed the authority of the national
state. Concludes that the constitutionalists had to
mobilize the rural population and win the alliance of
popular caudillos. Northern leaders confiscated haciendas
to finance their campaigns and reward their followers, not
to improve the condition of the peasantry. It was only
in the 1930s that the national party sought to incorporate
the peasants as clients that a program of agrarian reform
was instituted in order to undermine the power of regional
caudillos. Contributors are: D.A. Brading, "Introduction";
Alan Knight, "Peasant and Caudillo in Revolutionary Mexico
1910-17"; Friedrich Katz, "Poncho Villa, Peasant Movements,
and Agrarian Reform in Northern Mexico"; Ian Jacobs,
"Rancheros of Guerrero: The Figueroa Brothers and the
Revolution"; Héctor Aguilar Camín, "The Relevant Tradition:
Sonoran Leaders in the Revolution"; Linda B. Hall, "Alvaro
Obregón and the Agrarian Movement 1912-20"; Dudley Anker-
son, "Santurnino Cedillo: A Traditional Caudillo in San
Luis Potosí 1890-1938"; Heather Fowler Salamini, "Revolu-
tionary Caudillos in the 1920s: Francisco Múgica and
Adalberto Tejeda"; Gilbert M. Joseph, "Caciquismo and the
Revolution: Carrillo Puerto in Yucatán"; Raymond Buve,
"State Governors and Peasant Mobilization in Tlaxcala";
and Hans Werner Tobler, "Conclusion: Peasant Mobilization
and the Revolution."

352   BUVE, RAYMOND Th. J. "Patronaje en las zonas rurales de
México." Boletín de Estudios Latinoamericanos y del Caribe
(Amsterdam) 16 (June 1974): 3-15.
A study of the impact of modernization upon the institution of rural patronage from the nineteenth century through
the Revolution. After 1867 the predominantly paramilitary
patron-client relationship gave way to the more stable

Political, Legal, and Military History

caudillaje of the Porfiriato. Patronage became more
permanent with military assistance being replaced by
political patronage and economic rewards. Medium and
large landowners acted as intermediate powerholders between
the rural village and the state. These local patrons are
replaced by rural caudillos during the first stages of the
Revolution. After 1916 revolutionary elites, as rural
caudillos, assume the positions of traditional patrons
and intermediate powerholders. This substitution process
leads to extreme forms of strife and violence at the village
level as traditional rural elites fought the revolutionary
elites. After 1934 the Central Government and the PNR sub-
jugate caudillos (military and state authorities) and
curtail landlords and revolutionary caudillos, leading to
new changes in political patronage. Author uses G.E.
Black's theory on the dynamics of modernization as his model.

353   CALVERT, PETER. "The Mexican Political System: A Case Study
      in Political Development." Journal of Development Studies
      4 (1968): 464-80.
          Describes the structure of the Mexican political system
      and government since the 1910 revolution and the 1917
      constitution, which presupposes the traditional customs
      of pre-Columbian and Spanish Mexico and the judicial forms
      and customs of Roman law. Emphasizes the crucial role of
      the presidency, conditions for election, and extent of
      powers; outlines the characters and policies of past and
      present officeholders. Also examines the roles of the
      legislature and judiciary, political parties, regional
      and federal government, and levels of force currently
      employed in social control. The conflict phase produced
      a three-way division of power, giving rise to a system of
      unusual freedom and stability. Primary and secondary sources.

354   CAMP, RODERIC A. Mexico's Leaders: Their Education and
      Recruitment. Tucson: University of Arizona Press, 1980.
          Draws on original data and personal contact with more
      than one hundred political figures to weigh the impact of
      education on career mobility and points to an integral
      relationship between career and educational patterns for
      the majority of Mexican leaders holding office between
      1935 and 1976.

355   _____. "Autobiography and Decision-Making in Mexican
      Politics." JISWA 19 (May 1977): 275-81.
          A review essay of the published memoirs and autobio-
      graphies of seven men who occupied important public
      positions in the political history of the Revolution.
      These men were generally involved in either party-electoral
      or public careers or were active in administration and the

bureaucracy. The authors are Práxedis Balboa (politician
from Tamaulipas), Alfredo Bremauntz (Michoacán politician),
Jaime Torres Bodet (foreign relations; public education),
Jesús Silva Herzog (public educator), Eduardo Villasenor
(consular service), Luis Garrido, and Manuel Rivera Silva.

356 _____. "A Reexamination of Political Leadership and
Allocation of Federal Revenues in Mexico, 1932-1973."
Journal of Developing Areas 10 (1976): 193-212.
    An explanation is sought for the uneven development
between states and regions of Mexico. The "favorite son"
explanation does not hold. There was no conclusive relationship between a high percentage of national leadership
from a state and federal spending in that state. There
is, however, a relationship between lack of representation
and lack of federal funds. The "president's home state"
explanation does not hold over time, though home states
have been politically overrepresented in the president's
own administration and that following. No significant
changes were found in patterns of socioeconomic development.
Analysis of the "party vote" hypothesis did find a relationship between low federal investment in a state and
low PRI votes. The "experience of the governor" argument
found support in those states where the governor was
appointed by the president at the time he took office.
In those states revenue surpluses consistently occurred.
The federal government contribution to regional development in Mexico is slanted in favor of the already developed
states. Four tables.

357 _____. "Mexican Governors Since Cárdenas: Education and
Career Contacts." JISWA 16 (Nov. 1974): 454-81.
    An examination of all Mexican governors who held office
between 1935 and 1973 reveals that these men were a part
of the federal bureaucracy before becoming governors.
Consequently they knew less about state problems than one
would expect. In addition, they had no competition from
other parties. The only opposition came from within the
PRI; nomination by the party was tantamount to election.
Finally, governors usually came from the middle class;
no workers or peasants were elected state governors in
the period under study. Based on newspapers, reports,
and secondary works; 9 tables; bibliography.

358 CAZES, DANIEL. Los revolucionarios. Mexico: Editorial
Grijalbo, 1973.
    This work is written from many of the materials of the
Archivo Sonora del Departamento de Investigaciones Histór-

Political, Legal, and Military History

icas del Instituto Nacional de Antropología e Historia.
Argues that the dictatorship of 1929 greatly resembles
the one that was overthrown in 1911. However, its immediate
external manifestation is that of an almighty, demagogic
and repressive party-government that substitutes the man
that represents it every six years.

359   CONKLIN, JOHN G. "Elite Studies: The Case of the Mexican
      Presidency." Journal of Latin American Studies 5(Nov. 1973):
      247-69.
          Delineates the characteristics of men who have become
      president of Mexico in the nineteenth and twentieth cen-
      turies in terms of birthplace, education, occupation, and
      age when assuming the presidency. As a group they are
      quite heterogeneous and represent political modernization.
      Methodologically, the author's approaches greatly reduce
      the problem of elite identification, lend themselves to
      comparative analysis, and are relatively easy to design.
      However, not all data are suitable for quantitative methods,
      although quantification does bring "a semblance of order
      to a large number of observations." Secondary sources;
      13 tables, 4 appendixes.

360   FERNANDEZ BRAVO, VICENTE. "La Revolución y la política:
      Los cambios operados en México a partir de la Revolución."
      Revista de Ciencias Sociales (Universidad de Puerto Rico,
      Río Piedras)7 (1963): 231-45.

361   GONZALEZ CASANOVA, PABLO. Democracy in Mexico. Translated
      by Danielle Salti. New York: Oxford University Press,
      1970.
          A classic in political sociology. Originally published
      in Spanish in 1965. Critical of the complacency surrounding
      the economic "miracle of Mexican development." Attacks
      the mythical view that Mexicans are revolutionaries and
      anticolonists.

362   GONZALEZ y GONZALEZ, LUIS. "Los balances periódicos de la
      Revolución Mexicana." Historia y Sociedad en el Mundo de
      Habla Española 5 (1970): 329-54.
          Deals with the reports presented each year by the
      presidents of the republic to the Congreso de la Unión.

363   LEAL, JUAN FELIPE. "The Mexican State, 1915-1973: A Histor-
      ical Interpretation." Latin American Perspectives 2
      (Summer 1975): 48-62.

Argues that the State was destroyed in 1914. By 1916
the country was characterized by the victory of the popular
armies of Carranza and Obregón, a developing bureaucracy,
and the nonexistence of a national state. The political-
military bureaucracy organized, through the Constitution
of 1917, a new State based on the capitalistic model with
three major characteristics: a representative democracy,
a presidential dictatorship, and corporatism. Between
1917 and 1940 the State subordinated the agrarian masses,
labor, and management. Since 1940 the government has
witnessed a weakening of its social base and has had to
resort to direct repression of peasants, workers, and even
small and medium capitalists. As a dependent capitalistic
State, its primary mission consists of promoting the
capitalistic development of the country under conditions
imposed by the imperialistic system.

364   _____ . La burguesía e el estado mexicano. Mexico:
Ediciones El Caballito, 1972.
A study of the development of the Mexican State, especially the transition from nineteenth-century liberalism
to the imperialism of the Porfiriato and the political
consolidation of the evolutionary regimes.

365   LIEUWEN, EDWIN. Mexican Militarism: The Political Rise and
Fall of the Revolutionary Army, 1910-1940. Albuquerque:
University of New Mexico Press, 1968.
Sequel to author's earlier study on Arms and Politics
in Latin America. Traces the transition of revolutionary
soldiers into praetorean regulars, and the civil-military
conflict that lasted until 1940.

366   LOZOYA, JORGE ALBERTO. "Breve historia del ejército mexicano."
Aportes (Paris) 20 (1971): 113-31.
Taking into consideration the political events of
Mexican history, this author analyzes the conduct of the
Mexican army up to the present. The last military president
was Avila Camacho, who together with Cárdenas, eliminated
the aforesaid group from the PRM. The author feels that
the use of the army in civil conflicts such as those in
1956, 1959, and 1968 is the responsibility only of the
president.

367   _____ . El ejército mexicano, 1911-1945. Mexico: El
Colegio de México, 1970.
Short description of military involvement in politics.
Contains some new material based on interviews.

Political, Legal, and Military History

368   OSORIO MARBAN, MIGUEL. El partido de la Revolución Mexicana
       (Ensayo). Mexico: Miguel Osorio Marbán, 1970.

369   REYES ESPARZA, RAMIRO et al. La burguesía mexicana: Cuatro
       ensayos. Mexico: Editorial Nuestro Tiempo, 1973.
              Four essays, in which the authors argue that the
       Mexican bourgeoisie has captured the Mexican State and
       has abandoned the principles of the Revolution.

370   SABLOFF, PAULA L.W. "El caciquismo en el ejido post revolu-
       cionario." América Indígena 37 (1977): 851-81.
              A study on caciquismo, or political bossism: a type
       of autocratic political organization found on the local
       level (village, hamlet, municipality) of many complex
       societies and which has been prevalent in rural agrarian
       Mexico for over 400 years. It has been especially noted
       in Mexican communities that have had corporate land-
       holding, i.e., where title to the agricultural lands,
       pasture, and woodlands has been held by the community,
       and usufruct rights to these lands have been granted to
       community members. Caciquismo exists in this type of
       community when one individual, with the help of a small
       group of followers, controls the economic, political, and
       sometimes even the social activity of the members of that
       community. The cacique gains and maintains control
       through various means--patronage, coercion, cooptation,
       or violence. Tracts have been written explaining why
       communities with this form of land tenure arrangement have
       been prey to autocratic or cacique rule in previous
       centuries. It is not so clear, however, why many post-
       Revolution communities in which most land is under ejido
       grant are still under cacique rule, for many parts of the
       1917 Constitution and subsequent laws purposefully built
       a democratic form into the government of these communities.

371   SCHMITT, KARL M. Communism in Mexico. Austin: University
       of Texas Press, 1965.
              Dispassionately discounts major communist influence
       on Mexican history after the Revolution; describes the
       increasingly anticommunist stance of the Mexican govern-
       ment; and analyzes the long-standing weaknesses of the
       Mexican communist movement.

372   SCOTT, ROBERT E. Mexican Government in Transition. Rev. ed.
       Urbana: University of Illinois Press, 1964.

Political, Legal, and Military History

A general political analysis of modern Mexico, including a chapter on the Mexican Revolution. Describes party and presidential system in the political evolution of Mexico.

373 SILVA, JOSE. Evolución agraria en México. Mexico: B. Costa-Amic, 1969.
A political history of the agrarian revolution and agrarian reform in Mexico. Reproduces several documents, including the Plan de Ayala, Plan of San Luis, Pacto de Xochimilco, and Artículo 27 Constitucional.

374 SILVA HERZOG, JESUS. "El presidente Echeverría y la derecha y la izquierda en México." Cuadernos Americanos 184 (Sept.-Oct. 1972): 7-21.
Indicates those who belong to the Left and those who belong to the Right throughout modern Mexican history. Appeals to the Mexican intelligensia to support Echeverría and not abandon him to the forces of the Right.

375 SMITH, PETER H. Labyrinths of Power: Political Recruitment in Twentieth-Century Mexico. Princeton: Princeton University Press, 1979.
An analysis of political careers and elite composition in Mexico since 1900. Suggests that the revolution was important in creating and institutionalizing a system of elite circulation that promised greater political mobility to the same stratum of the population from which pre-revolutionary elites were chosen. Contains socioeconomic and career information on more than six hundred individuals who have held high-level office. Analyzed in terms of prerevolutionary (1900-1911), revolutionary (1917-1940), and postrevolutionary elites (1946-1971). All three groups recruited from the privileged middle class.

376 _____. "The Mexican revolution and the transformation of political elites." Boletín de Estudios Latinoamericanos y del Caribe (Amsterdam) 25 (Dec, 1978): 3-20.
Analysis of political elites in prerevolutionary Mexico (1900-1911), revolutionary Mexico (1917-1940), and postrevolutionary Mexico (1946-1971). Concludes that "the Mexican Revolution, at least regarding leadership, was a bourgeois movement that sought to modernize, not overthrow, the country's capitalist system." The central discovery of this study is the prevalence, persistence, and preeminence of Mexico's relatively privileged middle class within the country's national political elites. Includes tables on social origins of elites; relationship between father's occupational class and professional title,

Political, Legal, and Military History

> by cohort; occupations of political elites, by cohort;
> relationship between father's occupational class and level
> of education, by cohort; and father's occupations for
> political elites, by cohort.

377 _____. "Continuity and Turnover within the Mexican
> Political Elite, 1900–1971." In Contemporary Mexico:
> Papers of the Fourth International Congress of Mexican
> History, edited by James W. Wilkie, Michael C. Meyer, and
> Edna Monzón de Wilkie, pp. 167-86. Los Angeles and Mexico:
> University of California Press and El Colegio de México, 1976.
>   Statistical study of Mexico's authoritarian one-party
> system in terms of continuity and turnover among the
> political elite. Evidence indicates that the Revolution
> cut the rate of continuity in half, so that during each
> presidential term approximately two-thirds of the high
> national offices have been held by complete newcomers to
> the elite circles. This revolving door has meant that
> political patronage has been constantly available, the
> potential for elite cooptation and corruption in office has
> remained high, and that stability has been at the expense
> of skilled experience. Additional evidence suggests that
> national elites in postrevolutionary Mexico have undergone
> ninety per cent renewal over the course of every three
> presidential terms, providing each regime with flexibility
> to move politically like a pendulum. The pattern of elite
> mobility has been up-or-out, with political careers being
> dependent on executive largesse. Tables on elite data;
> appended notes on methodology.

See also the following: federal expenditures, entries 311–12;
international politics, entry 381; politics of development, entry
400; immigration policy, entry 403; political changes and foreign
investment, entries 399, 406, and 427; political economy, entries
413 and 415; political causes of the Revolution, entry 409; political
relationship to agrarian reform, entries 419–21, 475, 489 and 504;
church-state relations, entries 432 and 507; political education,
entries 435–36; government and intellectuals, entries 433 and 458;
and political biographies, entries 588, 611, and 667.

DIPLOMATIC HISTORY AND INTERNATIONAL AFFAIRS

378 CECEÑA, JOSE LUIS. México en la órbita imperial: Las empresas
> transacionales. Mexico: Ediciones "El Caballito," 1975.
>   A study of the impact of international business and
> global capitalism on Mexico's economy from 1821 to 1969,

Diplomatic History and International Affairs

with emphasis upon the Porfiriato and the Mexican Revolution
to Cárdenas. Appendixes contain useful data concerning
foreign ownership of Mexican properties and foreign capital
investments in Mexico.

379 GARCIA CANTU, GASTON. Las invasiones norteamericanas en
     México. Mexico: Ediciones Era, 1971.
        A history of North American intervention in Mexico from
     the early 1800s to the 1960s. Interprets Mexican history
     as a process of colonization and struggle for independence
     in which the internal economic history of Mexico is part
     of the external history of capital accumulation and develop-
     ment in the United States.

380 LEVENSTEIN, HARVEY A. Labor Organizations in the United
     States and Mexico: A History of Their Relations.
     Conn.: Greenwood Publishing Co., 1971.
        Monograph surveying seven decades of Mexican-American
     labor relations since 1900. Focus is upon the leadership,
     with emphasis upon the roles of Samuel Gompers, John Murray,
     Luis Morones, and Vicente Lombardo Toledano. Based upon
     the private letters and public statements of these men
     with a heavy reliance upon U.S. archival sources.

381 QUINTANILLA, LUIS. "La política internacional de la Revolución
     Mexicana." Revista de la Universidad de Yucatán 6 (July-
     Aug. 1964): 17-39.
        The international politics of the Mexican Revolution.
     Previously published in Foro Internacional 5 (July-Sept.
     1964): 1-26.

382 RODRIGUEZ, ERWIN. "Las proyecciones mexicanas de la crisis
     general del capitalismo (elementos para su estudio)."
     Estudios Políticos 2 (1976): 5-14.
        An examination of the relationship between the general
     crisis of world capitalism and the Mexican economy (1929-
     76). The general crisis of capitalism is caused by the
     lack of international solvency, which causes "stagflation"
     in the highly industrialized economies of Western Europe
     and the United States. The inflationary component of
     this malaise has been exported to Mexico through the
     sale of capital goods at inflated prices. At the same
     time, recession in the United States has caused that nation
     to reduce its imports of Mexican primary products. The
     combination of inflation and falling exports in Mexico
     weakened demand for domestic manufactured goods, causing
     recession in the industrialized sector. This recession

Diplomatic History and International Affairs

reduced the tax base of the Mexican government, impeding
its public sector spending to stimulate the economy.
Based on economic studies and the statistics of private
and governmental institutions.

383   SCHMITT, KARL M.   Mexico and the United States, 1821-1973:
      Conflict and Coexistence.   New York: John Wiley & Sons,
      1974.
          Concludes that Mexico's primary concern during the last
      one hundred years has been one of dealing with neocolonial-
      ism in the guise of economic dependency.   Suggests that
      since the 1920s a trend has developed that has limited the
      crisis diplomacy of the early Revolution.   This trend has
      been accelerated since 1940, with Mexico developing internal
      unity and United States attention being attracted primarily
      towards Europe and outside the Western Hemisphere.

384   ZORRILLA, LUIS G.   Historia de las relaciones entre México
      y los Estados Unidos de América, 1800-1958.   2 vols.
      Mexico: Porrúa, 1965-66.
          Standard narrative of United States-Mexico relations.
      Vol. 2, part 3 treats of the revolutionary period from
      Madero to Cortines.

See entry 96 for research problems peculiar to the topic of United
States-Latin American relations.   For U.S. policy responses to the
Mexican Revolution see entry 335.   For an indispensable source of
printed documents for diplomatic history see entry 515.

                    ECONOMIC AND SOCIAL HISTORY

385   BERNSTEIN, MARVIN.   The Mexican Mining Industry, 1890-1950.
      Albany: State University of New York, 1964.
          A thorough and scholarly study of the interaction of
      politics, economics, and technology in Mexico from 1890
      to 1950.   Appendixes include U.S. tariff rates from 1897
      to 1958.

386   CARMONA AMOROS, SALVADOR.   La economía mexicana y el nacional-
      ismo revolucionario.   Mexico: Ediciones "El Caballito,"
      1974.
          Revolutionary nationalism and the Mexican economy.

387   CASO, ALFONSO.   "El indigenismo mexicano."   Cahiers d'histoire
      mondiale 10 (1967): 438-44.

Brief account of the importance of diverse racial groups
in the history of Mexico. Focus is upon the Mexican Revolution as a period of indigenous revindication, and the
role of the Instituto Nacional Indigenista in transforming
the life and culture of the Indian.

388 CAYTAN, CARLOS. La Revolución Mexicana y sus monedas.
     Mexico: Ed. Diana, 1969.
     The Revolution and coinage.

389 DELARBE, RAUL TREJO. "The Mexican Labor Movement: 1917-
     1975." Latin American Perspectives 3 (1976): 133-53.
     A history of the labor movement in Mexico. Considers
     the important role of the State and its impact on organized
     labor. The state-party-union formula has been fundamental
     to the Mexican system and is basic to an understanding of
     the Mexican labor movement.

390 FOX, DAVID J. "Mexico: The Development of the Oil Industry."
     Bank of London & South America Review 11 (Oct. 1977): 520-
     32.
     Traces the history of the Mexican oil industry from the
     law of 1884 to date.

391 GALLAGA, ROBERTO. "La historia del trabajo de los campesinos
     cañeros en el siglo XX." In El trabajo y los trabajadores
     en la historia de México, compiled by Elsa Cecilia Frost,
     Michael C. Meyer, and Josefina Zoraida Vázquez, pp. 565-
     98. Mexico and Tucson: El Colegio de México and the
     University of Arizona Press, 1979.
     A study of the exploitative nature of the sugar industry
     with regard to its labor force from colonial times to
     the present. Focus is on the socioeconomic conditions of
     the sugar producer. Despite his change from peon and day
     laborer before the Revolution of 1910 to ejidatario and
     minifundista by 1940, his earned income and dependence
     on the mill owner was not changed significantly. Only the
     strikes of 1941 and 1972 won for him a national contract.

392 GAMIO, MANUEL. Mexican Immigration to the United States.
     1927. Reprint; with a new introduction by John H. Burma.
     New York: Dover Press, 1971.
     This work remains a definitive (if outdated) study of
     the initial Mexican immigrant experience in the United
     States. Contains statistical data.

Economic and Social History

393   GLADE, WILLIAM P. "Revolution and economic development: A
      Mexican reprise." In The Political Economy of Mexico,
      edited by William P. Glade and Charles W. Anderson, pp.
      1-101. Madison: University of Wisconsin Press, 1963.
         Sketches broad historical, political, and economic
      patterns in Mexican revolutionary history, including a
      positive assessment of agrarian reform.

394   GOMEZ JARA, FRANCISCO. El movimiento campesino en México.
      Mexico: Editorial Campesina, 1970.

395   GONZALEZ NAVARRO, MOISES. Población y sociedad en México,
      1900-1970. 2 vols. Mexico: UNAM, 1974.
         These volumes continue the author's earier work on
      social conditions during the Porfiriato. The first
      volume covers population problems and social issues such
      as health, nutrition, housing, and water supplies.
      Volume two deals with international migration to and from
      Mexico, including a discussion on Mexican workers in the
      United States. Based on national censuses, newspapers,
      federal government reports, and statistical yearbooks.
      A major work in the area of demographic history.

396   _____. "Social Aspects of the Mexican Revolution."
      Cahiers d'histoire mondiale 8 (1964): 281-89.
         Social and economic history from the Porfiriato to the
      Díaz Ordaz regime.

397   GONZALEZ RAMIREZ, MANUEL. La Revolución social de México.
      3 vols. Mexico: Fondo de Cultura Económica, 1960, 1965,
      and 1966.
         Vol. 1, Las ideas. La violencia. A study of the ideas
      that brought the Revolution to birth and the social
      antecedents which shaped it. Concludes with Carranza's
      death at Tlaxcalantongo. Vol. 2, Las instituciones
      sociales. El problema económico. The Revolution as
      reflected through the nation, the family, and the indi-
      vidual. Vol. 3, El problema agrario. A history of the
      agrarian movement. Concludes that the history of land
      ownership is the tortured history of the Mexican people.

398   GONZALEZ ROA, FERNANDO. El aspecto agrario de la Revolución
      Mexicana. Mexico: Liga de Economistas Revolucionarios de
      la República Mexicana, 1975.
         Agrarianism.

Economic and Social History

399   GORDON, WENDELL C. The Expropriation of Foreign-owned
      Property in Mexico. Westport, Conn.: Greenwood Press
      Publishers, 1975.
         Introduction by Samuel Guy Inman.

400   HANSEN, ROGER D. The Politics of Mexican Development.
      Baltimore and London: Johns Hopkins Press, 1971.
         An historical analysis of the Mexican "miracle" or
      growth rate of contemporary Mexico. Notes the tremendous
      income inequalities of today's Mexico and examines their
      development. Concludes that today's Mexico can best be
      understood in terms of the nineteenth-century mestizo
      political heritage which construed politics as an avenue
      to socio-economic mobility and personal power. Because of
      the activities of a modernizing yet traditional elite,
      economic development has occurred with political values
      not unlike those held by Porfirio Díaz. Appendix:
      balance of payments data. Select bibliography.

401   HUIZER, GERRIT. La lucha campesina en México. Mexico:
      Centro de Investigaciones Agrarias, 1970.
         Mentioned are the principal peasant representatives
      and the political development of the agrarian organizations
      at the time of the Revolution.

402   KEESING, DONALD B. "Structural Change Early in Development:
      Mexico's Changing Industrial and Occupational Structure
      from 1895 to 1950." Journal of Economic History 29
      (Dec. 1969): 716-38.
         According to historian John Womack, Jr., this is a
      "key article on modern Mexico's occupational history."

403   McWILLIAMS, CAREY. North from Mexico: The Spanish-Speaking
      People of the United States. 1948. Reprint. New York:
      Greenwood Press, 1968.
         Classic but now dated study of the history of Mexican
      Americans.

404   MENDIETA ALATORRE, MARIA de los ANGELES. "Galería de mujeres
      mexicanas en la Revolución." Revista de la Universidad
      de México 28 (1973): 15-21.
         Presents women in Mexican Revolution who were not only
      anonymous soldadas and passive heroines, but who partic-
      ipated actively as journalists, ideologues, benefactors,
      etc. Sketches twenty-two women. A sequel to her book
      on La mujer en la Revolución Mexicana.

General Works

Economic and Social History

405 _____. La mujer en la Revolución Mexicana. Mexico: In-
stituto Nacional de Estudios Históricos de la Revolución
Mexicana, 1961.
A study of the role of the Mexican woman during the
Revolution.

406 MEYER, LORENZO. "Cambio político y dependencia: México en
el siglo XX." Foro Internacional 13 (1972): 101-38.
Surveys the relationship between political changes
and dependence on foreign investment in Mexico since 1910.
Concludes that political and industrial modernization
nullified political changes designed to end Mexico's
dependence on foreign investment. Primary and secondary
sources; table.

407 MROZIEWICZ, ROBERT. "El problema campesino en la Revolución
Mexicana." Estudios Latinoamericanos (1972): 13-44.

408 NEYMET, MARCELA de. "El movimiento obrero y la Revolución
Mexicana." Historia y Sociedad 3 (1967): 56-73.
Labor history.

409 OCHOA CAMPOS, MOISES. La Revolución Mexicana. 4 vols. Mexico:
Instituto Nacional de Estudios Históricos de la Revolución
Mexicana, 1966-70.
Vol. 1, Sus causas económicas. A study of the economic
causes of the Mexican Revolution. Five part division:
neofeudalism in the countryside; the exploitation of labor
by industrial capital; the pervasive foreign investor;
the unbalanced structure of the national economy; and the
uneven progress of the country. Vol. 2, Sus causas
sociales; vol. 3, Sus causas políticas; El reeleccionismo;
vol. 4, Sus causas políticas; La dictadura.

410 REYNOLDS, CLARK W. The Mexican Economy: Twentieth-Century
Structure and Growth. New Haven: Yale University Press,
1970.
A comprehensive survey of Mexico's economic history
from 1900 to 1965. Major attention devoted to structural
changes in the economy, land reform and agricultural productivity, urbanization, public finance, and trade policy.
Extensive statistical documentation, appendices, including
a discussion of the "opportunity cost" of the Mexican
Revolution.

411 RIPPY, MERRILL. Oil and the Mexican Revolution. Leiden:
E.J. Brill, 1972.

90

Concerns itself with the problem of Mexican oil and foreign companies. Dates back to the colonial period. A translation of the 1954 "El Petróleo y la Revolución Mexicana" in Problemas Agrícolas e Industriales de México. Scholarship is limited and has not been updated since the original publication.

412   SAMUEL, A.   "Le Mexique ou la Révolution Embourgeoisée: Croissance des Jeunes Nations." Jano (1963): 7-15.

413   SILVA HERZOG, JESUS.   La economía política en México: 1810-1974. Mexico: Cuadernos Americanos, 1975.

414   _____.   El agrarismo mexicano y la reforma agraria. Mexico: Fondo de Cultura Económica, 1964.
The agrarian problem and the socioeconomic development of the Revolution. Won the 1960 (first edition, 1959) prize of the Banco Nacional de Mexico, S.A. Massive work emphasizing legal and political aspects of Mexican agrarian history. Presents details on the prerevolutionary Mexican agrarian structure (particularly the Porfiriato), on agrarian aspects of the revolution, and on the postrevolutionary period. Separate sections present the positions of numerous Mexican intellectuals and politicians.

415   SOLIS, LEOPOLDO.   "La política económica y el nacionalismo mexicano." Foro Internacional 9 (1969): 235-48.
Distinguishes two periods in the economic nationalism fostered by Mexico's revolution of 1910. The most constructive era lasted to 1940. The subsequent period had been characterized by strong national interest, a favoring of the middle class, and xenophobia. Recommends modifying present policies to alleviate harmful economic isolation and social inequalities. Secondary sources.

416   STAVENHAGEN, RODOLFO.   "Collective Agriculture and Capitalism in Mexico: A Way Out or a Dead End." Latin American Perspectives 2 (1975): 146-63.
Analyzes ejidos, landholding units which sponsor cooperative farming enterprises under government auspices in Mexico, 1925-1975. The institution is not really a viable one due to the basically capitalist nature of the Mexican economy.

417   _____.   "L'evoluzione storica della riforma agraria messicana." Annali della Fondazione Luigi Einaudi 4 (1970): 415-41.

Economic and Social History

> Studies land distribution in Mexico, 1910–1966. Reform
> did not favor the bulk of the rural population that had
> been deprived of meaningful representation in decision-
> making. Discusses unemployment and the standard of living
> among farm workers. Six tables.

418 TANNENBAUM, FRANK. The Mexican Agrarian Revolution. 1929.
Reprint. Hamden, Conn.: Archon Books, 1968.
Classic study of agriculture, land tenure, and agrarian
laws in Mexico prior to 1929.

419 TOBLER, HANS WERNER. "Agrarevolution und politischgesell-
schaftliche Stabilitaet Mexikos." Lateinamerika-
Nachrichten 5, no. 2 (Mar.–Apr. 1977): 25–37.
A study in agrarian reform and its relationship to
political and social relations from the Porfiriato to 1940.
Work derived from previous studies on the ejido by
François Chevalier, labor and haciendas by Friedrich
Katz, agrarian revolts by Paul Friedrich and Luis González,
and John Womak on Zapata.

420 _____. "Agrarrevolution und politischgesellschaftliche
Stabilitaet Mexikos." Berichte zur Entwicklung in Spanien,
Portugal und Lateinamerika 2 (1976): 10–18.
A study in agrarian reform and its relationship to
political and social relations from the Porfiriato to 1940.

421 _____. "Bauernerhebungen und Agrarreform in der Mexikanischen Revolution." In Mexico: Die institutionalisierte
Revolution, by Manfred Mols and H.W. Tobler, pp. 115–70.
Cologne and Vienna: Böhlau Verlag, 1976.
An analysis of peasant revolts and agrarian reform
during the Mexican Revolution from the Porfiriato through
1970 in four parts: conditions during the Porfiriato;
the Revolution, 1910–1920; later revolts, political stab-
ilization, peasants' organizations, and agrarian reform,
1920–1940; and problems since 1940.

422 Trabajo y los trabajadores en la historia de México. Compiled
by Elsa Cecilia Frost, Michael C. Meyer, and Josefina
Zoraida Vázquez. Mexico and Tucson: El Colegio de México
and the University of Arizona Press, 1979.
Papers of the Fifth meeting of Mexican and North
American Historians meeting in Pátzcuaro, 12–15 October
1977, on the theme of "Labor and Laborers through Mexican
history." The work is divided into two sections. The
first, consisting of twelve chapters, is on labor history.

The second part consists of four chapters on historiography, methodology, research themes, and archives. Of particular interest to students of the Revolution are the following: "Movilización campesina y reforma agraria en los valles de Nativitas, Tlaxcala (1917-1923)," by Raymond Th.J. Buve (pp. 553-64); "La historia del trabajo de los campesinos cañeros en el siglo XX," by Roberto Gallaga (pp. 565-98); "The Historiography of Mexican Labor," John Womack, Jr. (pp. 739-55); "Political and Military History of the State of Michoacán, 1910-1940," by Lyle C. Brown (pp. 801-805); "Importancia y problemas de la historiografía de Michoacán en el siglo XX," by David L. Raby (pp. 806-809); "Questions in Search of Historians," by John H. Coatsworth (pp. 870-73); "The Casa del Obrero Mundial, Constitutionalism and the Pact of February 1915," by Barry Carr (pp. 603-31); and "Coyuntura y conciencia: Factores convergentes en la fundación de los sindicatos petroleros de Tampico durante la década de 1920," by Lief Adleson (pp. 632-60).

423 TURNER, FREDERICK C. The Dynamic of Mexican Nationalism. Chapel Hill: University of North Carolina Press, 1968; London: Oxford University Press, 1971.
    A detailed social history beginning with 1810, including a review of the role of literature and art.

424 _____. "Los efectos de la participación femenina en la Revolución de 1910." HM 16 (Apr.-July 1967): 603-20.
    Sees Mexican Revolution of 1910 as a favorable catalyst to expanding role of women in national affairs. Participation altered family, regional, ecclesiastical and strict sex role loyalty patterns. Traces struggle for women's rights, including desire to improve conditions of prostitutes. Based on newspapers and public documents.

425 VERNON, RAYMOND. The Dilemma of Mexico's Development. Cambridge, Mass.: Harvard University Press, 1963.
    A general economic history of Mexico that focuses on the roles of private and public sectors. Chapter 3 is on "The Revolution and After, 1910-1940" (pp. 59-87). Argues that by the close of the 1930s the division of responsibilities between the public and the private sectors that characterizes modern-day Mexico had already been largely established.

426 WILKIE, RICHARD W. "Urban Growth and the Transformation of the Settlement Landscape of Mexico, 1910-1970." In Contemporary Mexico: Papers of the Fourth International Congress of Mexican History, edited by James W. Wilkie,

Economic and Social History

> Michael C. Meyer, and Edna Monzón de Wilkie, pp. 99-134.
> Los Angeles and Mexico: University of California Press
> and El Colegio de México, 1976.
> A study in the changes in the spatial structure of
> settlement patterns that have resulted from population
> growth between 1910 and 1970. Author discards traditional
> categories of rural and urban and speaks of urbanization
> trends in terms of dispersed populations, villages, simple
> urban, complex urban, and metropolitan. In 1910 most
> regional settlement patterns were either village-dispersed
> or village-simple; about 1930 the pattern of complex urban
> settlements dominated Mexico City and the northern border
> areas; by 1960 a complex urban-village and metropolitan-
> village pattern was established along the northern fron-
> tier and the Yucatán peninsula and was spreading south.
> Even so, the age structure of the country has stayed the
> same from 1910 to 1960, while in absolute numbers the
> number of rural villagers has grown. Appendix: tables
> on rural-urban distributions for 1910, 1930, 1960, and
> 1970.

427   WIONCZEK, MIGUEL S. El nacionalismo mexicano y la inversión
      extranjera. Mexico: Siglo XXI, 1975.
      A most competent analysis of interaction between Mexican
      nationalism and foreign investment after 1910.

428   WOLF, DONNA M. "Women in Modern Mexico." Studies in History
      and Society 1 (1976): 28-53.
      Discusses the women suffrage movement in Mexico, 1916-
      53, and related political events. Reviews nineteenth-
      century laws on women's relationship to the family and
      the important changes made after the Revolution of 1910,
      principally the Civil Code of 1928. The Mexican Revolu-
      tionary Party resisted full suffrage in the 1920s and
      1930s because of the strong influence of the Church, and
      hence the Right, on women. Machismo, as shown by the
      increasing divorce rate, has been on the decline, while
      women's role in the work force has expanded along with
      their educational achievements. Despite modernization
      the socially ingrained role of subservience in women has
      continued to be the norm.

429   WOLF, ERIC R. Las luchas campesinas del siglo XX. Mexico:
      Siglo Veintiuno Editores, 1972.
      See entry 430.

430 _____. "Mexico." In <u>Peasant Wars of the Twentieth Century</u>,
pp. 3-48. New York: Harper & Row, 1969.
A survey of the Revolution from colonial times to 1940.
Notes that many of the causes of the Revolution had their
origin in the colonial countryside with its landscape of
haciendas and republics of Indians. Focus is upon the
agrarian revolts of Zapata and Villa. Concludes that
"Initial success went to the peasant guerrillas of Morelos
and the Cowboy armies of the north, but final victory
rewarded an elite which had created a viable army, demonstrated bureaucratic competence, and consolidated its
control over the vital export sector of the economy."
Based on secondary sources.

See also the following: bibliographies on labor and economic history, entries 149-50 and 251; federal expenditures and social change
in Mexico, entries 311-12; nineteenth-century economic history,
entry 342; caudillos and peasants, entries 351-52; the bourgeoisie
and the Mexican state, entries 362 and 369; the relationship of
economic history to military intervention, entry 379; Mexico-U.S.
labor relations, entry 380; global capitalism and Mexico, entries
378 and 382; ideology, capitalism, and Mexico, entry 441; indigenism,
entries 440 and 463; the Chinese in Sonora, entry 488; and for
biographies of Mexican women <u>see</u> entry 685.

RELIGIOUS AND CHURCH HISTORY

431 CASTRO VILLAGRAN, BERNARDO et al. <u>La iglesia, el subdes-</u>
<u>arrollo y la Revolución</u>. Mexico: Editorial Nuestro
Tiempo, 1968.
The church, underdevelopment, and the Revolution.

432 TURNER, FREDERICK C. "The Compatability of Church and State
in Mexico." JISWA 9 (1967): 591-619.
Survey of Church-State relations since the late nineteenth century. Cites the Mexican oil controversy of 1938
as an example of religion coming to terms with nationalism
(when the clerical hierarchy urged the people to support
the government's nationalization campaign).

For Church-State relations in Veracruz, 1840-1940, <u>see</u> entry 507.

History of Education

HISTORY OF EDUCATION

433   BURKE, MICHAEL E. "The University of Mexico and the Revolu-
       tion, 1910-1940." Americas 34 (Oct. 1977): 252-73.
            A study of the relationship between academics and pol-
       iticians during the Revolutionary era. Concludes that the
       political environment affected the National University's
       role, resulting in teaching and research that concentrated
       on subjects indigenous to Mexico and realizing such revolu-
       tionary goals as cultural independence, self-identity,
       and national dignity.

434   COMAS, JUAN. "Manuel Gamio en la antropología mexicana."
       América Indígena 34 (1974): 863-80.
            A clear tendency exists among some Mexican anthropol-
       ogists toward establishing a new theoretical and method-
       ological orientation, in teaching as well as research,
       disregarding completely the work of their pioneering
       predecessors. There is even distortion and falsification
       of their views and activities. The author vindicates
       Manuel Gamio, whose work was of primary importance for the
       subsequent development of anthropology, archaeology,
       ethnology, and Indian studies in Mexico. In evaluating
       Gamio's personality, notes the historical and political
       circumstances during which he carried out his anthro-
       pological activities.

435   MONROY HUITRON, GUADALUPE. Política educativa de la Revolución
       (1910-1940). Mexico: SepSetentas, 1975.
            A study of political education under various governments
       between 1910 and 1940 in which the system of education
       established in Mexico reflected the distinct styles of
       the politicians and the social order.

436   _____. "Los gobiernos de la Revolución: Su política
       educativa, 1910-1940." In Extremos de México, pp. 257-98.
       Mexico: El Colegio de México, 1971.
            Contents: "El legado," "Los años de lucha," "La con-
       stitución de 1917," "Las primeras realizaciones," "Nuevas
       inquietudes," "El conflicto político-religioso," "La
       educación sexual," "Lo positivo," "La dictadura del pro-
       letariado," "La opinión pública," "Las realizaciones."

For a current bibliography which includes the history of education
see entry 35. For a study on the impact of education on political
mobility see entry 354.

CULTURAL AND INTELLECTUAL HISTORY

437   ALBA, VICTOR. "The Mexican Revolution and the Cartoon."
       Comparative Studies in Society and History 9 (1967): 121-
       36.
            An examination of the transformation of Mexican political
       ideas as exemplified in the Mexican cartoon from the period
       prior to the Revolution to the present. Prerevolutionary
       cartoons, because of the dominance of the political inter-
       ests of the public, included no social satires, while
       postrevolutionary cartoons reflect the dominance of cultural
       rather than political nationaliom. Social criticism rather
       than criticism of a person, party, or issue has become
       the fundamental theme.

438   BLANCO-AGUINAGA, CARLOS. "El laberinto fabricado por Octavio
       Paz." Aztlán 3 (1972): 1-12.
            Criticizes Octavio Paz's existentialism as expressed in
       The Labyrinth of Solitude (1947) and Posadata (1970), in
       which Paz asserts that there is a fundamental opposition
       between history and mythology, and only mythical or poetic
       understanding can reveal man's true existence.

439   CASASOLA, GUSTAVO. Historia gráfica de la Revolución
       Mexicana, 1900-1970. 5 vols. Mexico: Editorial F.
       Trillas, 1965-71.
            A photographic history of the Revolution interspersed
       with text and documentary extracts. Last volume covers
       the years 1961-1970.

440   CAZES, DANIEL. "Indigenismo en México: Pasado y presente."
       Historia y Sociedad 5 (Spring 1966): 66-85.
            The first section of this study is a commentary on
       Luis Villoro's Los grandes momentos del indigenismo; the
       second part is an outline sketch of the history of Mexican
       indigenism. Author is critical of the official theories
       and practices of indigenismo.

441   CORDOVA, ARNALDO. La ideología de la Revolución Mexicana:
       La formación del nuevo régimen. Mexico: Ediciones Era,
       1975.
            An intellectual history of the Revolution from the
       Porfirian background to the Calles era. Focus is upon
       liberalism, positivism, populism, zapatismo, villismo,
       floresmagonismo, and the populist dimensions of
       caudillismo. Argues that a bourgeois state evolved in
       which the ideas of capitalism and private property served

Cultural and Intellectual History

as the basis for social organization. As a result, the
Mexican Revolution was not a social revolution but a logical
continuation of the Díaz period.

442   DESSAU, ADALBERT. La novela de la Revolución Mexicana. Mexico:
       Fondo de Cultura Económica, 1972.
          A study of the historical development of the novel of
       the Revolution and the relationship of the revolutionary
       novel to Mexican literature in general.

443   DIAZ-GUERRERO, ROGELIO. Psychology of the Mexican: Culture
       and Personality. Austin: University of Texas Press, 1975.
          An anthology of ten essays, the most recent being
       published in Spanish in 1967. Although a contemporary
       psychological analysis of Mexican personality, the work
       is a good example of the "lo mexicano" Freudian tradition
       which uses a "historico-psychobio-sociocultural" approach.

444   FERNANDEZ BRAVO, VICENTE. El ideario de la Revolución Mexicana:
       Del programa del Partido Liberal a Lázaro Cárdenas.
       Mexico: B. Costa-Amic, 1973.
          A biographical catalog of the political and social
       thought of leading Mexican revolutionaries to Cárdenas.
       Well illustrated with etchings of several revolutionary
       artists.

445   _____. Política y administración. Mexico: B. Costa-Amic,
       1965.
          A history of Mexican political ideas from the time of
       the Revolution to the present.

446   FROST, ELSA CECILIA. Las categorías de la cultura mexicana.
       Mexico: UNAM, 1973.
          Divided into two parts: a) contemporary philosophy
       and the idea of Mexican culture; B) political culture of
       the Mexican Revolution; religious culture as expressed in
       the cristero conflict; literary culture as seen in the
       Revolutionary novel and the corrido; the arts, especially
       Rivera and Orozco.

447   FUENTES, CARLOS. "Mexico and Its Demons." New York Review
       of Books 20 (20 Sept. 1973): 16-21.
          A literary review of Octavio Paz's The Other Mexico
       and a critique of the Mexican Revolution by one of Mexico's
       greatest living novelists.

448   _____. Where the Air is Clear. Translated by Sam Hileman.
       New York: Ivan Obolensky, 1960.

Translation of La regiôn más transparante [1958],
a novel of social criticism that is an indictment of the
Revolution. The character Robles, a revolutionary turned
banker, personifies the Revolution as a creation of the
upper bourgeoisie. According to Fuentes, the Revolution
resulted only in a new privileged class, a paralyzing of
internal political life, and economic domination by the
United States.

449 GORTARI, ELI de. La ciencia en la historia de México.
     Mexico: Fondo de Cultura Económica, 1963.
        A general history of science in Mexico. See Chapter
     12 for "Participación de México en la ciencia contempor-
     ánea," (pp. 338-85). Bibliography; index.

450 HILLMAN, JACQUELIN K. Ideological Aspects of the Mexican
     Revolution. Albuquerque: University of New Mexico, 1962.

451 LANGFORD, WALTER. The Mexican Novel Comes of Age. Notre
     Dame: University of Notre Dame Press, 1972.
        A blend of literary history and criticism. Briefly
     discusses the nineteenth-century novel before Azuela,
     summarizes the history of the novels of the Revolution,
     describes a dozen more novelists born between 1925 and
     1944, and concludes by assessing the Mexican publishing
     industry. Bibliographies, plot summaries and appraisals,
     personal interviews and biography.

452 LANGLE RAMIREZ, ARTURO. Vocabulario, apodis, seudónimos,
     sobrenombres y hemerografía de la Revolución. Mexico:
     UNAM, 1969.
        Nicknames and pseudonyms of the Revolution.

453 MONSIVAIS, CARLOS. "La cultura mexicana en el siglo XX."
     In Contemporary Mexico: Papers of the Fourth International
     Congress of Mexican History, edited by James W. Wilkie,
     Michael C. Meyer, and Edna Monzón de Wilkie, pp. 624-70.
     Los Angeles and Mexico: University of California Press
     and El Colegio de México, 1976.
        A survey of cultural life in twentieth-century Mexico,
     including art, music, literature, and cinema.

454 PAREDES, AMERICO. "Los Estados Unidos, México y el machismo."
     JISWA 9 (Jan. 1967): 65-84.
        Critical of traditional view of Octavio Paz and the
     "lo mexicano" school which argues that machismo (the

Cultural and Intellectual History

Mexican cult of masculinity) has its origins in the violation of Aztec women by Spanish conquistadores (e.g., the
cortez and La Malinche legend). Compares machismo in the
United States and Mexico. Notes recent origins of
Mexican machismo (e.g., Camacho in the 1940s), and suggests
that several antecedents can be traced to the "cowboy
culture" of the American Southwest.

455 PAZ, OCTAVIO. The Other Mexico: Critique of the Pyramid.
New York: Grove Press, 1972.
Written in 1969, shortly after the democratic movement
led by Mexican students was abruptly ended with the massacre
of between 300 and 400 students and workers at Tlatelolco.
Through the use of literary metaphors and historical images,
Paz offers a critique of the Mexican Revolution, the
Revolutionary government, and the Revolutionary Party. A
collection of three essays, the book is a sequel to The
Labyrinth of Solitude (see entry 456). Translated by
Lysander Kemp from Postdata (Mexico: Siglo XX, 1970).

456 _____. The Labyrinth of Solitude: Life and Thought in
Mexico. London: Evergreen Books; New York: Grove Press, 1961.
A classic work of genius by one of Mexico's greatest
living poets. Nine essays or chapters in narrative form.
A collection of interpretative and theoretical essays
unified by a common theme of solitude; an existential
essay on Mexican-ness using historical and psychological
symbols, including the symbol of the Revolution. Translated by Lysander Kemp from El laberinto de la soledad
(Mexico: Fondo de Cultura Económica, 1959).

457 RODRIGUEZ, ANTONIO. A History of Mexican Mural Painting.
Translated from the Spanish and German by Marina Corby.
London: Thames & Hudson, 1969.
Well-documented book that explains mural painting in
its social context. Concentrates on Rivera, Siqueiros,
and Orozco.

458 ROSS, STANLEY R. "La protesta de los intelectuales ante
México y su Revolución." HM 26 (Jan.-Mar. 1977): 396-437.
Noting that Mexico's Revolution lacked theoreticians,
the author examines relationship between intellectuals
and government from anti-Díaz critics of the late Porfiriato to intellectual opponents of Echeverría.

459 SILVA HERZOG, JESUS. El pensamiento económico, social y
político de Mexico, 1810-1964. Mexico: Instituto Mexicano
de Investigaciones Económicas, 1967.

General Works

Cultural and Intellectual History

Social, economic, and political thought, 1810–1964.

460   SIMMONS, MERLE E. The Mexican Corrido as a source for Interpretative Study of Modern Mexico, 1870–1950: With a
Consideration of the Origins and Development of the Corrido
Tradition. Bloomington: Indiana University Press, 1957;
New York: Kraus Reprint Co., 1969.
      Demonstrates the corrido as a historical source for
the Revolution and shows how the corrido both shaped and
reflected public opinion.

461   SOMMERS, J. "Novels of a Dead Revolution." Nation 197 (1963):
114–15.

462   STAMATA, HORIA. "Die 'revolution' und die Literatur Mexikos
im 20 Jahrhundert." Sacculum (Berlin) 16 (1965): 191–255.

463   ZANTWIJK, R.A.M. van. "Indigenismo: A Philosophy and a
Method of Guided Development of the Aboriginal Minorities
in Mexico: Historical Background and Actual Orientations."
Plural Societies 7 (1976): 95–103.
      Presents historical background, since 1521, for the
development of attitudes toward Indian peoples in Mexico
and assesses active government Indian policies that
integrate indigenismo into the national character, 1948–76.

For a current bibliography which includes history of science see
entry 35. For a bibliography of intellectual history see entry 153.
For methodology and the novel see entry 223. For comparative studies
in revolutionary ideology see entry 347. For corridos see entries
529 and 540. For biographies of "cultural caudillos," see entry 644.

IV. Regional and State History

464　AGUILAR, JOSE ANGEL. La Revolución en el estado de México.
Patronato series, no. 68. Mexico: Instituto Nacional de
Estudios Históricos de la Revolución Mexicana, 1976.
　　　State history of the Revolution in the state of México.
Part of the Patronato series. The Patronato is a consult-
ative body to the Secretaría de Gobernación. The Association of the National Institute of Historical Studies of
the Mexican Revolution is composed of scholars, writers,
and literary figures including Florencio Barrera Fuentes,
Martín Luis Guzmán, and Jesús Romero Flores. Of the more
than seventy works in the series, over a dozen relate to
regional and state history.

465　AGUILAR CAMIN, HECTOR. La frontera nomada: Sonora y la
Revolución Mexicana. Mexico: Siglo XXI Editores, 1977.
　　　Regional history of the Revolution in Sonora that makes
good use of local and state archives.

466　_____. La Revolución sonorense, 1910-1914. Mexico: El
Colegio de México, 1975.
　　　The Revolution in Sonora, 1910-1940.

467　ALMADA; FRANCISCO R. La Revolución en el estado de Sonora.
Patronato series, no. 52. Mexico: Instituto Nacional de
Estudios Históricos de la Revolución Mexicana, 1971.
　　　State history of the Revolution, 1910-1946, in the north-
western state of Sonora by the dean of regional historians.

468　_____. La Revolución en el estado de Chihuahua. 2 vols.
Patronato series, no. 35. Mexico: Instituto Nacional de
Estudios Históricos de la Revolución Mexicana, 1964-65.
　　　Volume one covers the antecedents of the revolution in
Chihuahua from the Porfiriato to the first months of 1913.
Contains reproductions of primary documents relating to
the Madero campaign, the Baja revolution, the government
of Abraham González, and the Orozco revolt. Volume two

treats the military, social, and political history of
Chihuahua from February 1913 to the reestablishment of
"constitutional order" in October 1920. Narrative history
by the dean of Mexican local historians. Based on primary
materials from Defensa Nacional and various state and
private archives. Each volume contains a table of contents
and a bibliography.

469   ALVAREZ SALINAS, GILBERTO. Pancho Villa en Monterrey.
      Monterrey, Nuevo León: Ediciones Continentes, 1969.
      Villa in Monterrey.

470   BEEZLEY, WILLIAM H. "Governor Carranza and the Revolution
      in Coahuila." Americas 33 (July 1976): 50-61.
          Evaluation of Madero's plan to decentralize the Revolu-
      tion using Carranza's governorship in Coahuila from 1911-
      13 as a case study. This experience convinced Carranza
      of the need to discard federalism in favor of a reform
      program under national government auspices. Based on
      archival sources.

471   _____. Insurgent Governor: Abraham González and the
      Mexican Revolution in Chihuahua. Lincoln: University
      of Nebraska Press, 1973.
          A study of the course of Francisco Madero's revolutionary
      movement at the local level. This account of the public
      life of Abraham González (revolutionary governor of
      Chihuahua in 1911) is the first to examine systematically
      the day-to-day functioning of the maderist organization
      in a state that played a crucial role in the insurgency.
      Well researched, derived from manuscripts in Mexican and
      U.S. archives, published documents, diaries, memoirs, and
      contemporary accounts.

472   _____. "State Reform During the Provisional Presidency:
      Chihuahua, 1911." HAHR 50 (Aug. 1970): 524-37.
      Reforms by Governor Abraham González as provisional
      governor of Chihuahua between November 1910 and August 1911.
      Reforms included equalizing taxes, curtailing the wealth
      of landowners, enforcing arbitration in labor disputes,
      public works projects, acts to eliminate gambling and
      restrain alcoholism, and reorganization of local government.

473   BERZUNZA PINTO, RAMON. "El constitucionalismo en Yucatán."
      HM 12 (Oct.-Dec. 1962): 274-95.
          Social, political, and economic history of Yucatán
      from 1910 to 1915.

474   BOLIO, EDMUNDO. Yucatán en la dictadura y la Revolución.
      Patronato series, no. 44. Mexico: Instituto Nacional de

Estudios Históricos de la Revolución Mexicana, 1967.
State history of Yucatán during the Porfiriato and
the early Revolution.

475 BUVE, RAYMOND Th. J. Boeren-mobilisatie en landhervorming
tijdens en na de Mexicaanse Revolutie: De vallei van
Nativitas, Tlaxcala tussen 1910 en 1940. Amsterdam: Inter-
universitair Centrum voor Studie Incidentele Publicaties,
no. 9, 1977.
A study in "controlled mobilization" and land reform
in Tlaxcala between 1910 and 1940, based on detailed
case studies of seven villages in the valley and municipio
of Nativitas. Describes the political struggles and socioeconomic changes of the revolutionary era. Stresses the
importance of peasant control for political power strategy
and the systematic application of "controlled mobilization"
during the implementation of land reform measures. Role
of zapatista caudillo Domingo Arenas (1914-1917) is noted,
as well as the activities of the constitutionalist and
later "Revolutionary" government. Concludes that the
peasant developed a client relationship with the new
"Revolutionary" governments, which were similar to and
derived from earlier hacendado and caudillo eras; that no
significant shift of power into the hands of peasants
took place, i.e., "the varieties of 'controlled mobilization' of peasants only accentuated the dependent position
of peasants vis-a-vis a mobilizing patron who often
tried to monopolize their political loyalty." Also concludes that peasant solidarity was virtually nonexistent.
Summary of contents in English and Spanish. Bibliography;
based on regional archives in Tlaxcala and materials from
the Institute of Social History in Amsterdam.

476 CARR, BARRY. "Las peculiaridades del nortemexicano, 1880-
1927: Ensayo de interpretación." HM 3 (Jan.-Mar. 1972):
320-46.
This article attempts to isolate and explore some of
the primary characteristics of the coalition of northern
revolutionary caudillos. Talks particularly about their
anticlerical tendencies, their radicalism, their vigorous
nationalism that was contiguous to the hatred of foreigners
and their highly creative opportunism.

477 CAVAZOS GARZA, ISRAEL. "Fichas para una biblio-hemerografía
histórica de Nuevo León, 1960-1969." Humanitas 11 (1970):
361-87.
This work is divided into fourteen sections: Bibliography and Archives; Biobibliographies; The History of
Nuevo León; Prehispanic Themes; The Colonial Era; Independence; Reform; The French Intervention; The Porfiriato and

the Revolution; Monterrey; Municipalities; The History
of Education; Genealogy and Heraldry; and a few other
minor categories.

478   CORNEJO CABRERA, EZEQUIEL. "Los ejidos de Veracruz, México:
Su situación social a mediados del siglo XX." Revista
Mexicana de Sociología 28 (1966): 337-55.
Socioeconomic study of the ejidos of Veracruz.

479   CUELLAR ABAROA, CRISANTO. La Revolución en el estado de
Tlaxcala. 2 vols. Patronato series, no. 65. Mexico:
Instituto Nacional de Estudios Históricos de la Revolución
Mexicana, 1975.
Survey of Mexican Revolution in Tlaxcala based on few
published sources.

480   DOMINGUEZ MILLAN, CARLOS. Tuxpan, capital provisional del
primer gobierno constitucionalista. Jalapa: Universidad
Veracruzana, 1964.

481   EISER-VIAFORA, PAUL. "Durango and the Mexican Revolution."
NMHR 49 (July 1974): 219-40.
In Durango, the disintegration and collapse of the old
order followed the coming of economic "modernization,"
especially the replacement of the traditional cattle
hacienda by the commercial agricultural plantation, accom-
panied by an increase in North American investment and
influence.

482   FRIEDRICH, PAUL. Agrarian Revolt in a Mexican Village.
Englewood Cliffs, N.J.: Prentice Hall, 1970.
A study of agrarian struggle in the Tarascan community
of Naranja, Michoacán, and the phenomenon of the leadership of peasant movements. Relates the emergence of Primo
Tapia as a community leader and his careful handling of
the interlocking network of local, state, and national
politics. Includes a historical sketch of economic and
social changes in the village between 1885 and 1920,
and an analysis of an agrarian revolt in the area in the
period from 1920 to 1926 that resulted in the establishment
of an ejido. Replete with anthropological data.

483   GAMIZ OLIVAS, EVERARDO. La Revolución en el estado de
Durango. Patronato series, no. 28. Mexico: Instituto
Nacional de Estudios Históricos de la Revolución Mexicana,
1963.
Covers the years 1909-1920 for the Revolution in Durango.

484   GARZA TREVIÑO, CIRO de la. La Revolución Mexicana en el
estado de Tamaulipas. Mexico: Librería de Manuel Porrúa,
1973.

The first part of this book discusses the events from 1885 to 1913 in chronological order. The second part consists of reproductions of fifty-five important documents.

485 GONZALEZ CALZADA, MANUEL. Historia de la Revolución Mexicana en Tabasco. Mexico: Talleres Gráficos de la Nación, 1972. The author considers that the events leading the people of Tabasco to join the Revolution were: that the government was in the hands of only one man during a sixteen-year period; the predominance of an economically powerful political group; and the consecutive re-elections of Porfirio Díaz.

486 _____. Historia de la Revolución en Tabasco. Patronato Series, no. 55. Mexico: Instituto Nacional de Estudios Históricos de la Revolución Mexicana, 1972. State history of the Revolution in Tabasco. See entry 485.

487 GONZALEZ y GONZALEZ, LUIS. San José de Gracia: Mexican Village in Transition. Austin: University of Texas Press, 1974. Translated by John Upton from Pueblo en villo: Una microhistoria de San José de Gracia (Mexico: El Colegio de México, 1972). A memoir and history of the municipio of San José (located in northwestern Michoacán) between 1861 and 1967. Revolutionary history organized in part 2 under the subheadings: "The Mexican Revolution, 1910-1924"; "The Cristero Revolution, 1925-1932"; "The Agrarian Revolution, 1933-1943." Concludes that the "triple revolution" brought the end of isolation for San José; the beginning of "Mexicanization;" an increase in the power of priests and warriors; the appearance of secular education and the ejido; an end of the rule of traditional patriarchs and family leaders; a rise in class consciousness; a continuation of general poverty; and an unchanging demography. Based on local and national archives, private and public; most important sources were parish registers, diaries, oral interviews, and personal recollections. Praised by reviewers for his craftsmanship, the book's author received the Haring Prize, awarded once every five years for the best book on Latin American history.

488 JACQUES, LEO M. "Have Quick More Money Than Mandarins: The Chinese in Sonora." Journal of Arizona History 17 (1976): 201-18. Thesis: In its efforts to bring rapid economic development of the country in the 1890s, Mexico gave official encouragement to Chinese immigration in order to build up the labor force. In Sonora especially, contrary to

Mexican expectations, the Chinese went into business, soon
became prosperous, and gradually came to dominate small-
scale mercantile activities. With their increase in
numbers and growing influence in the state's economy,
public opposition intensified, with anti-Chinese arguments
stemming largely from racial and cultural antagonisms.
They suffered violence during the revolution and increasing
legal harassment. The antiforeign provisions of the constitution of 1917 encouraged intensification of the anti-
Chinese campaign, which soon spread to all Mexico, especially while the 'Sonoran Dynasty' governed the country.
The 1931 decree that expelled most of the Chinese from
Sonora shook the state's already weakened economic
structure.

489   JOSEPH, GILBERT M. "The Fragile Revolution: Cacique Politics
       and Revolutionary Process in Yucatán." Latin American
       Research Review 15, no. 1 (1980): 39-64.
           A study of the phenomenom of caciquismo using the example
       of Felipe Carrillo Puerto's rise and fall in the Yucatán
       between 1922 and 1924. Carrillo's career, first as a local
       agrarian cacique and later as a regional caudillo, was
       distinguished by the essential characteristics of caciquismo:
       the rise to power from a local base; the development of
       informal political networks structured by bonds of kinship
       and personalistic patron-client arrangements (especially
       with Obregón and Calles in Mexico City); the tactical use
       of violence (or threat of violence); the manipulation of
       ideological symbols (derived from Maya nationalism, Marxism,
       and socialism); and the performance of "middleman" roles
       in dealing with state and national officials and local
       campesinos. Carrillo, the counterpart of Zapata in Morelos
       and Primo Tapia in Michoacán, lost power and his life due
       to a failure to control social bandit caciques and a
       decline in the Mexico City patron-client relationship.
       The Carrillo case verifies the generalization that the
       Epic Revolution found its energies in small towns and
       villages by people who fought, not simply for the promise
       of land reform, but to break the political and economic
       stranglehold of local bosses and power-brokers. Based on
       Obregón branch of Archivo General Nacional; Archivo
       General del Estado de Yucatán; and Mérida newspapers.

490   _____. "Apuntes para una nueva historia regional: Yucatán
       y la Revolución Mexicana, 1915-1940." Revista de la
       Universidad de Yucatán 29 (Jan.-Feb. 1977): 12-35.
           Careful, well-documented study of the Mexican Revolution
       in Yucatán. Notes regional differences from national
       trends, e.g., an increase in population between 1910-1920;
       limited violence and greater radicalism; a direct

dependency relationship upon the United States, which
excluded Mexico City; a periodization in which Yucatán
had two revolutionary phases, 1915-1924 and 1934-1940.
Includes an historiographical discussion of sources.

491   MARTINEZ NUÑEZ, EUGENIO. La Revolución en el estado de
      San Luiz Potosí. Patronato series, no. 37. Mexico:
      Instituto Nacional de Estudios Históricos de la Revolución
      Mexicana, 1964.
          State history of the Revolution in San Luis Potosí.

492   NUÑEZ, RICARDO B. La Revolución en el estado de Colima.
      Patronato series, no. 56. Mexico: Instituto Nacional de
      Estudios Históricos de la Revolución Mexicana, 1973.
          Tells of how life was in Colima for the clergy,
      politicians, and great latifundistas before the Revolution.
      Mentions the involvement of Eugenio Aviña and Miguel García
      Topete in the Revolution and the opposition that the state
      of Colima showed towards Huerta. Finishes with the
      proclamation of the constitution of 1917. Included is
      a list of revolutionaries from Colima.

493   OLEA, HECTOR R. Breve Historia de la Revolución en Sinaloa.
      Patronato series, no. 36. Mexico: Instituto Nacional de
      Estudios Históricos de la Revolución Mexicana, 1964.
          State history of the Revolution in Sinaloa.

494   PASQUEL, LEONARDO. La Revolución en el estado de Veracruz.
      2 vols. Patronato series, no. 53. Mexico: Instituto
      Nacional de Estudios Históricos de la Revolución Mexicana,
      1971.
          State history of the Revolution in the east coast state
      of Veracruz.

495   RAMIREZ; ALFONSO FRANCISCO. Historia de la Revolución en
      Oaxaca. Patronato series, no. 48. Mexico: Instituto
      Nacional de Estudios Históricos de la Revolución Mexicana,
      1970.
          State history of the Revolution in the southern
      Indian state of Oaxaca.

496   RICHMOND, DOUGLAS W. "Factional Political Strife in Coahuila,
      1910-1920." HAHR 60 (Feb. 1980): 49-68.
          A study in the regional aspects of the Mexican Revolution,
      1910-1920. Focuses upon rival administrations in Coahuila
      to show that Madero endured in Coahuila because Carranza
      (1911-1913) was an effective governor; that Huerta failed
      because of excessive taxation (1913-1914); that Villistas
      lacked a strong administration at the top (1915); and
      that Carranza as a national leader (1915-1920) had the
      support of Coahuila because of the effective efforts of

governor Gustavo Espinosa Mireles. Describes Carranza as
a nationalist reformer whose primary appeal was to rural
and urban middle-class groups. Based on papers in the
Archivo General del Estado de Coahuila, Saltillo.

497 RIVERA, ANTONIO G. La Revolución en Sonora (Sonora en la
integracion de la nacionalidad mexicana; El maderismo;
La Revolución constitucionalista). Mexico: Imprenta
Arana, 1969.
The Epic Revolution in Sonora.

498 ROMERO FLORES, JESUS. Historia de la Revolución en Michoacán.
Patronato series, no. 31. Mexico: Instituto Nacional de
Estudios Históricos de la Revolución Mexicana, 1964.
A history of the Revolution, 1910-1917, in the state
of Michoacán, by a Michoacán historian known for his
earlier publications of historical annals and corridos.

499 RONFELDT, DAVID. Atencingo: The Politics of Agrarian
Struggle in a Mexican Ejido. Stanford: Stanford University Press, 1973.
A detailed analysis of a postrevolutionary ejido.
This study focuses on the struggles of the "ejiditarios"
of Atencingo, a sugar-producing community near Puebla,
to win possession and control of the land from 1919 to
1969. A case study of Mexican agrarian reform since
the Revolution. Based upon taped interviews, private
files, government archives, "ejiditario" documents, published works, and participant observation.

500 SANDELS, ROBERT. "Antecedentes de la Revolución en
Chihuahua." HM 24 (Jan.-Mar. 1975): 390-402.
Describes the socioeconomic conditions in Chihuahua
prior to the 1910 revolution, particularly the discontent
caused by the dominant local elites, the Luis Terrazas and
Enrique Creel families, who were supported by Porfirio
Díaz. Although substantial progress occurred after the
entry of railroads, increased concentration of landholdings
restricted employment and created social unrest among
industrial workers. Progress was largely ephemeral and
economic depression, beginning in 1907, created an
atmosphere conducive to revolt.

501 TARACENA, ALFONSO. Historia de la Revolución en Tabasco.
Villahermosa: Ediciones del Gobierno del Estado, 1974.
A native son's narrative history of the Revolution in
Tabasco that reads like an epic poem on Tabasco.

502   VILLARELLO VELEZ, ILDEFONSO. Historia de la Revolución
       Mexicana en Coahuila. Patronato series, no. 49. Mexico:
       Instituto Nacional de Estudios Históricos de la
       Revolución Mexicana, 1970.
       State history of the Revolution in Coahuila.

503   VISCAYA CANALES, ISIDRO. Los orígenes de la industrialización
       de Monterrey (1867-1920): Una historia económica y social
       desde la caída del segundo imperio hasta el fin de la
       Revolución. Monterrey, N.L.: Instituto Tecnológico
       y de Estudios Superiores de Monterrey, 1969.

504   WARMAN, ARTURO. Y venimos a contradecir: Los campesinos de
       Morelos y el estado nacional. Mexico: Ediciones de la
       Casa Chata, 1976.
           Divides study of eastern Morelos peasantry into four
       periods: Porfiriato; Revolution (1910-20); redistribution
       of land (1920-40); and the 1940-72 era. Concludes that
       peasantry has been able to maintain a traditional economic
       base and life style in face of pressure from large land-
       owners, big business, and government because of the
       endurance of local values and community structure.

505   WASSERMAN, MARK. "The Social Origins of the 1910 Revolution
       in Chihuahua." Latin American Research Review 15, no. 1
       (1980): 15-38.
           Well-documented study of the causes of revolution in
       Chihuahua identified as the result of depression, drought,
       political repression and unrest under the Terrazas-Creel
       regime, and a massive and unparalleled assault on the land
       after 1905, which directly affected in an adverse way the
       tough inhabitants of the former military colonies. Careful
       use of Anuarios demonstrates that economic development
       before 1907 led to an expansion of the middle sector,
       especially small industrial establishments and artisan
       shops. Improvements in standard of living also occurred
       for miners, agricultural workers and industrial workers
       as well. The depression of 1907 struck all of these
       groups hard, especially the middle sector from which
       emerged revolutionary chieftains such as Toribio Ortega,
       Pascual Orozco, and Porfirio Talamantes.

506   _____. "Oligarquía en intereses extranjeros en Chihuahua
       durante el porfiriato." HM 2 (Oct.-Dec. 1973): 279-319.
           Deals mainly with the Terrazas-Creel family, which
       owned millions of hectares of land and also controlled
       a number of businesses like the telephones, steel foundries,
       and sugar refineries. Enrique Creel, Terraza's son-in-law,
       was governor of Chihuahua from 1904-1910. At the same
       time he was the Secretary of Foreign Relations and

Ambassador to the United States. All of the British and U.S. economic interests are studied.

507 WILLIAM, JOHN B. La iglesia y el estado en Veracruz, 1840–1940. Mexico: SepSetentas, 1976.
     A study of Church-State relations in Veracruz. Beginning with the 1840s, the emphasis is upon the chaos and violence of the decade after 1925, especially the 1931-1932 period.

508 ZUNO, JOSE G. Historia de la Revolución en el estado de Jalisco. Patronato series, no. 34. Mexico: Instituto Nacional de Estudios Históricos de la Revolución Mexicana, 1964.
     A state history of the Revolution in Jalisco.

For bibliography relating to regional history see entries 7, 12, 33, 35, 73, and 167-70. For regional archives see entries 73, 94, 98, 110 and 116. For historiography see entries 180, 182, 186, 190, 200-201, 222, and 239. For regional studies of caudillos and peasants see entry 351. For documents relating to Jalisco see entry 535. For regional studies of the Revolution see the following: Chihuahua, entries 789, 807, and 897; Sonora, entry 836; San Luis Potosí, entry 838; Yucatán, entry 898; Coahuila, entry 887; Tlaxcala, entries 475 and 995-96; Tampico, entry 1116, Oaxaca compared to Morelos, entry 1039; Veracruz, 1123 and 1133-35.

V. Documentary Sources

509   AVRICH, PAUL. "Prison Letters of Ricardo Flores Magón to
       Lilly Sarnoff." International Review of Social History
       22 (1977): 379-422.
              Ricardo Flores Magón (1874-1922), the foremost Mexican
       anarchist of the twentieth century, spent the last nine-
       teen years of his life in the United States. During half
       of that time he was imprisoned, and he died at Leavenworth
       penitentiary. While there he began his long correspondence
       with Lilly Sarnoff, a young New York anarchist and member
       of the defense committee working for his release. From
       the files of the International Institute of Social History
       in Amsterdam, twenty-one letters of Magón to Sarnoff,
       covering the period from October 1920 to November 1922,
       are reprinted here in their original form. Written in
       English, these letters reveal the horrors of prison life,
       Magón's attitudes toward the Bolshevik Revolution, and
       a florid style characteristic of an age of romantic
       revolutionism.

510   BARTRA, ARMANDO, comp. Regeneración, 1900-1918: La corriente
       más radical de la Revolución de 1910 a través de su
       periódico de combate. Mexico: HADISE, 1972.
              Collection of 126 articles published in Regeneración,
       El Hijo del Ahuizote, Revolución, and Punto Rojo between
       1900-1918 by Ricardo Flores Magón and other magonistas.

511   CARRILLO AZPEITIA, RAFAEL, comp. Siqueiros. Mexico:
       SepSetentas, 1974.
              A collection of quotations by the great muralist
       Siqueiros over a variety of topics--political, social,
       and artistic. Includes an introduction that traces the
       art and life of the artist.

512   CONGRESS. MEXICO. Constituyente de la Revolución Mexicana,
       1916-1917: 50 discursos doctrinales.... Mexico: Instituto
       Nacional de Estudios Históricos de la Revolución Mexicana,
       1967.

Work divided into three parts: a) transcripts of fifty
speeches pronounced in the constituent congress of 1917;
b) journals and diaries (Nov. 1916–Jan. 1917); c) a biographical section of the individuals whose speeches are
reproduced.

513   CONTRERAS, MARIO. México en el siglo XX: 1900–1913. Mexico:
      UNAM, 1975.
            An anthology of documents. Jesús Tamayo aided in
      writing the text and gathering the documents.

514   "Documentos inéditos de José Ives Limantour." Trimestre
      Politico 1 (July–Sept. 1975: 125–38.
            Limantour's notes of discussions with President Díaz
      concerning transfer of power. Also includes discussion
      with Madero's father and Francisco Vázquez Gómez over
      revolutionaries' terms.

515   FABELA, ISIDRO, and FABELA, JOSEFINA E. de. Documentos
      históricos de la Revolución Mexicana. 27 vols. Mexico:
      Fondo de Cultura Económica (vols. 1–5), 1960–64; Editorial
      Jus (vols. 6–27), 1965–73. Indice cronológico de la
      colección de documentos históricos de la Revolución Mexicana.
      Mexico: Editorial Jus, 1976.
            Indispensible source of printed documents for the
      magonista, maderista, villista, zapatista, and carrancista
      phases of the Revolution, especially for political and
      diplomatic history. A monumental series edited and com-
      piled by the members of the Comisión de Investigaciones
      Históricas de la Revolución Mexicana. Project was initi-
      ated by the Director of the Comisión, Isidro Fabela, and
      brought to completion (beginning with vol. 6) by Josefina
      E. de Fabela. The published documents have been primarily
      taken from five major research centers: a) Archivo
      General de la Nación; b) Archivo Isidro Fabela; c) Archivo
      Histórico de la Defensa Nacional; d) Archivo de la
      Secretaría de Relaciones Exteriores; and e) Biblioteca
      Isidro Febela. Each volume contains a general documents
      index, and all documents are preceded by a brief synopsis
      with a reference to the archival source of the document.
      The earliest volumes (1–5) contain several illustrations.
      The series index (vol. 28), available since 1976, describes
      all documents individually and is a general guide to the
      twenty-seven volumes.
            Contents: vol. 1 and vols. 14–18, Revolución y Régimen
      constitucionalista; vol. 2, La intervención norteamericana
      en Veracruz (1914); vol. 3, Carranza, Wilson y el A.B.C.;
      vol. 4, El Plan de Guadalupe; vols. 5–9, Revolución y
      régimen maderista; vol. 10, Actividades políticas y revo-
      lucionarias de los hermanos Flores Magón; vol. 11, Pre-

cursores de la Revolución Mexicana, 1906-1910; vols. 12-13, Expedición punitiva; vol. 19, Testimonio sobre los asesinatos de Don Venustiano y Jesús Carranza; vol. 20 (in two books), Las relaciones internacionales en la Revolución y régimen constitucionalista y la cuestión petrolera; vol. 21, Emiliano Zapata: El Plan de Ayala y su política agraria; vols. 22-27, La convención: debates de las sesiones de la Soberana Convención Revolucionaria (1914-1916); vol. 28, Indice cronólogico. Forthcoming: "Mis Memorias de la Revolución," by Isidro Fabela.

516   FABELA, ISIDRO, comp. Arengas revolucionarias: Discursos y
        artículos políticos. Mexico: Editorial Jus, 1975.
            Revolutionary speeches. Edited by the Comisión de
        Investigaciones Históricas de la Revolución Mexicana.

517   FLORES MAGON, RICARDO. Semilla libertaria. Mexico: Liga
        de Economistas Revolucionarios de la República Mexicana,
        1975.
            Magonista editorials and articles from Regeneración,
        1910-1918.

518   _____. Epistolario revolucionario e íntimo de Ricardo
        Flores Magón. Mexico: Ediciones Antorcha, 1975.
            Leavenworth correspondence (1919-22) of Flores Magón.
        Includes Harry Weinberger letters. Chronology chart,
        1874-1922.

519   _____. "Plan del partido liberal." Revista de la Facultad
        de Derecho de México 25 (1975): 277-99.
            Reprints the text of the Plan of Mexico's Liberal
        Party written by Richardo Flores Magón, and promulgated
        on 1 July 1906.

520   _____. "Testimonio: Textos...." Historia Obrera 1
        (1974): 18-38.
            The contents of these little-known articles speak out
        against some of the foreign anarchists.

521   _____. Epistolario y textos.... Mexico: Fondo de Cul-
        tura Económica, 1973.
            Letters and excerpts from the works of one of Mexico's
        foremost anarchist revolutionaries. For this volume
        Manuel González Ramírez has organized and edited the
        writings and letters of RFM and his colleagues in the
        United States. Consists primarily of prison correspondence
        after 1908 taken from articles in Regeneración, the
        Mexican Foreign Relations Archives, and the Archivo
        General de la Nación. First edition appeared in 1964.

522 _____. Antología. Mexico: UNAM, 1970.
Introduction and selections by Gonzalo Aguirre Beltrán.
Drawings by Alberto Beltrán.

523 _____, and FLORES MAGON, JESUS. Batalla a la dictadura:
Textos políticos. Mexico: Empresas Editoriales, 1967.
Political documents of Ricardo Flores Magón and his
older brother, Jesús.

524 GONZALEZ RAMIREZ, MANUEL, comp. Fuentes para le historia de
la Revolución Mexicana. 4 vols. Mexico: Fondo de
Cultura Económica, 1974.
Vol. 1, Planes políticos y otros documentos; vol. 2,
La caricatura política; vol. 3, La huelga de Cananea;
vol. 4, Manifiestos políticos 1892-1912. Compiled with an
introduction to each volume with notes by González Ramírez.
Vol. 2 reproduces a large number of political caricatures.
Vol. 3 is the authoritative work on the Cananea strike.
All volumes contain either correspondence or primary
sources. First editions between 1954 and 1957.

525 HANRAHAN, GENE Z., ed. Documents on the Mexican Revolution.
2 vols., 4 pts. Salisbury, N.C.: Documentary Publications,
1976.
Photographic copies of selected documents from U.S.
National Archives, especially Departments of State and
Justice. Vol. 1, The Origins of the Revolution in Texas,
Arizona, New Mexico, and California: 1910-1911; vol. 2,
The Madero Revolution as Reported in the Confidential
Dispatches of U.S. Ambassador Henry Lane Wilson and the
Embassy in Mexico City, June 1910 to June 1911.

526 LUNA CASTRO, HILARIO. México en 1911. Mexico: Librería de
Manuel Porrúa, 1967.
A collection of caricatures, the majority of which are
unedited and political in nature. Some of these cartoons
are taken from those published by Cabral in Multicolor.

527 MADRAZO, CARLOS A. Madrazo: Voz postrera de la Revolución.
discursos y comentarios. Mexico: Costa-Amic, 1971.
Compilation of Madrazo's speeches where he criticizes
the official political party.

528 MEJIA ZUÑIGA, RAUL. La Revolución Mexicana. Mexico: Librería
Ariel, 1967.
An enlarged compilation of the articles published in
the newspaper, El Universal during January 1967 under
the heading, "Radiografía de la Revolución Mexicana."

529   MENDOZA, VICENTE T. El corrido mexicano. Mexico: Fondo de
      Cultura Económica, 1974.
            Second edition of 1954 publication. 172 corridos, or
      popular ballads, many of which relate to history, Revolu-
      tion, politics, the cristero revolt, agrarianism, and
      religion.

530   MONJARAS-RUIZ, JESUS, ed. "Una versión alemana de los
      inicios de la Revolución de 1910." Anuario de Historia
      8 (1976): 205-48.
            Collection and translation into Spanish of materials
      concerning the Mexican Revolution which appeared in
      several German newspapers in 1910.

531   MORALES JIMENEZ, ALBERTO. 20 encuentros históricos en la
      Revolución Mexicana. Mexico: Departamento del Distrito
      Federal, 1973.
            A series of historical interviews, beginning with one
      between Porfirio Díaz and Elihu Root and concluding with
      that of Villa and Obregón.

532   MUÑIZ, DANIEL, and GARCIA PRADO, GEORGINA. Antología: Cuentos
      en la política mexicana. Córdoba, Veracruz: Imprenta
      Ruiz, 1969.
            A collection of anecdotes and jokes about Mexican
      politicians.

533   NOVO, SALVADOR. La vida en México en el período presidencial
      de Lázaro Cárdenas: La vida en México en el período de
      Manuel Avila Camacho. 2 vols. Mexico: Empresas Editor-
      iales, 1964 and 1965.
            Compilation of articles which appeared in Hoy (27 Feb-
      ruary 1937 to 7 December 1940) and Mañana (25 August 1943
      to 20 October 1946) about Presidents Cárdenas and Camacho
      respectively. Author and general indexes.

534   PACHECO MENDEZ, GUADALUPE et al. Cárdenas y la izquierda
      mexicana. Mexico: Juan Pablos Editor, 1975.
            A collection of essays, interviews, and documents on
      Cárdenas and the Mexican Left.

535   PARRES ARIAS, JOSE. Estudio de la legislación constitucion-
      alista de Jalisco y sus decretos constitutivos, 1914-1915.
      Guadalajara: Universidad de Guadalajara. Instituto Jalis-
      ciense de Antropología e Historia, 1969.
            Made up of 133 decrees that include eighteen from
      June 1914 to December 1915. Sixty-nine of them were
      issued by Manuel M. Diéguez while he was governor and
      military commander of Jalisco. Fifty-six were issued
      by Manuel Aguirre Berlanga and eight by Tomás López

Linares, both of whom were acting governors during Diéguez's absence. An analysis is given of each decree.

536 REYES H., ALFONSO. Emiliano Zapata: Su vida y su obra con documentos inéditos. Mexico: Libros de México, 1963.

537 RICHMOND, DOUGLAS W., comp. El régimen de Carranza y la frontera norte durante la época revolucionaria, 1910-1920. Mexico: Secretaría de Relaciones Exteriores de México, 1980.
Anthology of 205 documents relating to immigration history and the revolution on the northern frontier during the Carranza era. Each document has an introduction. Preface, notes, illustrations.

538 ROMERO CERVANTES, ARTURO. "Nueva documentación inédita de Ricardo Flores Magón." Boletín Bibliográfico de la Secretaría de Hacienda y Crédito Público 17 (1971): 454.
Documents taken from the Archivo General de la Nación.

539 _____. "Documentación inédita del magonismo." Boletín Bibliográfico de la Secretaría de Hacienda y Crédito Público 15 (1969): 408, 410, 412-13.
Documents reproduced from the series "¡Revoltosos magonistas!" Taken from the Archivo General de la Nación. First letters are dated July 1907.

540 ROMERO FLORES, JESUS. Corridos de la Revolución Mexicana. Mexico: B. Costa-Amic, 1977.
Collection of over one hundred corridos composed between 1879 and 1938, with an introduction.

541 ROSOFF, ROSALAND. Así firmaron el Plan de Ayala. Mexico: Secretaría de Educación Pública, 1976.
Consists of interviews with the last three signatories to Zapata's Plan of Ayala. Appendixes: Text of Plan de Ayala; Zapata-Magaña correspondence calling for publication of the Plan.

542 TENA RAMIREZ, FELIPE, comp. Leyes fundamentales de México, 1808-1975. Rev. ed. Mexico: Editorial Porrúa, 1975.
Fundamental laws of Mexico. Includes texts of Mexican constitutions and related documents. Expanded edition that has been brought up to date.

543 THIERCELIN, RAQUEL. La Revolución Mexicana. Paris: Masson et Cie, 1972.
Designed for classroom use in secondary schools, this book is a collection of readings on the Mexican Revolution. Includes: Plans of San Luis Potosí, Ayala, and Guadalupe; Ricardo Flores Magón's attack on Díaz; Carrancista ejido

law of 6 January 1915; and key sections of the Constitution
of 1917. Also includes selections from Pablo González
Casanova, Martín Luis Guzmán, and Jesús Silva Herzog.
Other items include corridos, poems, and excerpts from
revolutionary novels.

544   VILLASEÑOR, JOSE, comp. "Diez y seis discursos de Francisco
      I. Madero." Boletín Bibliográfico de la Secretaría de
      Hacienda y Crédito Público 479 (1972): 3-8.
         The first speech is that of 24 December 1909 and the
      last one included here is that of 29 May 1910.

545   WILKIE, JAMES W., and MICHAELS, ALBERT L., comps.
      Revolution in Mexico. New York: A. Knopf, 1969.
         Anthology of 1910-1940 period. Forty-eight short
      readings. Sources include extracts from the Plan of San
      Luis Potosí and the Plan of Ayala, Magaña's account of the
      meeting between Madero and Zapata, Zapata's open letter to
      Carranza, Morrow on Calles and the oil controversy, and
      Carleton Beals on Joaquín Amaro. Interspersed with these
      are extracts from leading modern historians. Two
      chronologies.

For a collection of documents and brief summary of educational
politics and policies see entry 435. For an anthology of the
Porfiriato, which includes documents, see entry 559.

VI. Contemporary History and Memoirs

546   BUICK, HARRY ARTHUR. The Gringoes of Tepehuanes. London: Longmans, Green, 1967.
     Narrative of the experience of an American who worked in the mines of Chihuahua during the Revolution in 1916.

547   CABRERA, LUIS. Obras completas. 4 vols. Mexico: Ediciones Oasis, 1975.
     Writings, speeches, political commentaries, legal essays, and literary thoughts of maderista and carrancista Luis Cabrera. Volumes 1 and 2 on law and literature respectively; vols. 3 and 4 entitled Obra política. Cabrera complete works include a brief biographical sketch by Eugenia Meyer and introductory essays to each of the four volumes by Leoncio Lara Sáenz, Felipe Remolina Roqueñí, María del Carmen Millán, and Eugenia Meyer. These voluminious writings of Luis Cabrera amount to over 3,758 pages.

548   CARDENAS, LAZARO. Diario político. Mexico: Ediciones Era, 1972.
     Speeches, interviews, messages and correspondence, etc. Covers the years 1895-1970.

549   _____. Epistolario. 2 vols. Mexico: Siglo XXI Editores, 1974-75.
     Collection of Cárdenas's personal and official correspondence from 1925-1970. Second part of multivolume Obras. Volume 1 contains letters to and from Cárdenas on internal and external matters: politics; agriculture; social, educational, and economic affairs; the petroleum and nationalization issues; and the war in Europe and Asia. Most material is on the political issues and agrarian and expropriation controversies of the 1934-1940 era. Volume 2 contains correspondence to and from Cárdenas on international themes such as world peace, national liberation movements, etc., most for the post-1940 era. Index.

550 _____. Ideario político. Mexico: Ediciones Era, 1972.
Selection of speeches and writings from during and
after his presidency.

551 _____. Obras. Vol. 1, Apuntes, 1913-1940. Mexico:
UNAM, 1972.
Personal correspondence, presidential and electoral
campaign memos and notes, and the private reflections
of "citizen" Cárdenas, for the 1913-1940 period. Not a
biography but a variety of comments and administrative
decisions on politics and society in Mexico. Especially
good for the Spanish Civil War and Mexico prior to World
War II. Some comments on Calles. The multivolume Obras
is the result of the cooperative efforts of the Cárdenas
family and the members of the Instituto Lázaro Cárdenas
de Estudios de la Revolución Mexicana. Volume 1 contains
a preface by Gastón García Cantu with an introduction by
Cárdenas's son, Cuauhtémoc Cárdenas.

552 _____. Obras. Vol. 2, Apuntes, 1941-1956. Mexico:
UNAM, 1973.
Correspondence and memos for the 1941-1956 period.
Collection of personal memoirs, diary entries, political
commentaries, administrative decisions, and philosophical
reflections of Lázaro Cárdenas. Arranged chronologically.

553 _____. Obras. Vol. 3, Apuntes, 1957-1966; vol. 4,
Apuntes, 1967-1970. 2 vols. Mexico: UNAM, 1974.
Part of the multivolume Obras. Correspondence and
memos for the 1957-1970 period. Volume 4 contains a
name, place, and analytical index to the four-volume
series.

554 CEJA REYES, VICTOR. Cabalgando con Villa. Mexico: Populibros
"La Prensa," 1961.
Collection of tales and episodes about Francisco Villa,
selected from the writings of popular novelists and the
recollections of surviving revolutionaries.

555 _____. Yo maté a Villa. Mexico: Populibros "La Prensa,"
1960.
Excerpts from articles published in La Prensa concerning the death of Francisco Villa. Included are interviews with three surviving participants in the ambush of
Villa, one of whom assigned to Calles the responsibility
for the crime.

556 CERVANTES, FEDERICO. Francisco Villa y la Revolución.
Mexico: Ediciones Alonso, 1960.

Friendly account of Villa's role in the Revolution by
the chief of staff of Villa's principal military adviser,
General Felipe Angeles. Scattered throughout are documents and memoirs representing the recollections of
Cervantes and fellow villistas, including official reports,
descriptions of military engagements, and correspondence
between the revolutionists.

557   FLANDRAU, CHARLES MACOMB. Viva Mexico! Edited, with an
      introduction by C. Harvey Gardiner. Urbana: University
      of Illinois Press, 1964.
          First published in 1908. Entertaining and informative
      travel book that has become a classic. Description of
      Mexican life immediately prior to the Revolution, including
      plight of the peon.

558   FUENTES MARES, JOSE. La revolución mexicana: Memorias de
      un espectador. Mexico: Joaquín Mortiz, 1971.
          Writing in the first person, the author acts as the
      narrator of the episodes of the Revolution of 1910.
      Polemical, in part.

559   GIL, CARLOS B., ed. The Age of Porfirio Díaz: Selected
      Readings. Albuquerque: University of New Mexico Press,
      1977.
          An anthology of twenty-seven excerpts from travelers'
      accounts and histories, journal articles, treatises, and
      monographs which describe conditions and attitudes during
      the Porfiriato. Also contains an introduction by Gil and
      a bibliographical essay by Anthony Bryan. Author suggests
      that modernization began with Díaz.

560   GONZALEZ, PABLO. Zapata: Reaccionario y traidor. Mexico:
      Textos de Cultura Historiográfica, 1974.
          Unfriendly account of Zapata by a participant in the
      Revolution.

561   GUERRERO YOACHAM, CRISTIAN, ed. "Un testigo chileno del
      asesinato del Presidente Madero." In Siete estudios,
      pp. 81-116. Santiago: University of Chile, 1975.
          Correspondence of Anselmo Hevia Riquelme, Chilean
      diplomat in Mexico during the "Decena trágica" of 1913.

562   GUISA Y AZEVEDO, JESUS. La Revolución y su Luis Cabrera.
      Mexico: Editorial Polis, 1975.
          Collection of commentaries by revolutionary participants
      on Carranza, constitutionalism, and matters relating to
      Cabrera. Includes short essays by José Vasconcelos,
      Antonio Villarreal, Martín Luis Guzmán, Antonio Díaz Soto
      y Gama, and others.

563   GUIZAR OCEGUERA, JOSE. Episodios de la guerra cristera.
      Mexico: B. Costa-Amic Editor, 1976.
      Memories of a cristero.

564   JIMENEZ, LUZ. De Porfirio Díaz a Zapata: Memoria náhuatl
      de Milpa Alta. Translated by Fernando Horcasitas. Mexico:
      UNAM, 1968.
      Memoirs of the Náhuatl-speaking Luz Jiménez of the
      Milpa Alta. Recollections concerning the late Porfiriato
      and the early Revolution, especially the zapatistas. Tes-
      timony to a Revolution that was devoid of measurable
      impact, at least to some of the inhabitants of the Milpa
      Alta region. See also entries 565-66.

565   _____. _____. Translated by Fernando Horcasitas.
      Mexico: Instituto de Investigaciones Históricas, 1974.
      Accounts of the life of Luz Jiménez and her recollections
      of the Mexican Revolution, as dictated to Fernando Horcas-
      itas. Introductory note by Miguel León-Portilla. In
      Náhuatl and Spanish.

566   _____. Life and Death in Milpa Alta: A Nahuatl Chronicle
      of Díaz and Zapata. Translated and edited by F. Horcasitas.
      Norman: University of Oklahoma Press, 1972.
      An Indian woman's account of life in Milpa Alta, a
      village near Mexico City, during the Díaz regime and the
      early revolution. Part 1 describes activities of villagers,
      education, religious customs, and legends; Part 2 relates
      impressions of various revolutionary groups (e.g.,
      zapatistas, carrancistas), her exile from and eventual
      return to her village in 1923. In Náhuatl and English.

567   LIMANTOUR, JOSE IVES. Apuntes sobre mi vida publica (1892-
      1911). Mexico: Porrúa, 1965.
      Autobiography of his public career as Minister of the
      Treasury under Porfirio Díaz. Denies the general public
      allegations that he supported the re-creation of the
      office of vice president and tries to absolve the
      cientificos of responsibility for the cabinet crisis of
      1911.

568   LOMBARDO TOLEDANO, VICENTE. Escritos sobre el movimiento
      obrero. Mexico: Universidad Obrera de México, 1975.
      Reflections on the workers' movement in Mexico by
      former labor leader Toledano.

569   LOPEZ PORTILLO y ROJAS, JOSE. Síntesis de la Revolución
      Mexicana, vivida y escrita por José López Portillo
      y Rojas. Cuernavaca, Morelos: privately printed, 1968.

This book has been written by a revolutionary who
participated in the battles of 1910. In his pages he
refers to the end of the Porfirio Díaz period, to the
politics which characterized his regime and to the democratic campaign of Francisco I. Madero. Later, he talks
about the resignation of General Díaz, the death of
Madero, the Plan de Guadalupe, the zapatista movement,
and the constitionalist period. A bilingual edition:
Spanish and English.

570   MADERO, FRANCISCO. Pensamiento y acción de F. Madero.
      Mexico: Instituto Nacional de Estudios Históricos de la
      Revolución Mexicana, 1973.
         Memoirs, correspondence, and speeches of Francisco
      Madero.

571   MANTEGON PEREZ, ADAM. Recuerdos de un villista: Mi
      campaña en la Revolución. Mexico: n.p., 1967.
         Recollections of a villista.

572   MARQUEZ STERLING, MANUEL. Los últimos díaz del Presidente
      Madero: Mi gestión diplomática en México. Mexico:
      Editorial Porrúa, 1975.
         Account of the overthrow and death of Madero by the
      then Cuban Ambassador to Mexico.

573   MILLETT, RICHARD. "John Wesley Butler and the Mexican
      Revolution, 1910-1911." West Georgia College Studies in
      the Social Sciences 17 (1978): 73-88.
         Describes John Wesley Butler's account of the events
      of the Mexican Revolution, 1910-11, which he experienced
      while carrying on missionary activities in Mexico. Based
      on excerpts from letters written to friends and the
      Methodist Church offices in New York.

574   MORENO, DANIEL, ed. Batallas de la Revolución y sus
      corridos. Mexico: Editorial Porrúa, 1978.
         Fifteen battles in Mexico's Revolution are sketched
      in this book, a series of eyewitness, official, participant,
      and recollected reports of the fighting between 1911 and
      1916. Includes a number of official dispatches of interest
      to students of military aspects of the Revolution. Also
      included are a number of corridos.

575   OBREGON, ALVARO. Ocho mil kilómetros en campaña. Mexico:
      Fuentes para la Historia de la Revolución Mexicana,
      1973.
         Recollections of the military phases of the Revolution.

576 O'HEA, PATRICK A. Reminiscences of the Mexican Revolution.
     Mexico: Centro Anglo-Mexicano del Libro, 1966.
     An eyewitness account of the happenings of the Laguna
     region during the second decade of the twentieth century.
     Detailed, but written from a broad and unbiased point
     of view.

577 PEÑA de VILLARREAL, CONSUELO. La Revolución en el norte.
     Puebla: Periodística e Impresora de Puebla, 1968.
     The episodes that surrounded the life of the author
     are written in the form of memoirs.

578 PORTES GIL, EMILIO. Polémicas. Mexico: B. Costa-Amic, 1975.

579 REED, JOHN. México Insurgente: La guerra en el desierto.
     3 vols. Mexico: Departamento del Distrito Federal,
     1973.
     Impressions of a U.S. war correspondent during the
     Mexican Revolution. Included is "El origen de las
     revoluciones en México," which is taken from La Revolución
     Mexicana by Jesús Romero Flores. The English version:
     Insurgent Mexico. Edited by Albert L. Michaels and
     James W. Wilkie. New York: Simon & Schuster, 1969.

580 REYES NEVARES, SALVADOR, comp. Relatos de la Revolución:
     Antología de Rafael F. Muñoz. Mexico: SepSetentas, 1974.
     Sixteen stories about the Revolution related to Reyes
     Nevares by Rafael F. Muñoz, a "norteño" eyewitness to the
     Revolution. Includes a prologue by Reyes Nevares.

581 SILVA HERZOG, JESUS. "Tríptico en la Revolución Mexicana."
     Cuadernos Americanos 173 (Nov.-Dec. 1970): 128-50.
     The author tells of his experiences in the Mexican
     Revolution, 1911-1915.

582 TAPIA, RAFAEL. Mi participación revolucionaria. Mexico:
     Suma Veracruzana, 1967.
     With a prologue by Leonardo Pasquel.

583 THORD-GRAY, I. Gringo Rebel (Mexico 1913-1914). Coral
     Gables: University of Miami Press, 1960.
     First-hand account by a man who served in the "rebel"
     cavalry between 1913-14. The career of Sancho Panchez
     is well described. Contemporary portraits. Poor
     bibliography and index.

584 VELA GONZALEZ, FRANCISCO. "La Quincena Trágica de 1913."
     HM 12 (Jan.-Mar. 1963): 440-53.
     Personal account of the author as a young medical
     student who was an eyewitness to the events which led
     to the overthrow of Madero.

585   WILKIE, JAMES W., and WILKIE, EDNA MONZON de. <u>México visto</u>
      <u>en el siglo XX</u>. Mexico: Instituto Mexicano de Investi-
      gaciones Económicas, 1969.
          Transcripts of well-organized interviews with Ramón
      Beteta (politician and hacendado), Marte R. Gómez
      (agrarista), Manuel Gómez Morín (founder of the Partico
      Acción Nacional), Vicente Lombardo Toledano (theoretician,
      labor leader, and militant Marxist), Miguel Palomar y
      Vizcarra (Catholic militant), Emilio Portes Gil (ex-president
      of Mexico), and Jesús Silva Herzog (economist and historian).
      The original tapes are at the Oral History Center for
      Latin America, Ohio State University.

For a bibliography of memoirs <u>see</u> entry 31. For autobiography and
decision-making in Mexican politics <u>see</u> entry 355. For the memoirs
of Francisco Madero's private secretary <u>see</u> entry 814. For a Casa
del Obrero Mundial testimonial <u>see</u> entry 1034.

VII. Biographies

586 ALCOCER ANDALON, ALBERTO. Librado Rivera: Ilustre potosino precursor de la Revolución Mexicana. San Luis Potosí: Academia de Historia Potosina, 1973.
    Study of Librado Rivera, the magonista precursor.

587 _____. "El General y Profesor Alberto Carrera Torres." Archivos de Historia Potosina (San Luis Potosí) 1 (1969): 32-48.
    Carrera Torres took up arms with Madero and later opposed Huerta. Born in Tamaulipas, his arena of action was in San Luis Potosí. When he rejoined the Convención in Aguascalientes he remained loyal to it even though Pablo González had invited him to join forces with Carranza. Moved from one prison to another, he was shot by a firing squad on 16 February 1917.

588 ALISKY, MARVIN. Who's Who in Mexican Government. Tempe, Arizona: Arizona State University, 1969.
    Short factual biographies of 245 public officials.

589 ALMADA, FRANCISCO R. Vida, proceso y muerte de Abraham González. Mexico: Instituto Nacional de Estudios Históricos de la Revolución Mexicana, 1967.
    Biography of maderista leader and revolutionary governor Abraham González.

590 ALONSO CORTES, RODRIGO. Francisco Villa el quinto jinete del apocalipsis. Mexico: Editorial Diana, 1972.

591 ALVEAR ACEVEDO, CARLOS. Lázaro Cárdenas: El hombre y el mito. Mexico: Editorial Jus, 1972.
    Cárdenas, the man and the myth.

592 ANGEL PERAL, MIGUEL. El vendadero Zapata. Mexico: Editorial PAC, 1975.

Diatribe against Zapata. Concludes that Zapata was
neither a revolutionary nor an idealist. Instead, he was
a rebel, a paranoid, a robber of property, a barbarian
against civilization, and a symbol of disorder and
anarchy.

593 ARELLANO, JOSEFINA G. de. "El general Bernardo Reyes, gobernador de Nuevo León." Capilla Alfonsina 13 (30 Sept. 1969):
16-20.
Study of Bernardo Reyes, governor of Nuevo León.

594 ARELLANO, LUZ de. Palomas, Torreón y Pancho Villa. Mexico:
n.p., 1966.

595 ARENAS GUZMAN, DIEGO. Alfredo Robles Domínguez en jornadas
culminantes de la Revolución. Mexico: Biblioteca del
Instituto Nacional de Estudios Históricos de la Revolución
Mexicana, 1974.
Biography of Robles Domínguez, military man and engineer
and a maderista who joined the Constitutional forces after
1913. Partido Republicano candidate for president in
1920, he died in Mexico City in 1928.

596 _____. José María Pino Suárez. Mexico: Secretaría de
Educación Pública, 1969.
Biography of Pino Suárez, vice-president of Mexico who
was assassinated with Madero in 1913.

597 AZUELA, SALVADOR. "Hacia una valoración de Madero." Revista
de la Universidad de México 28 (1973): 22-24.
Argues that Francisco I. Madero's stature is based on
the fact that he sacrificed everything for Mexico: tran-
quility, fortune and life itself.

598 BARRERA FUENTES, FLORENCIO. Ricardo Flores Magón, el apóstol
cautivo. Mexico: Instituto Nacional de Estudios Históricos de la Revolución Mexicana, 1973.
Biography of one of the precursors of the Mexican Revolution. Well-documented study of the life, thought, and
activity of Flores Magón by a distinguished historian
of the Revolution.

599 BEALS, CARLETON. Porfirio Diaz: Dictator of Mexico. 1932.
Reprint. Westport, Conn.: Greenwood Press, 1972.
Classic study by a científico.

600 BELTRAN, ENRIQUE. "Fantasía y realidad de Pancho Villa."
HM 16 (July-Sept. 1966): 71-84.

601 BERUMEN, FIDENCIO. Semblanza del general de división Francisco Villa. Zacatecas: Talleres Linotipográficos del Gobierno del Estado, 1966.

602 BLANCO MOHENO, ROBERTO. Zapata. Mexico: Editorial Diana, 1973.
Argues that Zapata, "the caudillo of the South," was neither a revolutionary nor a bandit; that zapatismo was neither a doctrine nor a system, but rather a mystique. No index or bibliography.

603 _____. Pancho Villa, que es su padre. Mexico: Editorial Diana, 1969.

604 BRADDY, HALDEEN. Cock of the Walk: Qui-qui-ri-quí! The Legend of Pancho Villa. Port Washington, New York, and London: Kennikat Press, 1970.
Lively account of Villa--bandit, gay caballero, and patriot betrayed by a pumpkin-seed vendor. First published in 1955. Based on newspapers, books, magazines, and numerous informants.

605 BRENNER, LEAH. The Boyhood of Diego Rivera. Illustrated by Diego Rivera. New York: Barnes & Noble; London: Yoseloff, 1964.
Five stories based on material, including conversations with Rivera's family, given to the author by Diego Rivera. Illustrations.

606 BULNES, PEPE. Pino Suárez: El caballero de la lealtad. Mexico: B. Costa-Amic, 1969.
Biography of Madero's vice-president.

607 CALCES, ALBERTO. Un marinero en la Revolución Mexicana: El Sr. Madero. Mexico: Editorial Litorales, 1968.

608 CALZADIAZ BARRERA, ALBERTO. Hechos reales de la Revolución: Gral. Ignacio L. Pesqueira. Mexico: Editorial Patria, 1973.
Biography of Ignacio Pesqueira, military man, governor of Sonora, and partisan of Carranza. Died in 1940 in France.

609 _____. Víspera de la Revolución: El abuelo Cisneros. Mexico: Editorial Patria, 1969.
Biography of Eligio Cisneros (1853-1947), a witness to various important events in the history of Mexico. A native of Chihuahua, he saw the collapse of Maximilian's empire, as well as that of the Díaz government and the Mexican Revolution headed by Madero.

Biographies

610 _____. Anatomía de un guerrero: El general Martín Lopez, hijo militar de Pancho Villa. Mexico: Editores Mexicanos Unidos, 1968.
A study of villista military man Martín López.

611 CAMP, RODERIC A. Mexican Political Biographies, 1935-1975. Tucson: University of Arizona Press, 1976.
Contains biographies of persons living and dead "who have been prominent in Mexican political life from 1935 to early 1974." Appendixes list government officials for the forty-year period covered. Virtually a government organizational manual for Mexico.

612 Carranza: Biografía del primer jefe del ejército constitucionalista. Mexico: Edición de Cultura y Ciencia Política, 1971.

613 CASASOLA, GUSTAVO. Biografía ilustrada del general Porfirio Díaz, 1830-1965. Mexico: Ediciones Gustavo Casasola, 1970.
Based on the newspaper archives of Casasola. Illustrated.

614 CASILLAS, JOSE ALBERTO. Sendero de un mártir: Anacleto González Flores. Mexico: Imprenta Juan Pablos, 1960.
Moralistic biography of the famed cristero leader who met his martyrdom in the Los Altos region of Jalisco in 1927.

615 CASTILLO, HERBERTO. Cárdenas el hombre. Mexico: Editorial Hombre Nuevo, 1974.

616 CEBALLOS MALDONADO, JOSE. Cárdenas: Infancia y juventud. Michoacan: n.p., 1970.

617 CEJA REYES, VICTOR. Yo decapité a Pancho Villa. Mexico: Costa-Amic, 1971.

618 CERVANTES M., FEDERICO. Felipe Angeles en la Revolución: Biografía, 1869-1919. Mexico: Ediciones Botas, 1964.
Biography of Villa's military adviser, general, and colleague.

619 CHAVEZ PERALTA, SAUL. Emiliano Zapata: Crisol de la Revolución Mexicana. Mexico: Ed. Renacimiento, 1972.
Sympathetic study of Zapata, "Crucible of the Mexican Revolution."

620 COVIAN MARTINEZ, VIDAL. Emilio Portes Gil, gobernador delahuertista de Tamaulipas. Cuidad Victoria, Tamaulipas: Ediciones Siglo XX, 1967.

Biographies

Portes Gil, governor of Tamaulipas, 1925–1928;
president of Mexico in 1929.

621 CRUZ, SALVADOR. *Francisco I. Madero: Un hombre, un libro,
un destino.* Mexico: Seminario de Cultura Mexicana, 1965.

622 _____. "Perfiles de Serdán y Madero." *El Libro y el
Pueblo* 6 (1965): 43–45.
   Profiles of Aquiles Serdán (1876–1910) and Francisco
Madero.

623 DUVALIER, ARMANDO. "Belisario Domínguez, héroe antiimperial-
ista." *Instituto de Artes y Ciencias de Chiapas* 10 (1963):
66–68.

624 FERRUA, PIETRO. *Gli anarchici nella rivoluzione messicana:
Práxedis G. Guerrero.* Ragusa: Giugno, La Fiaccola, 1976.
   Study of the ideology and career of Práxedis G.
Guerrero, magonista poet, theoretician, and revolutionary
guerrilla.

625 FLORES TAPIA, OSCAR. *Madero.* Mexico: Cultura y Ciencia
Política, 1971.
   Sympathetic biography of Madero from his birth to his
death. Concludes with confession of Francisco Cárdenas
to the effect that Victoriano Huerta ordered the murder
of Madero.

626 FOIX, PERE. *Pancho Villa.* Mexico: Trillas, 1968.

627 FUENTES AGUIRRE, ARMANDO. *Madero: Caudillo civil de la
Revolución.* Mexico: Biblioteca del Instituto Nacional
de Estudios Históricos de la Revolución Mexicana, 1973.

628 GOMEZ, MARTE R. *Pancho Villa: Un intento de semblanza.*
Mexico: Fondo de Cultura Económica, 1972.
   Biography of Villa by the political revolutionary Gómez.

629 GONZALEZ, PABLO. *Zapata, reaccionario y traidor.* Saltillo,
Coahuila: Textos de Cultura Historiográfica, 1974.
   Didactic and polemical, this work attempts to demonstrate
that Zapata was a traitor and reactionary who was allied
with latifundistas, foreign petroleum companies, and the
White House.

630 GUANDIQUE, JOSE SALVADOR. "Perfiles sobre Caso y Vasconcelos."
Humanitas 15 (1974): 135–90.
   Profiles of idealistic philosophers Antonio Caso and
José Vasconcelos.

631   GUILLEN, FLAVIO. <u>Dos estudios: Francisco I. Madero y Fray</u>
      <u>Matías de Córdova</u>. Mexico: Departamento del Distrito
      Federal, 1975.

632   GUILLEN, PEDRO. <u>Vasconcelos "Apresurado de Dios."</u> Mexico:
      Organización Editorial Novarro, 1975.

633   _____. <u>Belisario Domínguez</u>. Mexico: Secretaría de
      Educación Publica n.d.
          Study about senatorial critic of Huerta who was
      assassinated in 1914.

634   GUISA y AZEVEDO, JESUS. <u>La Revolución y su Luis Cabrera</u>.
      Mexico: Editorial Polis, 1975.

635   _____. <u>Me lo dijo Vasconcelos</u>. Mexico: Editorial Polis,
      1965.

636   GUITERREZ CRESPO, HORACIO. <u>Monroy, el diputado guerrillero</u>.
      Mexico: Textos de Rescate Histórico, 1975.
          Concerning Nestor Enrique Monroy (1879-1913).

637   GUZMAN, MARTIN LUIS. <u>Memoirs of Pancho Villa</u>. Translated
      by Virginia H. Taylor. Austin and London: University of
      Texas Press, 1975.
          One of Mexico's leading writers details a life of
      Francisco Villa to 1915 in autobiographical form. A
      sympathetic insight into the revolutionary leader. Based
      on villista documentary materials and the author's
      recollections of his participation in the movement.

638   HADDOX, JOHN H. <u>Antonio Caso: Philosopher of Mexico</u>.
      Austin and London: University of Texas Press, 1971.
          Biography that spans the life of one of Mexico's
      great teachers and idealist philosophers (1883-1946).

639   _____. <u>Vasconcelos of Mexico: Philosopher and Prophet</u>.
      Austin and London: University of Texas Press, 1967.
          According to the author, "Vasconcelos considered
      himself an inventor, a creator, and not at all a pedantic
      philosopher." Appendixes illustrate his formation and
      thought; bibliography.

640   HEFLEY, JAMES C. <u>Aaron Sáenz: Mexico's Revolutionary</u>
      <u>Capitalist</u>. Waco, Tex.: Word Books, 1970.
          Biography of a sugar industry magnate and supporter of
      Calles and Obregón. He was at one point a candidate for
      the presidency.

641 HERNANDEZ GARCIA, BEATRIZ. Vida y obra de Adolfo Cienfuegos
     y Camus. Mexico: Secretaría de Educación Pública, 1968.
        Life and work of Cienfuegos y Camus, educator,
     revolutionary, and diplomat. Ambassador to Chile and
     Guatemala in the 1930s.

642 JAVIER ARENAS, FRANCISCO. Emiliano Zapata: El intransigente
     de la Revolución. Mexico: B. Costa-Amic, 1975.
        Sympathetic account of Zapata and Mexico's población
     campesina from early times in Anenecuilco to the "crime
     of Chinameca." No notes or index.

643 KARSEN, SONJA P. Jaime Torres Bodet. New York: Twayne
     Publishers, 1971.
        Life and literary activity of the Mexican educator,
     UNESCO director, and public servant.

644 KRAUZE, ENRIQUE. Caudillos culturales en la Revolución
     Mexicana. Mexico: Siglo XXI, 1976.
        A study of the political life and creative passions of
     several "cultural caudillos," including José Vasconcelos,
     Antonio Caso, Palacios Macedo, Narciso Bassols, Daniel
     Cosío Villegas, and Vázquez del Mercado.

645 LANSFORD, WILLIAM DOUGLAS. Pancho Villa: Historia de una
     Revolución. Barcelona: Editorial Argos, 1967.
        Biography of Villa in story form. Through this work
     the author tries to separate the man from the legend that
     surrounds him. The author refers to written documents
     and speeches by Pancho Villa, his friends, and even his
     enemies. A popular account. Translated from English
     version of Pancho Villa (see entry 646).

646 _____. Pancho Villa. Los Angeles, Calif.: Sherbourne
     Press, 1965.

647 LAVRETSKII, IOSIF ROMUAL'DOVICH. Pancho Vil'ia, 1878-1923.
     Moscow: Molodaya Gvardiya, 1962.
        Study of Pancho Villa, 1878-1923, by a Soviet writer.
     A sympathetic biography of Villa, who is portrayed as a
     saint, a social bandit, and as apostle and martyr of the
     Revolution. Includes bibliography.

648 _____. Pancho Villa. Santiago: Quimantú, 1973.

649 _____. Pancho Villa. Translated into Spanish from Russian
     by S. T. de Constantin. Buenos Aires: Editorial Lautaro,
     1965.

650   LEAL, LUIS. <u>Mariano Azuela</u>. New York: Twayne Publishers,
      1971.
      A biography and literary analysis of Mexico's best-
      known novelist and his novels. In addition to the novels
      of the Revolution (<u>Andrés Péres, maderista</u>, 1911; <u>Los
      de abajo</u>, 1915; <u>Los caciques</u>, 1917; <u>Las moscas</u>, 1918),
      Leal studies and examines the later political novels
      and posthumous works.

651   LIST ARZUBIDE, GERMAN. <u>Emiliano Zapata: Exaltación</u>.
      Mexico: B. Costa-Amic, 1969.

652   LLANAS FERNANDEZ, ROBERTO. <u>Antonio I. Villareal</u>. Mexico:
      Secretaría de Educación Pública, 1968.
      Villarreal was one of the principal opponents to the
      Díaz regime on the side of the Flores Magón brothers.
      He was imprisoned for speaking out against the regime
      of the dictator through his articles published in the
      newspaper, <u>Regeneración</u>. Convinced that nothing could
      be done im Mexico, he emigrated to the United States in 1905.
      Accused of conspiracy, he was imprisoned in 1906. When the
      maderista revolution broke out, Villarreal separated from
      the Flores Magón brothers. After the death of Madero
      he united with Carranza. He died in 1914.

653   LOPEZ DIAZ, PEDRO. <u>Madero, hombre y héroe</u>. Mexico: Cámara
      de Diputados, 1969.

654   <u>Luis Cabrera: Semblanzas y opiniones</u>. Mexico: Instituto
      Nacional de Estudios Históricos de la Revolución Mexicana,
      1976.
      A publication in honor of the revolutionary and legal
      theorist Luis Cabrera on the centennial of his birth in
      Zacatlán, Puebla, 17 July 1876. Twenty-five essays by
      various authors on Cabrera as thinker, lawyer, and
      government minister. Appendix: Correspondence and speeches
      of Cabrera.

655   LOPEZ PORTILLO y WEBER, JOSE. "Lázaro Cárdenas, presidente
      civil." <u>Memorias de la Academia Mexicana de la Historia</u>
      25, no. 1 (1966): 5-29.

656   MAGNER, JAMES ALOYSIUS. <u>Men of Mexico</u>. 1942. Reprint.
      Freeport, N.Y.: Books for Libraries Press, 1968.
      Biographies of leading figures from Moctezuma to
      Porfirio Díaz, Venustiano Carranza, Plutarco Elías Calles,
      and Lázaro Cárdenas. Bibliographical footnotes.

657   MANZUR OCAÑA, JUSTO. <u>La Revolución permanente: Vida y obra
      del general Cándido Aguilar</u>. Mexico: Costa-Amic, 1972.

Cándido Aguilar took an active part in the constitutionalist revolution. A follower and son-in-law of Carranza, he was banished from his country in the 1920s.

658 MARTINEZ de la VEGA, FRANCISCO. Heriberto Jara: Un hombre de la Revolución. Mexico: Diálogos, 1964.
Biography of the famous revolutionary general and member of the Congreso Constituyente of 1916-1917.

659 MARTINEZ NUNEZ, EUGENIO. Juan Sarabia: Apóstol y mártir de la Revolución Mexicana. Mexico: Biblioteca del Instituto Nacional de Estudios Históricos de la Revolución Mexicana, 1965.
Biography of PLM leader Juan Sarabia.

660 MEDIZ BOLIO, ANTONIO. Salvador Alvarado. Mexico: Secretaría de Educación Pública, 1968.
Mentions all socially and culturally important works written during the government of General Alvarado, a maderista and carrancista who at one time commanded the Army of the Southeast. Opposed Obregón in 1923; killed in 1924.

661 MEJIA ZUÑIGA, RAUL. Venustiano Carranza en la Revolución constitucionalista. Mexico: Secretaría de Educación Pública, 1964.

662 MENA, MARIO. Zapata. Mexico: Editorial Jus, 1969.
Argues that intellectuals like Antonio Soto y Gama misled Zapata, the Catholic populist chief.

663 MENDIETA ALATORRE, MARIA de los ANGELES. Carmen Serdán. Puebla: Centro de Estudios Históricos de Puebla, 1971.
Attempts to provide authentic biography of revolutionary heroine Carmen Serdán. Places her in a sociopolitical context just before the Revolution. Documented. Includes her letter of 18 November 1910, which resulted from her interview with Ignacio Herrerías.

664 MENENDEZ DIAZ, CONRADO. "La trayectoria política de Felipe Carrillo Puerto." Revista de la Universidad de Yucatán 3 (1961): 42-55.
Biography of Felipe Carrillo Puerto, campesino leader, worker, and revolutionary from Yucatán. Founded the Socialist Party of the Southeast, which worked for women's rights, popular education, and zapatista agrarianism. As governor of the state he was in charge of the delahuertista revolt in his region. Killed in 1924.

665   MEYER, EUGENIA W. de. Luis Cabrera: Teórico y crítica de la
      Revolución. Mexico: SepSetentas, 1972.
            Sixty-page discussion of Cabrera as theorist under
      Carranza and critic under Cárdenas. Remainder of the
      volume consists of carefully selected samplings of major
      writings.

666   MONDRAGON, MAGDALENA. Cuando la Revolución se cortó las
      alas. Mexico: Costa-Amic, 1967.
            A documented biography of General Francisco J.
      Múgica (1884-1954).

667   MORALES JIMENEZ, ALBERTO. Hombres de la Revolución: Cincuenta
      semblanzas biográficas. Mexico: Instituto Nacional de
      Estudios Históricos de la Revolución Mexicana, 1960.
            Fifty biographical sketches of the men of the Revolution.
      Includes bibliography.

668   MURIA, JOSE MARIA. "Jose Vasconcelos y la Revolución
      Mexicana." Boletín Histórico 12 (1974): 238-55.
            Argues that the Mexican historian and philosopher José
      Vasconcelos Calderón, noted particularly for La raza
      cósmica (1925) and Breve historia de México (1940), is
      a controversial figure in Mexico's history. Author notes
      that although Vasconcelos's inconsistent attitudes and
      biased perspective weaken the effectiveness of his writings,
      his thought is typical of that of the first half of the
      twentieth century. Vasconcelos charged the United States
      with attempting to obliterate all traces of Spain's
      influence in Spanish America. Exiled four times by the
      leaders of the Mexican Revolution, all of whom he opposed
      except for Francisco Madero, Vasconcelos criticized
      their rigidity, persecution of the Church, and land
      reform.

669   OLEA, HECTOR R. Vida de Belisario Domínguez. Mexico:
      Cámara de Sandores, 1965.

670   OROZCO, ELENA. Wistano Luis Orozco: Un precursor de la
      Revolución agraria. Mexico: Secretaría de Educación
      Pública, 1968.
            A study of the life and ideas of Wistano Luis Orozco,
      Zacatecas lawyer and thinker who published Legislación
      y jurisprudencia sobre terrenos baldíos. A critic of
      inequity of wealth and the tiendas de raya system,
      Orozco suffered various persecutions, including incar-
      ceration, under the old regime.

Biographies

671 PALACIOS, PORFIRIO. Emiliano Zapata: Datos biográficos-históricos. Mexico: 1960.
     A balanced study of Zapata's career, written in a plain and clear style. Based on important secondary works, interviews with zapatista veterans, and the archives of the Frente Zapatista.

672 PALMER, FREDERICK. John J. Pershing, General of the Armies: A Biography. Westport, Conn.: Greenwood, 1970.

673 PARKINSON, ROGER. Zapata: A Biography. New York: Stein & Day, 1975.
     Popular account, derived from secondary sources, with traditional view of Zapata as the reluctant rebel and skilled military leader who found victory in death.

674 PINEDA, HUGO. José Vasconcelos: Político mexicano, 1928-1929. Mexico: Ediciones Edutex, 1975.
     A study of one of Mexico's greatest twentieth-century philosophers and educators.

675 PORRAS Y LOPEZ; ARMANDO. Luis Cabrera: Revolucionario e intelectual. Mexico: Librería de Manuel Porrúa, 1968.

676 PORTILLA GIL de PARTEARROYO, SANTIAGO. "La personalidad política de Francisco León de la Barra." HM (Oct.-Dec. 1975): 232-70.
     León de la Barra was interim president in 1913.

677 RAUSCH, GEORGE J., Jr. "The Early Career of Victoriano Huerta." Americas 21 (Oct. 1964): 136-45.
     Important, scholarly study.

678 _____. "The Exile and Death of Victoriano Huerta." HAHR 42 (May 1962): 133-51.

679 REYES H., ALFONSO. Cauce 17: Un hombre en el crisol constitucional y progreso revolucionario. Mexico: Editorial del Autor, 1970.
     Deals with Francisco J. Múgica (1884-1954), maderista, constitutionalist, and Cárdenas cabinet member.

680 _____. Emiliano Zapata: El caudillo de la tierra. Mexico: Secretaría de Educación Pública, 1969.

681 RIVAS LOPEZ, ANGEL. El verdadero Pancho Villa. Mexico: B. Costa-Amic, 1970.

682 ROMERO FLORES, JESUS. Don Francisco I. Madero: "Apóstol de la democracia." Mexico: Instituto Nacional de Estudios Históricos de la Revolución Mexicana, 1973.

A biographical summary of Madero. Also includes other
historical figures from the time of the Díaz government.

683   _____ . Lázaro Cárdenas: Biografía de un gran mexicano.
       Mexico: Costa-Amic, 1972.
       A sympathetic study of the life, thought, and activities
       of Lázaro Cárdenas.

684   ROUVEROL, JEAN. Pancho Villa: A biography. Garden City,
       N.Y.: Doubleday, 1972.
       One of many biographies of Villa to appear since a
       1966 resolution of the Mexican Cámara de Diputados that
       officially declared Villa a hero-patriot. A work written
       for a popular audience that will overlook the inadequate
       bibliography and be entertained by revolutionary remin-
       iscences and vivid images.

685   SAENZ ROYO, ARTEMISA. Semblanzas: Mujeres mexicanas,
       revolucionarias y guerreras, revolucionarias ideólogicas.
       Mexico: Año de la Patria, 1960.
       Contains small biographies of important women from the
       time of the Mexican Revolution in 1910.

686   SALAZAR SALAZAR, ANTONIO. Esteban Baca Calderón. Mexico:
       Secretaría de Educación Pública, 1968.
       Calderón began as an elementary school teacher in Tepic
       and Sonora. He later entered the Cananea Consolidated
       Copper Company as a barrel-maker in order to propagate
       the ideas of the newspaper, Regeneración. He took an
       active part in the movement at Cananea, risking years of
       imprisonment. Later he became a diputado of the Constitu-
       yente of 1916-17, a general, and three times a senator.
       He was decorated with the Belisario Domínguez Medal.
       Died in 1957.

687   SANTOS VALDES, JOSE. Madero: Razón de un martirologio.
       Mexico: privately printed, 1968.

688   SAYEG HELU, JORGE. Pastor Rouaix. Mexico: Secretaría de
       Educación Pública, 1968.
       A revolutionary who fought with Madero and Carranza.
       One-time governor of Durango known for passing the first
       agrarian law on 3 October 1913. Published a number of
       works among which is the well-known Diccionario geográfico,
       histórico y biográfico del Estado de Durango.

689   SEDANO PEÑALOZA, MIGUEL ANGEL. Emiliano Zapata. Revolucion-
       arios surianos y memorias de Quintín González. En el 59º
       aniversario de la proclamación del Plan de Ayala (28 de
       noviembre de 1911-29 de 1970). Mexico: Editorial
       Magisterio, 1970.

690 SERRALDE NIETO, HUBERTO. "Silviano Macedonio González
     Sánchez (1884-1967)." Boletín del Instituto de Investig-
     aciones Bibliográficas [UNAM] no. 1 (1969): 117-90.
     Fought in the army of Madero and later in that of
     Carranza.

691 SIERRA, CARLOS J. Zapata: Señor de la tierra, capitán de los
     labriegos. Mexico: Secretaría de Hacienda y Crédito
     Público, 1967.

692 SILVA HERZOG, JESUS. Lázaro Cárdenas: Su pensamiento
     económico, social y político. Mexico: Editorial Nuestro
     Tiempo, 1975.
     A two-part study of the social philosophy of Cárdenas
     from 1913 to 1970. The first section contains excerpts
     from Cárdenas's four-volume Obras, while the second is
     an interpretative commentary on his presidency. The
     author, a prominent Mexican political economist, was a
     member of the team of advisors to the Cárdenas presidency.

693 _____. "La vida y obra de Narciso Bassols." Memoria de
     El Colegio Nacional 5 (1963): 57-70.
     Introduction to the complete works of Narciso Bassols
     (1897-1959). Examines Bassols contributions to Mexican
     life and thought, as Secretary of Public Education (1931-
     1934), as minister to London and Paris, as ambassador to
     the USSR, as founder of the Partido Popular, as champion
     of agrarian reform and author of the agrarian law of 1927,
     and as defender of the rights of Indians.

694 SONNICHSEN, C.L. Colonel Greene and the Copper Skyrocket.
     Tucson: University of Arizona Press, 1974.
     Biography of the Copper King, William Cornell Greene,
     owner of the Cananea Company in Sonora. This was the
     site of the famous strike of June 1906, a major event
     leading to the Revolution.

695 SUAREZ, IGNACIO G. Carranza: Forjador del México actual.
     Mexico: B. Costa-Amic, 1965.
     An uncritical study of Carranza.

696 TARACENA, ALFONSO. Zapata: Fantasía y realidad. Mexico:
     B. Costa-Amic, 1976.
     Third edition of a brief study originally published
     in 1970. An attempt to present diverse opinions on the
     life and work of Zapata. This edition contains an intro-
     ductory chapter critical of John Womack's Zapata and the
     Mexican Revolution. Criticizes Womack for excluding
     fundamental facts and for not being critical with his
     sources.

697   . Francisco I. Madero: Biografía. Mexico:
Editorial Porrúa, 1973.
     Sympathetic and polemical biography of "el Presidente
Mártir," designed to answer all the "counterrevolutionary"
charges of bad faith journalists and Porfirian políticos.
Second edition of a work originally published in 1969.
Uses a multitude of documents to demonstrate that Madero,
the Apostle, did not seek personal success but worked
and died only for the national cause.

698   . Vida de acción y sacrificio de Francisco I.
Madero. Mexico: Manuel Quesada Brandi, 1969.

699   . Venustiano Carranza. Mexico: Editorial Jus,
1963.
     Subjective biography of Carranza.

700 TORRES, ELIAS L. Hazañas y muerte de Francisco Villa.
Mexico: Editorial Epoca, 1975.

701 UROZ, ANTONIO. Los hombres de la Revolución. Mexico:
Talleres de Impr. Arana, 1968.
     Derived from a series of articles published in El
Universal.

702 VALDES, JOSE de la LUZ. El mito de Zapata. Mexico:
Ediciones Espigas, 1974.

703 VILLA, LUIS. Vasconcelos: Pensador y educador mexicano.
Mexico: Centro de Estudios Educativos, 1968.

704 YOUNG, DESMOND. Member for Mexico: A Biography of Weetman
Pearson. London: Cassell, 1966.
     Biography of a Yorkshire contractor and empresario in
Mexico (d. 1927) known for the Grand Canal (29.5 miles
long) that drained Mexico City, the conversion of Veracruz harbor into a modern deep-water port, and the rebuilding
of the railway across the Tehuantepec Isthmus, linking
the Atlantic and the Pacific. Pearson also had a big
stake in Mexican oil and as such he incurred the enmity
of Woodrow Wilson. Analytical index.

705 ZEVADA, RICARDO J. Calles, el presidente. Mexico: Editorial
Nuestro Tiempo, 1971.

For related biographical items see entry 202 and sections VIII, IX,
X, and XI. For revisionist studies of Madero, Villa, Carranza,
Obregón, and Cárdenas see entry 313. For a biographical catalog
of political and social thought of revolutionaries see entry 444.

VIII. Background to Revolution: The Porfiriato

706 ALBRO, WARD S. "El secuestro de Manuel Sarabia." HM 18 (Jan.-Mar. 1969): 400-407.

A study in governmental harassment: the kidnapping of magonista Manuel Sarabia by Mexican officials in Douglas, Arizona, during 1907.

707 ANDERSON, RODNEY D. Outcasts in Their Own Land: Mexican Industrial Workers, 1906-1911. De Kalb:. Northern Illinois University Press, 1976.

Well-researched study of Mexican industrial workers on eve of Revolution. Argues that Spanish anarchists and PLM had little influence on Mexican workers and stresses workers' concern for equality, respect, and dignity. They sought aid from the Díaz government when employers ceased to perform traditional duties of the patrón, and when the government failed them, its legitimacy was lost.

708 _____. "Díaz y la crisis laboral de 1906." HM 19 (April-July 1970): 513-35.

Author argues that there is no evidence to support the contention that Díaz had a broad and well-defined program of action for dealing with labor. In reality, because there was no labor policy, Díaz tended to rely upon the police powers of the state to resolve labor problems.

709 ANKERSON, DUDLEY. Some Aspects of Economic Change and the Origins of the Mexican Revolution, 1876-1910. Working Papers, no. 12. Cambridge: Centre of Latin American Studies, University of Cambridge, 1974.

Argues that it was not the urban maderista clubs, but rather changes in the lot of the agricultural communities which gave strength and momentum to the 1910 Revolution. Emphasis upon Chihuahua and Sonora. Statistics on agricultural populations and "Indian" populations.

143

710 ARAGON, AGUSTIN. Porfirio Díaz: estudio histórico-
filosófico. 2 vols. Mexico: Clásica Selecta, Editorial
Literaria, 1964.
A classic work authored by a Porfirian positivist.

711 ARENAS GUZMAN, DIEGO. Proceso democrático de la Revolución
Mexicana (Antecedentes). Mexico: Biblioteca del Instituto
Nacional de Estudios Históricos de la Revolución Mexicana,
1971.
The antecedents of the Revolution. Finished with the
convention at Tivoli on 15 April 1910.

712 AUB, MAX. Guía de narradores de la Revolución Mexicana.
Mexico: Fondo de Cultura Económica, 1968.
Begins with the year 1890 when the Mexican people first
opposed Porfirio Díaz. Mentions the principal reelection-
ists and the different publications that opposed the
dictatorship.

713 BAZANT, JAN. Cinco haciendas mexicanas: Tres siglos de
vida rural en San Luis Potosí (1600-1910). Mexico:
El Colegio de México, 1975.
A study of five haciendas, including the Hacienda de
Ipiña y Verástegui in the era of Porfirio Díaz. A
respected historian and award-winning author, Bazant analyzes family finances, productivity, and the impact of
the railroads on the hacienda. Contains pictures,
graphics, maps, illustrations, and an appendix of
statistics. Taken together these case studies present the
reader with three centuries of rural life in San Luis
Potosí.

714 _____. "Peones, arrendatarios y aparceros: 1868-1904."
HM 24 (July-Sept. 1974): 94-121.
A study of landless peones and small tenants on the
hacienda of Bocas north of San Luis Potosí. Indicates
that after 1876, peones, who had been relatively better
off before that date, suffered a greater loss in their
level of living from low salaries and high prices than
did tenants.

715 BEEZLEY, WILLIAM H. "Opportunity in Porfirian Mexico."
North Dakota Quarterly 40 (Spring 1972): 30-40.
Shows that beneath the Porfirian patina, Chihuahua's
gentry (especially the Terrazas clan) found enough flexibility within established institutions to contest for
political and economic opportunities.

716   BELLINGERI, MARCO. "L'economia del latifondo in Messico:
       L'hacienda San Antonio Tochatlaco dal 1880 al 1920."
       <u>Annali della Fondazione Luigi Einaudi</u> 10 (1976): 287-428.
          Examines production and labor organization on Mexican
       haciendas and considers the penetration of foreign capital
       in agriculture under Porfirio Díaz, as well as the con-
       sequences of railroad extension into central Mexico. Also
       considers the state of Hidalgo and the hacienda San
       Antonio Tochatlaco, specifying four different periods in
       the rise and the evolution of new internal and external
       contradictions in the traditional system of agricultural
       production. The Mexican Revolution laid the bases for the
       definitive overthrow of this system through land distribu-
       tion. Based on official sources, reviews, and publications;
       27 statistical tables, 3 graphs, bibliography, appendix.

717   BENJAMIN, THOMAS. "International Harvester and the Henequen
       Marketing System in Yucatan, 1898-1915." Inter-American
       <u>Economic Affairs</u> 31 (Winter 1977): 3-19.
          Examination of traditional interpretation that domination
       of henequen market by International Harvester was respon-
       sible for decline in henequen prices in early 1900s. Argues
       that decline was due to movements in world fiber market,
       fluctuations in business cycles, Mexican monetary reforms,
       and decline in U.S. agricultural production and resulting
       drop in demand for henequen.

718   BONFIL BATALLA, GUILLERMO. "Andrés Molina Enríquez y la
       Sociedad Indigenista Mexicana: El indigenismo en vísperas
       de la Revolución." <u>Anales del Instituto Nacional de
       Antropología e Historia</u> 8 (1967): 217-32.
          A study of agrarianism and indigenism.

719   BRYAN, ANTHONY T. "El papel del General Bernardo Reyes en
       la Política nacional y regional de México." <u>Humanitas</u>
       (Nuevo León) 13 (1972): 331-49.
          Case study of state and local government under Por-
       firiato, especially that of Bernardo Reyes. Argues that
       governors were not puppets. Maintenance of local order
       and solution of local problems were crucial to success
       of Porfirian regime nationwide.

720   BULLEJOS S., JOSE. "El pensamiento social de la Revolución
       Mexicana." <u>Cuadernos Americanos</u> 47 (Mar.-Apr. 1961): 43-46.
          Brief examination of the social and ideological ante-
       cedents of the Mexican Revolution.

721   BULNES, FRANCISCO. <u>The Whole Truth About Mexico: The
       Mexican Revolution and President Wilson's Part Therein</u>, as
       Seen by a Científico. Detroit, Michigan: Blaine Ethridge
       Books, 1972.

A reprint of a lengthy, lively polemic written by a close witness of the era. Argues that the old regime was not a reservoir of evil.

722 _____. El verdadero Díaz y la evolución. 1920. Reprint. Mexico: Editora Nacional, 1967.
Reprint of an early classic written by a científico.

723 BUVE, RAYMOND Th. J. "Protesta de obreros y campesinos durante el Porfiriato." Boletín de Estudios Latinoamericanos y del Caribe (Amsterdam) 13 (Dec. 1972): 1-20.
Argues that worker unrest during the late Porfiriato was related to peasant unrest and grew out of resentment against worsening living conditions and the privileged status of foreign workers. European influence and non-worker leadership brought about ideological mobilization.

724 CADENHEAD, IVIE E., Jr. "The American Socialists and the Mexican Revolution of 1910." Southwestern Social Science Quarterly 43 (Sept., 1962): 103-17.
Examines the reactions of the socialist groups in the United States toward events in Mexico during the years 1908 to 1917.

725 CARBO DARNACULLETA, MARGARITA. El magonismo en la Revolución Mexicana. Mexico: UNAM, 1965.
A study of the radical anarchist philosophy of Flores Magón and his followers.

726 CARDERO GARCIA, MARIA ELENA. "Evolución financiera de México: Porfiriato y Revolución." Revista Mexicana de Sociología 38 (Apr.-June 1976): 359-87.
Overview of financial stagnation fostered by Porfirian policy of elitist concentration of capital and dependence upon foreign economic catalysts.

727 CASILLAS, MIKE. "The Cananea Strike of 1906." Southwest Economy and Society 3 (Winter 1977/78): 18-32.
Concludes that although the Cananea strike was a tactical failure, the event had several important consequences: (1) it led to renovation of the Mexican mining laws; (2) it resulted in an Anglo walkout and a decline in the Anglo work force; (3) it led to an increase in Mexican wages; and (4) as an integral part of Mexican and Chicano labor history in the Southwest, disenchanted revolutionaries trained at Cananea later participated in the Clifton-Morenci strike of 1915-16. Based on secondary sources and newspapers.

728 COATSWORTH, JOHN H. El impacto económico de los ferrocarriles en el Porfiriato: Crecimiento y desarrollo. 2 vols. Mexico: SepSetentas, 1976.

Utilizes econometric techniques to measure impact of
railroads upon Porfirian economy. Concludes that railroads
in Mexico sparked greater economic activity in countries
already possessing industrial establishment. Railroads
contributed little to growth, however, because freight
consisted primarily of raw materials for export. Also
notes a correlation between frequency and location of
agrarian protests, land appropriations, and the influence
of new or projected railroad lines. Well-documented.

729 _____. "Anotaciones sobre la producción de alimentos
durante el Porfiriato." HM 26 (Oct.-Dec. 1976): 167-87.
Argues that the living and nutrition standards of
Mexicans did not decline during the dictatorship, as there
is no evidence that the production of traditional food
crops declined. Maize production kept pace with population
growth. Mexicans did not eat better in 1907 than in 1877,
but they ate no worse. Based on statistical sources.

730 _____. "Los orígenes del autoritarismo moderno en México."
Foro Internacional 16 (1975): 205-32.
Examines the origins of modern Mexican authoritarian
government, 1800-1910, in light of models proposed by
Barrington Moore in Social Origins of Dictatorship and
Democracy (Boston: Beacon Press, 1966).

731 COCKCROFT, JAMES D. Precursores intelectuales de la Revolución
Mexicana (1900-1913). Translated by María Eunice Barrales.
Mexico: Siglo XXI, 1971.
This Spanish edition (originally published in English
in 1968) was greeted with some skepticism and controversy
in Mexico, especially in conservative nationalist circles.
Author dedicated the Mexican edition to "los presos
políticos." See entry 732.

732 _____. Intellectual Precursors of the Mexican Revolution,
1900-1913. Austin: University of Texas Press, 1968.
Well-documented, "pioneering" study of the "precursor"
movement in Mexico. Focus is upon the intellectuals of
San Luis Potosí, the ideologues of the PLM (Partido Liberal
Mexicano), and Francisco Madero. Especially good for
studying the ideas of Camilo Arriaga, Juan Sarabia,
Librado Rivera, and Ricardo Flores Magón. Narrative
continues beyond 1910 to discuss the relationship of
magonistas to maderistas and the schisms within maderista
ranks. Appendix includes an English translation of the
PLM manifesto of 1906. Bibliography includes newspaper
sources and rare published memoirs.

733   COLE, GAROLD L.   "The Birth of Modern Mexico, 1867-1911:
       American Travelers' Perceptions." North Dakota Quarterly
       45 (1977): 54-72.
            Examines attitudes expressed by American tourists and
       missionaries upon their visits to Mexico, 1867-1911.
       Examines thought on the predominance of the Catholic Church,
       structured social differences, haciendas, and railroads,
       and modernization attempts by the Mexican government.

734   COSÍO VILLEGAS, DANIEL, ed.   Historia moderna de México.
       9 vols. in 10. Mexico: Editorial Hermes, 1955-72.
            A collaborative work by several researchers and at
       least thirteen authors. A major historiographical achieve-
       ment, this multivolume history provides massive documenta-
       tion of the forty-three years prior to the Revolution of
       1910. For the Porfiriato see: Moisés González Navarro,
       El Porfiriato: La vida social, vol. 4 (1957); D. Cosío
       Villegas, El Porfiriato: La vida política exterior,
       vol. 5 (1960) and vol. 6 (1963), pts. 1 and 2; Luis
       Nicolau d'Olwer et al., El Porfiriato: La vida económica,
       vol. 7 (1965), pts. 1 and 2; D. Cosío Villegas, El
       Porfiriato: La vida política interior, vol. 8 (1970),
       pt. 1, and vol. 9 (1972), pt. 2.

735   COUTURIER, EDITH BOORSTEIN.   "Modernización y tradición en
       una hacienda (San Juan Hueyapan, 1902-1911)." HM 18
       (July-Sept. 1968): 35-55.
            A study in the modernization of a traditional hacienda
       in Zacatecas during the last decade of the Porfiriato.

736   DAVIS, THOMAS.   "Porfirio Díaz in the Opinion of His North
       American Contemporaries." Revista de Historia de América
       63/64 (1967): 79-116.
            Expressions of praise for Díaz collected by a member
       of the Mexican diplomatic staff in 1909. Leading
       educators, politicians, and public figures in the United
       States admired his administration for its domestic peace
       and economic prosperity.

737   GIBBS, WILLIAM E.   "Díaz' Executive Agents and United States
       Foreign Policy." JISWA 20 (May 1978): 165-90.
            Examines the role played by various secret agents of
       Porfirio Díaz in awakening the United States from a semi-
       dormant state with regard to U.S. commercial potential
       in Mexico. Acting as "catalytic agents," these Mexican
       commercial agents gave direction and intensity to political
       and economic factors which led to the decision to extend
       diplomatic recognition to Díaz in 1876.

738 GOLDFRANK, WALTER L. "Inequality and Revolution in Rural
Mexico." Social and Economic Studies 25 (1976): 397-410.
Describes social and economic conditions in three
different areas in late-nineteenth-century Mexico.
Inequality and oppression do not necessarily produce revolt,
and the opportunity to revolt occurs less often than
conditions that might lead to revolt.

739 _____. "World System, State Structure, and the Onset of
the Mexican Revolution." Politics and Society 5 (1975):
417-39.
Applies a macro-approach to an analysis of the regime
of Porfirio Díaz (1830-1915) and the coming of the Revolution, 1876-1910. The development of foreign investments,
class conflicts that were fostered by the regime's dependency upon foreign investment, and the resulting state of
internal politics produced a climate of internal affairs
that made the Mexican state susceptible to changes in the
world system that occurred prior to World War I and were
largely beyond the control of the Díaz regime. Secondary
sources.

740 GOMEZ MONTERO, SERGIO. "Ricardo Flores Magón y la palabra
política." Solidaridad 36 (1970): 33-34.
Flores Magón, precursor.

741 COMEZ-QUIÑONES, JUAN. Las ideas políticas de Ricardo Flores
Magón. Mexico: Serie Popular Era, 1977.
Intellectual history and biography of Ricardo Flores
Magón. Spanish version of Sembradores. See entry 743.

742 _____. "Piedras contra la luna, México en Aztlán y Aztlán
en México: Chicano-Mexican Relations and the Mexican
Consulates, 1900-1920." In Contemporary Mexico: Papers
of the Fourth International Congress of Mexican History,
edited by James W. Wilkie, Michael C. Meyer, and Edna
Monzón de Wilkie, pp. 494-527. Los Angeles and Mexico:
University of California Press and El Colegio de México,
1976.
A study of the thirty-one consulates in the United
States between 1900 and 1920, in which it is noted that
the Mexican consuls were usually more interested in
promoting commerce and performing intelligence tasks than
in protecting the Chicano community from discrimination
and exploitation. Bibliography.

743 _____. Sembradores: Ricardo Flores Magón y el Partido
Liberal Mexicano, A Eulogy and Critique. Los Angeles:
Aztlan Publications, 1973.

Intellectual history and biography of Ricardo Flores
Magón, leader of the PLM. Documents and bibliography.

744 GONZALEZ NAVARRO, MOISES. Las huelgas textiles en el
     Porfiriato. Puebla: Editorial José M. Cajica, 1970.
        Reprint in book form of periodical articles about strikes
     in the textile industry during the Porfiriato.

745 GUY, ALAIN. "Le bergsonisme en Amérique latine." Cahiers
     du monde Hispanique et Luso-Brésilien (University of
     Toulouse, France) 1 (1963): 121-39.
        Argues that Bergsonism was introduced to Mexico with the
     formation of the Ateneo de la Juventud, founded in 1909.
     Antonio Caso and José Vasconcelos as well as others were
     members of this group who dedicated themselves to this
     philosophy. Caso was mainly responsible for introducing
     Bergsonism to Mexico and destroying positivism. The
     Spanish philosophers Joaquín Nirau and Eduardo Nicol,
     and others, are also mentioned.

746 HAMON, JAMES L., and NIBLO, STEPHEN R. Precursores de la
     Revolución agraria en México: Las obras de Wistano Luis
     Orozco y Andrés Molina Enríquez. Mexico: SepSetentas, 1975.
        A study of the ideas of agrarianism and social conflict
     in two of the more important precursors of the revolution
     in the countryside: Wistano Luis Orozco and Andrés Molina
     Enríquez. Also includes sketches of the agrarian views of
     Francisco Madero, Toribio Esquivel Obregón, Alberto García
     Granados, Oscar Braniff, Lauro Viadas, Pastor Rouaix,
     Gustavo Durán, Rómulo Escobar, and Luis Cabrera. A com-
     pendium of agrarian thought.

747 HART, JOHN MASON. Los anarquistas mexicanos, 1860-1900.
     Mexico: SepSetentas, 1974.
        An intellectual history of anarchism in Mexico from
     1860 to 1900. Early chapters treat of the European
     background, the organization of the first campesino and
     labor groups, and the initial efforts of Plotino Rhoda-
     kanaty and others. Details the limits of anarchist success
     during the late nineteenth century and argues for a con-
     tinuity and similarity between the doctrines of Chávez
     López and Zapata. Well researched; based on Mexican
     archival sources, private and public, and newspapers.

748 _____. "Nineteenth-Century Urban Labor Precursors of
     the Mexican Revolution: The Development of an Ideology."
     Americas 30 (Jan. 1974): 297-318.
        Mexican anarchist movement of 1860s and 1870s. Maintains
     that anarchist followers of Plotino C. Rhodakanaty made
     significant contributions to the ideology of the Revolution
     of 1910, especially the Casa del Obrero Mundial.

749 _____. "Agrarian Precursors of the Mexican Revolution:
The Development of an Ideology." Americas 29 (Oct. 1972):
131-50.
Beginning with an agrarian uprising in 1849, and con-
tinuing through the utopian socialist peasant revolts of
the 1860s, agrarian agitation led to the development of
an agrarianist ideology that found its expression in the
Ley del Pueblo of Alberto Santa Fe during the Porfiriato.
All of this was background to the Revolution of 1910.

750 HENDRICKS, WILLIAM. The Flores Magón Brothers and the
Mexican Revolution. Los Angeles: University of Southern
California, 1964.

751 HERNANDEZ, SALOME. "Innocence or Guilt? Mexico's Arrest of
the Yaquis, 1099-1909." Journal of the West 14 (1975):
15-26.
Supplies the historical background of the inharmonious
relationship between the Yaquis of Sonora and the Mexican
government; synopsizes the anti-Yaqui policy and actions
of the Mexican government, 1533-1909.

752 HERNANDEZ MOLINA, MOISES. Los partidos políticos en México,
1892-1913. Puebla, Mex.: José M. Cajica, 1971.
A comprehensive study of the underlying social, economic,
political, and legal causes of the Revolution, beginning
with the last decade of the nineteenth century with the
themes of foreign capital and popular class exploitation
by the bourgeoisie. Appendix includes reproductions of
documents, manifestos, proclamations, and plans of
government. A large number of notes and bibliographical
references aid the text.

753 HERNANDEZ R., ROSAURA. "Las campañas de Porfirio Díaz en el
estado de Guerrero." Estudios de Historia Moderna y Contemporánea de México 2 (1967): 147-56.
The Guerrero campaigns of Porfirio Díaz.

754 ITURRIBARRIA, JORGE FERNANDO. "La versión de Limantour."
HM 16 (Jan.-Mar. 1967): 382-418.
Critically examines José Ives Limantour's account of
his public career as Secretary of Treasury under Porfirio
Díaz.

755 KATZ, FRIEDRICH, ed. La servidumbre agraria en México en la
época profiriana. Mexico: SepSetentas, 1976.
A selection of essays on the life and condition of
work of peones and arrendatarios on haciendas during the
Porfiriato, an era when the hacienda reached its maximum
extension under the influence of internal and external

capitalistic penetration. Several issues are dealt with in this volume: the extent of indebted peonage, the influence of the colonial past as well as the capitalist nineteenth century on the economy of the hacienda, and the pros and cons of capitalist influences. Katz authored the introduction and submitted one of his own essays on "Condiciones de trabajo en las haciendas de México durante el porfiriato."

756 _____. "Labor Conditions on Haciendas in Porfirian Mexico: Some Trends and Tendencies." HAHR 54 (Feb. 1974): 1-47.
A comprehensive assessment of laboring conditions in Mexican haciendas from 1876 to 1910. Concludes that the acasillado (the resident, indentured hacienda worker) was relatively better off than peons and far better off than the wretched laborers of Yucatán and the Valle Nacional, Oaxaca.

757 _____. "Plantagenwirtschaft und Sklaverei: Der Sisalanbau auf der Halbinsel Yucatán bis 1910." Zeitschrift für Geschichtswissenschaft 7: 1002-27.
A study of sisal plantations and slavery in Yucatán peninsula until 1910.

758 KELLEY, JAMES R. "The Education and Training of Porfirian Officers: Success or Failure?" Military Affairs 39 (1975): 124-28.
Examines the military education and training of Mexican army officers during the dictatorship of Porfirio Díaz (1830-1915). The vital core of the Porfirian officer corps achieved a high degree of professionalism on the eve of the revolution against Díaz. The shortcomings of the Federal Army resulted from a competent bulk of officers sandwiched between a thin layer of nonprofessionals at the top and a thick layer of conscripted illiterate and dispirited troops at the bottom. Primary and secondary sources.

759 KITCHENS, JOHN W. "Some Considerations on the Rurales of Porfirian Mexico." Journal of Latin American Studies 9 (1967): 441-55.

760 KNOWLTON, ROBERT J. Church Property and the Mexican Reform: 1856-1910. De Kalb: Northern Illinois Press, 1976.
Detailed study of the disamortization and nationalization of ecclesiastical property between 1856 and 1910. Bibliography and index.

761 LANGLE RAMIREZ, ARTURO. "Porfirio Díaz y la agitación popular." Estudios de Historia Moderna y Contemporánea de México 2 (1967): 157-66.

762 LAVROV, NIKOLAI M. "Padenie diktatury Porfirio Diasa."
     Latinskaja Amerika (Moscow) 3 (1972): 104-21.
         A study of the fall of Porfirio Díaz based on Mexican
     Foreign Relations documents, newspaper sources in Mexico
     and the United States, the Serdán archive in Puebla,
     printed documents, and secondary works like Michael
     Meyer's Orozco and Cosío Villegas's El Norte de Porfirio
     Díaz.

763 LEAL, JUAN FELIPE. "El estado y el bloque, 1867-1914."
     Latin American Perspectives 2 (Summer 1975): 34-47.
         Uses the notion of a "hegemonic power bloc" as a tool
     for understanding the role of the State. Argues that after
     1857 the Mexican State played the role of the State of a
     capitalist society. After 1880 democratic freedoms were
     restricted as capitalism became predominant by the turn
     of the century. At this time the State also became a semi-
     colonial state dominated primarily by the United States.
     This predominance of capitalism was brought about largely
     by the intrusion of the imperialist faction of the bour-
     geoisie, with local bourgeoisie and landowners losing
     hegemony to the foreigner. Between 1908-1914 one witnessed
     the disintegration of the traditional power bloc and the
     destruction of the liberal state began in 1867.

764 _____. "Las clases sociales en México: 1880-1910." Revista
     Mexicana de Ciencia Política 17 (July-Sept. 1971): 45-57.
         A neo-Marxist social and class analysis of the Porfiriato,
     dividing Mexico's society into la burguesía, la clase media,
     la pequeña burguesía, el proletariado industrial, los
     terratenientes (rural workers, managers, farmers, and
     rancheros), and el campesinado. Concludes that three
     significant developments occurred during the Porfiriato:
     1) the emergence of an industrial bourgeoisie (and an
     industrial proletariat; 2) a deterioration in the relative
     power of the terrateniente; and 3) the establishment of
     foreign enclaves (and increased dependency).

765 LOPEZ PORTILLO y ROJAS, JOSE. Evaluación y caída de Porfirio
     Díaz. 1921. Reprint. Mexico: Editorial Porrúa, 1975.
         Prologue written by Atenedoro Monroy.

766 LOPEZ PORTILLO y WEBER, JOSE. "Primera decada del petróleo
     en la última del Porfiriato." Memorias de la Academia
     Mexicana de la Historia 28 (1969): 410-31.
         Describes the political and social conditions during
     the last decade of the Díaz government.

767 LUNA, JESUS. La carrera pública de Don Ramón Corral.
     Translated by Antonietta S. de Hope. Mexico: SepSetentas,
     1975.

Documented study of Ramon Corral's public careers.

768   MARTINEZ NUNEZ, EUGENIO. Historia de la Revolución Mexicana:
       Los Mártires de San Juan de Ulóa. Mexico: Talleres
       Gráficos de la Nación, 1968.
       A study of the "martyrs" who suffered imprisonment at
       San Juan de Ulúa during the Porfiriato.

769   MEYER, JEAN A. Problemas campesinos y revueltas agrarias
       (1821-1910). Mexico: SepSetentas, 1973.
       Well-documented reconstruction of the history of crisis
       of the nation's countryside from 1821 to 1910.

770   MEYERS, WILLIAM K. "Politics, Vested Rights, and Economic
       Growth in Porfirian Mexico: The Company Tlahualilo in
       the Comarca Lagunera, 1885-1911." HAHR 57 (Aug. 1977):
       425-54.
       In 1888 Compañía Agrícola del Tlahualilo was granted a
       concession by the Government of Porfirio Díaz to develop
       Laguna area of northern Mexico for cotton. Disputes with
       local planters over water rights and takeover of the
       company by British and American investors in 1903
       illustrate Díaz's problem in trying to encourage investment
       while favoring national interests.

771   MONJARAS-RUIZ, JESUS. Los primeros días de la Revolución:
       Testimonios periodísticos alemanes. Mexico: SepSetentas,
       1975.
       From information published in the German newspaper
       Kölnische Zeitung, three subjects are developed: the
       fiesta of the Centennial in 1910; the events between
       November 1910 at the beginning of the Madero revolt
       and the fall of Díaz in May 1911; and images of Mexico
       during this period presented to German readers.

772   PASQUEL, LEONARDO. El conflicto obrero de Río Blanco en 1907.
       Mexico: Editorial Citlaltépetl, 1976.
       Short treatment of Río Blanco textile strike of 1907
       drawn from published primary and secondary sources.

773   PEÑA SAMANIEGO, HERIBERTO. Río Blanco: El Gran Círculo de
       Obreros Libres y los sucesos del 7 de enero de 1907.
       Mexico: Centro de Estudios Históricos del Movimiento
       Obrero Mexicano, 1975.
       The Río Blanco textile industry strike of 1907.

774   PESCHARD, JACQUELINE. "La dinastía revolucionaria: Person-
       ificación de la autoridad monárquico-republicana." Estudios
       Políticos 3 (1978): 123-37.

Disputes the traditional interpretation that post-revolutionary Mexican governments represent an abrupt break with the regime of Porfirio Díaz; in fact, they are its heirs. The Díaz regime imposed federal political authority throughout Mexico through a network of personal bonds connecting the dictator with regional caudillos. Although governing by extraconstitutional means, Díaz scrupulously respected constitutional norms. His only major political failure was his inability to provide for the peaceful and orderly transition of power. After the fall of Díaz, the Constitution of 1917 established centralized government which permitted participation of new social forces in national politics. The paramount problem of post-1917 regimes was to convert personal bonds uniting its leaders into institutional means of transferring and exercising power. This was done through the creation of a single political party, uniting all political factions in support of the revolutionary leadership. Secondary sources.

775 POHL, HANS von, and MERTENS, HANS-GUNTHER. "Die Entwicklung der Mexikanischen Landwirtschaft während des Porfiriats." Ibero-Amerikanisches Archiv (Berlin)1 (1975): 61-103.
A description of the development of Mexican agriculture (production, capital formation, land concentrations, and social problems) during the Porfiriato. During the first years of the Porfiriato external and negative influences were eliminated, i.e., disintegration of local markets, insufficient infrastructure, political instability, and the predominance of a subsistence economy. This resulted in the expansion of primary materials for the internal markets such as sugar cane, cotton, cocoa, and tobacco, and an increase in export items such as fibers, coffee, and vanilla. Modernization of agriculture was limited to the production of primary materials for industry and the external market. All of this resulted in the concentration of land in the hands of a few latifundistas who were disinterested in the low level of living of the masses. Modernization also created a proletarianization of the country person. Thus progress in agriculture created social tensions which became the underlying causes of the Mexican Revolution.

776 PRIDA, RAMON. Los sucesos de Río Blanco en 1907. Mexico: Editorial Citlaltépetl, 1970.
Río Blanco strike in the textile industry of Veracruz, 1907. Prologue written by Leonardo Pasquel.

777 RAAT, WILLIAM DIRK. "The Antipositivist Movement in Pre-revolutionary Mexico, 1892-1911." JISWA 19 (Feb. 1977): 83-98.

Thesis: By the 1890's the antipositivists in Mexico had significantly altered the nature of their critique of Mexican society. No longer fearful of the dangers to Catholic theology and the morality of youth, the antipositivists had become more concerned about the problems developing out of the urbanization and industrialization of Mexico; social problems like drunkenness, prostitution; and such dangerous ideologies as anarchism and socialism. Demonstrates liberal, Reyista, labor, and clerical expressions of antipositivism in the anti-Científico politics of the late Porfiriato.

778 _____. "The Diplomacy of Suppression: Los revoltosos, Mexico, and the United States, 1906-1911." HAHR 56 (Nov. 1976): 529-50.
Indicates that the Roosevelt and Taft administrations cooperated with Díaz in operating an extensive police and espionage network on both sides of the border. Official and semiofficial pursuit and harassment was effective against floresmagonistas and other "amateur" revolutionaries in the United States; less so against maderistas who had a compact, well-financed, "professional" operation. Based on U.S. and Mexican archival sources.

779 _____. El positivismo durante el Porfiriato: 1876-1910. Mexico: SepSetentas, 1975.
Revisionist analysis of intellectual currents of the Porfiriato. Distinguishes between Comtean positivism, Darwinism, and "scientism." Argues that Comtean positivism was limited to education, while "scientism" was the attitude and belief system of the Científicos and others.

780 _____. "Ideas and Society in Don Porfirio's Mexico." Americas 30 (July 1973): 32-53.
A survey of the variety of ideas, and the relationship of ideas to socioeconomic groups that existed during the Porfiriato. Author differentiates ideas, concepts, and philosophies, including ideologies of protest, Indianism, liberal indigenism, anticlericalism, antipositivism, reforming Darwinism, scientism, positivism, Krausism, Spencerianism, orthodox positivism, and utilitarianism.

781 _____. "Los intelectuales, el positivismo y la cuestión indígena." HM 20 (Jan.-Mar. 1971): 412-27.
Studying the ideas of "key" Científicos, the author argues that, while they shared the conservative views of other twentieth-century elites of the day concerning the Indian, they were not simple racists. This is also true for orthodox positivists like Agustín Aragón. In other words, the simplistic traditional view of equating

Científico thinking with positivism and positivism with racism must be revised.

782 _____. "Agustín Aragón and Mexico's Religion of Humanity." JISWA 11 (July 1969): 441-57.
A study of secular religion and orthodox positivism in Díaz's Mexico.

783 READ, JOHN LLOYD. The Mexican Historical Novel, 1826-1910. 1939. Reprint. New York: Russell and Russell, 1973.
Detailed and comprehensive account. All quoted Spanish texts are given literal translation in footnotes.

784 RODRIGUEZ EGUIA, JOSE. El desarrollo capitalista y la Revolución de 1910. Puebla: UAP, 1975.
The development of capitalism during the Porfiriato as an underlying cause of revolution.

785 ROEDER, RALPH. Hacia el México moderno: Porfirio Díaz. Mexico: Fondo de Cultura Económica, 1972.
A well-documented description of social conditions that gave rise to the dictator Díaz.

786 ROMERO CERVANTES, ARTURO. "Algunas consideraciones sobre el magonismo, sus discrepancias y sus consecuencias." Boletín Bibliográfico de la Secretaria de Hacienda y Crédito Público 417 (1969): 9-11.
The author considers that one of the causes of the failure of magonismo was violation of PLM correspondence on the part of the American and Mexican authorities. Reproduces two letters found in the Archivo General de la Nación.

787 ROSENZWEIG HERNANDEZ, FERNANDO. "Las exportaciones mexicanas de 1877 a 1911." IIM 9 (Jan.-Mar. 1966): 394-413.
A study of Mexican exports from 1877 to 1911. Reveals the way in which international economic fluctuations affected an underdeveloped economy.

788 SALOMON, NOEL. "Féodalisme et capitalisme au Mexique de 1856 à 1910." Amérique latine 32 (July-Aug. 1962): 180-96.
Marxist analysis of the transition from feudalism to capitalism under the Reform and the Porfiriato.

789 SANDELS, ROBERT. "Silvestre Terrazas and the Old Regime in Chihuahua." Americas 28 (1971): 191-205.
Studies the family of Silvestre Terrazas. Special attention is given to Enrique Creel, Terrazas's son-in-law who was at one time ambassador to Mexico in the United States.

790 SERNA MATYORENA, M.A. "Santa: México, Federico Gamboa y
la realidad histórica del Porfiriato." Cuadernos Americanos
182 (May-June 1972): 168-83.
Presents a study from the point of view of novelist
Gamboa of the respective social evils that afflicted the
province and the capital. Analysis emphasizes the identity
of the heroine Santa with the city of Mexico as revealed
in Gamboa's 1903 novel Santa.

791 SILVA HERZOG, JESUS. "Lo positivo y lo negativo en el
porfirismo." Cuadernos Americanos 170 (May-June 1970):
124-41.
A summary of the government of Porfirio Díaz. Reprint.
See entry 792.

792 _____. "Lo positivo y lo negativo en el porfirismo."
Memoria del Colegio Nacional 6 (1967/68): 23-41.
Considers the positive and negative effects on Mexico
of the policies of the presidency of Porfirio Díaz (1830-
1915). There was progress but no social justice for the
proletariat. Porfirismo encouraged foreign investment,
especially in mining and railway construction. As part
of Díaz's land policy, cattle ranches were established
in the north and large grain-producing haciendas in
central Mexico. The author provides comparative statistics,
1877-1910, and focuses attention on foreign investment,
the land question, laborers' wages, and the myth of peace
under the regime. Primary and secondary sources.

793 SIMS, HAROLD D. "Espejo de caciques: Los Terrazas de
Chihuahua." HM 18 (Jan.-Mar. 1969): 379-99.
A study in regional power demonstrating how local
cacique interests, in this instance the Terrazas family
of Chihuahua, maintained their wealth and power during
the Porfiriato. Supplemented with an analysis of the
economic interests of Enrique C. Creel, Terrazas's son-
in-law, who engineered reconciliation between Terrazas
and Díaz in 1903.

794 SMITH, CORNELIUS C. Emilio Kosterlitzky: Eagle of Sonora
and the Southwest Border. Glendale, Calif.: Arthur
H. Clark Co., 1970.
A study of the "fighting Tartar" who exercised the
"mailed fist" of Díaz along the Sonoran border. Full-length
biography; includes photographs of the Cananea revolt of
1906.

795 SONNICHSEN, C.L. "Colonel William C. Greene and the Strike at
Cananea, Sonora, 1906." Arizona and the West 13 (1971):
343-68.

Arizona promoter William Cornell Greene (1851-1911) built
the operations of the Cananea Consolidated Copper Company
into a multi-million-dollar business. On 1 June 1906,
a walkout paralyzed the entire mining camp. The strike was
over by June 4, but not before an invasion of Arizona
Rangers and Bisbee miners made the incident an international
affair. Mexican historians consider the Cananea affair
to be an important beginning of the Revolution of 1910.

796 _____. "Col. W.C. Greene and the Cobre Grande Copper
Company." Journal of Arizona History 12 (1971): 73-100.
A study in business history--the founding of the Cobre
Crande Copper Company by George Mitchell and William
Greene in 1899.

797 THEISEN, GERALD. "La mexicanización de la industria en la
época de Porfirio Díaz." Foro Internacional 12 (Apr.-June
1972): 497-506.
Argues that Mexico's economy was near "take off point"
on eve of Revolution. Manufacturing was attracting more
Mexican capital than foreign; Díaz government was promoting
this trend as well as curtailing foreign, especially
American, capital; and a group of modernizing nationalist
leaders, such as Limantour and his associates, was emerging.

798 TISCHENDORF, ALFRED. Great Britain and Mexico in the Era of
Porfirio Díaz. Durham, N.C.: Duke University Press, 1961.
A history of commercial investments in Mexico, 1878-
1910. Contents. the renewal of diplomatic relations;
British enterprise during the diplomatic imbroglio; rails,
rivalries, and pools, 1885-1910; the mining story, 1885-
1910; a disastrous adventure in real estate and rubber;
some British investments in the later Díaz period (utilities,
factories, and petroleum); the loss of British commercial
preeminence; the balance sheet. Appendix: brief financial
statements on companies concerned. Selected bibliography
and analytical index.

799 TOWNER, MARGARET. "Monopoly Capitalism and Women's Work
During the Porfiriato." Latin American Perspectives 4
(1977): 90-105.
Concentrates on Mexican industrialization between 1880
and 1900 and the profound changes in the relationship of
women to productive work brought about by that process.
Women were brought into the system of productive labor
as they were needed by emergent capitalism in Mexico and
this had an impact on women's consciousness and political
activity. The author analyzes the crisis of 1907 on the
employment of women, forcing them out of the active labor
force to form a reserve army of unemployed to be drawn
upon only when needed.

800   TURNER, JOHN KENNETH. <u>Barbarous Mexico</u>. 2d ed. 1910.
      Reprint. Introduction by Sinclair Snow. Austin: Univer-
      sity of Texas Press, 1969.
          The classic critique of the Porfiriato by "muckraker"
      John Kenneth Turner.

801   VALADES, JOSE C. <u>Breve historia del porfirismo, 1876-1911</u>.
      Mexico: Editores Mexicanos Unidos, 1971.
          The author previously published two other volumes dealing
      with the same period of history: <u>El nacimiento y esplendor</u>
      <u>del porfirismo</u>. Like his earlier works, this is an attempt
      to bring some semblance of balance to an interpretation
      of the period.

802   VANDERWOOD, PAUL J. "Mexico's Rurales: Reputation Versus
      Reality." <u>Americas</u> 34 (July 1977): 102-12.
          Demythologizing of don Porfirio's rural police force;
      e.g., Rurales were seldom accomplished horsemen and were
      often inept in "getting their man."

803   _____. "Responses to Revolt: The Counter-Guerrilla
      Strategy of Porfirio Díaz." HAHR 56 (Nov. 1976): 551-79.
          Military history of Madero revolt in North discussed
      in context of guerrilla warfare theory. Díaz understood
      well enough the strategy and tactics of counterinsurgency
      warfare but lacked the necessary and expensive resources
      that successful counterinsurgency tactics require. He was
      also hindered by a thirty-year history of accumulated
      grievances against his regime which hurt him on the
      political front.

804   _____. "Los rurales: Producto de una necesidad social."
      HM 22 (July-Sept. 1972): 34-51.
          Contrary to revolutionary propaganda and rhetoric, the
      Rurales was a reputable institution widely admired by
      contemporaries. Individual members were sometimes guilty
      of excesses and abuses, but the force never knowingly
      recruited from among criminal elements, was rarely as
      strong as supposed, helped pacify some outlying areas,
      was most effective in Mexico City, and was held indispensable
      for keeping order at festivals and during holidays.
      Francisco Madero's expansion of the Rurales contributed to
      his downfall, and the organization played an important
      role in the Revolution until General Venustiano Carranza
      dismantled it. Primary and secondary sources.

805   _____. "Genesis of the Rurales: Mexico's Early Struggle
      for Public Security." 50 (May 1970): 325-44.
          Deals with the services provided by the Rurales from
      their beginning in 1861 to the end of the Díaz regime.

806   VELASCO VALDES, MIGUEL. La prerevolución y el hombre de
       la calle. Mexico: Costa-Amic, 1964.

807   WASSERMAN, MARK. "Foreign Investment in Mexico, 1876-1910:
       A Case Study of the Role of Regional Elites." Americas
       36 (July 1979): 3-21.
           An examination of native elite relations with foreign
       entrepreneurs at the regional level using the example of
       the Terrazas in Chihuahua. Concludes that the influx
       of foreign investment helped to perpetuate ruling groups
       who were able to take advantage of the opportunities
       it provided. Based on Mexican newspapers and consular
       reports and despatches.

808   WOLF, ERIC R., and HANSEN, EDWARD C. "Caudillo Politics:
       A Structural Analysis." Comparative Studies in Society
       and History 9 (1967): 168-79.
           Study of Porfirio Díaz when he began his slogan,
       "order and progress."

809   YEAGER, GENE. "Porfirian Commercial Propaganda: Mexico in
       the World Industrial Expositions." Americas 34 (Oct. 1977):
       230-43.
           Thesis: During the era of Porfirio Díaz (1876-1910),
       Mexico was the Latin American country most committed to
       active participation in international industrial and
       commercial exhibits and expositions. This effort was
       undertaken for its propaganda value at home and abroad
       as well as its direct contribution to attracting trade
       and investment. The latter effect is impossible to measure
       precisely, but there are indications that Mexico's exposi-
       tion policy did produce results. Based on official reports
       and other published sources.

810   ZAYAS ENRIQUEZ, RAFAEL de. Apuntes confidenciales al presi-
       dente Porfirio Díaz. 1906. Reprint. Mexico: Editorial
       Citlaltépetl, 1967.
           Recent edition of Zayas Enríquez's confidential report
       on the sources of disorder in Mexico. The study was
       originally commissioned by Díaz in 1906.

811   ZEA, LEOPOLDO. Positivism in Mexico. Austin: University of
       Texas Press, 1974.
           A translation of El positivismo en México, which was
       originally published in 1943 (and, along with Apogeo y
       decadencia del positivismo en México, again in 1968).
       Traces the transformation of Positivism from a post-1867
       doctrine of idealistic liberals to that of a defense of
       neocolonial dependency by the bourgeoisie of the Porfiriato.
       This translated version contains a new preface in which

Zea responds to three of his North American critics:
Harold E. Davis, Charles A. Hale, and William D. Raat.

812   ZONN, LEO E.   "The Railroads of Sonora and Sinaloa, Mexico:
      A Historical Survey." Social Science Journal 15 (1978):
      1-16.
         Analyzes the interrelation between economic and noneco-
      nomic factors contributing to the development of railroad
      systems in Sonora and Sinaloa, Mexico, 1877-1920.

For a research review of the Porfiriato see entry 54; for the Díaz
archive see entry 109. For historiography of the Porfiriato see
entries 187, 226, 228, 231, 236-38, and 247. For a general political
history see vol. 3 of the work listed under entry 409. For a comparative study of nineteenth-century economic growth see entry 342. For
regional studies see entries 476, 500-501, and 506.

   For biographical studies of Díaz see entries 599 and 613. Other
biographical studies include those for Weetman Pearson (entry 704),
Colonel Greene (entry 694), Bernardo Reyes (entry 593), and Winstano
Luis Orozco (entry 670). For autobiography and documents of
Limantour see entries 567 and 514 respectively. Magonista biographies
include R. Flores Magón, entry 598; L. Rivera, entry 586; J. Sarabia,
entry 659; Guerrero, entry 624; and A. Villarreal, entry 652. For
magonista documents see entries 509-10, 517-23, and 538-39.

   For Porfiriato travel literature see entries 557 and 559. For an
anthology of the Porfiriato see entry 559. For Náhuatl memoirs of
the late Porfiriato see entries 564-66. For German influence in
Díaz's Mexico see entry 955. For anarchism, 1860-1931, see entry
1008. For Andrés Molina Enríquez and agrarianism see entry 1023.
For the primary schoolteacher as "precursor" see entry 1048. And
for printmaking during the Porfiriato see entries 1066 and 1073.

IX. The Epic Revolution, 1910-1920

POLITICAL, LEGAL, AND MILITARY HISTORY

813   AGUIRRE BENAVIDES, LUIS. Las grandes batallas de la División
      del Norte al mundo del general Francisco Villa. Mexico:
      Editorial Diana, 1960.
         Military history of Villa's Division of the North; the
      great battles.

814   _____. De Francisco I. Madero a Francisco Villa: Memorias
      de un revolucionario. Mexico: A. del Bosque, Impresor,
      1966.
         The author, one-time a private secretary for Gustavo
      A. Madero and Francisco Villa, begins his story with
      the first contact that he had with the Madero family
      in 1903. Finishes with the assassination of his brother,
      Eugenio, in June of 1915. Work includes a prologue by
      Martín Luis Guzmán.

815   AMAYA C., LUIS FERNANDO. La Soberana Convención Revolucionaria,
      1914-1916. Mexico: Editorial F. Trillas, 1966.
         Monograph of the Soberana Convención Revolucionaria,
      which, in spite of its failure to unify the factions in
      conflict, did succeed in structuring the Programa de
      Reformas Político-Sociales de la Revolución which was the
      basis of the Constitution of 1917.

816   ARELLANO GARCIA, CARLOS: "Cincuenta años de la Constitución
      de 1917." Lecturas Jurídicas (Universidad Facultad de
      Derecho, Chihuahua) 30 (1967): 27-36.
         Commentary on the major principles of the Constitution
      of 1971 and their application to the present.

817   ARENAS GUZMAN, DIEGO. El régimen del general Huerta en
      proyección histórica. Mexico: Biblioteca del Instituto
      Nacional de Estudios Históricos de la Revolución Mexicana,
      1971.

Political, Legal, and Military History

History and life of Victoriano Huerta (1854-1916).

818 _____. La Revolución Mexicana: Eslabones de un tiempo
histórico. Mexico: Fondo de Cultura Económica, 1969.
Covers the years 1903-1917.

819 ATKIN, RONALD. Revolution! Mexico 1910-20. London:
Macmillan & Co., 1969.
A compendium of social, political, military, and diplo-
matic history from Díaz to Carranza. Illustrations and maps.

820 BASSOLS BATALLA, NARCISO. "Zapata maderista." Solidaridad
49 (1971): 23-27.
Argues that Zapata wanted an understanding with Madero
and aspired to become part of a great historical cause;
he did not want to be merely an opportunist in a turbulent
era.

821 BECK, BARBARA, and KURNITZKY, HORST. Zapata: Bilder aus der
Mexikanischen Revolution. Berlin: Wagenbach, 1975.
A short narrative history of Zapata's movement, primarily
derived from John Womack's work, followed by a collection
of documents and interviews with participants. Chronology,
glossary, and brief bibliography.

822 BEER, GABRIELLA de. "Los cien años de Luis Cabrera: Actualidad
de su pensamiento revolucionario." Cuadernos Americanos
209 (Nov.-Dec. 1976): 80-91.
Homage to Cabrera on centennial of his birth. Discusses
his political thought beginning with his criticism of the
Científicos in 1909 and emphasizing his theories on the
Mexican Revolution.

823 BEEZLEY, WILLIAM H. "Madero: The 'Unknown' President and
His Political Failure to Organize Rural Mexico." In Essays
on the Mexican Revolution: Revisionist Views of the
Leaders, edited by George Wolfskill and Douglas W. Richmond,
pp. 1-24. Austin and London: University of Texas Press,
1979.
An examination of the Madero phase of the Revolution.
Argues that Madero was unknown in the rural villages of
Mexico for lack of an adequate message and program.
Outside of the actions of a few state governors, a program
of rural regeneration was absent during the period of the
Madero government. Madero failed to develop both formal
and informal contacts on the regional level, and thus
failed in the villages. Based on printed works and
Coahuila archives.

Political, Legal, and Military History

824 BENSON, NETTIE LEE. "La carta de triunfo de Huerta."
     Extremos de México (1971): 89-106.
     Argues that Huerta tried to protect the sovereignty
     of Mexico.

825 BRANDT, NANCY. "Pancho Villa: The Making of a Modern
     Legend." Americas 23 (July 1966): 146-62.
     A well-documented work which analyzes the legend of
     Pancho Villa.

826 BUSTILLO BERNAL, ANGEL. La Revolución Mexicana en el Istmo de
     Tehuantepec y realidades en las muertes del C. Gral. don
     Jesús Carranza, su hijo y sobrino, y del C. Lic. D. José
     F. Gómez ("Che Gómez"), caudillo juchiteco. Mexico:
     Editora Mexicana de Periódicos, Libros y Revistas, 1968.
     Revolution in the isthmus of Tehuantepec and the murder
     of Jesús Carranza, brother of Venustiano.

827 CALDERON, JOSE MARIA. Genesis del presidencialismo en
     México. Mexico: Ediciones "El Caballito," 1972.
     Studies the nineteenth-century and early revolutionary
     antecedents to the Constitution of 1917, and "constitutional
     dictatorship" or presidencialismo. Analyzes Artículos 27
     and 123. Concludes that the constitutional power of the
     executive office developed intimately from and with the
     historical development in Mexico of "national dependency
     capitalism." Bibliography.

828 CALZADIAZ BARRERA, ALBERTO. Hechos reales de la Revolución:
     El fin de la División del Norte. Mexico: Editorial
     Patria, 1972.
     Narrates the events of the Revolution from the last
     months of 1915 to the first few months of 1916; that is,
     to the defeat of Villa's Division of the North.

829 _____. Por que Villa atacó Columbus (intriga inter-
     nacional). Mexico: Editores Mexicanos Unidos, 1972.
     An anti-United States account of the international
     intrigue of the Wilson administration, which was the
     underlying context for Villa's raid on Columbus. Anti-
     semitic interpretation of Columbus raid; also adheres to
     Germany conspiracy theory.

830 COUTINO MUÑOZ, EZEQUIEL. Revolución Mexicana: La lucha
     armada 1913-1914. Mexico: Talleres Gráficos de la
     Nación, 1968.
     The armed struggle, 1913-1914.

Political, Legal, and Military History

831   CUMBERLAND, CHARLES CURTIS. La Revolución Mexicana: Los
       anos constitucionalistas. Mexico: Fondo de Cultura
       Económica, 1975.
          Introduction by David C. Bailey. Translation into
       Spanish by Héctor Aguilar Camín. See entry 832.

832   _____. Mexican Revolution: The Constitutionalist Years.
       Austin and London: University of Texas Press, 1972.
          A sequel to his study of the Madero years, this is the
       last research work by Cumberland before his death (the
       manuscript was completed by David C. Bailey, who wrote
       the introduction and the epilogue and added material on
       Zapata to the text). A vital reference work for the
       political, military, and diplomatic history of the
       constitutionalist movement (1913-1920).

833   _____. Mexican Revolution: Genesis under Madero.
       2d ed. 1952. New York: Greenwood Press, 1969.
          Cumberland's classic study of Francisco Madero (1873-
       1913). Bibliography.

834   _____. La Revolución Mexicana. Buenos Aires: Siglo
       Veinte, 1968.
          Spanish version of entry 833.

835   DAVLIN, THOMAS R. Days of Discord: A Brief Chronology of
       the Mexican Revolution, 1910-1920. El Paso: American
       Print Co., 1974.

836   DEEDS, SUSAN M. "José María Maytorena and the Mexican
       Revolution in Sonora." Arizona and the West 18 (Spring/
       Summer 1976): 21-40, 125-248.
          A well-documented study of the political career of José
       María Maytorena, revolutionary governor and Maderista
       in Sonora between 1910 and 1915. Maytorena is portrayed
       as a political liberal of the Madero stripe whose political
       ineptitude was no match for his formidable adversaries,
       Alvaro Obregón and Plutarco Elías Calles.

837   DIAZ de LEON, MIGUEL ROMAN. Algunos constituyentes notables
       de 1917. Mexico: Secretaría de Educación Pública, 1966.
          Gives summarized biographies of the following constit-
       uents and mentions their proceedings in the Congress of
       1917: Luis Manuel Rojas, Heriberto Jara, Pastor Rouaix,
       Carlos L. Garcidas, and Francisco J. Mújica.

Political, Legal, and Military History

838 FALCON VEGA, ROMANA. "¿Los orígenes populares de la Revolu-
     ción de 1910? El caso de San Luis Potosí." HM 29 (Oct.-
     Dec. 1979): 197-240.
     A regional study of the popular dimensions of the
     maderista revolt of 1910 in the province of San Luis
     Potosí.

839 FERNANDEZ de CASTRO y FINCK, JORGE. Madero y la democracia:
     Estudio sobre la doctrina de la superación. Mexico:
     Secretaría de Educación Pública, 1966.
     A work selected by the Secretary of Public Education
     to celebrate the fiftieth anniversary of the Mexican
     Revolution. The work defends Madero from all the attacks
     that have been made on him.

840 FERRER de MENDIOLEA, GABRIEL. Presencia de Don Francisco
     I. Madero y un apendice documental. 2 vols. Mexico:
     Departamento del Distrito Federal, Secretaría de Obras
     y Servicios, 1973.

841 FIGUEROA URIZA, ARTURO. Ciudadanos en armas: Antecedencia
     y datos para la historia de la Revolución Mexicana. 2 vols.
     Mexico: B. Costa-Amic, 1960.
     Sympathetic account of the Figueroas, revolutionary
     leaders in Guerrero during the initial decade of the Revolu-
     tion. Author relies primarily on Andrés Figueroa's
     memoirs as well as Figueroa family papers.

842 GARCIA, RUBEN. "Don Venustiano, el gobernador de hierro."
     Boletín Bibliográfico 198 (28 Nov. 1960): 1, 4.
     Study of Carranza's governorship in Coahuila at the
     time of the Huerta coup.

843 GARZA, CIRO R. de la. "Madero y Huerta: La trágica decena
     de febrero de 1913." Humanities 8 (1967): 479-95.
     Study of the huertista coup and overthrow of Madero.

844 GERLACH, ALLEN. "Conditions Along the Border 1915: The Plan
     of San Diego." NMHR 43 (1968): 195-212.
     A study of the 1915 secessionist movement in southern
     Texas and the relationship of the Plan of San Diego to
     huertista and orozcista invasion schemes of Mexico.

845 GILDERHOUS, MARK T. "Carranza and the Decision to Revolt,
     1913: A Problem in Historical Interpretation." Americas
     33 (Oct. 1976): 298-310.

Political, Legal, and Military History

An attempt to resolve conflicting interpretations of Carranza's political motives. Rejects extreme view that Carranza was a political opportunist in favor of an interpretation in which Carranza was a moderate committed to liberalism but "not prepared to sacrifice himself needlessly on the altar of high principle."

846   GONZALEZ, PABLO. El centinela fiel del constitucionalismo. Saltillo, Coahuila: Textos de Cultura Historiográfica, 1971.
       A sympathetic account of the revolutionary career of Pablo González, commander of the carrancista Division of the Northeast, by his son. Includes over 400 facsimiles of historical documents and photographs. Pro-González account which argues, among other things, that Zapata was a hopeless reactionary; that González deserves to be ranked as a precursor along with Flores Magón; that Obregón was allied with reactionary científico groups; that González, not Obregón, should be given the credit for the defeat of Villa; and that González made the Constitution of 1917 possible.

847   GONZALEZ RAMIREZ, MANUEL. "La muerte del general Zapata y la práctica de las emboscadas." Estudios de Historia Moderna y Contemporánea de México 2 (1967): 211-47.
       The ambush and death of General Zapata.

848   GRIEB, KENNETH J. "The Causes of the Carranza Rebellion: A Reinterpretation." Americas 15 (July 1968): 25-32.
       Argues that Carranza's rebellion against Huerta was motivated by a desire for political power, not revolutionary idealism or an honorable attempt to avenge the assassination of Huerta.

849   GUZMAN, MARTIN LUIS. Muertes históricas. Vol. 1, Tránsito sereno de Porfirio Díaz; Ineluctable fin de Venustiano Carranza. 2d ed. Mexico: Compañía General de Ediciones, 1969.
       First edition appeared in 1958.

850   _____. Febrero de 1913. Mexico: Empresas Editorialies, 1963.
       Narrative of Huerta's overthrow of Madero.

851   HALL, LINDA B. "The Mexican Revolution and the Crisis of Naco: 1914-1915." Journal of the West 16 (1977): 65-89.

Political, Legal, and Military History

There was much fighting between the villista and the maytorena forces for the control of Naco, Sonora. Citizens of Naco, Arizona, were outraged over the effects of this fighting on the U.S. side of the border. Several Americans were killed by stray bullets and there was much property damage. President Wilson tried to avoid intervention. José María Maytorena and the villistas were finally driven from Sonora by Alvaro Obregón in 1915.

852 HARRER, HANS-JURGEN. Die Revolution in Mexiko 1910 bis 1917. Koln: Pahl-Rugenstein, 1973.
      A history of the 1910-1917 period, based mostly on printed documents and secondary sources.

853 HOUSTON, DONALD E. "The Oklahoma National Guard on the Mexican Border, 1916." Chronicles of Oklahoma 53 (1975-76): 447-62.
      Contents: On 18 June 1916, President Woodrow Wilson ordered the entire National Guard to the Mexican border while General John Pershing pursued Pancho Villa deep inside Mexico. Oklahoma responded with enthusiasm as civic leaders and veterans offered their services. Oklahoma units served in south Texas and underwent training exercises, but saw only limited action against bandits. Withdrawn from border duty only a short time before U.S. entry into World War I, the guardsmen had gained valuable experience which would aid them on the battlefields of Europe. Primary sources; 3 photos, map.

854 KATZ, FRIEDRICH. "Villa: Reform Governor of Chihuahua." In Essays on the Mexican Revolution: Revisionist Views of the Leaders, edited by George Wolfskill and Douglas W. Richmond, pp. 26-45. Austin and London: University of Texas Press, 1979.
      A revisionist characterization of Villa's rule in Chihuahua, 1913-1915. Suggests that Villa was neither a single-minded bandit, nor the single-minded agrarian reformer other historians have called him. He did manage to gain popular support among the poorer and middle classes and to confiscate the properties of the very wealthy in order to keep his Division of the North in the field. Villa was a complete mixture of social bandit, peasant leader, traditional caudillo, charismatic spokesman for the poor, and a manager and administrator. This study is part of a larger biographical enterprise.

Political, Legal, and Military History

855 KNUDSON, JERRY W. "When Did Francisco I. Madero Decide on
     Revolution?" Americas 30 (Apr. 1974): 529-34.
         Reprint in its entirety of Madero's letter to William
     Randolph Hearst, 25 April 1911.

856 LANGLE RAMIREZ, ARTURO. "El significado de la toma de
     Zacatecas." Estudios de Historia Moderna y Contemporánea
     de México 1 (1965): 125-34.
         Divided into three sections: "The Battle of Zacatecas
     in Accordance with Military Science;" "The Historical
     Significance;" and "The Involvement of the División
     del Norte."

857 LAVROV, NIKOLAI M. Meksikanskaia revoliutsiia, 1910-1917.
     Moscow: Nauka, 1972.
         Well-researched study of 1910-1917 period by an
     experienced Soviet historian. Extensive use of Mexican
     archival resources and sophisticated Marxist analysis.
     Especially good for anarchosyndicalism and rural villista
     and zapatista movements.

858 LIST ARZUBIDE, GERMAN. Madero: El México de 1910, Homenaje
     a los 100 anos de su nacimiento. Mexico: Sociedad
     Mexicana de Geografía y Estadística, 1973.
         Brief descriptions of the main events of the Mexican
     Revolution. Included are twenty-four articles by
     different authors concerning episodes of that era. These
     articles deal with the strikes of Cananea, Río Blanco,
     General Ramón Corona, Camilio Arriaga, Germán List
     Arzubide, Ramón Puente, etc.

859 McNELLY, JOHN H. "Origins of the Zapata Revolt in Morelos."
     HAHR 46 (May 1966): 153-69.
         Relates events beginning 1909 and ending in 1911.
     Zapata presented as the supreme example of an agrarian
     reformer.

860 MASON, J. ALDEN. "La quincena furiosa: Diario de la batalla
     de la cuidad de México, fabrero de 1913." Ciencias
     Políticas y Sociales [UNAM] 9, no. 32 (1963): 223-55.
         Diary of events during the "Decena Trágica," which took
     place in Mexico City in February of 1913.

861 MELO de REMES, MARIA LUISA. ¡Alerta, Baja California!
     Mexico: Editorial Jus, 1964.
         Narrative history based upon interviews with survivors
     of events in 1911 in Baja California. Unfriendly to
     magonista activities there.

Political, Legal, and Military History

862   MENA BRITO, BERNARDINO. Ocho diálogos con Carranza. 2d ed.
      Mexico: Editores Mexicanos Unidos, 1964.
      Eight conversations with Carranza. First ed. 1933.

863   MENDIETA y NUÑEZ, LUCIO. El sistema agrario constitucional:
      Explicación e interpretación del artículo 27 de la consti-
      tución política de los Estados Unidos Mexicanos en sus
      preceptos agrarios. 2d ed. Mexico: Editorial Porrúa,
      1975.
      First ed. 1932.

864   MEYER, EUGENIA W. de, et al. La vida con Villa en la
      Hacienda de Canutillo. Mexico: Instituto Nacional de
      Antropología e Historia, 1974.
      This study of Villa was developed through the Programa
      de Historia Oral.

865   MEYER, JEAN A. "Grandes compañías, ejércitos populares y
      el ejército estatal en la Revolución Mexicana (1910-1930)."
      Anuario de Estudios Americanos 31 (1974): 1005-30.
      Contents: The regular Mexican army of 1910 resembled
      that of the nineteenth century with enforced enlistment,
      archaic maneuvers, and widespread graft. Its real purpose
      was domestic control. With the outbreak of the revolution,
      this organization disintegrated; and with victory for
      the revolution assured, civilian soldiers of the people's
      armies disbanded while professional soldiers continued
      their service. Today, as under Díaz, the army guards the
      civilian populace. Its volunteers indicate reluctance
      to enter the service, and officers continue to find irreg-
      ular profits.

866   MEYER, MICHAEL C. Huerta: A Political Portrait. Lincoln:
      University of Nebraska Press, 1972.
      First scholarly study of Victoriano Huerta and his
      regime based on archival research, especially the National
      Defense Archive. It covers Huerta's entire career but
      emphasizes the period of his presidency, February 1913
      to July 1914. Combines descriptive narrative with inter-
      pretation to study Mexico's public policy. Revisionist
      conclusions concerning the regime, suggesting that
      Huerta's regime was not counterrevolutionary. This
      reassessment of Huerta overcomes two obstacles: (1) the
      lack of a personal archive of Huerta's correspondence;
      (2) the emotional traditional picture of Huerta as
      a counterrevolutionary monster. Confirms that there is
      little evidence for Huerta's direct complicity in Madero's

Political, Legal, and Military History

assassination and that Huerta's administration was easily
as reformist as that of earlier "revolutionary" regimes.

867 _____. "The Militarization of Mexico, 1913-1914."
Americas 27 (Jan. 1971): 293-306.
Argues that the system of recruiting soldiers from
among citizens was a method that had been enforced since
the Colonial period but never more so than in the summer
of 1913. Huerta went further to increase war production,
mobilize troops, transform Mexico City police into
regiments, introduce forced conscription, and increase
the budget of the armed forces. Militarization would
continue after Huerta with Carranza pursuing the same
policies.

868 _____. Mexican Rebel: Pascual Orozco and the Mexican
Revolution, 1910-1915. Lincoln: University of Nebraska
Press, 1967.
Biography of the revolutionary Orozco and the course of
the revolution in Chihuahua. Based on documentary
material, including the records of the Mexican Ministry
of Foreign Relations and the Archivo Histórico de la
Defensa Nacional.

869 MORENO, DANIEL. "Nuestra tradición jurídica: El programa
del partido liberal y la constitución de 1917." Revista
de la Facultad de Derecho de México 25 (1975): 273-76.
Discusses the influence of the Liberal Party program
of 1906 and especially the influence of Ricardo Flores
Magón on the Mexican Constitution of 1917.

870 MROZIEWICZ, ROBERT. Rewolucja meksykańska 1910-1917:
Zarys historii politycznej. Warsaw: Państwowe
Wydawnictwo Naukowe, 1973.
An outline political history of the Mexican Revolution,
1910-1917. This book is the first in Polish literature
to make an attempt at explaining the causes and presenting
the course of events and their results in Mexico in the
second decade of the twentieth century. Focus is primarily
upon the Revolution as a striving to restructure Mexican
agriculture or as agrarian reform. Argues that the
Porfirian State was founded on two incompatible pillars:
capitalism as a superstructure capping the age-old
feudalistic hacienda system. Capitalism in conflict with
feudalism was the prime cause of the revolution. Concludes
with an epilogue on the Revolution from 1917 through
Cárdenas. Based on printed documents (debates, legislación,
decretos) and secondary works.

Political, Legal, and Military History

871 MUNOZ y PEREZ, DANIEL. "El general Torres en la decena
     trágica." Memoria de la Academia Nacional de Historia
     y Geografía 2, no. 184 (1961): 39-43.
       Role of Torres during huertista coup of 1913.

872 NAYLOR, THOMAS H. "Massacre at San Pedro de la Cueva: The
     Significance of Pancho Villa's Disastrous Sonora Campaign."
     Western Historical Quarterly 8 (Apr. 1977): 125-50.
       A study of Villa and his Division of the North during
     the Sonoran invasion of October 1915-January 1916.
     Defeated by Woodrow Wilson and Calles at Agua Prieta,
     Villa's troops marched through Hermosillo to San Pedro
     de la Cueva. There Villa personally directed and carried
     out an unjust slaughter of nearly eighty noncombatants.
     The Sonora campaign, a reflection of Villa's defeats and
     weakened condition, marked his end as a viable national
     revolutionary leader—several months before the infamous
     Columbus, New Mexico, raid. Based on primary materials,
     including the Cananea Company papers. The 1976 Herbert
     E. Bolton Award winner for the best essay in Spanish
     Borderlands history.

873 NIEMEYER, E.V., Jr. Revolution at Queretaro: The Mexican
     Constitutional Convention of 1916-1917. Austin:
     University of Texas Press, 1974.
       Not a systematic analysis of the Convention of 1916-
     1917 or a definitive biographic study of delegates. Rather,
     an attempt to relate the unfolding of ideas expressed
     during the debates, especially the humanitarian concern
     of the delegates, their idiosyncrasies, attitudes, and
     individual contributions. Attempts to show how the
     ideals of the Revolution were written into fundamental
     law. Focuses on anticlericalism (Articles 3, 5, and 130),
     labor reform (Article 123), property rights (Article 27),
     municipal reform, prohibition, women's suffrage, and the
     abolition of the death penalty.

874 OLIVERA de BONFIL, ALICIA, and MEYER, EUGENIA [W. de].
     Jesús Sotelo Inclán y sus conceptos sobre el movimiento
     Zapatista. Mexico: Instituto Nacional de Antropología
     e Historia, 1970.
       Pamphlet; the result of an oral history project that
     included this interview with Jesús Sotelo Inclán, the
     biographer of Zapata who first published his work on
     Zapata in 1934.

875 OROSA DIAZ, JAIME. Madero y la revolución mexicana. Mérida:
     Universidad de Yucatán, 1969.

Political, Legal, and Military History

876   OWEN, ROGER C. "Indians and Revolution: The 1911 Invasion
       of Baja California, Mexico." Ethnohistory 10 (1963):
       373-95.
          Concludes that from the Indian standpoint, magonismo
       was a matter of Indian fighting Indian, eventually causing
       the collapse of the Baja insurgency. Based on interviews
       with surviving Indians.

877   PASQUEL, LEONARDO. Manuel y José Azueta, padre e hijo:
       Héroes en la gesta de 1914. Mexico: Editorial Citlal-
       tépetl, 1967.

878   PASTOR y CARRETO, LUIS G. La Revolución los Serdán, el
       protomártir y la historia: Ensayo histórico crítico
       sociológico. Mexico: Editorial Casa Poblana, n.d.

879   PENA, RODOLFO F. "Zapata: El mito contra la historia."
       Solidaridad 3 (1960): 29-31.
          Mythical versus historical views of zapatismo.

880   PENICHE VALLADO, LEOPOLDO. "El idealismo pragmático de
       Salvador Alvarado." Cuadernos Americanos 213 (July-
       Aug. 1977): 47-66.
          Analysis of Alvarado's term as Governor of Yucatán
       between 1915-18.

881   PETIT, ARTHUR. "Emiliano Zapata's Revolt Against the
       Mexican Government, 1908-1911." Historian 31 (1969):
       233-50.
          Investigations made among the survivors of the Zapata
       movement to discover the means by which this caudillo
       moved. Also studies the break between Madero and
       Zapata.

882   PORRAS OROPEZA, PEDRO. Eslabones de la Revolución: Los
       Figueroa en el sur, en el centro y en el norte del país;
       Breves apuntes de mi contribución en la lucha armada
       durante los años de 1910 a 1920. Mexico: 1971.
          Tells of the deeds of the Figueroa brothers. Ambrosio,
       the most well-known of them, was shot by a firing squad
       at the orders of Huerta.

883   QUIRARTE, MARTIN. "Ensayos de interpretación sobre Madero."
       Revista de la Universidad de México 28 (1973): 11-14.
          A review essay of Imaginación y realidad de Francisco
       I. Madero, by José C. Valadés. See entry 912.

Political, Legal, and Military History

884   QUIRK, ROBERT E. The Mexican Revolution, 1914-1915: The
       Convention of Aguascalientes. Bloomington: Indiana
       University Press, 1960.
          Origin, development, program and collapse of the
       revolutionary Convention of Aguascalientes, 1914-1915.
       Based upon documentary sources, including the papers of
       Convention leader Roque González Garza.

885   _____. "La Convención en Cuernavaca." HM 9 (Apr.-June
       1960): 571-81.
          The history of the Convention from its removal from
       Mexico City to Cuernavaca in late January 1915, to its
       return to Mexico City in mid-March.

886   RAMIREZ REYES, MANUEL. "La vigencia de Juárez en la
       Constitución de 1917." Voces sobre Juárez (1972): 9-20.
          According to the author the thoughts of Juárez are found
       in Articles 3, 5, 13, 24, and 130 of the Constitution.

887   RICHMOND, DOUGLAS W. "Carranza: The Authoritarian Populist
       as Nationalist President." In Essays on the Mexican
       Revolution: Revisionist Views of the Leaders, edited by
       George Wolfskill and Douglas W. Richmond, pp. 47-80.
       Austin and London: University of Texas Press, 1979.
          A revisionist synthesis of the Carranza years of the
       Revolution. Assesses the nationalistic ideology and social
       programs of the Carranza era--labor policy, agrarian
       reform, economic nationalism, progressive taxation, and
       the doctrine of nonintervention--and concludes that
       Carranza was more of an "authoritarian populist" than
       a political moderate. It was his violation of the populist
       political process which led to his violent end. Based
       on Carranza telegrams and newspapers.

888   ROJAS, BASILIO. La Soberana Convención de Aguascalientes.
       Mexico: n.p., 1961.
          Aguascalientes convention of 1913-1914.

889   ROMAN, RICHARD. "Political Democracy and the Mexican Con-
       stitutionalists: A Re-Examination." Americas 34 (July
       1977): 81-89.
          Examines the debates of the Mexican Constitutional
       Congress of 1916-1917 on the four issues of suffrage,
       literary requirements to serve as a Deputy, directness of
       electing officials, and no re-election. Concludes that
       the Constitutionalist delegates were not radical democrats,
       but rather elitists fearful of mass participation in
       government.

Political, Legal, and Military History

890   _____. Ideología y clase en la Revolución Mexicana: La
       Convención y el Congreso Constituyente. Mexico: Sep-
       Setentas, 1976.
          A study of the ideas expressed in the Constitutional
       Congress of 1916-1917, in which the content of the
       Revolution was defined. Based on analysis of various
       debates on social, economic, and political questions.

891   ROMERO FLORES, JESUS. Anales históricos de la Revolución
       Mexicana. Mexico: Libro Mex, 1960.
          Narrative history from Porfiriato to Constitution of
       1917 and first revolutionary governments.

892   ROSS, STANLEY R. Francisco I. Madero: Apostle of Mexican
       Democracy. New York: AMS Press, 1970.
          One of the more scholarly biographies of Madero.
       Reprint of the 1955 edition.

893   RUDENKO, BORIS T. "Ricardo Flores Magón y la corriente
       democrática revolucionaria en la Revolución mexicana de
       los años 1910-1917." América Latina (Academy of Sciences
       of the USSR) 1 (1975): 99-121.
          Soviet interpretation of Ricardo Flores Magón as
       undergoing transformation after 1910 from a petty
       bourgeois reformer to a democratic revolutionary who lost
       out to the bourgeois liberal revolution led by Madero.

894   RUIZ, RAMON EDUARDO. The Great Rebellion: Mexico 1905-1925.
       New York: W.W. Norton Co., 1980.

895   _____. Mexican Revolution 1910-1923. San Diego:
       University of California, 1972.
          Narrative history; documented.

896   SALDANA, JOSE P. "Madero y su época." Humánitas 16 (1975):
       393-417.
          Discusses the life and epoch of Francisco Madero (1873-
       1913), emphasizing his politics and travels in the early
       twentieth century and his influence on the course of the
       Mexican Revolution, resulting in his election to the
       presidency of Mexico in 1911.

897   SANCHEZ LAMEGO, MIGUEL A. Historia militar de la Revolución
       Mexicana en la época maderista. Mexico: Instituto Nacional
       de Estudios Históricos de la Revolución Mexicana, 1976.
          A military history of the Maderista revolution. Although
       all geographical regions of the country are represented,
       emphasis (two-thirds of the book) is upon the Revolution

Political, Legal, and Military History

in the North, especially Chihuahua. Based on primary
materials in expedientes in the Archivo Histórico de la
Secretaría de Defensa Nacional. First volume of a projected
multivolume study. Notes; no index.

898   SILVA HERZOG, JESUS. "Las ideas económicas, sociales y
       políticas de Salvador Alvarado." Cuadernos Americanos
       213 (July-Aug. 1977): 67-82.
            Discussion of Alvarado's actions as Governor of Yucatán
       between 1915-18, especially agrarian reform, Indian policy,
       and treatment of women.

899   _____. Breve historia de la Revolución Mexicana. 2 vols.
       Vol. 1, Los antecedentes y la etapa maderista, vol. 2, La
       etapa constitucionalista y la lucha de facciones. Mexico:
       Fondo de Cultura Económica, 1972.
            Seventh edition since originally published in 1966 of
       a classic in the literature of the Mexican Revolution by
       one of Mexico's best-known economists, sociologists, and
       historians. Volume one is a social history of the Revolu-
       tion from the Porfiriato through Madero; volume two covers
       Huerta, the Plan of Ayala, Carranza, and the Constitution
       of 1917.

900   _____. "La constitución mexicana de 1917." Cuadernos
       Americanos 151 (Mar.-Apr. 1967): 178-91.
            Refutes the contention that the constitution of 1917
       was the work of the national bourgeoisie. Argues that
       the Revolution between 1910 and 1917 was antibourgeois,
       popular, agrarian, and nationalist. Peasants, workers,
       professionals, and the military at Querétaro modified
       Articles 27 and 123 to oppose bourgeois values.

901   _____. "Un esbozo de la Revolución Mexicana (1910-1917)."
       Cuadernos Americanos 113 (Nov.-Dec. 1960): 135-64.
            Analysis of the Revolution, 1910-1917, based on the
       assumption that the Porfirian peon was in a feudal
       condition not unlike the serfs of twelfth-century Europe.

902   SMITH, PETER H. "La política dentro de la Revolución: El
       Congreso Constituyente de 1916-1917." HM 3 (Jan.-Mar.
       1973): 363-95.
            Study of the social origin of the diputados. Through
       quantitative analysis Smith discusses the social origins
       of the delegates to the Congress, the issues, and the
       relationship of social origin to areas of conflict.

Political, Legal, and Military History

903   SOTELO INCLAN, JESUS. Raíz y razón de Zapata. 2d ed. Mexico:
Fondo de Cultura Económica, 1970.
Zapata and the village of Anenecuilco. Includes biblio-
graphical references, illustrations, and maps.

904   SUAREZ GAONA, ENRIQUE. "La legitimación del poder en México:
Madero y Carranza ante el poder revolucionario." In
Extremos de México, pp. 481-500. Mexico: El Colegio de
México, 1971.
According to this description, neither Madero nor
Carranza were the presidents who legitimized their power
through the historical phenomena of the Mexican Revolution.
Instead, the movements of Zapata and Villa are described
as those that clearly legitimized the Revolution.

905   TARACENA, ALFONSO. Madero, víctima del imperialismo yanqui.
Mexico: privately printed, 1973.
Polemical study written by a well-known maderista
apologist in order to show that Madero was a victim of
Yankee imperialism.

906   _____. ...Y a hierro murieron: La forma trágica como
terminaron los asesinos de Madero y Pino Suárez.
Mexico: Botas, 1972.

907   TORRES, ELIAS L. Vida y hechos de Francisco Villa. Mexico:
Editorial Epoca, 1975.

908   _____. Twenty Episodes in the Life of Pancho Villa.
Translated by Sheila M. Ohlendorf. Austin: Encino Press,
1973.
Torres, who played a minor role in the Revolution,
published his vignettes of Villa eight years after Villa's
assassination in 1923. These episodes, translated here
for the first time, span the period between 1913-1920,
with three of them referring to the controversial murder
of British subject William Benton.

909   ULLOA ORTIZ, BERTA. "Días trágicos." Dialogos 48 (1972):
33-36.
Deals with the overthrow of Madero and the rise of
Huerta.

910   URQUIZO, FRANCISCO L. Carranza: El hombre, el político,
el caudillo, el patriota. Mexico: Secretaría de
Gobernación, 1970.
Official history and eulogy of Carranza.

The Epic Revolution, 1910-1920

Political, Legal, and Military History

911   VALADES, JOSE C. "La pureza constitucional de Madero."
       Revista de la Universidad de México 28 (1973): 7-10.
          Study based on the postulates put forth by Madero:
       "Effective suffrage" and "No reelection."

912   _____. Imaginación y realidad de Francisco I. Madero.
       2 vols. Mexico: Antigua Librería Robredo, 1960.
          Analyzing the appearance and reality of Madero, the
       author makes extensive use of manuscript materials and
       provides considerable new material on Madero's family
       antecedents. Considered one of the better Mexican
       biographies of the initiator of the Mexican Revolution.
       For review, see entry 883.

913   VALERO SILVA, JOSE. "La Decena Trágica." Estudios de Historia
       Moderna y Contemporánea de México 3 (1970): 89-116.
          Argues that Huerta was lucky in that he was in charge
       of making a counterrevolution by attacking Zapata and
       Pascual Orozco with federal troops. Exposes the plan
       that Huerta had in order to seize power. This plan
       included the compromise with the rebels of the Ciudadela.

914   _____. "Al pueblo Mexicano (15 de abril de 1919)."
       Estudios de Historia Moderna y Contemporánea de México
       3 (1970): 117-33.
          Contains the opinions of Zapata's armed forces concerning
       his death.

915   _____. "Relación de los hechos que dieron por resultado
       la muerte de Emiliano Zapata, jefe de la rebelión del
       sur." Estudios de Historia Moderna y Contemporánea de
       México 2 (1967): 197-210.

916   VELA GONZALEZ, FRANCISCO. Diario de la Revolución: Año de
       1913. Monterrey, Nuevo León: El Patronato Universitario
       de Nuevo León, 1971.
          A detailed chronology of the Revolution during 1913,
       with a day-by-day "diary-like" account from 10 February
       1913 to December 31. Written in honor of the author's
       father, Lázaro Vela Hinojosa, a constitutionalist soldier,
       who died at the battle of Monterrey on 23 October 1913.
       Traditional account with emphasis upon the positive virtues
       of Madero and Carranza. Appendixes: PLM Program; Plan of
       San Luis Potosí; 1913 Pact of the Empassy; Plan of Ayala;
       Decreto of the state of Coahuila; Plan of Guadalupe;
       "Discurso" by Carranza, 24 Sept. 1913.

Political, Legal, and Military History

917   VIGIL, RALPH H. "Revolution and Confusion: The Peculiar
         Case of José Inés Salazar." NMHR 53 (1978): 145-70.
         Recounts the changeable political and military career
         of José Inés Salazar, a notorious figure in U.S.-Mexican
         borderlands history during the course of the Mexican
         Revolution, 1910-17.

918   VILANOVA FUENTES, ANTONIO. Muerte de Villa. Mexico:
         Editores Mexicanos Unidos, 1966.
         The death of Villa (1878-1923). Includes bibliography.

919   WEINSTEIN, IRVING. Land and Liberty: The Mexican Revolution
         (1910-1919). New York: Cowles Book Co., 1971.
         Entertaining account of the Mexican Revolution from
         1910 to 1915 (the title notwithstanding). No notes,
         bibliography, or original research.

920   WHARFIELD, H.B. "The Affair at Carrizal." Montana 18
         (1968): 24-39.
         A study of the battle of Carrizal; the major battle of
         General John J. Pershing's punitive expedition into
         Mexico in 1916 was against Carranza's troops, not those
         of Villa. Author concludes that Pershing ordered the
         march purposely to escalate the conflict and inflame
         American opinion in favor of total invasion. Based on
         information from participants.

921   WHITE, E. BRUCE. "The Muddied Waters of Columbus, New
         Mexico." Americas 32 (July 1975): 72-98.
         Discusses the events, 1913-16, leading up to Pancho
         Villa's attack on Columbus, New Mexico, 9 March 1916.

For bibliographies of the Epic Revolution see entries 14-15 and 31.
For historiography on Zapata see entry 203. For a Marxist critique
of the Epic Revolution see entry 275. For revisionist studies of
Madero, Villa, and Carranza see entry 313. See entry 409 for a
multivolume political and socioeconomic history of the Epic Revolution. For the Revolution in the Yucatán see entry 490. For
documentary sources on the late Porfiriato and the Epic Revolution
see entries 515, 524-25, 530-31, and 544-45. For documents on Zapata
see entries 536 and 541. For a documentary collection on Carranza
see entry 537. For biographies of Madero see entries 597, 607,
621-22, 625, 627, 631, 653, 682, 687, and 697-98. For biographies
of Abraham González see entries 471 and 589. For Pino Suárez see
entries 596 and 606. For biographies of Zapata see entries 592,
602, 619, 629, 642, 651, 662, 671, 673, 680, 689, 691, 696, 702, and
1042. For biographies of Villa see entries 590, 594, 600-601, 603-
604, 617, 626, 628, 637, 645-49, 681, 684, 700, and 1072. For

Diplomatic History and International Affairs

Felipe Angeles see entry 618. For biographies of Carranza
see entries 612, 661, 695, and 699. For Huerta see entries 677-78
and 969. For contemporary accounts about Madero see entries 570,
572, 584, and 961. For Villa's death see entry 555; as revolutionary,
see entry 556; and for recollections of villistas see entries 554, 556,
and 571. For the memoirs of a Zapatista see entries 564-66. For
works and materials relating to Luis Cabrera see entries 547, 562,
634, 654, 665, 675, 934, and 1054. For the Epic Revolution in
Coahuila see entries 470 and 496; for Chihuahua see entries 471
and 505. For the Convention of Aguascalientes, 1914-1915, see entry
973.

DIPLOMATIC HISTORY AND INTERNATIONAL AFFAIRS

922 AL'PEROVICH, M.S., and RUDENKO, BORIS T. La Revolución
     Mexicana de 1910-1917 y la política de los Estados Unidos.
     Translated from the Russian by Makedonio Garza, María
     Teresa Francés, and Alejo Méndez García. Mexico: Ediciones
     de Cultural Popular, 1976.
        Classic study of the struggle between the Mexican
     people (represented by Zapata and Villa) and the reactionary
     clerical-latifundista forces allied with North American
     imperialism. Authors are two noted Soviet historians.
     Having gone through several Spanish editions, the original
     was published in Moscow in 1958.

923 BAECKER, THOMAS. Die deutsche Mexicopolitik 1913-14.
     Berlin: Colloquium Verl., 1973.
        Germany's Mexican policy for 1913-1914. A study of
     Huerta's German connections.

924 _____. "The Arms of the Ypiranga: The German Side."
     Americas 30 (July 1973): 1-17.
        Short history of the Ypiranga incident of May 1917
     when the U.S. Navy detained the ship at Veracruz after the
     seizure of Veracruz. When the ship was released it
     delivered its arms to another Mexican port, causing an
     anti-German outcry in the United States. Based on the
     archives of the German government and the Hamburg-
     American Lines.

925 BAEZ GOROSTIZA, JORGE. La Revolución Mexicana (ensayo).
     Mexico: Editorial Epoca, 1972.
        Analyzes the influence that England and the United
     States exerted over Mexico. Marxist analysis of the
     early Revolution.

Diplomatic History and International Affairs

926   BLAISDELL, LOWELL L.   "Harry Chandler and Mexican Border
       Intrigue, 1914-1917." Pacific Historical Review 35
       (1966): 385-93.
          A study of the filibustering activities of Chandler
       in the area of Baja California.

927   _____. The Desert Revolution: Baja California 1911.
       Madison: University of Wisconsin Press, 1962.
          Magonista military and political campaign launched
       from Los Angeles. Based on printed documents, newspapers,
       interviews and secondary sources.

928   BLASIER, COLE. "The United States and Madero." Journal of
       Latin American Studies 4 (Nov. 1972): 207-31.
          Examines the role of Henry Lane Wilson in the overthrow
       of Francisco Madero in Mexico. Wilson worked to overthrow
       Madero by using the protection of American interests as
       an excuse to meddle and as a pretext to threaten U.S.
       intervention, 1911-13. These efforts did not cause
       Madero's overthrow, but his position was weakened, while
       the military officers were encouraged to make their
       coup d'etat. There is no evidence that Wilson sought
       Madero's death. Wilson did not reflect U.S. policy in
       Mexico, but, because he was not recalled by the State
       Department, the United States is responsible for his
       activities. Based on the secret report of William Bayard
       Hale; the memorandum of the Spanish Minister, Bernardo
       Cólogan y Cólogan; records in the British Foreign office;
       and diary and dispatches of the German minister, Paul
       von Hintze.

929   BRADDY, HALDEEN. Pershing's Mission in Mexico. El Paso:
       Texas Western Press, 1966.
          About the punitive expedition against Mexico that
       began in 1916. Argues that the Pershing expedition
       succeeded in that it fostered renewed hostilities between
       Villa and Carranza, which ended harassment on the Mexican
       border. Based on Pershing and Scott papers at the Library
       of Congress and on materials from the municipal libraries
       of Chihuahua City, Juárez, and Parral.

930   _____. Pancho Villa at Columbus: The Raid of 1916.
       El Paso: Texas Western Press, 1965.
          Argues that the Columbus raid was the inevitable result
       of genuine operations by villistas along the border.

Diplomatic History and International Affairs

931   CALVERT, PETER.   The Mexican Revolution, 1910-1914:   The
      Diplomacy of Anglo-American Conflict.   Cambridge:
      Cambridge University Press, 1968.
      A study of the development of the Mexican Revolution
      between 1910-1914, and the associated diplomatic conflict
      which arose between Britain and the United States.
      Examines the relationship between the British and American
      oil companies in Mexico and the way in which this was
      reflected in the underlying assumptions of British and
      American diplomatic action (of special interest is the
      author's treatment of the relationship of Standard Oil
      to Madero's revolution).   Derived from archival sources
      in Mexico, the United States, and Britain.

932   _____.   "Francis Stronge en la decena trágica."   HM 15
      (July-Sept. 1965)· 47-68
      Role of the British Minister in Mexico during the
      tragic ten days which led to Madero's overthrow and death.

933   CARMAN, MICHAEL DENNIS.   United States Customs and the Madero
      Revolution.   El Paso: University of Texas at El Paso,
      1976.
      Shows that U.S. customs officials were unable to control
      flow of munitions into Mexico during Madero revolution
      because of confusion over neutrality laws.   Based on
      records of Departments of Treasury and State.

934   CLEMENTS, KENDRICK A.   "Emissary From a Revolution: Luis
      Cabrera and Woodrow Wilson,"   Americas 35 (Jan. 1979):
      353-71.
      A study of Luis Cabrera's three diplomatic missions to
      the United States between 1914-1916 as a special agent
      for Carranza and the Constitutionalists in Washington.
      Concludes that Cabrera's activity had an impact on
      American policy, making Wilson more tolerant than he had
      been of Mexican radicalism.   Based on State Department
      materials, especially correspondence from the Foreign
      Relations series.

935   _____.   "'A Kindness to Carranza':   William Jennings
      Bryan, International Harvester, and Intervention in
      Yucatán."   Nebraska History 57 (Winter 1976): 478-90.
      Description of incident in which Bryan, opponent of
      "harvester trust," was prepared to intervene militarily
      in Mexico to protect interests of International Harvester.
      Author sees event as illustrative of Bryan's "moral
      imperialism."

Diplomatic History and International Affairs

936   CLENDENEN, CLARENCE C. The United States and Pancho Villa:
       A Study in Unconventional Diplomacy. Ithaca: Cornell
       University Press, 1961.
           Well-documented and researched study of the villista
       phase of revolutionary international relations. Sympathetic
       yet objective account of how Villa shaped and was con-
       ditioned by his relationship with the United States.

937   COKER, WILLIAM S. "Naval Diplomacy During the Mexican
       Revolution: An Episode in the Career of Admiral Frank
       Friday Fletcher." North Dakota Quarterly 40 (Spring 1972):
       51-64.
           United States-British relations during the Tampico and
       Veracruz incidents of 1913-14. Notes the acknowledgement
       of U.S. hegemony by the British there. Based on Naval
       Records Collection of the Office of Naval Records and
       Library, the National Archives.

938   _____. "Mediación británica en el conflicto Wilson-
       Huerta." HM 17 (1968): 244-57.
           British mediation in the Wilson-Huerta conflict.

939   FORSTER, MERLIN H. "U.S. Intervention in Mexico: The 1914
       Occupation of Veracruz." Military Review 57 (1977): 88-96.
           Narrates the U.S. military occupation of Veracruz; its
       success and failures. The action was carried out with
       very few casualties, and the occupation administration
       was extremely efficient.

940   FURMAN, NECAH S. "Vida Nueva: A Reflection of Villista
       Diplomacy, 1914-1915." NMHR 53 (1978): 171-92.
           Traces the change from pro-American, anti-Carranza
       propaganda of Pancho Villa's newspaper Vida Nueva, to its
       anti-American position of November 1915, a process reflecting
       Villa's rise and fall, 1914-15. In spite of the Tampico
       and Veracruz incidents, Villa and his newspaper voiced
       no criticism to the U.S. occupation of Veracruz and opposed
       Venustiano Carranza's treatment of Americans as inter-
       ventionists. Diplomatically weakened by military defeats,
       Villa and Vida Nueva attributed raids on the U.S. southern
       borders to Carranza's forces, said to be seeking U.S.
       recognition. Carranza won that recognition in October
       1915, as well as an embargo on arms and munitions to
       Villa. A disillusioned Villa, who had respected and
       protected American interests and espoused American ideals,
       correctly predicted the revolution's continuance
       "according to...the bandido tactics of an earlier day."

Diplomatic History and International Affairs

Based on memoirs, published American documents, <u>Vida Nueva</u>, and secondary sources.

941 GERHARDT, RAY C. "Inglaterra y el petróleo mexicano durante la primera guerra mundial." HM 11 (July-Sept. 1975): 118-42.
England and Mexican oil during World War I.

942 GILDERHUS, MARK T. <u>Diplomacy and Revolution</u>. Tucson: University of Arizona Press, 1977.
A study of Woodrow Wilson's diplomatic initiatives with Mexico in the 1915-1921 period. The author argues that U.S. policy was designed to circumscribe the Revolution within the bounds of liberal capitalism, while Carranza's were designed to preserve Mexico's right to national self-determination. Unable to reconcile liberal capitalism with self-determination, Wilson's Mexican policy was inconsistent and vexing to the leaders of both countries. Based on archival materials, the work contains an excellent bibliographical essay.

943 _____. "Senator Albert B. Fall and 'The Plot Against Mexico.'" NMHR 48 (1973): 299-311.
Study of allegations that Senator Fall of New Mexico and American oil producers sought military intervention in 1919 against the government of Carranza.

944 GRIEB, KENNETH J. "Sir Lionel Carden and the Anglo-American Confrontation in Mexico: 1913-1914." Ibero-Amerikanisches Archiv 1 (1975): 201-16.
A study in Anglo-American relations in Mexico during the Huerta regime. British "realism" was confronted with Wilsonian "idealism." Desiring to secure Mexican oil reserves for its navy, yet wanting friendly relations with the United States, Carden was dispatched to seek a solution for British problems by promoting rapprochement between Huerta and Wilson. The victory of Carranza and the fall of Huerta led to Carden's departure from Mexico, a departure which symbolized the failure of British policy. Based on U.S. State Department papers, British Foreign Office papers, the <u>New York Times</u>, and the <u>London Times</u>.

945 _____. "Standard Oil and the Financing of the Mexican Revolution." <u>California Historical Society Quarterly</u> 50 (Mar. 1971): 59-71.
Makes a case from circumstantial evidence for involvement of the company in Madero's revolt.

Diplomatic History and International Affairs

946   _____. The United States and Huerta. Lincoln: University
       of Nebraska Press, 1969.
           A very detailed work on the diplomatic conflict between
       Huerta and the United States based on archival materials
       from both countries.

947   _____. "El caso Benton y la diplomacia de la Revolución."
       HM 19 (Oct.-Dec. 1969): 282-301.
           Narrative of the Benton incident. William S. Benton,
       a British citizen, was killed by villistas in 1914. This
       led to an unfriendly foreign press reaction to the Mexican
       Revolution. Washington pressured Carranza to name a
       British commission to investigate the incident. Instead,
       Carranza, maintaining national dignity, appointed a
       Mexican commission.

948   HALEY, P. EDWARD. Revolution and Intervention: The Diplomacy
       of Taft and Wilson with Mexico, 1910-1917. Cambridge,
       Mass., and London: Massachusetts Institute of Technology
       Press, 1970.
           Affirms that Carranza used the Germans in order to gain
       greater advantages with the United States. Based primarily
       upon manuscripts in the Library of Congress and National
       Archives State Department records.

949   HARPER, JAMES W. "Hugh Lenox Scott y la diplomacia de los
       Estados Unidos hacia la Revolución Mexicana." HM 27
       (Jan.-Mar. 1978):   427-45.
           The response of Woodrow Wilson to the Mexican Revolution
       was the first chapter in the response of North American
       diplomacy to the nationalist revolutions of the twentieth
       century. Through Hugh Lenox Scott, Wilson rejected full-
       scale direct intervention and sought to establish a
       reasonably efficient and friendly government in Mexico
       through support of Pancho Villa and his partisans. This
       objective was frustrated by Carranza's victory over Villa
       in central Mexico in 1915. Recognizing the failure of
       indirect intervention, Scott still maintained a moderate
       position and opposed military intervention. Scott's
       rejection of military intervention in Mexican affairs
       belies usual claims that Wilson engaged in "idealistic
       imperialism."

950   HARRIS, CHARLES H. III, and SADLER, LOUIS R. "The Plan of
       San Diego and the Mexican-United States War Crisis of 1916:
       A Reexamination." HAHR 58 (Aug. 1978): 381-408.

Diplomatic History and International Affairs

The Plan of San Diego called for a Mexican American
rebellion and the establishment of an independent republic
in the Southwest. Guerrilla raids on Anglos in South
Texas followed, February 1915 to July 1916. These were
fomented by Mexican leader Venustiano Carranza (1859-1920)
in a move first, to force U.S. recognition of his government, and later, to force the removal of American troops
that had pursued raiders into Mexico. There is no solid
evidence of German involvement in the plan. The plan
left a legacy of racial tension in South Texas.

951 _____, and SADLER, LOUIS R. "Pancho Villa and the Columbus
Raid: The Missing Documents." NMHR 1 (Oct. 1975):
335-46.
For years historians have known of the existence of
missing documents thought to have originally been in the
saddlebags of one of the dead invaders at Columbus. These
were recently located by the authors in the National
Archives in Washington, D.C.

952 HILL, LARRY D. Emissaries to a Revolution: Woodrow Wilson's
Executive Agents in Mexico. Baton Rouge: Louisiana
State University Press, 1973.
A study in unconventional diplomacy: Wilson's attempt
to comprehend the Mexican Revolution through the use of
eleven formally accredited executive agents. Some were
factfinders and negotiators; some were private individuals;
some were consular or state department officers. Most
had little influence on Wilson's policy (or the Department
of State), as Wilson failed to develop a satisfactory
revolutionary diplomacy. Based on research in U.S. and
Mexican archives.

953 HINKLE, STACY C. Wings and Saddles: The Air and Cavalry
Punitive Expedition of 1919. El Paso: Texas Western
Press, 1967.

954 KATZ, FRIEDRICH. "Pancho Villa and the Attack on Columbus,
New Mexico." American Historical Review 83 (Feb. 1978):
101-30.
In-depth analysis of the reasons and circumstances that
led Villa to attack Columbus, New Mexico, on 9 March 1916.
Concludes that the primary motivation was Villa's belief
that Woodrow Wilson had concluded an agreement with Carranza
that would virtually convert Mexico into a U.S. protectorate.
Introduction relates Villa to the constitutionalist movement, and Villa's changing relations with the U.S.

Diplomatic History and International Affairs

government and U.S. business interests. Villa's final
actions were more the calculated moves of a thoughtful
independence fighter than the reckless acts of a desperado.
Well-documented, with informative notes.

955   . Deutschland, Diaz und die mexikanische Revolution:
Die deutsche Politik in Mexiko 1870-1920. Berlin: VEB
Deutscher Verlag der Wissenschaften, 1964.
Studies mostly the relations between Mexico and Germany,
and to a lesser degree Mexico's relations with other
European governments. The book is divided into three parts:
the Porfirio Díaz Era; the first four years of the Mexican
Revolution; World War I; and postwar years. Treats Huerta's
German policy. For the late Díaz era, Katz notes how
North American assistance and participation was necessary
for economic development in both central Mexico and the
northern frontier. Also shows how economic nationalism
developed under Díaz with his ministers negotiating with
German investors in an attempt to build a German counter-
weight to U.S. investment.

956   . "Alemania y Francisco Villa." HM 12 (July-Sept.
1962): 83-103.
Germany and Francisco Villa.

957 KERIG, DOROTHY PIERSON. Luther T. Ellsworth: U.S. Consul on
the Border During the Mexican Revolution. El Paso: Texas
Western Press, 1975.
Examines espionage and intelligence activities of
American Consul assigned to Ciudad Porfirio Díaz, 1907-1913.

958 KNIGHT, ALAN S. International Aspects of the Mexican Revolution 1913-1917. Oxford: University of Oxford, 1971.

959 LAPSHEV, E.G. "Meksikanskaia revolutsiia i SShA." Novaia i
noveishaia istoriia 5 (May 1962): 155-56.
The Mexican Revolution and the United States: a review
of Alfonso Taracena's Madero, víctima del imperialismo
yanqui (Mexico: Editora Librera, 1960) by a Soviet writer.
See item 982.

960 MANNO, FRANCIS J., and BEDNARCIK, RICHARD. "El incidente de
Bahía Magdalena." HM 19 (Jan.-Mar. 1970): 365-87.
A study of the rumors and incidents surrounding U.S.
interests in Magdalena Bay in 1911-1912 and U.S. fear
of Japanese involvement--fears that led to the Lodge
Resolution.

Diplomatic History and International Affairs

961 MARQUEZ STERLING, MANUEL. Los últimos días del Presidente
     Madero: Mi guestión diplomática en México. 3d ed.
     Mexico: Editorial Porrúa, 1975.
          Cuban ambassador's point of view concerning the overthrow
     and death of Madero. Márquez was a participant in the
     events he describes. First edition appeared in 1958.

962 MASON, HERBERT MOLLOY. The Great Pursuit. New York: Random
     House, 1970.
          Problems from the era of the Revolution. The Pershing
     expedition and Villa's incursions to the United States.

963 MELO de REMES, MARIA LUISA. Veracruz martir: la infamia de
     Woodrow Wilson, en memoria de los caídos cuyos nombres
     nadie se ha acordado de recordar. Mexico: 1967.
          Based on newspaper articles.

964 MEYER, MICHAEL C. "Villa, Sommerfeld, Columbus y los
     Alemanes." HM 28 (Apr.-June 1979): 546-66.
          A study of the mysterious German agent Félix Sommerfeld
     and his activities in relation to Villa's raid on Columbus,
     New Mexico, in 1916. Establishes that Sommerfeld was a
     double agent who proposed a plan, later approved by the
     highest levels of the German government, to provoke U.S.
     intervention in Mexico through the manipulation of Villa.
     Also notes that Sommerfeld was well financed by German
     authorities. Does note that documents are lacking to make
     other than a circumstantial case for the German connection
     at Columbus. Based on Foreign Relations materials,
     printed documents, and secondary sources.

965 _____. "The Arms of the Ypiranga." HAHR 50 (Aug. 1970):
     543-56.
          Narrates all of the mishaps experienced by the crew of
     the ship Ypiranga in disembarking arms brought from
     Hamburg and delivering them to Huerta.

966 _____. "The Mexican-German Conspiracy of 1915." Americas
     23 (July 1966): 76-89.
          Well-documented study of the conspiracy of Mexican
     exiles in the United States (Orozco, Salazar, Campa et al.)
     and in Spain (Creel, Huerta) between 1914-1915. Discusses
     Plan of San Diego, Texas; the huertista revolt; and
     German involvement in Mexico prior to World War I.

967 MUNCH, FRANCIS J. "Villa's Columbus Raid: Practical Politics
     or German Design?" NMHR 44 (1969): 189-214.

Diplomatic History and International Affairs

Following a detailed study of Mexican-American provocations and Mexican-German provocations, the author concludes
that "Villa's raid on Columbus, New Mexico, combined
Mexican-American provocations with a Mexican-German
conspiracy." Based on State Department materials in the
National Archives.

968   O'BRIEN, DENNIS J. "Petróleo e intervención: Relaciones
      entre los Estados Unidos y México, 1917-1918." HM 27
      (July-Sept. 1977): 103-40.
         Well-written examination of American petroleum policy
      toward Mexico during World War I. Flow of oil to United
      States and Allies was maintained due to effective diplomacy
      and Carranza's acquiescence.

969   O'SHAUGHNESSY, EDITH. Huerta y la Revolución vistos por la
      esposa de un diplomático en México: Cartas desde la
      Embajada norteamericana en México que refieren al dramático
      período comprendido entre el 8 octubre de 1912 y el rompi-
      miento de relaciones que tuvo lugar el 23 de abril de 1914,
      junto con un resumen sobre la ocupación de Veracruz.
      Prologue and notes by Eugenia Mayer. 1916. Reprint.
      Mexico: Editorial Diógenes, 1971.
         Original version published by O'Shaughnessy, a diplomat's
      wife; covers the 1913-1914 period.

970   PARKER, MARJORIE C. "Diary of a Revolution: A United States
      Ambassador's Involvement in the Intrigue of Mexico's
      'Tragic Ten Days.'" American West 10 (1973): 4-9, 57-59.
         Narrates Henry Lane Wilson's involvement in the "Tragic
      Ten Days," which led to the overthrow of Madero, on a
      daily basis, 9-22 February 1913.

971   PATERSON, THOMAS C. "California Progressives and Foreign
      Policy." California Historical Society Quarterly 47
      (1968): 329-42.
         American-Mexican relations during the Mexican Revolution
      and the preparedness controversy before American entry
      into World War I. Illustrates the interrelationship of
      domestic reform and international affairs. Only a few
      progressives favored intervention in the Mexican Revolution.
      Based on original papers in the Bancroft Library at
      Berkeley.

972   QUIRK, ROBERT E. An Affair of Honor: Woodrow Wilson and the
      Occupation of Veracruz. New York: Norton, 1967.

Diplomatic History and International Affairs

Well-documented account of the American occupation of
Veracruz in 1914. Concludes that the Wilson policy, however
admirable in theory, was impossible in practice.

973 _____. The Mexican Revolution 1914-1915: The Convention
of Aguascalientes. New York: Citadel Press, 1963.
    Well-written monograph, based on extensive archival
research. Relates the critical events of 1914-1915,
especially the Convention of Aguascalientes. Suggests
the Convention thinking was critical in the evolution of
revolutionary ideology. Central to the author's treatment
is the role played by the United States, particularly by
Woodrow Wilson.

974 RAUSCH, GEORGE J., Jr. "Poison-Pen Diplomacy: Mexico, 1913."
Americao 24 (Jan. 1968): 272-80.
    Details how Woodrow Wilson's Mexican policy was based
on scant information received from the "poison pen" of
confidential agent William Bayard Hale.

975 RYAN, PAUL B. "Ten Days at Veracruz." U.S. Naval Institute
Proceedings 98 (1972): 64-73.
    Discusses the reasons behind the U.S. landing at Veracruz
in April 1914, including the Tampico and Ypiranga incidents.
Also describes the Navy's performace at Veracruz--
operations, logistics, communications, and acts of individual
valor.

976 SANDOS, JAMES A. "German Involvement in Northern Mexico,
1915-1916: A New Look at the Columbus Raid." HAHR 50
(Feb. 1970): 70-88.
    Argues that a German conspiracy to provoke American
intervention was behind the attacks that Villa led on
border towns. The person responsible for this was a
German of Austrian descent, Dr. Rausenbaum.

977 SCHOLES, WALTER V., and SCHOLES, MARIE V. "Wilson, Grey
and Huerta." Pacific Historical Review 37 (1968): 151-58.
    Anglo-American Mexican relations, 1913.

978 SESSIONS, GENE A. "Nonintervention and the Fall of Ciudad
Juárez, 1911." Revista Interamericana 5 (1975): 236-49.
    Argues that President William H. Taft's administration
has often been described as one willing to use force to
impose its will on Latin America. Yet Taft's decision not
to intervene in Mexico after the seizure of Ciudad Juárez
in 1911 by rebel forces, even when American life and property
suffered, sheds doubt on this old interpretation.

Diplomatic History and International Affairs

979   SMITH, ROBERT FREEMAN. <u>The United States and Revolutionary</u>
      <u>Nationalism in Mexico, 1916-1932</u>. Chicago: University
      of Chicago Press, 1972.
         A study of the protracted crisis between the United
      States and Mexico over the North American effort to protect
      the property rights and investments of its citizens,
      especially those private interests involved in banking
      and the oil industry. Well-researched, thoroughly
      documented, and gracefully written.

980   _____. <u>Los Estados Unidos y el nacionalismo revolucionario</u>
      <u>en México 1916-1932</u>. Translated by Ernesto de la Pena.
      Mexico: Editorial Extemporáneos, 1972.
         <u>See</u> above entry 979.

981   SWEETMAN, JACK. <u>The Landing at Veracruz, 1914: The First</u>
      <u>Complete Chronicle of a Strange Encounter in April 1914,</u>
      <u>When the United States Navy Captured and Occupied the City</u>
      <u>of Veracruz, Mexico</u>. Annapolis: United States Naval
      Institute, 1968.

982   TARACENA, ALFONSO. <u>Madero, víctima del imperialismo yanqui</u>.
      2d. ed. Mexico: n.p., 1973.
         Argues that Madero was a faultless victim of American
      imperialism. First ed. 1960.

983   TATE, MICHAEL L. "Pershing's Punitive Expedition: Pursuer
      of Bandits or Presidential Panacea?" <u>Americas</u> 32 (July
      1975): 46-71.
         Maintains that the original goal of the expedition--
      dispersal of Villa's troops--soon gave way to a desire to
      protect foreigners and influence Carranza's tax measures.

984   TEITELBAUM, LOUIS M. <u>Woodrow Wilson and the Mexican</u>
      <u>Revolution, 1913-1916</u>. New York: Exposition Press, 1967.
         A less-than-satisfactory venture into diplomatic
      history by a practicing lawyer.

985   ULLOA ORTIZ, BERTA. <u>La Revolución intervenida: Relaciones</u>
      <u>diplomáticas entre México y Estados Unidos, 1910-1914</u>.
      Mexico: El Colegio de México, 1971.
         Scholarly and well-written work. Author makes extensive
      use of Mexican Foreign Relations papers, U.S. Naval
      Archives materials, Library of Congress manuscripts, and
      British Foreign Office papers. The author has also
      utilized a previously untapped source of important docu-
      ments, the papers of the Spanish Embassy in Mexico City.

Diplomatic History and International Affairs

Deals with the development of the Mexican Revolution, 1910-1914, within the international community, and specifically with the interposition of the United States. Supersedes much previous writing on this subject both in Mexico and the United States.

986 _____. "Taft y los antimaderistas." Historia y Sociedad en el Mundo de Habla Espanola. Edited by Bernardo García Martínez, pp. 319-28. Mexico: El Colegio de México, 1970. Brief analysis taken from the previously published work, La Revolución intervenida. See entry 985.

987 _____. "Carranza y el armamento norteamericano." HM 17 (1968): 253-62.

988 WHITE, E. BRUCE. "The Muddied Waters of Columbus, New Mexico." Americas 32 (July 1975): 72-92. See entry 921.

989 WHITTAKER, WILLIAM G. "Samuel Gompers, Labor and the Mexican-American Crisis of 1916: The Carrizal Incident." Labor History 17 (1976): 551-67. Study of response of Gompers and AFL to Pershing's Punitive Expedition of 1916.

990 ZILINSKAS, RAYMOND. "Japanese at Turtle Bay, Lower California, 1915." Southern California Quarterly 60 (1978): 45-58. Analyzes the reasons for the Japanese naval presence at Turtle Bay, Baja California, in 1915. Stories circulated, especially by the Los Angeles Times, to the effect that Japan was forming an alliance with Mexico and that Turtle Bay was being occupied and colonized as part of a grand Japanese military-political strategy. The ostensible reason for Japan's presence at the bay was the salvaging of the cruiser Asama, which had run aground. War scare stories notwithstanding, the Asama did need extensive repairs requiring the assistance of other vessels and many men. Primary and secondary sources.

For bibliography of diplomacy of the Revolution see entries 147-48. For Mexican consulates in the United States, 1900-1920, see entry 742. For Villa's attack on Columbus, see entry 829. For Soviet-Mexican relations see entry 1100. For U.S. relations with Obregón the revolutionary between 1913-1917 see entry 1104. For the United States, Mexico, and the oil controversy, 1917-1942, see entries 1202-1203.

ECONOMIC AND SOCIAL HISTORY

991 ALONSO, JORGE. Los campesinos de la tierra de Zapata.
     Vol. 2, Subsistencia y explotación. Mexico: Secretaría
     de Educación Pública, 1974.
     Agrarianism.

992 BADURA, BOHUMIL. "Agrarní otázka a názory na v Mexicke
     Revoluci 1910-1917." Sbornik Historicky (Czechoslovakia)
     14 (1966): 135-86.
     Views on the agrarian question in the Mexican Revolution
     1910-1917. Concludes that the agrarian issue was fundamental
     and that the agrarian revolution in Mexico was a protest
     against all the contradictions within the society.

993 BASSOLS BATALLA, NARCISO. "La trayectoría agrarista de
     Zapata." Solidaridad 44 (1971): 37-44.
     A study of the proclamations of Zapata that speak of
     political liberty, social equality, respect for the public
     vote and of improved institutions for the people.
     Agrarianism.

994 BUTTREY, T.V. "The Silver Coinage of Zapata, 1914-1915."
     HAHR 52 (Aug. 1972): 456-62.
     The Mexican Revolution produced a variety of coinages
     as the central government temporarily suspended mintage.
     The Zapata series is easily recognized by its legend.
     Neutron analysis of Zapata peso pieces suggests that
     Zapata attempted to produce a coinage equalling the
     government's in intrinsic value. Zapatista coinage was
     conventional, suggesting a traditional view of financial
     and commercial affairs. Based on neutron analysis of
     Zapatista coins and printed sources.

995 BUVE, RAYMOND Th. J. "Movilización campesina y reform agraria
     en los valles de Nativitas, Tlaxcala (1917-1923): Estudio
     de un caso de lucha por recuperar tierras habidas durante
     la revolución armada." In El trabajo y los trabajadores
     en la historia de México, compiled by Elsa Cecilia Frost,
     Michael C. Meyer, and Josefina Zoraida Vázquez, pp. 533-64.
     Mexico and Tucson: El Colegio de México and the University
     of Arizona Press, 1979.
     Details the struggle among villagers, landlords, and
     landless laborers in Tlaxcala's Nativitas Valley, 1917-
     1923. Notes the differences between these rural inhabitants
     and concedes that even when their rural organizations were
     at their strongest, national politics was overwhelming.
     Based on primary materials.

Economic and Social History

996 _____ . "Peasant Movements, Caudillos and Land Reform
During the Revolution, 1910-1917: Tlaxcala, Mexico."
Boletín de Estudios Latinoamericanos y del Caribe
(Amsterdam) 18 (June 1975):112-52.
    Study of agrarian revolt in Tlaxcala during the military
phase of the Revolution. Due to proximity to urban centers
and retention of land ownership, peasants of Tlaxcala
occupied a "take-off" position for effective revolt, an
advantage they exercised when social controls broke down.
Their revolt was expressed through the mechanism of classic
caudillaje.

997 CARDOSO, LAWRENCE A. "Labor Emigration to the Southwest,
1916-1920: Mexican Attitudes and Policy." Southwestern
Historical Quarterly 79 (Apr. 1976): 400-416.
    War in Europe and Revolution in Mexico encouraged massive
emigration of Mexican workers to the United States. Although
opposed by revolutionary nationalists in Mexico, political
realities forced the Carranza administration to pursue a
moderate course of anti-bracero propaganda and consular
protection for braceros. Based upon extensive primary
documentation.

998 CARR, BARRY. "The Casa del Obrero Mundial, Constitutionalism
and the Pact of February 1915." In El trabajo y los
trabajadores en la historia de México, compiled by Elsa
Cecilia Frost, Michael C. Meyer, and Josefina Zoraida
Vázquez, pp. 603-31. Mexico and Tucson: El Colegio de
México and the University of Arizona Press, 1979.
    Examines the famous pact between the Constitutionalist
Army and the Casa del Obrero Mundial. Concludes that
the members of the Casa were able to distinguish between
a short-term tactical alliance and the long-term goals
of social revolution. If the Casa failed to develop an
independent workers' movement, it was not due to its
anarchist affiliations but to the small size of the
working class, its youth, and the institutional framework
of the Revolution. Bibliographical essay.

999 _____ . El movimiento obrero y la política en México,
1910-1929. 2 vols. Mexico: SepSetentas, 1976.
    Vol. 1 is a study of economic and labor history from
the Porfiriato through the administration of Obregón in
the early 1920s. Traces the development of labor in prerevolutionary Mexico and the relationship of revolutionary
caudillismo to radical labor between 1910 and 1917. Notes
the organization of labor (CROM) in 1918, the role of labor

Economic and Social History

in the Constitution of 1917, and the patron-client
relationship of government to labor under Obregón.
Well-documented; based on archives, interviews, government
publications, newspapers, and secondary works. For
Volume 2 see entry 1120.

1000 CHEVALIER, FRANCOIS. "Un facteur décisif de la révolution
agraire au Mexique: Le soulèvement de Zapata. 1911-1919."
Annales: Economies, Sociétés, Civilisations 16 (1961):
66-82.
The result of a 1959 round table discussion at the
Instituto Nacional de la Juventud Mexicana. Argues that
Zapata was a genuine agrarian reformer. Based on primary
documents (e.g., Zapata archive) and testimonies (especially
General Gildardo Magana). See entry 1001.

1001 _____. "Un factor decisivo de la reforma agraria de
México: El levantamiento de Zapata (1911-1919)." Cuadernos
Americanos 113 (1960): 165-87.
Zapata's movement in the state of Morelos and its
agrarian content. The author is one of France's leading
social historians. Original version of entry 1000 above.

1002 CUMBERLAND, CHARLES C. "The Sonora Chinese and the Mexican
Revolution." HAHR 40 (May 1960): 191-211.
A study of the anti-Chinese attitudes and actions of
northern revolutionaries between 1910-1932; based
primarily on U.S. consular despatches from Mexico.

1003 DAMBOURGES, JACQUES LEO M. "The Chinese Massacre in Torreón
(Coahuila) in 1911." Arizona and the West 16 (1974):
233-46.
An account of the infamous Torreón massacre of 1911,
the first of a series of anti-Chinese incidents in northern
Mexico during the Epic Revolution, 1910-1920.

1004 GOMEZ, MARTE R. La reforma agraria en las filas villistas,
anos 1913 a 1915 y 1920. Mexico: Biblioteca del
Instituto Nacional de Estudios Históricos de la Revolución
Mexicana, 1966.
Discusses the agrarian content of Francisco Villa's
revolutionary movement.

1005 GONZALEZ NAVARRO, MOISES. "Xenofobia y xenofilia en la
Revolución Mexicana." HM 18 (Apr.-June 1969): 569-614.

Economic and Social History

With careful use of statistical data on investments,
immigration, murders, and antiforeign legislation the
author delineates the ambivalent Mexican reactions towards
North American, Spanish, Chinese, and Guatemalan intrusions.

1006 _____. "Zapata y la Revolución Agraria Mexicana." Cahiers
du monde Hispanique et Luso-Brésilien (University of
Toulouse, France) (1967): 5-31.

1007 CUERRA, XAVIER. "De l'Espagne au Mexique: Le milieu
anarchiste et la révolution mexicaine (1910-1915)."
Mélanges de la Casa de Velázquez 9 (1973): 653-87.
A panoramic view is given of the Spanish anarchist
movement in Mexico to demonstrate the influence it exercised
after the foundation of the Primera Internacional. Magonismo is dealt with in the context of the international
worker's movement. The first unions founded after the
revolution and the creation of the Casa del Obrero Mundial
are mentioned. The author finishes with the creation of
the CROM.

1008 HART, JOHN M. Anarchism and the Mexican Working Class, 1860-
1931. Austin & London. University of Texas Press, 1978.
A study of agrarian and urban anarchism in Mexico from
the proselytizer Plotino Rhodakanaty in the nineteenth
century to the anarchosyndicalist Casa del Obrero Mundial
of the early Revolution. Focuses upon the conflict
between the urban working class and the new revolutionary
elite. Argues that the Casa was dissolved by the Carranza
government, that organized labor was soon purged of its
radicalism, and that anarchosyndicalism was relegated to
history with the reformism of the Obregón, Calles, and
Cárdenas regimes. Based on primary sources; the bibliography contains a definitive list of anarchist and radical
working-class newspapers for the period. Illustrated with
photographs--a gift to the author from Ingeniero Ernesto
Sánchez Paulín.

1009 _____. "The Urban Working Class and the Mexican Revolution:
The Case of the Casa del Obrero Mundial." HAHR 58 (Feb.
1978). 10-20.
Analysis of the coalition of the upper classes, urban
workers, and peasants in the politics of Mexico from 1910
to 1971. Indicates that the strike of 31 July-2 August
1916, was the turning point that led to the decline of the
anarchosyndicalist Casa and the victory of a resurgent
upper class--Mexico's new "Revolutionary" elite.

Economic and Social History

1010   HERNANDEZ, SALVADOR. "La Revolución Mexicana y el movimiento
        obrero: 1900-1925." Revista de la Universidad de México
        28 (1973): 34-42.
            Contents: "The Resurgence of the Worker's Movement in
        Mexico (1900);" "The Worker's Movement during the Revolu-
        tion of 1910," "The Casa del Obrero Mundial;" "Carranza and
        the Casa del Obrero Mundial;" "Towards the Formation of the
        Confederación Regional Obrera Mexicana (CROM;" "Obregón
        and the Worker's Movement."

1011   HUITRON, JACINTO. Orígenes e historia del movimiento obrero
        en México. Mexico: Editores Mexicanos Unidos, 1974.
            History of early labor movement by one of Mexico's
        leading anarchists and labor agitators. Mostly on pre-
        1920 period. Narrative goes from colonial times to the
        dissolution of the Confederación General de Trabajadores
        (CGT) in 1931. The author, an anarchosyndicalist, was
        cofounder of the "Grupo Luz" of the Casa del Obrero
        Mundial. The pre-Revolutionary sections are derived
        mostly from newspaper sources, while the latter chapters
        include Huitrón's memories and recollections.

1012   KATZ, FRIEDRICH. "Innen- und Aussenpolitische Ursachen Des
        Mexikanischen Revolutionsverlaufs." Jahrbuch für
        Geschichte von Staat, Wirtschaft und Gesellschaft Latein-
        amerikas 15 (1978): 95-101.
            Argues that despite the destruction of the federal army
        during the Mexican Revolution, 1910-1920, few social
        changes occurred. Nonetheless, the events of these years
        did influence the ultimate social revolution accomplished
        during the administration of Lázaro Cárdenas.

1013   _____. "Agrarian Changes in Northern Mexico in the Period
        of Villista Rule, 1913-1915." In Contemporary Mexico:
        Papers of the Fourth International Congress of Mexican
        History, edited by James W. Wilkie, Michael C. Meyer,
        and Edna Monzón de Wilkie. pp. 259-73. Los Angeles
        and Mexico: University of California Press and El
        Colegio de México, 1976.
            Notes that except for large-scale confiscations of a
        few wealthy estates, there were no revolutionary changes
        in the countryside during Villa's administration of
        Northern Mexico; no massive occupations of hacienda lands
        by peasants and no fundamental changes in working and
        living conditions. Most income from confiscated estates
        helped the Division of the North. Land was granted to
        his generals to gain support. Division of land would

have reduced the funds at Villa's disposal, funds which
were used to buy arms and supplies from the United States.
Katz also notes that there was a lack of pressure from
below for land reform since Chihuahua peasants were
few in number compared to miners and cowboys who did not
seek to acquire their own lands. Supporters were promised
land when the fighting was over, but when it was over
Villa was not a victor in a position to redistribute
lands. Based on Terrazas papers.

1014 _____. "Peasants in the Mexican Revolution of 1910." In
Forging Nations: A Comparative View of Rural Ferment and
Revolt, edited by Joseph Spielberg, Joseph Whiteford,
and Scott Whiteford. East Lansing: Michigan State University Press, 1976.
    A study of the role of the peasant in the Epic Revolu-
tion of 1910. Notes that the pattern of peasants subord-
inating their movements to nonpeasant leadership was
visible in most of Mexico; this was the pattern for
Chihuahua and Sonora. Morelos would be an exception to
the above. Large-scale distribution of lands lagged two
decades behind constitutional mandate of 1917 due to
early cooptation of peasantry in support of political ends
of nonpeasants. Meaningful change does not occur before
the 1930s.

1015 LAFUENTE, RAMIRO. "El artículo 123, el Congreso obrero de
Tampico y el Congreso de industriales en el ano de 1917."
Historia Obrera 1 (1974): 39-44.
    Studies three groups of workers which existed in 1917:
the anarchosindicalistas, the catholic workers, and those
that proclaimed a conciliation between capital and work.
The attitude of the workers, the industrialists and
the government are analyzed.

1016 LAMARTINE YATES, PAUL. El desarrollo regional de México.
Mexico: n.p., 1962.
    Economic development in the Mexican provinces.

1017 LEVENSTEIN, HARVEY A. Labor Organizations in the United
States and Mexico. New York: Greenwood Publishing Co.,
1971.
    A study of U.S.-Mexican labor movements. Demonstrates
how Samuel Gompers and the AFL used its influence to
affect Wilson's diplomacy with Mexico, the direction of
Mexico's revolution, and the role of labor in the United
States. Interesting account of how the AFL fought the

Economic and Social History

IWW (Industrial Workers of the World), and later
communism, in Mexico as well as the United States.

1018   LOPEZ ROSADO, DIEGO G. Historia del Peso Mexicano. Mexico:
        Fondo de Cultura Económica, 1975.
        A brief history of the Mexican peso in five chapters
        from pre-Columbian times to the Revolution. Last two
        sections deal with the Porfiriato and the early Revolution.

1019   MACHADO, MANUEL A., Jr. "The Mexican Revolution and the
        Destruction of the Mexican Cattle Industry." Southwestern
        History Quarterly 79 (1975): 1-20.
        An analysis of the effects of the Mexican Revolution
        on the Mexican cattle industry. The assorted revolutionary
        groups perceived that cattle would serve both as food and
        as an exchange medium for acquiring weapons. The U.S.
        government confused the situation further by regulating beef
        imports so as to favor one or another group. The Mexican
        government attempted to prevent shipments, for they served
        to arm its enemies. By 1923, the once flourishing industry
        was in tatters.

1020   MAGANA, GILDARDO. Emiliano Zapata y el agrarismo en México.
        Prologue and selection by Guillermo Perez Velasco.
        Mexico: LER, 1975.

1021   MARTINEZ de la VEGA, FRANCISCO. "México: una huelga
        general en 1916." Solidaridad 48 (1971): 36-40.
        Deals with the strike decreed on 26 May 1916. The
        strike began with the streetcar drivers, electricians,
        and other trade unions and resulted in a general strike
        on June 30 of the same year.

1022   MEYER, JEAN A. "Los obreros en la Revolución Mexicana:
        Los 'Batallones rojos.'" HM 21 (July-Sept. 1971): 1-37.
        According to article 8 of the pact between carrancismo
        and the Casa del Obrero Mundial, the workers who take up
        arms in favor of the Constitutionalist Army will be
        named the "rojos." The author offers the explanation that
        they were not workers but artisans. Unionism in Mexico
        was born dead because it appeared under the tutelage of
        the State.

1023   MOLINA ENRIQUEZ, ANDRES. La Revolución agraria en México.
        Mexico: Liga de Economistas Revolucionarios de la
        República Mexicana, 1976.
        Classic analysis of agrarian problems in Mexico during
        the late Porfiriato and the early Revolution. Originally
        published in five volumes in 1932.

Economic and Social History

1024   NEYMET, MARCELA de. "Rabochii Klass v Meksikanskoi
        Revoliutsii 1910-1917." Novaia i noveishaia istoriia
        11, no. 3 (1967): 90-99.
            Role played by the Mexican workers in the bourgeois-
        democratic revolution of 1910-1917. Emphasis on strike
        movements and the Casa de Obrero Mundial. Concludes with
        a history of the creation of the Mexican Communist Party
        in 1919.

1025   NICKEL, HERBERT J. "Zur Immobilität Und Schuldknechtschaft
        Mexikanischer Landarbeiter Vor 1915." Saeculum 27 (1976):
        289-328.
            Thesis: The system of hereditary debts for Mexican
        agricultural laborers caused an immobility of the rural
        proletariat that could only be overcome by escape or, in
        less frequent cases, by transfer of payments.

1026   NUNES, AMERICO. Les Révolutions du Mexique. Paris:
        Flammarion, 1975.
            A history of the agrarian problem from the Porfiriato
        through the civil war era of 1910-1917. Last section
        treats several interpretative problems such as the nature
        of the Villa-Carranza conflict; whether Zapata was an
        agrarian reformer or a traditionalist; whether or not the
        Mexican Revolution was without ideology and ideas; and
        whether the Revolution was socialist or bourgeois-democratic;
        and Mexico and the theory of dependency. The author tends
        to homogenize and synthesize the various views in forming
        his conclusions. Bibliography and chronology.

1027   PALACIOS, PORFIRIO. El Plan de Ayala: Sus orígenes y su
        proclamación. Mexico: n.p., 1969.
            A summary of the beginnings of the agrarian movement
        headed by Emiliano Zapata. Covers the differences he had
        with Madero and the proclamation of the Plan de Ayala.

1028 PECHURO, E.E. "Novye materialy o krest'anskom vosstanii
        pod rukovodstvom Emiliano Sapaty." Voprosy istorii 10
        (1961): 187-89.
            New materials on the peasant movement led by Zapata
        by a Soviet author.

1029   PERAZA LIZARRAGA, LUIS F. "Zapata, libertador campesino."
        Revista de la Universidad de Yucatán 3 (1961): 89-99.
            Pro-zapatista account of agrarianism.

Economic and Social History

1030   RICHMOND, DOUGLAS W.   "El nacionalismo de Carranza y los
          cambios socioeconómicos: 1915-1920."   HM 26 (July-Sept.
          1976): 107-31.
               Well-researched article on Venustiano Carranza's
          program of economic nationalism. Contends that this
          nationalism was the basis of Carranza's reforms in agri-
          culture, labor, and banking, as well as his efforts to
          increase business opportunities for native capitalists.
          Argues that Carranza's influence as a national leader can
          be traced to his Coahuilan background. Describes him as
          a reformist with a highly legal approach to problems of
          reform. His socioeconomic reforms rewarded the urban
          and rural middle class with economic opportunities,
          political order, education, progressive legislation, and
          administrative efficiency.

1031   ROSS, STEVE.   "Zapata and the Revolt of the Morelos
          'Indians.'"   Mankind 5 (1975): 28-37.
               Thesis: Emiliano Zapata shared the views of his fellow
          Indian peasants in southern Mexico regarding the necessity
          for shared democratic civilian rule. His example fostered
          in the Mexican people a sense of pride and a desire to
          fulfill the egalitarian aims of the Mexican Revolution.
          His own authority originated in a village council and he
          remained true to the aims of the people's revolution for
          land and bread in southern Mexico.

1032   RUIZ, RAMON EDUARDO.   Labor and the Ambivalent Revolutionaries:
          Mexico, 1911-1923.   Baltimore, Md.: Johns Hopkins Univ-
          ersity Press, 1976.
               Study of Mexican labor movement during the early Revolu-
          tion. Demonstrates continuing efforts by government--
          whether under Madero, Huerta, or Carranza--to control
          labor movement by favoring certain groups and repressing
          others. Argues that "the views of current revisionist
          scholars, who doubt the existence of a revolution defined
          in terms of a fundamental socioeconomic change, are close
          to the truth....No revolutionary regime faithfully
          mirrored labor's aspirations...." Based on Carranza
          papers and Fomento records.

1033   _____.   "Madero's Administration and Mexican Labor."   In
          Contemporary Mexico: Papers of the Fourth International
          Congress of Mexican History, edited by James W. Wilkie,
          Michael C. Meyer, and Edna Monzón de Wilkie, pp. 187-203.
          Los Angeles and Mexico: University of California Press
          and El Colegio de México, 1976.

Concludes that Madero's administration failed to
improve the lot of labor. Despite the rhetoric of
democracy, maderista leaders distrusted independent
labor organizations, reacting to labor in a paternalistic
fashion. Official benevolence curtailed and hampered
attempts at unionization. By 1913 the morale of labor
was low, as was its faith in the Madero administration.
Based on primary materials from the Archivo General de
la Nación.

1034   SALAZAR, ROSENDO. La Casa del Obrero Mundial. Mexico:
        Costa-Amic, 1962.
        A member of the Casa narrates the history of Mexican
        unionism in general and of the Casa in particular. Woven
        into the text are accounts of personal experiences as well
        as documents and testimonials.

1035   SILVA HERZOG, JESUS. "Opiniones heterodoxas sobre la
        Revolución Mexicana." Memoria del Colegio Nacional 7
        (1970): 21-39.
        According to the author, "the Mexican Revolution was
        not a bourgeois revolution, rather it was a revolution
        against the national and foreign bourgeoisie. It was a
        popular, peasant, and nationalist revolution that ended
        in May 1917."

1036   , director. La cuestión de la tierra, 1910-1917:
        Colección de folletos para la historia de la Revolución
        Mexicana. 4 vols. Mexico: Instituto Mexicano de
        Investigaciones Económicas, 1960-1962.
        An important collection of historical materials and
        pamphlets on topics related to the Mexican Revolution,
        1910-1917. Vol. 1, 1910-1911; vol. 2, 1911-1913; vol. 3,
        1913-1914; vol. 4, 1915-1917.

1037   TARACENA, ALFONSO. La labor social del presidente Madero.
        Saltillo, Coahuila: 1966.
        Apologetic and sympathetic account of Madero's public
        sacrifices and service by a pro-vasconcelista.

1038   TURNER, FREDERICK C. "Los efectos de la participación
        feminina en la Revolución de 1910." HM 16 (Apr.-June
        1967): 603-20.
        The participation of women in the Revolution as
        soldiers, unofficial commissaries, and replacements in
        business and industry. Based largely on newspapers and
        secondary works.

Economic and Social History

1039 WATERBURY, RONALD. "Non-revolutionary Peasants: Oaxaca
      Compared to Morelos in the Mexican Revolution." Compara-
      tive Studies in Society and History (The Hague) 17
      (Oct. 1975): 410-42.
          Compares very different historical experiences of
      Morelos and Oaxaca. Concludes that a determining factor
      in motivating peasants to revolt is perception of threats
      to personal survival rather than sympathy with or under-
      standing of the national movement. The strong partici-
      pation of the peasants of Morelos in the Mexican Revolution,
      1910-1920, versus the inertia of the Oaxaca Indians, is
      attributed to the marked disintegration of traditional,
      community-oriented, and agrarian life in Morelos beginning
      in 1880 with economic modernization, the impact of which
      was not so strongly felt in Oaxaca.

1040 WOMACK, JOHN, Jr. Sterban für die Indios: Zapata und die
      mexikanische Revolution. Zurick: Atlantis, 1972.
          German edition of Womack's definitive work on Zapata.
      See entry 1042.

1041 _____. Zapata y la Revolución Mexicana: Hombre y época.
      Havana: Editorial de Ciencias Sociales, 1971.
          Cuban edition of Womack's definitive work on Zapata.
      See entry 1042.

1042 _____. Zapata and the Mexican Revolution. New York:
      Knopf, 1969.
          Definitive narrative history of Zapata and zapatismo.
      Excellently written and researched; derived from materials
      in the Archivo de Zapata and a wide variety of public and
      private collections. Chronology extends from the last
      years of the Porfiriato to the mid-1960s, with emphasis on
      the violent social revolution from 1910 to 1920. 1930s
      witnessed the rise of new village leaders, the decline of
      the hacienda and plantation class, and the institutionali-
      zation of land reforms.

1043 _____. Zapata y la Revolución Mexicana. Translated by
      Francisco González Aramburu. Mexico: Siglo XXI Editores,
      1969.
          Mexican edition of Womack's definitive work. See
      entry 1042.

For historiography of economic history, 1910-1920, see entry 251.
For revisionist studies of Madero, Villa and Carranza see entry 313.

Religious and Church History

For revisionist studies of caudillos and peasants <u>see</u> entry 351.
For a socioliterary approach to the Revolution of 1910 <u>see</u> entry
1068.

RELIGIOUS AND CHURCH HISTORY

1044   COX, DWAYNE. "Richard Henry Tierney and the Mexican Revolu-
        tion, 1914-1917." <u>Mid-America</u> 59 (Apr.-July 1977):
        93-101.
            A study of Richard Henry Tierney, editor of the Jesuit
        weekly <u>America</u> from March 1914 to February 1925. Tierney
        campaigned against the anti-Catholic stance of the Mexican
        Revolution during his first three years at this post. He
        especially opposed the leadership of Venustiano Carranza,
        whom he saw as a threat to Catholicism everywhere. His
        crusade was carried out through editorials and speeches
        until the spring of 1917, when American entry into World
        War I became the major issue. Although he toiled actively
        on behalf of the Catholic Church in denouncing governmental
        practices in Mexico, he did little to influence American
        foreign policy in this direction.

1045   DARDY, CARMON B. "Cultural encystment as a cause of the
        Mormon exodus from Mexico in 1912." <u>Pacific Historical
        Review</u> 34 (1965): 439-54.
            A study of Mormons who established themselves in Mexico
        in 1885 and then abandoned the country in 1912; they
        "broke out" of the "cyst" of revolution and violence.

1046   ROMAN, RICHARD. "Church-state Relations and the Mexican
        Constitutional Congress, 1916-1917." <u>Journal of Church
        and State</u> 20 (Winter 1978): 73-88.
            Considers the concern of the Constitutional Congress of
        1916-17 with relations between Church and State, and
        traces the roots of extreme and bitter anticlericalism
        in Mexico with emphasis on the period between 1910 and 1916.

For Church-State relations, 1910-1929, <u>see</u> entry 1155. For Veracruz
<u>see</u> entry 507.

HISTORY OF EDUCATION

1047 BRITTON, JOHN A. "Indian Education, Nationalism, and
      Federalism in Mexico, 1910-1921." Americas 32 (Jan. 1976):
      445-58.
          Argues that interest in rural education had been growing
      even before the Revolution of 1910, in part as a means of
      integrating the Indians into Mexican society. It intensified
      in the following decade, though revolutionary disturbances,
      inadequate funding, and disputes over federal versus state
      control of schools hampered progress. Reestablishment of
      a national educational ministry in 1921 under José
      Vasconcelos (1882-1959) resolved the latter conflict and
      opened the way to further efforts. Based on the Mexican
      press and other published materials.

1048 COCKCROFT, JAMES D. "El maestro de primaria en la Revolución
      Mexicana." HM 16 (Apr.-June 1967): 565-87.
          Using the example of Alberto Carrera Torres, the author
      investigates the influence that primary schoolteachers had
      through their actions and ideas in initiating and developing
      the Revolution, 1900-1917.

CULTURAL AND INTELLECTUAL HISTORY

1049 ARENAS GUZMAN, DIEGO. El periodismo en la Revolución
      Mexicana: De 1876 a 1917. 2 vols. Mexico: Instituto
      Nacional de Estudios Históricos de la Revolución Mexicana,
      1966.
          Journalism in the history of the Revolution to 1917.

1050 AZUELA, MARIANO. Los de abajo: Novela de la Revolución
      Mexicana. Mexico: Fondo de Cultura Económica, 1966.
          A new (fifth) edition of Azuela's famous novel which
      first appeared in El Paso in 1915. This edition includes
      a copy of the song la Adelita and a chronology divided
      into three parts: a) Azuela's life; b) a cultural pano-
      rama; and c) historical data on Mexico.

1051 BEEZLEY, WILLIAM H. "Shooting the Mexican Revolution."
      Americas 28 (1976): 17-19.
          A study of Texas photographer Otis Aultman who traveled
      with revolutionaries in Mexico in order to photograph
      the events of the Mexican Revolution, 1910-16 (which
      later earned him a job in Hollywood as a cameraman
      during the 1920s).

Cultural and Intellectual History

1052   BOYD, LOLA E.   "Zapata in the Literature of the Mexican
       Revolution." Hispania 52 (Dec. 1969): 903-10.
           Descriptive bibliographical survey of studies treating
       Zapata written before John Womack's study (see entry 1042).

1053   CARRERAS GONZALEZ, OLGA.   "La naturaleza y el hombre en Los
       de abajo." Norte: Revista Hispanica de Amsterdam 14
       (Nov.-Dec. 1973): 136-42.
           Illustrates how naturalism was used by Mariano Azuela in
       his revolutionary novel Los de abajo [The Underdogs] not
       only to develop the images of the Mexican landscape, but
       through metaphors and similes, the personalities of his
       characters.

1054   De BEER, GABRIELLA.   "Luis Cabrera ensayista y teórico de la
       Revolución Mexicana." Cuadernos Americanos 202 (Sept.-
       Oct. 1975): 155-60.
           A study of the political thought of one of Mexico's
       foremost revolutionary theorists. Argues that Cabrera
       (1876-1954) should be considered one of Hispanic America's
       great essayists in the tradition of Sarmiento or Martí.

1055   DESSAU, ADALBERT.   La novela de la Revolución Mexicana.
       Mexico: Fondo de Cultura Económica, 1973.
           The author distinguishes between the novel of the
       Revolution and the revolutionary novel. Among the first
       are Mariano Azuela, Martín Luis Guzmán et al. In the
       second group are Xavier Icaza, Enrique Othón Díaz, Raúl
       Carrancá y Trujillo, Gregorio López y Fuentes et al.

1056   GRISWOLD del CASTILLO, RICHARD.   "The Mexican Revolution and
       the Spanish-Language Press in the Borderlands." Journalism
       History 4 (Summer 1977): 42-47.
           A study of the editorial opinion appearing in the Spanish-
       language press published in the United States between 1910-
       1914. Concludes that the New Mexico press was the most
       apolitical and that the Mexican-American editors helped,
       through their publication of revolutionary corridos,
       novelas, and art, to develop a sense of Mexican nationalism.
       Survey does not include Arizona publications.

1057   GUISA y AZEVEDO, JESUS.   "José Vasconcelos, el hombre de un
       pueblo, de una raza, de una civilización." Lectura 165
       (1965): 3-8.

Cultural and Intellectual History

1058   HUBBEL, LINDA S. "Historocity Study of Mexican Corridos
        About Zapata." Kroeber Anthropological Society Papers
        (University of California) 38 (1968): 68-81.
            Comparative study of two corridos about Zapata, one
        in favor and one against him.

1059   KIRCHNER, LOUISA D. México, en busca de su identidad: La
        faz cultural de su Revolución. Madrid: Ediciones Ibero-
        americanas, 1973.
            This study, a Spanish translation of the author's
        dissertation, "Mexico in Four Founders of the Ateno"
        (Columbia University, 1969), concerns itself with the
        eclectic descriptions of Mexico written by the four most
        prominent members of the Ateneo de la Juventud (founded
        on 28 October 1909)--José Vasconcelos, Antonio Caso, Pedro
        Henríquez Urena, and Alfonso Reyes.

1060   KNUDSON, JERRY W. "The Press and the Mexican Revolution of
        1910." Journalism Quarterly 46 (1969): 760-66.
            The press played a vital role in the early history of
        the Revolution. Madero's vacillating leniency facilitated
        attacks that led to his downfall. Zapata suffered from
        an adverse press. Huerta suppressed all newspaper
        opposition. Based on primary sources.

1061   KRAUZE, ENRIQUE. Caudillos culturales en la Revolución
        Mexicana. Mexico: Siglo XXI Editores, 1976.
            Study of relationship between intellectuals and political
        power, focusing on entrance of student "generation of
        1915" into politics and government.

1062   MILLON, ROBERT PAUL. Zapata: The Ideology of a Peasant
        Revolutionary. New York: International Publishers,
        1972.
            Seeks to determine the nature of the ideology which
        Zapata's movement formulated for itself amid a welter of
        philosophical crosscurrents.

1063   MONTANO, OTILIO E. "El Zapatismo ante la filosofía y ante
        la historia." Estudios de Historia Moderna y Contemporánea
        de México 2 (1967): 185-96.
            A study of the philosophy and ideology of zapatismo.

1064   OJEDA, ABELARDO, and MALLEN, CARLOS. Ricardo Flores Magón:
        Su idea y su obra frente al origen y las proyecciones de
        la Revolución Mexicana; Estudios crítico-biográficos.
        Mexico: Secretaría de Educación Pública, 1967.

The book is divided into two parts: the first is a
biography; the second is a study of the ideas that
influenced Ricardo Flores Magón.

1065   POSADA, GERMAN. "La generación mexicana de 1910." HM 12
        (July-Sept. 1962): 147-53.
        Study of some aspects of the lives and works of the
        great members of the Mexican "Generation of 1910." Emphasis
        is upon José Vasconcelos, Alfonso Reyes, and Pedro
        Henríquez Urena.

1066   POSADA, JOSE GUADALUPE. La Revolución Mexicana vista por
        José Guadalupe Posada: Recopilación y presentación de
        Jaled Muyaes. Mexico: Talleres "Policromia," 1960.
        A pictorial history of the Revolution, 1910-1929.
        Sixty-two plates. Posada is often described as Mexico's
        greatest printmaker.

1067   RENN, LUDWIG. Trini. Munich: Weismann Verlag, 1973;
        Berlin (DDR): Der Kinderbuchverlag, 1979.
        Novelistic treatment of the civil war era of Mexico's
        Revolution centering around the main character Trinidad
        (Trini) and the themes of zapatismo and peasant revolt.
        Illustrated with reproductions of works by Diego Rivera
        and Alfaro Siqueiros. Afterword, describing the Revolution
        and Mexico's contemporary history, by Henio Cano (Munich
        edition).

1068   RUTHERFORD, JOHN. Mexican Society during the Revolution:
        A Literary Approach. Oxford: Clarendon Press, 1971.
        A socioliterary approach which surveys the various
        revolutions within the Revolution. In the introductory
        chapter ("Novels as Historical Sources"), the inter-
        dependence between the disciplines of the social historian
        and the literary critic is set forth. Study of the
        Revolution, 1910-1917, is based on an analysis of thirty
        novels written by Mexicans before 1925, including Mariano
        Azuela, José López-Portillo y Rojas, Alfonso Teja Zabre,
        José Vasconcelos, Martín Luis Guzmán, Alfonso López
        Ituarte, and others. Author successfully combines the
        disciplines of literary criticism, historiography, and
        sociology to illustrate the Revolution in concrete,
        human terms. Zapatista phase mostly excluded for lack
        of sources.

1069   SILVA HERZOG, JESUS. Trayectoria ideológica de la Revolución
        Mexicana 1910-1917 y otros ensayos. Mexico: Secrataría de
        Educación Pública, 1973.

Cultural and Intellectual History

The three essays included here were published during three different eras. Only the first deals with revolutionary ideology from 1910 to 1917. The second essay is entitled "La Epopeya del Petróleo en México"; the third is "Meditaciones sobre México."

1070 STARKWEATHER, JAMES A., Jr. "The Ateneo de la Juventud: The Formulation of a Quest." North Dakota Quarterly 40 (Spring 1972): 41-50.
Study of an attempt on the part of young intellectuals to renovate Mexican intellectual life between 1906 and 1911. Their objective was to form an aesthetic appropriate to the Mexican experience.

1071 STEIN, HARRY H. "Lincoln Steffens and the Mexican Revolution." American Journal of Economics and Sociology 34 (1957): 197-212.
Discusses the involvement of Lincoln Steffens (1866-1936) in Mexico's revolution and in Mexican-American relations, 1913-27, estimating the consequences of his journalism. Primary and secondary sources.

1072 TUDELA, MARIANO. Pancho Villa: Vida, leyenda, aventura. Barcelona: Plaza y Janés editores, 1971.
Biography written in the form of a novel.

1073 TYLER, RON, ed. Posada's Mexico. Washington: Library of Congress, 1979.
A study of José Guadalupe Posada's work. Posada (1852-1913) was one of Mexico's great printmakers and an artist whose work personified the Mexican Revolution. This work, intended to accompany an exhibition of Posada's prints, contains over 250 illustrations and five essays which discuss the Mexican popular press, Posada's life and work, the sources of Posada's imagery, and the historical and social context of Mexico during Posada's life. The illustrations are organized into four sections: the Porfiriato; the Centennial and the Revolution; Calaveras (skeleton caricatures); and Posada and Mexican graphic traditions. Index; bibliography; five appendixes.

1074 VALADES, EDMUNDO, and LEAL, LUIS. La Revolución y las letras. Mexico. Instituto Nacional de Bellas Artes, 1960.
Two studies on the early Revolution and literature. One by Valadés on the revolutionary novel, the other by Leal on the short story.

Cultural and Intellectual History

1075   VALDES, JOSE de la LUZ. El mito de Zapata. Saltillo,
        Coahuila: Ed. "Espigas," 1974.
            Attacks the falsification of the history of Zapata
        and zapatismo. Argues that Zapata was not a true hero of
        the Revolution; rather he was an anarchist, rebel, and
        "terrible bandolero" who caused over 10,000 deaths.

1076   VALERO SILVA, JOSE. "El zapatismo ante la filosofía ante
        la historia, por Otilio E. Montano." Estudios de Historia
        Moderna y Contemporánea de México 2 (1967): 185-96.

1077   YANEZ, AGUSTIN. The Lean Land. Translated by Ethel Brinton
        Austin and London: University of Texas Press, 1968.
            Translation of Las tierras flacas (Mexico: J. Mortiz,
        1962), a sociological novel describing the aftermath of
        the Revolution of 1910. Yánez is one of Mexico's better
        novelists known also for his work as an educator and public
        servant. Translator Brinton is Yánez's former student,
        herself the director of the Anglo-Mexican Institute.

For a biography of Mariano Azuela see entry 650. For biographies
of philosophers Vasconcelos and Caso see entries 630, 632, 635,
638-39, 668, 674, and 703. For the Ateneo de la Juventud see
entry 745. For intellectual "precursors" see entries 732 and 746.

X. The Northern Dynasty, 1920-1934

POLITICAL, LEGAL, AND MILITARY HISTORY

1078   BAILEY, DAVID C. "Obregón: Mexico's Accommodating President."
        In Essays on the Mexican Revolution: Revisionist Views
        of the Leaders, edited by George Wolfskill and Douglas
        W. Richmond, pp. 82-99. Austin and London: University
        of Texas Press, 1979.
            A study of the politics of accommodation that Obregón
        practiced in the 1920s with labor, agrarians, landowners,
        the army, political opponents (like Francisco Villa),
        the church, and the government of the United States.
        Obregón's political skills provided stability and made
        possible the consolidation of the political and social
        system that prevails in Mexico today. Based on printed
        works.

1079   CAMP, RODERIC A. "La campana presidencial de 1929 y el
        liderazgo político en México." HM 27 (Oct.-Dec. 1977):
        231-59.
            Argues that José Vasconcelos, as an aspirant to the
        presidency in 1929 (in a campaign of opposition to Pascual
        Ortiz Rubio), served as a "catalyst" for a generation of
        younger political activists who were first initiated into
        politics during the 1929 campaign. Demonstrates that most
        of the then vasconcelistas were later either official party
        members of the government's bureaucracy, or were important
        members of Mexico's two opposition parties, which developed
        after 1929.

1080   CARRILLO FLORES, ANTONIO. "La suprema corte de justicia como
        tribunal federal de última instancia: Un testimonio de
        Antonio Carrillo Flores." Memoria del Colegio Nacional
        8 (1978): 75-99.
            Thesis: The Supreme Court of Mexico hears cases involving
        disputes between states; lower federal tribunals; state and
        federal courts, and cases concerning diplomatic personnel;

Political, Legal, and Military History

cases concerned with maritime law; cases between a state and residents of another state; and controversies over people claiming damages due to the application of federal laws. These powers are commonly thought to have originated mainly since 1930, but in actuality they were in use before then. Based on primary and secondary sources.

1081   DULLES, JOHN W.F. Yesterday in Mexico: A Chronicle of the Revolution, 1919-1936. Austin: University of Texas Press, 1967.
A political narrative of Mexico's northern dynasty, 1919-1936, based on John Dulles's sixteen-year experience in Mexico as a metallurgical engineer. An encyclopedic account of epic proportions, the work is detailed and written without passion. Generously illustrated with photographs. Based upon interviews and the recollections of survivors.

1082   GARCIADIEGO DANTAN, JAVIER. La revuelta de Agua Prieta. Mexico: UNAM, 1974.
1920 Agua Prieta revolt.

1083   HALL, LINDA B. "Alvaro Obregón and the Politics of Mexican Land Reform, 1920-1924." HAHR 60 (May 1980): 213-38.
A study of the way Obregón put into practice the revolutionary goal of agrarian reform within the framework of his plans for national reconstruction. Political manipulation of agrarian reform fell into three categories: areas where Francisco Villa, an old adversary, had supporters who needed to be coopted (Durango and Chihuahua); zapatista regions that had supported Obregón (Puebla, Guerrero, and, to a lesser extent, Morelos); regions of delahuertista strength (San Luis Potosí, Jalisco, Veracruz). The politics of land reform involved Obregón placing himself in the center of the distribution process, thus strengthening his position and the office of president.

1084   HANSIS, RANDALL. "The Political Strategy of Military Reform: Alvaro Obregón and Revolutionary Mexico, 1920-1924." Americas 36 (Oct. 1979): 199-233.
A study of Obregón's military reforms, which sought to insure, first, Army loyalty to the office of President and, second, military effectiveness when the Army was called upon to protect the Federal Government. Based on Obregón-Calles papers.

Political, Legal, and Military History

1085   IDUARTE, ANDRES. "Antireeleccionismo." Cuadernos Americanos
       26 (1967): 252-57.
       Personal account of student life during the reelection
       of Alvaro Obregón.

1086   LEON de PALACIONS, ANA MARIA. Plutarco Elías Calles, creador
       de instituciones. Mexico: Instituto Nacional de Admin-
       istración Pública, 1975.
       A study of Calles's political activities from 1911
       to 1928 (emphasis upon the events between 1924 and 1928),
       concluding with the creation of the Partido Nacional
       Revolucionario. Generally uncritical of Calles government.
       Winner of first prize in competition called "Plutarco
       Elias Calles, Creador de Instituciones." Based primarily
       on secondary sources. Includes bibliography.

1087   MARQUEZ FUENTES, MANUEL, and RODRIGUEZ ARAUJO, OCTAVIO.
       "El régimen de Obregón." Cuadernos Americanos 158 (May-
       June 1968): 179-93.
       A study of labor dependency and governmental control
       over labor during the obregonista era, 1920-1923.

1088   MARTINEZ AVELEYRA, AGUSTIN. No volverá a suceder. Mexico:
       Imprenta Novedades, 1972.
       A chronicle of events in 1927 under Alvaro Obregón.
       Talks about Obregón's assassination. Also discussed is
       the judgment brought against the assassin, Juan Toral,
       and his friends.

1089   MICHAELS, ALBERT L. Mexican Politics and Nationalism from
       Calles to Cárdenas. Philadelphia: University of Penn-
       sylvania, 1966.
       Scholarly study by a competent historian. Reproduction
       of typescript.

1090   OCHOA CAMPOS, MOISES. Calles el estadista. Mexico: Editorial
       Trillas, 1976.
       A study of Calles as the creator of institutions: CROM,
       Comisión Nacional de Irrigación, Comisión Nacional de
       Caminos, La Universidad de México, La Ley de Petróleo
       (1925), Banco de México, Comisión Monetaria, Comisión
       Nacional Bancaria, the Bancos Agrícolas Ejidales, and the
       Partido Nacional Revolucionario.

1091   PALACIOS, GUILLERMO. "Calles y la idea oficial de la
       Revolución Mexicana." HM 3 (Jan.-Mar. 1972): 261-78.
       Calles gives birth to the idea of a "revolution on the
       march."

Political, Legal, and Military History

1092   PINEDA, HUGO. José Vasconcelos: Político Mexicano, 1928–
        1929. Mexico: Edutex, 1975.
            A study of the role of José Vasconcelos and vasconcelismo
        in the presidential election of November 1929. Studies
        the political and social ideas of Vasconcelos and analyzes
        his economic program. Details the campaign and official
        intimidation of 1929. Bibliographical essay; appendix
        includes copies of correspondence and newspaper accounts.
        No index.

1093   PORTES GIL, EMILIO. Autobiografía de la Revolución Mexicana.
        Mexico: Instituto Mexicano de Cultura, 1964.
            An "official" view of the Revolution, including the
        traditional account of the conflict between the Catholics
        and the State in the 1920s as a struggle between the
        Revolution's defenders and a reactionary clergy allied
        with prerevolutionary elites. Personal and highly
        partisan account.

1094   SHULGOWSKI, ANATOLY. "El caudillismo después de la Revolución
        1917-1930." Historia y Sociedad 3 (1967): 3-20.
            The institution of the caudillo during the 1920s.

1095   SILVA HERZOG, JESUS. "Durante la presidencia del General
        Plutarco Elías Calles: Sucesos que es menestar recordar."
        Memoria del Colegio Nacional 8 (1978): 45-72.
            Presents a number of events during the presidency of
        Calles in Mexico, 1924-28. Some of the topics covered
        include the creation of a national party, attempts to
        separate the military from politics, the separation of
        Church and State, relations with the United States, relations
        with other foreign countries, Calles and labor, Calles and
        the foreign oil interests, and the internal policies of
        Calles on various fronts.

1096   SOKOLOV, ANDREJ ALEKSANDROVIC. Rabocee dvizenie Meksiki:
        (1917-1929). Moscow: Izd-vo Moskovsko, 1978.
            The Mexican Revolution, 1917-1929.

1097   SOSA FERREYRO, ROQUE ARMANDO. El crimen del miedo; Reportaje
        histórico: Cómo y por qué fue asesinado Carrillo Puerto.
        Mexico: B. Costa-Amic, 1969.
            Assassination of Carrillo Puerto in 1924. He was a
        revolutionary in the Yucatán.

Diplomatic History and International Affairs

1098   VALADES, JOSE C. <u>Historia general de la Revolución Mexicana.</u>
       Vols. 6-10. Mexico: M. Quesada Brandi, 1967.
       These volumes cover the time from the government of
       Carranza to that of Cárdenas.

For caudillismo in northern Mexico <u>see</u> entry 476; for caciquismo in
the Yucatán in the 1920s <u>see</u> entry 489; for caudillos and peasants
in general <u>see</u> entry 351. For the Revolution in Michoacán <u>see</u> entry
487; for the Yucatán <u>see</u> entry 490. For a revisionist study of
Obregón <u>see</u> entry 313; for military descriptions by Obregón <u>see</u>
entry 575. For Portes Gil <u>see</u> the following: writings by, entry
578; interview with, entry 585; biography of, entry 620. For a
biography of Calles <u>see</u> entry 705. For the Mexican military, 1910-
1930, <u>see</u> entry 865.

DIPLOMATIC HISTORY AND INTERNATIONAL AFFAIRS

1099   BERBUSSE, EDWARD J. "The Unofficial Intervention of the United
       States in Mexico's Religious Crisis, 1926-1930." <u>Americas</u>
       23 (July 1966): 28-62.
       U.S. officials deplored the anticlerical measures of
       the Mexican state, but a policy of noninterference prevented
       intervention. Ambassador Dwight Morrow subsequently used
       his personal friendship with Calles to promote an amicable
       settlement.

1100   CARDENAS, HECTOR. <u>Las relaciones mexicano-soviéticas:</u>
       <u>Antecedentes y primeros contactos diplomáticos (1789-1927).</u>
       Mexico: Secretaría de Relaciones Exteriores, 1974.
       A general diplomatic history of Russian-Mexican relations
       to 1927.

1101   CARRERAS de VELASCO, MERCEDES. <u>Los mexicanos que devolvió</u>
       <u>la crisis, 1929-1932.</u> Mexico: Secretaría de Relaciones
       Exteriores, 1974.
       Mexican government's perspective on the repatriations from
       the United States during the Great Depression, 1929-1932.
       A favorable view of the intents and actions on the repat-
       riations by the Secretaría de Relaciones Exteriores. Based
       on diplomatic sources and newspaper materials.

1102   DAVIS, MOLLIE C. "American Religious and Religiose Reaction
       to Mexico's Church-State Conflict, 1926-1927: Background
       to the Morrow Mission." <u>Journal of Church and State</u> 13
       (Winter 1971): 79-96.

Diplomatic History and International Affairs

In 1926, when Calles imposed anticlerical provisions
of the Constitution, American Catholics and oil interests
called for intervention. In general, the public mood was
antiwar. Coolidge, at first influenced by the inter-
ventionists, cautiously changed policy in the direction
of cooperation, especially through the appointment of
Dwight W. Morrow as U.S. ambassador to Mexico.

1103   FUENTES MARES, JOSE. "Los diplomáticos espanoles entre
        Obregón y el maximato." HM 24 (Oct.-Dec. 1974): 206-29.
        Notes that Spanish diplomats in the 1920s maneuvered
        to protect the interests of Spanish landowners faced with
        expropriation by Mexican agrarian reforms. They moved also
        to protect Spanish clergymen determined to maintain influence
        in the Mexican Church despite the Revolution. The author
        describes Mexican politics and gives a detailed account of
        Alvaro Obregón's (1880-1928) reelection, his political
        opposition, and the consequences of his assassination
        while president-elect. Gives accounts of anti-Spanish
        public opinion in Mexico and analyzes the position of the
        United States during the same period.

1104   HINDMAN, E. JAMES. "¿Confusión o conspiración? Estados
        Unidos frente a Obregón." HM 25 (Oct.-Dec. 1975): 271-
        301.
        Argues that U.S. policy in 1920 was conditioned by
        Woodrow Wilson's earlier experiences with Obregón between
        1913 and 1917; that is, Obregón the president was remembered
        by Washington as Obregón the revolutionary. Based on
        Wilson papers and the National Archives (U.S. State Depart-
        ment) materials.

1105   HORN, JAMES J. "Mexican Oil Diplomacy and the Legacy of
        Teapot Dome." West Georgia College Studies in the Social
        Sciences 17 (1978): 99-112.
        Thesis: Threats of military intervention in Mexico over
        enactment of legal provisions forbidding foreign ownership
        of lands, particularly oil land, died when public disclosure
        of the Teapot Dome Scandal made headlines, 1926-27.

1106   _____. "U.S. Diplomacy and the 'Specter of Bolshevism'
        in Mexico (1924-1927)." Americas 32 (July 1975): 31-45.
        Discusses the U.S. fear of Mexican Bolshevism, a
        manifestation of a strong "Mexico for Mexicans" movement
        that incorporated nationalism and a particular sovereignty
        consciousness, and contributed to the deterioration of
        diplomatic relations between Mexico and the United States.

Diplomatic History and International Affairs

1107   _____. "Did the United States Plan an Invasion of Mexico in 1927?" JISWA 15 (Nov. 1973): 454-71.

The United States did not seriously contemplate an invasion of Mexico, as some historians have contended. Rumors of that year concerning the invasion came from Mexican suspicion after some 300 documents, including contingency plans, were stolen from the U.S. Embassy in Mexico City. Calles used the incident of the stolen documents to strengthen his hand with the United States. Based on Mexican government documents and U.S. State Department materials.

1108   _____. "El embajador Sheffield contra el presidente Calles." HM 20 (Oct.-Dec. 1970): 265-84.

Discusses James R. Sheffield's role as U.S. Ambassador to Mexico in 1925, when Secretary of State Frank R. Kellogg stated that Mexico was on trial before the world. Sheffield's racism and hostility to Mexico's revolution contributed to the spread of the spurious notion of a Bolshevik government running Mexico. Based on Sheffield manuscripts at Yale University.

1109 KANE, N. STEPHEN. "Corporate Power and Foreign Policy: Efforts of American Oil Companies to Influence United States Relations with Mexico, 1921-1928." Diplomatic History 1 (1977): 170-98.

Demonstrates from two case studies of the interaction between American oil companies and the U.S. Department of State that the companies failed to exert effective influence on foreign policy in their efforts to protect their investments in Mexico. The State Department's position concerning Mexico's petroleum legislation was actually based on "the Department's long-standing commitment to the concept of fair treatment of United States citizens and their capital abroad in the fields of trade and investment within the framework of generally accepted principles of international law." Based on primary and secondary sources.

1110   _____. "American Businessmen and Foreign Policy: The Recognition of Mexico, 1920-1923." Political Science Quarterly 90 (1975): 293-313.

Presents a case study of the influence of the business community between 1920 and 1923 on the question of recognition of the Obregón regime in Mexico. Businessmen had little effective influence on that foreign policy decision.

Diplomatic History and International Affairs

1111 _____. "Bankers and Diplomats: The Diplomacy of the
    Dollar in Mexico, 1921-1924." Business History Review
    47 (1953): 335-52.
        Examines the cooperative relations between American
    investment bankers, the U.S. State Department, and Mexico,
    illustrating the interdependency of the dollar and diplomacy
    in the 1920s. Secretary of State Charles Evans Hughes used
    conditional recognition and financial pressure in the form
    of loan bans and closed markets to force Mexico to come
    to terms with the United States both politically and
    economically. The International Committee of Bankers on
    Mexico, representing holders of defaulted securities and
    working closely with the diplomats, achieved their goals
    of a settlement with Mexico wherein the debt would be paid.
    Diplomatic recognition came later. Mexican political
    instability hindered financial relations and eventually the
    Lamont-de la Huerta Agreement (1922) was suspended by
    Mexico. Dollar diplomacy achieved immediate American ends,
    but later proved self-defeating. Based on U.S. government
    documents, bankers' committee papers, contemporary news-
    paper reports, and other primary and secondary sources.

1112 SAENZ, AARON. La política internacional de la Revolución:
    Estudios y documentos. Mexico: Fondo de Cultura Económica,
    1961.
        A study of the international problems of the Mexican
    Revolution, including the oil issue, land disputes, and the
    various claims against Mexico. Authored by a former
    Secretary of Foreign Relations. Contents include the
    Bucareli Conferences, the Conventions of Claims, the Oil
    Regulations, and the Acquisition of Lands. Appendixes of
    the international Mexican-American question during the
    Obregón era and official correspondence between the govern-
    ments of Mexico and the United States about the Bylaws of
    section 1 of Article 27 of the Constitution. Fundamentally
    a partisan defense of Mexico's international policy in
    the Obregón administration.

1113 SCHOLES, WALTER, and SCHOLES, MARIE V. "Gran Bretana, los
    Estados Unidos y el no reconocimiento de Obregón." HM 19
    (Jan.-Mar. 1970): 388-96.
        The struggle in 1921-1922 between Obregón and the
    governments of the United States and Great Britain over
    Article 27 and recognition. Indicates that Great Britain
    supported the U.S. policy of nonrecognition of Obregón in
    1921-1922. Based on Foreign Office Records.

Economic and Social History

1114   SMITH, ROBERT FREEMAN.   "Estados Unidos y las reformas de la
        Revolución Mexicana, 1915-1928."   HM 19 (Oct.-Dec. 1969):
        189-227.
            A study of the application of "International Laws" to
        Mexico by the U.S., especially over the content of Article
        27 of the Constitution of 1917 and the "rights" of U.S.
        oil companies. Argues that "international law" favors the
        interests of developed, industrial creditor nations.

1115   _____. "The Morrow Mission and the International Committee
        of Bankers on Mexico: The Interaction of Finance Diplomacy
        and the New Mexican Elite." Journal of Latin American
        Studies 1 (Nov. 1969): 149-66.
            The deradicalization of the Revolution by Dwight Morrow
        and the international financial community in the late 1920s.
        A study in the working relationship between Ambassador
        Dwight Morrow (who had worked for J.P. Morgan & Co.) and
        Thomas W. Lamont of the International Committee of Bankers
        on Mexico (a former colleague of Morrow at J.P. Morgan
        Co.), and the development-oriented Mexican officials led
        by Secretary of Hacienda [Alfredo] Adolfo Pani--all of whom
        wanted to form and encourage the development of an autonomous
        middle class, not a socialist levelling.

For diplomacy and revolutionary nationalism, 1916-1932, see entries
979-980. For U.S., Mexico, and the oil controversy, 1917-1942,
see entries 1202-1203.

                        ECONOMIC AND SOCIAL HISTORY

1116   ADLESON, S. LIEF.   "Coyuntra y conciencia: Factores conver-
        gentes en la fundación de los sindicatos petroleros de
        Tampico durante la década de 1920."   In El trabajo y los
        trabajadores en la historia de México, compiled by Elsa
        Cecilia Frost, Michael C. Meyer, and Josefina Zoraida
        Vázquez, pp. 632-61. Mexico and Tucson: El Colegio de
        México and the University of Arizona Press, 1979.
            A study of labor agitation, strikes, and organization
        among the oil workers of the "El Aguila" company in
        Tampico, Tamaulipas (1923-1924). Concludes that the
        workers' success was due to outside aid and solidarity by
        municipal, state, and federal workers, and the militancy
        of the local workers. Based on local archives, newspapers,
        and secondary sources.

Economic and Social History

1117   ARRIOLA, ENRIQUE. "Los intereses petroleros, Calles, y los
        conflictos de 1924." Boletín del Archivo General de la
        Nación 1 (1977): 26-30.
            Reprints four letters between American businessmen
        Vernon J. Rose and Arthur C. Rath on the attitude of U.S.
        corporations toward the Mexican oil policies of President
        Plutarco Elías Calles, 1924-28. Based on documents in
        the Archivo General de la Nación.

1118   BASURTO, JORGE. El proletariado industrial en México,
        1850-1930. Mexico: UNAM, 1975.
            The industrial proletariat in Mexico, 1850-1930.

1119   CARDOSO, LAWRENCE A. "La repatriación de braceros en época de
        Obregón: 1920-1923." HM 26 (Apr.-June 1977): 576-95.
            Examination of repatriation of Mexican workers in the
        early 1920s caused by recession in the United States
        following World War I. Concludes that intensity and
        direction of population movement is primarily a function of
        U.S. economic needs.

1120   CARR, BARRY. El movimiento obrero y la política en México,
        1910-1929. 2 vols. Mexico: SepSetentas, 1976.
            Vol. 2 is a study of regional labor conflicts and the
        relationship of syndicalism to anticlericalism, agrarianism,
        and politics during the administration of Calles, 1924-1929.
        Well-documented, based on original research in Mexican
        archives. For vol. 1 see entry 999.

1121   CASTRO, JOSE RIVERA. "Le Syndicalisme Officiel et le Syndical-
        isme Révolutionnaire au Mexique dans les Années 1920."
        Mouvement Social 103 (1978): 31-52.
            Study of two rival labor movements in Mexico in the
        1920s. The Action group established a labor movement called
        the Confederación Regional Obrera Mexicana (CROM) and its
        political arm, the Labor Party. CROM and the army were the
        two pillars of the state. Simultaneously, anarchosyn-
        dicalists and communists organized an independent labor
        movement, the General Confederation of Labor (CGT). They
        both found themselves in conflict with the State. Revolu-
        tionary and official unions struggled for control over
        industrial workers, especially in the petroleum, transport,
        and textile industries. The CGT stimulated strikes, whereas
        CROM tried to break them.

1122   CUMBERLAND, CHARLES C. "The Sonora Chinese and the Mexican
        Revolution." HAHR 40 (May 1960): 191-211.

Causes and effects of the expulsion of the Chinese from Sonora during the early 1930s. A study in Mexican xenophobia. Based on U.S. consular dispatches.

1123   FALCON VEGA, ROMANA. El agrarismo en Veracruz: La etapa radical, 1928-1935. Mexico: El Colegio de México, 1977.
       Demonstrates that the agrarian movement of Veracruz during Adalberto Tejeda's governorship was carried out in conflict with less radical agrarian programs of the national government.

1124   GOMEZ, MARTE R. "La reforma agraria de México: Su crisis durante el período 1928-1934." Mexico: Porrúa, 1964.
       Consists of an account of the political and social furor over the agrarian issue in the years 1928-1934, and the text of a lecture on Mexican agrarian reform read in 1929. Appendix lists the amounts of land redistributed.

1125   GONZALEZ NAVARRO, MOISES. "Efectos sociales de la crisis de 1929." HM 19 (Apr.-June 1970): 536-58.
       Examines social effects of the 1929 economic crisis, particularly the exclusion of foreign workers and the repatriation of Mexicans from the United States. Based on official reports.

1126   HOFFMAN, ABRAHAM. "El cierre de la puerta trasera norteamericana: restricción de la inmigración mexicana." HM 25 (Jan.-Mar. 1976): 403-22.
       Analysis of administrative restriction of immigration from Mexico beginning in 1929.

1127   ITURRIAGA de la FUENTE, JOSE. La revolución hacendaria: La hacienda pública con el presidente Calles. Mexico: SepSetentas, 1976.
       A study of the economic revolution under Calles from 1925 to 1928. Argues that Plutarco Elías Calles was hindered from effective action by obstacles posed by the cristero opposition, the United States and oil interests, and the majority of congressmen who were for obregonismo.

1128   LEVENSTEIN, HARVEY A. "The AFL and Mexican Immigration in the 1920's: An Experiment in Labor Diplomacy." HAHR 48 (1968): 206-19.
       Narrates efforts by Samuel Gompers and AFL to restrict Mexican immigration and AFL-CROM relations to 1928.

Economic and Social History

1129   LOMBARDO TOLEDANO, VICENTE. La libertad sindical en México
        1926. Mexico: Universidad Obrera de México, 1974.
        Personal account of syndicalism in the 1920s by CTM
        labor leader Toledano.

1130   MACHADO, MANUEL A., Jr. "An Industry in Limbo: The Mexican
        Cattle Industry, 1920-1924." Agricultural History 50
        (Oct. 1976): 615-25.
        Notes that the Mexican cattle raising industry in the
        1920s suffered from government expropriation of large
        estates, cattle rustling, disease, and U.S. import and
        sanitary restrictions, and the number of cattle in Mexico
        remained well below prerevolutionary levels. Exports to
        the United States dropped sharply.

1131   PAZ, GUILLERMINA BAENA. "La confederación general de traba-
        jadores (1921-1931)." Revista Mexicana de Ciencias Políticas
        y Sociales 22 (Jan.-Mar. 1976): 113-86.
        A study of the Mexican CGT (General Confederation of
        Workers) during its anarchosyndicalist stage from 1921 to
        1931. Origins, history, structure and function of the CGT.
        Heavy reliance upon the pioneering works of Rosendo
        Salazar.

1132   REISLER, MARK. "Always the Laborer, Never the Citizen: Anglo
        Perceptions of the Mexican Immigrant during the 1920s."
        Pacific Historical Review 45 (May 1976): 231-54.
        Analysis of how Americans viewed Mexican workers during
        the 1920s. Notes that both sides on the immigration
        restriction debate operated from similar stereotypes of
        Mexican workers as docile, backward, and indolent. Based
        primarily on government reports and Congressional hearings.

1133   SALAMINI, HEATHER FOWLER. Agrarian Radicalism in Veracruz,
        1920-38. Lincoln: University of Nebraska Press, 1978.
        A political history and political sociology of Adalberto
        Tejeda and agrarismo in Veracruz. Analyzes how Tejeda and
        others created paramilitary tools in order to institute a
        program of radical reform which included obtaining land
        grants, controlling the clergy and the landlords, and
        applying tax laws to the oil companies. Indicates that
        the Tejeda program for Veracruz (1929-1932) paralleled
        Cárdenas's agrarian program in Michoacán, and that Cárdenas's
        national oil industry reforms had been initiated by Tejeda.
        Based on primary sources--interviews, local newspapers,
        national archives.

Economic and Social History

1134 _____. "Adalberto Tejeda and the Veracruz Peasant Movement." In Contemporary Mexico: Papers of the Fourth
International Congress of Mexican History, edited by James
W. Wilkie, Michael C. Meyer, and Edna Monzón de Wilkie,
pp. 274-92. Los Angeles and Mexico: University of
California Press and El Colegio de México, 1976.
Notes that the Veracruz agrarian movement passed through
four distinctive phases between 1906 and 1940: the first
phase, 1906-1923, was characterized by a spontaneous,
loosely organized mobilization of isolated groups; the
second phase, 1923 to 1928, saw the Peasant League organized
under the charismatic leadership of Ursulo Galván, radical-
ized by Galván's Marxist convictions, and militarized by
the revolt of 1923--i.e., institutionalization of the
peasant movement; phase three (1928-1932) saw the apogee
of peasant politization under the leadership of reform
governor Adalberto Tejeda (the "golden age of agrarianism");
and phase four (1932-1940) witnessed the hostility and
repression of the national government under Calles and disintegration for the peasant movement. Calles and the
official party curbed regional caudillos, and Tejeda became
another instance in history of a "case of political
marginality." Based on previous field work, especially
the Archive of A. Tejeda.

1135 _____. "Los orígenes de las organizaciones campesinas en
Veracruz: Raíces políticas y sociales." HM 22 (July-
Sept. 1972): 52-76.
Labor-farmer unrest in Veracruz was tense by 1923,
when armed violence occurred between campesinos and landowners in Puente Nacional. Governor Adalberto Tejeda
responded by fostering creation of the League of Agrarian
Communities and Farmers Syndicate of Veracruz State. The
combined talents of Ursulo Galván Reyes and Manuel Almanza
García advanced the cause. Results of the first league
convention in March produced notably moderate declarations
and resolutions, which contrasted sharply with those adopted
in other states. Tejeda's leadership and influence served
to neutralize Marxist-Syndicalist agitation and compared
favorably with similar developments in Michoacán under
Governor Lázaro Cárdenas. The league continued to operate
under official protection until the PNR was organized.
Based on the Tejeda papers; other primary and secondary
sources.

1136 TANNENBAUM, FRANK. The Mexican Agrarian Revolution. 1929.
Reprint. Hamden, Conn.: Archon Books, 1968.

Economic and Social History

Reproduction of a classic work on Mexican agrarian structure and the Revolution. Discusses historical development of the landholding system, the grouping and character of rural population, organization of the hacienda, the causes of the Revolution, the chronology of agrarian reform, and the influence of the Revolution on land distribution, 1915-1926. Appendixes contain population and land statistics and agrarian legislation.

1137 TOBLER, HANS WERNER. "Alvaro Obregón und die Anfänge der Mexikanischen Agrarreform, Agrarpolitik und Agrarkonflikt, 1920-1924." Jahrbuch für Geschichte von Staat, Wirtschaft und Gesellschaft Latein Amerikas 8 (1971): 310-65.
Obregón and the beginnings of agrarian reform, agrarian politics, and agrarian conflict, 1920-24.

1138 _____. "Las paradojas del ejército revolucionario: Su papel social en la reforma agraria mexicana, 1920-1936." HM 21 (July-Sept. 1971): 38-79.
According to the author, "the army resulted in not being a decisive instrument in the agrarian reconstruction, as there was room for hope in its popular revolutionary origin, but...to the contrary, it came to be one of the principal obstacles to progressive politics of reform and an important factor in the preservation of the old agrarian structures."

For caudillos and peasants see entry 351. For agrarian reform in Tlaxcala see entries 475 and 995; for agrarian conflict in Atencingo (Puebla) see entry 499; for agrarian revolt in Michoacán see entry 482; and for campesinos of Morelos see entry 504. For anarchism and the working class, 1860-1931, see entry 1008; and for labor history to 1931, see entry 1011.

RELIGIOUS AND CHURCH HISTORY

1139 ANDA, JOSE GUADALUPE de. Los cristeros: La guerra Santa en los Altos. Mexico: ANDA, 1974.
Traditional study of the cristero era.

1140 BAILEY, DAVID C. ¡Viva Cristo Rey! The Cristero Rebellion and the Church-State Conflict in Mexico. Austin and London: University of Texas Press, 1974.
Argues that during the State-Church conflict of the 1920s the Church was a reformed institution committed to social justice, not a reactionary body. Further, the author

points out that the hacendado class and the old Catholic
upper class supported the government. Notes that the
Vatican sought to preserve priestly functions more than
the position of the Mexican Church, and that U.S. intervention in the form of Dwight Morrow was decisive for
the government's victory. Based on newspapers, League
archives, memoirs and tracts of League members, accounts
and interpretations of government officials, U.S. State
Department papers, and recent secondary works.

1141 _____. "Alvaro Obregón and Anticlericalism in the 1910
Revolution." Americas 26 (Oct. 1969): 183-98.
Obregón's relations with the Church is studied during
various phases: his early career as a military revolutionary; the period of his presidency; and after 1924.
Obregón believed that organized religion had no useful
role to play in the future of the nation and dealt
harshly with clergymen during the violent phase of the
Revolution. After 1920, as president, he showed some
flexibility in enforcing anticlerical provisions of the
1917 Constitution. The Church could continue to function
and exist, but on terms set by the State.

1142 BARBA GONZALEZ, SILVANO. La rebelión de los cristeros.
Mexico: Manuel Casas Impresor, 1967.

1143 BONFIL, ALICIA O. de. La literatura cristera. Mexico:
Instituto Nacional de Antropología e Historia, 1970.
Proclamas and corridos of the cristero movement.

1144 DOOLEY, FRANCIS PATRICK. Los cristeros, Calles y el
catolicismo mexicano. Mexico: SepSetentas, 1976.
A study of the conflict between Catholics and
"Revolutionaries" from 1913 to the cristero era of Calles
in 1926 and 1927. Notes how the government of Carranza
accused the Church of supporting both Porfirio Díaz and
Victoriano Huerta and justified government persecution on
this ground, an argument used by other governments up to
and including Calles. Narrates the reaction by Catholics,
especially the leadership of French Jesuit Bernardo Bergoend,
who prepared his followers for social and political action
through use of arms.

1145 HILTON, STANLEY E. "The Church-State Dispute over Education
in Mexico from Carranza to Cárdenas." Americas 21
(Oct. 1964): 163-83.

Religious and Church History

Divides the history of Church-State relations into
three periods: era from 1917 to 1926 was quiescent owing
to moderation of Carranza; the period from 1926 to 1933
saw a positive campaign by the State to eradicate religious
influences at secondary and higher levels; the Cárdenas
era saw strong Church resistance to official "socialistic"
education. Based on published materials and U.S. State
Department dispatches.

1146   LARIN, NICOLAS. La rebelión de los cristeros (1926-1929).
       Translated by Angel C. Tomás. Mexico: Ediciones Era, 1968.
       Russian scholar who treats the cristero rebellion from
       a Marxist-Leninist framework. Sees the Church as a
       reactionary, fanatical force tied to Porfirian elites,
       hacendados, the new Mexican capitalists, and imperialist
       interests in the United States. The cristero revolt was
       a struggle between bourgeois elements represented by the
       government and quasi-feudalistic groups backed by the
       imperialists in the United States. Does not include
       United States or Mexican archives. Originally published
       as Borba tzerkvi s gosudarstvom v Meksike (Moscow, 1965).

1147   McDOWELL, JOHN HOLMES. "The Cristero Rebellion of Mexico: /
       A Sociological Approach." Austin: University of Texas
       Student Conference, 12 April 1974.
       Limited edition of a publication of the Student Conference
       on Latin America.

1148   MEYER, JEAN A. The Cristero Rebellion: The Mexican People
       between Church and State 1926-1929. Translated by Richard
       Southern. Cambridge Latin American Studies, no. 24.
       New York and London: Cambridge University Press, 1976.
       Abridged, translated English version of a massive study
       that appeared previously in two published forms: La
       Cristiada. 3 vols. Mexico: Siglo Veintiuno Editores,
       1973-4 [La guerra de los cristeros; El conflicto entre la
       iglesia y el estado, 1926-1929; Los cristeros] and
       Apocalypse et Révolution au Mexique: La guerre des
       Cristeros, 1926-1929. Paris: Editions Gallimard/Juilliard,
       1974.
       Revision of the history of the cristero rebellion and
       the Mexican Revolution. Contrary to traditional liberal
       and Marxist accounts, the author sees the cristero revolt
       as an authentic peasant movement and a Catholic resistance.
       Presents the Mexican Revolution as another stage in the
       growth of political absolutism, authoritarian statism, and
       capitalism. Argues that after 1910 a secular and armed

State collided with a reformed Church that offered an
alternative Mexican revolution. Cristeros came from the
rural poor as peons, small proprietors, and Indian
communeros; heirs of the agrarian, Catholic, rural world
of the zapatistas of 1910. Abandoned by urban Catholics
and the church hierarchy, they became another of history's
"losers." Well-researched, the product of seven years'
labor; based on personal interviews of survivors and local
and church documents--a major historiographical achievement
in the Annales tradition.

1149   . La cristiada. Translated by Aurelio Garzón del
Camino. 3 vols. Mexico: Siglo XXI Editores, 1973 74.
        Vol. 1, The War of the Cristeros. Vol. 2, The Conflict
Between Church and State 1926-1939. Vol. 3, The Cristeros.
This book contains many public and private documents from
the cristero movement.

1150   . "La cristiada." In Extremos de México, pp. 225-40.
Mexico: El Colegio de México, 1971.
        The author designates the period from 1926-1929 as
"La cristiada."

1151 MOCTEZUMA, AQUILES [pseud.]. El conflicto religioso de 1926.
Mexico. Editorial Jus, 1968.

1152 NAVARRETE, HERIBERTO. El voto de Chema Rodríguez: Relato de
ambiente cristero. Mexico: Jus, 1964.
        The author gives an historical account of the cristero
campaign. He participated in the rebellion in order to
revenge the death of his father, who was assassinated by
a government official.

1153 OLIVERA SEDANO, ALICIA. "La iglesia en México, 1926-1970."
In Contemporary Mexico, pp. 295-316. Berkeley: University
of California Press, 1976.
        A general study of the Church in Mexico. Discusses the
military aspects of the cristero conflict and concludes that
the cristeros could not have won.

1154   . Aspectos del conflicto religioso de 1926 a 1929:
Sus antecedentes y sus consecuencias. Mexico: Instituto
Nacional de Antropología e Historia, 1966.
        Argues that the Catholic Church was counterrevolutionary
and opposed to the secular revolution. Notes that there
were progressive Catholic elements which did oppose the
State, that the Catholic group was not monolithic, and that

Religious and Church History

the leadership was divided into an urban-based group
directed by the National League for the Defense of Religious
Liberty and a rural-based group composed of campesinos.
Based on league archives.

1155   QUIRK, ROBERT E.   The Mexican Revolution and the Catholic
Church, 1910-1929.   Bloomington and London: Indiana
University Press, 1973.
Quirk sees the Church as a threat to the revolutionary
ideal because it offered a romanticized version of medieval
corporatism and social justice that was irrelevant to the
masses, who saw the Church as foreign and exploitative.
The Church-State conflict of the 1920s was a victory for
the Revolution and resulted in a defeat for the corporatist
ideal.   Derived from the Canon García Gutiérrez collection,
the National League for the Defense of Religious Liberty
archives, and U.S. State Department materials.   Omits
cristero material.   Revised version of dissertation.

1156   SNOW, SINCLAIR.   "Protestants versus Catholics: U.S. Reaction
to the Mexican Church-State Conflict of 1926-29."   North
Dakota Quarterly 39 (1971): 68-80.
Discusses the American reaction, Protestant and Catholic,
to the conflict between Church and State in Mexico in the
late 1920s.   Protestants supported the Mexican government
and Calles.   American Catholics tried to develop a "red
scare" to stir American intervention and opposition to
Calles.   The Knights of Columbus was the principal source
of pro-Catholic agitation in the United States.   Based on
published materials.

1157   WILKIE, JAMES W.   "The Meaning of the Cristero Religious War
Against the Mexican Constitution."   Journal of Church and
State 8 (Spring 1966): 214-33.
Reexamines the cristero conflict, aiming to identify its
causes and to explain the strange outcome of the Church-
State conflict in 1929 which resulted in a victory for the
government even though there was no decisive defeat of
the Catholics.

For historiography of the cristeros see entry 211.   For Church-State
relations in Veracruz, 1840-1940, see entry 507.   For the memoirs of
a cristero see entry 563.   For a biography of a cristero leader see
entry 614.   For U.S. involvement in the religious crisis see entries
1099 and 1102.

HISTORY OF EDUCATION

1158   BRITTON, JOHN A. Educación y radicalismo en México. Vol. 1,
Los anos de Bassols (1931-1934). Mexico: SepSetentas,
1976.
    A history of the Secretaría de Educación Pública from
1931 to 1934, when Narciso Bassols was the Secretary of
Education, a time when the SEP underwent intensive Marxist
influence. See also entry 1233.

1159   _____. "Moisés Saénz: Nacionalista mexicano." HM 22
(July-Sept. 1972): 77-97.
    Analysis of the writings of Moisés Saénz (1880-1941)
indicates that, as Undersecretary of Public Education,
1923-33, he sought mainly to instill an intellectual
defense of Mexican economic sovereignty and to promote
social and cultural integration. Actual experience at
Carrapan, Michoacán, and in San Luis Potosí, and with
Mexico's difficulty in regaining control over its natural
resources, encouraged a certain pessimism. Saénz never
abandoned the ideal of an integrated Mexico, but was
obliged to admit that the process would take longer than
earlier anticipated. Based on primary and secondary sources.

1160   RABY, DAVID L. "Ideology and State-Building: The Political
Function of Rural Education in Mexico, 1921-1935." Ibero-
Amerikanisches Archiv (Berlin) 4 (1978): 21-38.
    Argues that the Sonoran regime of Obregón and Calles
promoted popular education in the rural zones for ideological purposes, i.e., an instrument of the government
for channeling the radical impulses of the petite bourgeoisie and workers. Studies also the anticlericalism of
the Sonorans, and argues for its ideological uses in
state-building.

1161   _____. Educación y Revolución social en México (1921-
1940). Mexico: SepSetentas, 1974.
    A study of the role of rural teachers in the social and
political history of the Revolution, 1921-1940. Focus is
upon the unionization of teachers, their role in agrarian
reform, hostility to them by conservative groups, and
their role in local history, especially literary campaigns.

1162   SCHOENHALS, LOUISE. "Mexico Experiments in Rural and Primary
Education: 1921-1930." HAHR 44 (Feb. 1964): 22-43.
    A discussion of the educational policies of the Mexican
government under Obregón, Calles, and Portes Gil.

History of Education

1163   VAUGHAN, MARK K. "Women, Class, and Education in Mexico,
        1880-1928." Latin American Perspectives 4 (Winter/Spring
        1977): 135-52.
            Thesis: Mexico modernized within the framework of
        capitalism, and the State gradually absorbed functions of
        the family for the purpose of increasing the productive
        capacity of society and ensuring the continuation of the
        existing social order. A particular ideology of the
        family prevails through the school system and other state
        bureaucracies in which the subordinate and primarily
        domestic role of women is reaffirmed. Both the public
        school system and the particular ideology of the family
        which the State elaborates are important tools in dampening
        working-class consciousness and organization.

1164   _____. "Education and Class Struggle in the Mexican
        Revolution." Latin American Perspectives 2 (Summer 1975):
        17-33.
            Chronicles elementary educational policy in Mexico,
        1890-1930. Programs were designed primarily to mold a
        labor force equipped with skills and social attitudes
        appropriate to the modernization process and with values
        which legitimized bourgeois rule.

For the Church-State dispute over education see entry 1145.

                CULTURAL AND INTELLECTUAL HISTORY

1165   BASSOLS BATALLA, NARCISO. El pensamiento político de Alvaro
        Obregón. Mexico: Editorial El Caballito, 1970.
            Obregón's political thought.

1166   JUAREZ, NICANDRO F. "José Vasconcelos and la raza cósmica."
        Aztlán 3 (1972): 51-82.
            José Vasconcelos (1882-1959) followed racist and pro-
        European ideas in his development of the ideology of La
        raza cósmica (1925): the ultimate superiority of the
        mestizo and Hispanic peoples. The contradictions in
        Vasconcelos's philosophy stemmed from his adherence to both
        environmental and racial determinism. Vasconcelos
        denigrated the native Indian culture in favor of the
        Hispanic, yet he also contributed to the development of
        Latin American nationalism. Based on Spanish language
        works of José Vasconcelos and secondary sources.

Cultural and Intellectual History

1167   MULLEN, EDWARD J., ed. Contemporáneos: Revista Mexicana de
       Cultura, 1928-1931. Madrid: Ediciones Anaya, 1972.
          Commentary on the Mexican literary journal Contemporáneos
       and its place in the history of twentieth-century Mexican
       literature. Contains a bibliography and a compilation
       of information on principal contributors for the 1928-
       1931 period.

1168   _____. "Contemporáneos in Mexican Intellectual History,
       1928-1931." JISWA 13 (Feb. 1971): 121-30.
          A study of the literary and cultural periodical
       Contemporáneos, founded in 1928 by a group of young
       intellectuals who desired to examine the Mexican character
       and analyze Mexican society.

1169   OROZCO, JOSE CLEMENTE. José Clemente Orozco: An Autobiography.
       Translated by Robert C. Stephenson. Austin: University
       of Texas Press, 1962.
          Autobiography by one of Mexico's greater muralists.
       Narrative ends at 1940. Includes accounts of his visits
       to the United States and Europe. Forty-four illustrations:
       paintings, cartoons, and murals.

1170   ROMANELL, PATRICK. Making of the Mexican Mind: A Study in
       Recent Mexican Thought. Foreward by Edgar S. Brightman.
       London and Notre Dame: University of Notre Dame Press,
       1967.
          A history of ideas from the positivism of the Porfiriato
       to the existentialism and perspectivism of contemporary
       Mexico, with emphasis on the "Christian Dualism" of Antonio
       Caso and the "Aesthetic Monism" of José Vasconcelos.
       Selected bibliography of recent Mexican thought. Paper
       version of 1952 edition.

1171   SCHMIDT, HENRY C. "Antecedents to Samuel Ramos: Mexicanist
       Thought in the 1920s." JISWA 18 (May 1976): 179-202.
          Theme: In 1934 Samuel Ramos wrote his provocative
       study entitled Profile of Man and Culture in Mexico.
       Basing his study on the works of four predecessors, Ramos
       presented a theory of Mexican society and its role in the
       outside world. Ramos's thought can be characterized as
       critical nationalism with a clearly humanistic tinge.
       Based on the work of Ramos and several other Mexican writers
       of the same genre.

1172   STAMATU, HORIA. "Die 'Revolución' und die Literatur Mexikos
       im 20. Jahrundert." Saeculum 16 (1965): 191-255.

Cultural and Intellectual History

From 1919–1930 a new generation of revolutionary writers started a renaissance in Mexican literature to the extent of creating a national literature.

For quotations from Siquerios see entry 511. For a biography of Diego Rivera see entry 605. For works relating to Vasconcelos see entries 630, 632, 635, 639, 668, 674, and 703. For Antonio Caso see entries 630 and 638. For Vasconcelos and the election of 1929 see entries 1079 and 1092.

XI. The Cárdenas Era, 1934-1940

1173 AGUILAR OCEGUERA, FRANCISCO JAVIER. El papel de los militares en la etapa cardenista. Mexico: UNAM, Facultad de Ciencias Políticas y Sociales, 1973.
Argues that Cárdenas began to weaken the power of the generals, many of whom were callistas in public positions, by replacing them with his own men. He also armed the campesinos and destroyed the power of the caudillos.

1174 ANGUIANO, ARTURO. El estado y la política obrera del cardenismo. Mexico: Ediciones Era, 1975.

1175 BENITEZ, FERNANDO. Lázaro Cárdenas y la Revolución Mexicana. 3 vols. Mexico: Fondo de Cultura Económica, 1977.
Vol. 1, El porfirismo; Vol. 2, El caudillismo; vol. 3, El cardenismo. Traditional chronology of the Revolution in which Cárdenas redirected what had been a stumbling incoherent Revolution and gave it authentic orientation as an economic and national Revolution. After 1940 the Revolution lapsed into bourgeois populism under misguided and devious men who abandoned Cárdenas's revolutionary nationalism. Volume 3 covers Cárdenas's presidency and the subsequent thirty years until his death in 1970.

1176 CALVERT, PETER. "The Institutionalisation of the Mexican Revolution." JISWA 11 (Nov. 1969): 503-17.
Attempts to answer the question of when the Mexican Revolution of 1910 became institutionalized. Suggests that the term "institutionalized" indicates that the government in this stage ruled without resorting to force. To accomplish this, agriculture, urban labor, the Church, foreign interests, and the military had to be satisfied with the government. The National Revolutionary Party attempted to incorporate these groups. Consequently, diverse elements in Mexico were able to work out their

Political, Legal, and Military History

differences through the party. The groundwork for this
cooperation was laid in the period from 1928 to 1934.

1177   "Cárdenas, Lázaro." Revista de la Universidad de México 25
       (1971).
           This issue is dedicated to the study of Cárdenas. The
       articles included are: "Los límites de la política
       cardenista: La presión externa," by Lorenzo Meyer;
       "Confusiones y aciertos de la educación cardenista," by
       Josefina V. de Knauth; "Cárdenas: Del maximato al presiden-
       cialismo," by Tzdi Medín; "Lázaro Cárdenas y el neutralismo
       actual," by Enrique Suárez Gaona; "Testamento político de
       Cárdenas" (speech given in Irapuato on 20 November 1969);
       "Los comunistas y el régimen de Cárdenas," by Lyle C. Brown.

1178   CORDOVA, ARNALDO. "La Transformación del PNR en PRM: El
       Triunfo del Corporativismo en México." In Contemporary
       Mexico: Papers of the Fourth International Congress of
       Mexican History, edited by James W. Wilkie, Michael C.
       Meyer, and Edna Monzón de Wilkie, pp. 204-27. Los Angeles
       and Mexico: University of California Press and El Colegio
       de México, 1976.
           A study of the transformation of the National Revolu-
       tionary Party (PNR) into the Party of the Mexican Revolu-
       tion (PRM) in the 1930s by Cárdenas. The PRM organized
       the people ("pueblo organizado") into corporative sectors
       such as the labor CTM or the agrarian CNC, and made these
       sectors tools for promoting State interests. Based on
       newspapers, primary documents, and secondary works.

1179   _____. La política de masas del cardenismo. Mexico:
       Ediciones Era, 1974.
           Argues that the success of Cárdenas lay in his recognition
       of the need to organize the masses. Cárdenas made of
       Mexico by 1935 an organized country; everyone, workers,
       peasants and capitalists, was organized under the PRM.
       Paradoxically it was the "populist" Cárdenas who created
       the vast Federal bureaucracy, effective in every region
       and state, which was a necessary substructure of the
       strong executive. The purpose was development: to
       change Mexico from a backward agricultural nation to a
       modern industrial one.

1180   HAMILTON, NORA. "Mexico: The Limits of State Autonomy."
       Latin American Perspectives 2 (1975): 81-108.

Political, Legal, and Military History

Analyzes attempts by the Lázaro Cárdenas administration, 1934-40, to implement revolutionary concepts of the auto- nomous state. Irreconcilable contradictions within the theory resulted in changes in class-state relations and ended by favoring the dominant social classes.

1181   HERMAN, DONALD L. "The Left Wing and the Communists in
       Mexico." Texas Quarterly 15 (1972): 116-33.
          A study of President Lázaro Cárdenas's administration
       in Mexico. Casts doubt on the thesis that a democratic
       left-wing government in Latin America offers the strongest
       resistance to Communist influence. The communists secured
       leadership of labor unions and the educational system
       during Cárdenas's term, as well as reaching a peak in
       membership. Primary and secondary sources.

1182   IANNI, OCTAVIO. El estado capitalista en la época de Cárdenas.
       Mexico: Ediciones Era, 1977.
          A study in the political economy of the Cárdenas state.
       Placed in the larger historical context of the developing
       revolutionary bourgeois state, Cárdenas is described as
       a man committed to the bourgeois notion of industrial
       progress and to the nationalist ideal of a Mexican revolu-
       tionary process. Threatened by North American intervention
       and presented with the opportunity for statist solutions
       to the problems of the Great Depression, Cárdenas consol-
       idated a fortified state which, as a vanguard, transformed
       and energized Mexican capitalism.

1183   Legado revolucionario de Lázaro Cárdenas. Mexico: B. Costa-
       Amic, 1971.
          A compilation of articles by several writers written
       in honor of Cárdenas on the first anniversary of his
       death. Eulogistic. Includes a speech by his son, Cuahtémoc
       Cárdenas Solórzano, given in front of the Monumento a la
       Revolución.

1184   LEPKOWSKI, TADEUSZ. "La Polonia de los coroneles y el México
       de Cárdenas (1934-1939)." Estudios Latinoamericanos
       (1972): 195-218.
          Polish military activities in Cárdenas's Mexico.

1185   LOPEZ-PORTILLO y WEBER, JOSE. "Primera decada del petróleo y
       última del porfiriato: Lázaro Cárdenas, presidente civil."
       Memorias de la Academia Mexicana de Historia 29 (1970):
       352-420.

Political, Legal, and Military History

Eulogistic and sympathetic tribute to Cárdenas: "Mexico is fortunate in counting itself as one of the more privileged countries because of its leader, Lázaro Cárdenas, who has not only been an honored revolutionary caudillo, but the Revolution itself."

1186   MEDIN, TZVI. Ideología y praxis política de Lázaro Cárdenas. Mexico: Siglo XXI Editores, 1972.
A significant account of the Cárdenas presidency, being both intellectual history and political biography. Well-researched, based on manuscript sources, oral history interviews, published documents, and important secondary works.

1187   MEYER, LORENZO. "La etapa formativa del estado mexicano contemporáneo (1928-1940)." Foro Internacional 17 (1977): 453-76.
Discusses the establishment of a one-party political system in Mexico through absorption, cooptation, and purges. The roles of Plutarco Elías Calles and Lázaro Cárdenas are stressed.

1188   MICHAELS, ALBERT L. "Las elecciones de 1940." HM 21 (July-Sept. 1971): 80-134.
Presents the characteristics of the first three candidates: Múgica, Almazán and Avila Camacho. Cárdenas selected Manuel Avila Camacho as his successor because he was the most appropriate candidate to meet the approaching political situation.

1189   _____. "The Crisis of Cardenismo." Journal of Latin American Studies 2 (May 1970): 51-79.
A study of the last year of the Cárdenas government focusing on the election of his successor. Notes that the movement towards Camacho and away from Francisco Múgica did not mean a betrayal of the Mexican Left. Cárdenas's acts in 1939, which included no more expropriations or labor conflicts, a decrease in land reform, the protection of small landowners from peasant land seizures, and the selection of Avila Camacho by the PRM, were designed to preserve the government's accomplishments, avoid civil war, institutionalize past reforms, and reduce hatred and anxiety among wealthy cardenistas, small landowners, foreign investors, and the growing urban middle class. The move to moderation was designed to preserve the various gains of the previous six years and avoid economic collapse.

Political, Legal, and Military History

1190 NOVO, SALVADOR. La vida en México en el período presidencial
de Lázaro Cárdenas. Mexico: Empresas Editoriales, 1964.
Collection of periodical articles portraying the last
three years of the Cárdenas administration. First of a
projected series of five volumes.

1191 RABY, DAVID L. "La contribución del cardenismo al desarrollo
de México en la epoca actual." Aportes (Paris) 26 (1972):
31-65.
Various hypotheses are presented about the policy
followed by Cárdenas during his term of office. The author
argues that a more adequate analysis of the cardenista era
can be made by seeing his regime as a kind of multiclass
alliance: the coalition of the national bourgeoisie, the
working class and peasants against the internal and external
reaction.

1192 RAMOS OLIBEIRA, ANTONIO. El asesinato de Trotski. Mexico:
Campanía General de Ediciones, 1972.
A narrative of the assassination of Trotsky in Mexico
on 20 August 1940; followed by a reproduction of Trotsky's
autobiographical essay entitled "Mi vida."

1193 SELVA, MAURICIO de la. "Los Apuntes de Lázaro Cárdenas."
Cuadernos Americanos 184 (Sept.-Oct. 1972): 66-72.
The writer concludes that "these Apuntes not only aided
the development of Mexican nationalism, but enabled Latin
Americans to develop a common goal of uniting against
the enemy--North American imperialism."

1194 SILVA HERZOG, JESUS. "Cárdenas en la presidencia." Cuadernos
Americanos 1/4 (Jan.-Feb. 1971): 91-104.
Sympathetic synopsis of the Cárdenas presidency that
likens Cárdenas to Benito Juárez.

1195 SUAREZ VALLES, MANUEL, comp. Lázaro Cárdenas. Mexico: B.
Costa-Amic, 1971.
A collection of writings on Lázaro Cárdenas by eighty
writers from Mexico and elsewhere, compiled and edited by
Suárez Valles, a Spanish "Republican" refugee who greatly
admired Cárdenas.

1196 TOWNSEND, WILLIAM CAMERON. Lázaro Cárdenas: Demócrata
mexicano. Mexico: Editorial Grijalbo, 1976.
Expanded Spanish language edition of a work first published in English in 1952. Six new chapters with material
on Cárdenas since the 1930s.

Political, Legal, and Military History

1197   VIDARTE, JUAN-SIMEON. Ante la tumba de Lázaro Cárdenas.
        Mexico: Ediciones "Valle de México," 1971.

1198   WILKIE, JAMES W. "El complejo militar-industrial en México
        durante la década de 1930: Diálogo con el general Juan
        Andreu Almazán." Revista Mexicana de Ciencias Políticas
        y Sociales 20 (July-Sept. 1974): 59-65.
            General Almazán explains how ambitious military men
        were coopted by Calles and Cárdenas through concessions of
        public works contracts. Claims decision to accept defeat
        in the election of 1940 was due to recognition that the
        United States favored Avila Camacho and would not tolerate
        a coup.

A multivolume work on events from 1933 to 1937 is entry 305. For a
revisionist study of Cárdenas see entries 313 and 1211. For bio-
graphies of Cárdenas see entries 591, 615-16, 655, 683, and 692.
For documentary sources on Cárdenas see entries 533-34. For the
Obras and memoirs of Cárdenas see entries 548-53. For the Revolution
in Michoacán, 1861-1967, see entry 487. For the Partido de Acción
Nacional see entries 1229 and 1231. For the political thought of
Cárdenas see entry 1246.

                DIPLOMATIC HISTORY AND INTERNATIONAL AFFAIRS

1199   CRONON, EDMUND DAVID. Josephus Daniels in Mexico. Madison:
        University of Wisconsin Press, 1960.
            An exemplary study of the diplomatic mission of Josephus
        Daniels in Mexico, 1934-1941. Focuses upon Daniels's
        handling of the sinarquista problem, the agrarian claims,
        and the petroleum expropriation. Reveals debate within
        the Roosevelt administration and the circumvention of the
        State Department by Daniels who was a personal friend of
        Roosevelt. A sympathetic account of Daniels, portrayed as
        a liberal and idealist who was friendly to Mexico's reform
        objectives. Based upon manuscript materials in the Daniels,
        Roosevelt, and State Department archives.

1200   HOFFMAN, ABRAHAM. Unwanted Mexican Americans in the Great
        Depression: Repatriation Pressures, 1929-1939. Tucson:
        University of Arizona Press, 1974.
            A short, well-documented historical investigation of the
        repatriation of Mexican nationals during the Great Depres-
        sion which clearly distinguishes between federal and local
        efforts to expatriate.

Diplomatic History and International Affairs

1201   MEYER, JEAN A.   "Los Estados Unidos y el petróleo mexicano:
Estado de la cuestión." HM 18 (1968): 79-96.
The oil question in Mexican-United States relations.

1202   MEYER, LORENZO. Mexico and the United States in the Oil
Controversy, 1917-1942. Austin & London: University of
Texas Press, 1977.
Explores the relationship between United States and
Mexico during the first half of the twentieth century,
with special attention to the Mexican nationalization of
the oil industry. Interpretation follows the dependency
theory. Based on Mexican archival material. Translated
from México y los Estados Unidos en el conflictor petrolero
(1917-1942), by Muriel Vasconcellos. First published by
Colegio de México.

1203   _____. México y los Estados Unidos en el conflicto
petrolero, 1917-1942. Mexico: El Colegio de México, 1972.
First published in 1968, this edition includes materials
from Mexican and U.S. archives not available in 1965-1967
when the first edition was completed. Meyer's book on the
conflict between Mexico and the United States over ownership
of oil companies operating in Mexico has become the standard
guide on the topic.

1204   _____. "El conflicto petrolero entre México y Los Estados
Unidos (1938-1942)." Foro Internacional 7 (1966): 99-159.
The oil controversy between Mexico and the United
States, 1938-1942.

1205   MORRISON, JOSEPH L. "Josephus Daniels, Simpático." JISWA
5 (Apr. 1963): 277-89.
Based on documents in the Southern Historical Collection
in Chapel Hill, North Carolina, the author demonstrates
the sympathies which Ambassador Daniels held concerning
the culture, people, and problems of Mexico.

1206   SMITH, ROBERT FREEMAN. "Who's Afraid of Sonj? Energy and
Nationalism in International Relations." Reviews in
American History 6 (1978): 394-99.
Review essay of Lorenzo Meyer's Mexico and the United
States in the Oil Controversy, 1917-1942. See entries
1202-1203.

1207   WALKER, WILLIAM O., III. "Control Across the Border: The
United States, Mexico, and Narcotics Policy, 1936-40."
Pacific History Review 47 (1978): 91-106.

Diplomatic History and International Affairs

> Argues that between 1936 and 1940 U.S. narcotic diplomacy transformed Mexican drug policy. The United States defined as illegal all nonmedical and nonscientific use of narcotics and made little distinction between users and peddlers. Although Mexico formally agreed to these policies in agreements signed in 1930 and 1932, its enforcement efforts did not gain American approval. In 1938, Leopold Salazar Viniegra became head of Mexico's Federal Narcotics Service. He did not believe in a punitive drug control program; instead he favored channeling the flow of illegal drugs through government controlled distribution centers. American diplomatic pressure led to Salazar's removal in August 1939 and to a more vigorous Mexican law enforcement policy. Based on documents in the National Archives, the Bureau of Narcotics Library, and Mexican newspapers.

ECONOMIC AND SOCIAL HISTORY

1208   ASHBY, JOE C. Organized Labor and the Mexican Revolution under Lázaro Cárdenas. Chapel Hill: University of North Carolina, 1967.
>   Well-documented economic history and case study of the role that organized labor may play as a tool for influencing industrial development in a lesser-developed economy. Major attention is given to the three chief areas of labor policy: the labor-National Railways difficulty; the labor-Laguna agricultural experiment question; and the labor-oil expropriations conflict.

1209   _____. "Labor and the Theory of the Mexican Revolution under Lázaro Cárdenas." Americas 20 (Oct. 1963): 158-99.
>   Examines the interpretation of the "general philosophy of the Revolution," during the Cárdenas government (1934-1940). Focuses on political, social and economic aspects, and puts emphasis on the "theory of work."

1210   BLANCO MOHENO, ROBERTO. Cuando Cárdenas nos dio la tierra. Mexico: Diana, 1970.
>   Agrarian reform under Cárdenas.

1211   BROWN, LYLE C. "Cárdenas: Creating a Campesino Power Base for Presidential Policy." In Essays on the Mexican Revolution: Revisionist Views of the Leaders, edited by George Wolfskill and Douglas W. Richmond, pp. 101-36. Austin & London: University of Texas Press, 1979.

The Cárdenas Era, 1934-1940

A study of the Cárdenas presidency, especially the foundation of the Confederación Nacional Campesina (CNC). The mobilization of the Mexican peasantry, opposed by several groups (most notably organized labor), helped Cárdenas to solidify his own position and enabled him to embark upon a series of social reforms. Based on printed sources and newspapers.

1212   CORDOVA, ARNALDO. La política de masas del cardenismo. Mexico: Ediciones Era, 1974.
        This study analyzes Cárdenas's position before the entrepeneurs purporting that his function was that of a counterbalance between the workers and the businessmen.

1213   CORONA, GUSTAVO. Lázaro Cárdenas y la expropiación de la industria petrolera en México. Mexico: 1975.
        Expropriation of the oil fields under Cárdenas. Prologue written by Salvador Calvillo Madrigal.

1214   DINWOODIE, D.H. "Deportation: The Immigration Service and the Chicano Labor Movement in the 1930s." NMHR 52 (July 1977): 193-206.
        Describes use of deportation as a weapon against labor organizers and distinguishes New Deal "liberalism" from repressive tactics actually implemented in the field. Based on a vast array of archival sources.

1215   FALCON VEGA, ROMANA. "El surgimiento del agrarismo cardenista: Una Revisión de las tesis populistas." HM 27 (Jan. Mar. 1978): 333-86.
        Challenges the traditional thesis that the agrarian populism of President Lázaro Cárdenas (1936-1940) represented an abrupt break with the policy of preceding regimes. Prior to the Cárdenas administration, the National Peasants Confederation, an organ of the official National Revolutionary Party, adopted a policy of moderate agrarianism and abolished laws limiting redistribution of land. Cárdenas's own agrarianism was a far more moderate version of that practiced in the states of Veracruz, Morelos, and Michoacán, 1928-32. Working within existing institutions and the law, this moderate agrarianism became Cárdenas's weapon to wrest control of the official party from followers of Plutarco Elías Calles. Reflecting a power struggle within the established political elite, this agrarianism never threatened existing political institutions. Based on secondary sources and documents in the Historical Archive of the Secretary of National Defense and the Archive of the Secretary of Agrarian Reform in Mexico, the National Archives, Washington, and the Public Records Office, London.

Economic and Social History

1216   . La participación campesina y el cambio político en
México: La influencia de los grupos agraristas en la
postulación del general Lázaro Cárdenas, 1928-1934.
Mexico: UNAM, 1975.
Agrarianism.

1217 GONZALEZ NAVARRO, MOISES. La Confederación Nacional Campesina:
Un grupo de presión en la reforma agraria mexicana. Mexico:
B. Costa-Amic, 1968.
A detailed study, well-documented, of the various ante-
cedents of the National Peasant Confederation (CNC).
Traces its origins, its relations with the official party,
and its struggle to defend the campesinos.

1218 LERNER, VICTORIA. "El reformismo de la década de 1930 en
México." HM 26 (Oct.-Dec. 1976): 188-215.
Essay on Mexican government's economic policies during
the 1930s, especially the roles of an "incipient industrial
bourgeoisie," and the small landed proprietors. Suggests
that there was a shift away from reformism in the late 1930s.

1219 LOMBARDO TOLEDANO, VICENTE. Carta a la juventud; sobre la
Revolución Mexicana: Su orígen, desarrollo y perspectivas.
Mexico: Sindicato Nacional de los Trabajadores del Estado,
1960.
Revolutionary history by CTM labor leader.

1220 MICHAELS, ALBERT L. "Nationalism and Internationalism in the
Mexican Labor Movement under the Government of Lázaro
Cárdenas, 1933-1940." Studies on Latin America (SUNY,
Buffalo) 9 (1968): 59-82.

1221   . "Lázaro Cárdenas y la lucha por la independencia
económica de México." HM 18 (July-Sept. 1968): 56-78.
Suggests that strident economic nationalism was delayed
during the years 1917-1934 because of the demands for a
stable economy. The Depression of 1929 made many Mexicans
argue for national self-sufficiency, which was expressed
in the Six-Year Plan of 1934, the Laws of Nationalization
(1934), and the Laws of Expropriation (1936). Concludes
that the nationalization of the oil industry and the railroads were unique cases forced on Cárdenas, rather than
part of a systematic policy to achieve autarky.

The Cârdenas Era, 1934-1940

Economic and Social History

1222 _____. "Fascism and Sinarquism: Popular Nationalism
Against the Mexican Revolution." Journal of Church and
State 8 (1966): 234-50.
A study of Dorados, right wing groups, and the Falange
in Mexico during the 1930s.

1223 MILLON, ROBERT PAUL. Mexican Marxist: Vicente Lombardo
Toledano. Chapel Hill: University of North Carolina
Press, 1966.
Describes and corroborates Toledano's orthodox Marxist
analysis of Mexican history, approves of his tactics, and
predicts the success of his movement. An intellectual
biography of the CTM's most important labor leader.

1224 ROSS, DELMER G. "The Workers' Administration of the National
Railways of Mexico." Revista Interamericana 2 (1973):
587-96.
Because of labor support for his government, President
Lázaro Cárdenas turned over control of the nationalized
railroads to their employees in 1938. By 1940 worker
administration had proven inefficient and responsible for
numerous accidents. As a result, the government assumed
direct control of the industry. The experience with the
railroads influenced the government not to try worker
administration of other nationalized industries. Based on
primary and secondary works.

1225 SILVA HERZOG, JESUS. La expropriación del petróleo en México.
Mexico: Cuadernos Americanos, 1963.
A well-documented study of the expropriation situation.
Presents a panorama of the circumstances that made possible
the action of the Mexican government. Author had firsthand
contact with the expropriation situation, and wrote his
UNAM thesis on this topic. Contains historical data on
the industry, the foreign companies, the texts of laws,
reports, contracts, etc.

1226 TANZER, MICHAEL. "Public Energy in a Private Economy: Mexico."
In The Political Economy of International Oil and the
Underdeveloped Countries, pp. 288-303. Boston: Beacon
Press, 1969.
Analysis of PEMEX's performance in developing Mexico's
economy. Includes tables on PEMEX exploration investment,
DFC rate of return on exploration investment (1938-1959),
and DFC rate of return on PEMEX refining investment (1938-
1967). Concludes that PEMEX is the model for other countries
wanting to nationalize their oil.

Economic and Social History

1227   ZAVALA ECHAVARRIA, IVAN. "El estado y el movimiento obrero
        mexicano durante el Cardenismo." Estudios Políticos 3
        (1978): 5-19.
            A systematic model of the relationship between the
        Mexican government and the labor movement during the admin-
        istration of Lázaro Cárdenas, 1936-40. Contrary to
        traditional interpretation, Cárdenas was neither an
        unequivocal foe of the Regional Confederation of Mexican
        Labor (CROM) nor an ardent ally of the Marxist Confederation
        of Mexican Workers (CTM). Presidential policy aimed at
        the creation of a strong centralized labor union and avoided
        direct confrontation with the CROM. The Cárdenas adminis-
        tration even sided with CROM during intraunion disputes
        with the larger CTM. However, because of CROM's past
        political affiliations, conservative ideology, and notorious
        corruption, Cárdenas relegated it to second place in the
        Mexican labor movement. CROM wavered between conditional
        support and reserved criticism of the president. Cárdenas,
        on the other hand, favored the CTM because its Marxist
        ideology supported his economic nationalism and regulation
        of private enterprise. He limited its influence, however,
        by forbidding it to organize the peasantry or the bureaucracy
        and denying it direct access to government policy-making.
        Based on published government and union records, memoirs,
        and secondary sources.

For reflections of Lombardo Toledano see entry 568; for an interview
with Toledano see entry 585. For agrarian conflict in Atencingo
see entry 499; for the campesinos of Morelos see entry 504. For the
social and economic thought of Cárdenas see entry 1246.

RELIGIOUS AND CHURCH HISTORY

1228   BROWN, LYLE C. "Mexican Church-State Relations, 1933-1940."
        Journal of Church and State 6 (Spring 1964): 202-22.
            Emphasizes the Church's opposition to the revision of
        the third constitutional article, as well as the advancement
        of relations between the Church and the State beginning
        in 1936. After 1936 Church-State relations improved slowly
        so that by the end of the decade a truce was effected
        which allowed Cárdenas to push reforms in other areas.

1229   MABRY, DONALD J. Mexico's Acción Nacional: A Catholic
        Alternative to Revolution. Syracuse, N.Y.: Syracuse
        University Press, 1973.

A history of the Partido de Acción Nacional (PAN) from
its beginnings in 1938 through 1972, with an analysis of
the party's doctrine, program, structure, membership, and
leadership. Considered as the Mexican response to the
twentieth-century Catholic reform impulse in Latin America;
that is, PAN was a Mexican Christian Socialist party.
Originally it was composed of Catholic dissidents, middle-
class groups, and captains of enterprise and finance opposed
to Cárdenas's socialism. Argues that PAN reached the limits
of its influence in the 1970s. Based on interviews with
party leaders and party records.

1230   MICHAELS, ALBERT L. "The Modification of the Anti-Clerical
Nationalism of the Mexican Revolution by General Lázaro
Cárdenas and its Relationship to the Church-State Détente
in Mexico." *Americas* 26 (July 1969): 35-53.
An analysis of the politics of the Mexican government
toward the Catholic Church between 1934-1940, with emphasis
upon the chaotic years of 1934-1936, when Cárdenas began
to change governmental policy from anticlericalism to
conciliation.

1231   SAUER, FRANZ von. The Alienated "Loyal" Opposition: Mexico's
Partido Acción Nacional. Albuquerque: University of New
Mexico Press, 1974.
A judicious account of PAN's origins, political history,
beliefs, and prospects.

For Church-State relations in Veracruz see entry 507. For the Church-
State dispute over education see entry 1145.

HISTORY OF EDUCATION

1232   BRITTON, JOHN A. "Teacher Unionization and the Corporate
State in Mexico, 1931-1945." HAHR 59 (Nov. 1979): 674-90.
A study of the extension of government influence over
Mexican education and the teachers' unions. In addition
to this political subordination, the government used
education as a means of spreading literacy and technical
training to both rural and urban lower classes.

1233   _____. Educación y radicalismo en Mexico. Vol. 2, Los
Años de Cárdenas. Mexico: SepSetentas, 1976.
Two themes are developed: a) the adoption of Marxism by
the Secretariat of Public Education and the conflict this
generated during the 1930s; b) the institutional development

History of Education

and expansion of the Secretariat and the issues associated
with the unionization of teachers during the Cárdenas era.
See also entry 1158.

1234 _____. "Urban Education and Social Change in the Mexican
Revolution, 1931-40." Journal of Latin American Studies
5 (Nov. 1973): 233-45.
Illustrates the shift in the Mexican Revolution from the
country to the city and industrialization in the activities
of the Ministry of Education. Four successive ministers
and their associates challenged the National University, the
Catholic school system, and public secondary schools. They
suggested that public institutions should no longer copy
the traditional liberal arts curriculum. They created a
three-stage technical school system, culminating in the
university-level Instituto Politécnico Nacional. They
increased the number of public and urban secondary schools
and gradually assumed control over many private secondary
schools. Finally, they attempted but failed to create a
complete and separate system of education for urban working-
class children. Marxism was the intellectual rationalization
for all four ministers, who "wanted to use urban education
to improve the condition of the lower classes and, at the
same time, counter the influence" of traditional, elitist,
conservative values. Based on ministers' Memorias in the
Secretaría de Educación Pública, newspapers, and secondary
works.

1235 CORDOVA, ARNALDO. Los maestros rurales como agentes del
sistema político en el cardenismo. Mexico: UNAM n.d.
Rural education under Cárdenas. A publication of the
Center of Latin American Studies at UNAM (Series avances
de investigación, no. 8).

1236 LERNER, VICTORIA. "Historia de la reforma educativa--1933-
1945." HM 29 (July-Sept. 1979): 91-132.
A study of the socioeconomic background to progressive
reforms in education, beginning with the reform legislation
of 1933 and ending with the overthrow of cooperative and
socialist education in 1945. Notes that most educational
reforms coincided with presidential campaigns, that is,
1934, 1939, and 1945.

1237 MORA FORERO, JORGE. "Los maestros y la práctica de la
educación socialista." HM 29 (July-Sept. 1979): 133-62.

Cultural and Intellectual History

A study of the role of teachers in attempting to
institute socialist education in Cárdenas's Mexico.
Indicates that the majority of teachers were either
indifferent or hostile to socialism and that implementation
of socialism was most limited in most of the states and
regions of the country.

1238   VAZQUEZ de KNAUTH, JOSEFINA Z. "La educación socialista de
        los años treinta." HM 18 (Jan.-Mar. 1969): 408-23.
        Discusses attempts in the 1930s to implement the 1934
        amendment to the constitution that called for public,
        socialist education. Despite a plethora of textbooks and
        teaching manuals, schoolmasters continued in their former
        methods. Moreover, there was no agreement on what
        socialist education was or how to implement it. Based on
        published education reports and secondary works.

For education and the Revolution, 1921-1940, see entry 1161.

CULTURAL AND INTELLECTUAL HISTORY

1239   BELTRAN, GONZALO AGUIRRE. "El pensamiento indigenista de
        Lázaro Cárdenas." América Indígena 31 (1971): 1007-19.
        Analyzes the Indianist policy of Lázaro Cárdenas, who
        promoted the first Inter-American Indian Congress, held
        in Patzcuaro, Michoacán, Mexico, in 1940. The Congress
        had important results, among them the creation of the
        Inter-American Indian Institute. Special emphasis is
        given to cardenista Indianism in relation to its importance
        for Mexico, analyzing it within an historical context.

1240   BLANCO MOHENO, ROBERTO. El cardenismo. Mexico: Editorial
        Libro Mex, 1963.
        Ideology of cardenismo.

1241   MUNOZ COTA, JOSE. "El mirador de la Revolución: Revolución
        y mexicanidad." El Nacional, 13 June 1962.
        Links "lo mexicano" with Revolution to show how they
        became virtually synonymous in meaning.

1242   ROMANELL, PATRICK. "Samuel Ramos on the Philosophy of Mexican
        Culture: Ortega and Unamuno in Mexico." Latin American
        Research Review 10, no. 3 (1975): 81-101.

Cultural and Intellectual History

A study of the thought of Samuel Ramos, Mexico's intellectual pioneer in the movement toward la mexicanidad. Compares Spanish thinkers José Ortega y Gasset and Miguel de Unamuno with Ramos, concluding that Ramos's starting point for his philosophy of Mexican culture was Ortega's point of departure.

1243   SCHMIDT, DONALD L. "The Indigenista Novel and the Mexican Revolution." Americas 33 (April 1977): 652-60.
        A study of the indigenista novel's evolution from a vehicle of social protest during the Cárdenas administration to that of ethnohistory in the 1960s--an evolution that dramatized the socioeconomic issues of the Revolution.

1244   SCHMIDT, HENRY C. The Roots of Lo Mexicano: Self and Society in Mexican Thought, 1900-1934. College Station and London: Texas A&M University Press, 1978.
        Schmidt examines the origins and development of lo mexicano in the works of Samuel Ramos's intellectual antecedents, particularly that of Justo Sierra, Antonio Caso, José Vasconcelos, Alfonso Reyes, and Daniel Cosío Villegas. Last chapter focuses on Ramos's Profile of Man and Culture in Mexico (1934), the work that launched the modern search for Mexico's national identity--an Adlerian psychoanalysis of Mexican culture. Overall, this is a study in the intellectual foundations of nationalism.

1245   SEGOVIA, RAFAEL. "El nacionaismo mexicano: Los programas políticos revolucionarios (1929-1964)." Foro Internacional 8 (1968): 349-59.
        Revolutionary nationalism.

1246   SILVA HERZOG, JESUS. Lázaro Cárdenas: Su pensamiento económico, social y político. Mexico: Editorial Nuestro Tiempo, 1975.
        Economic, social, and political thought of Cárdenas from 1931 until September, 1970.

For a bibliography of works produced by Samuel Ramos see entry 154.

Subject Index

Name Index

Guillén, Flavio, 631
Guillén, Pedro, 632-33
Guisa y Azevedo, Jesús, 562, 634-35, 1057
Guizar Oceguera, José, 563
Gurría Lacroix, Jorge, 203
Gustafson, Milton O., 91
Gutiérrez Crespo, Horacio, 636
Guy, Alain, 745
Guzmán, Martín Luis, 637, 849-50

Haddox, John H., 638-39
Haigh, Roger M., 81
Hale, Charles A., 204-206, 811
Hale, Richard W., Jr., 92
Haley, P. Edward, 948
Hall, Linda B., 351, 851, 1083
Hallewell, Laurence, 107
Hamer, Philip M., 93
Hamilton, Nora, 1180
Hammond, George P., 94
Hamon, James L., 746
Hancock, Richard, 244
Hanrahan, Gene Z., 525
Hansen, Edward C., 808
Hansen, Roger D., 337, 400
Hansis, Randall, 1084
Haro, Robert P., 59
Harper, James W., 949
Harrer, Hans-Jurgen, 852
Harris, Charles H., III, 950-51
Harrison, John P., 117
Hart, John Mason, 747-49, 1008-1009
Hetley, James C., 640
Hellman, Judith Adler, 277
Henderson, Peter V.N., 95
Hendricks, William, 750
Hennessy, Alistair, 207
Herman, Donald L., 1181
Hernández, Octavio, 254
Hernández, Salomé, 751
Hernández, Salvador, 1010
Hernández García, Beatriz, 641
Hernández Molina, Moisés, 752
Hernández R., Rosaura, 753
Hileman, Sam, 448
Hill, Larry D., 952
Hillman, Jacqueline K., 450
Hilton, Stanley E., 1145
Hindman, E. James, 1104

Hinkle, Stacy C., 953
Hoffman, Abraham, 1126, 1200
Horcasitas, Fernando, 564-66
Horn, James J., 1105-1108
Houston, Donald E., 853
Hubbel, Linda S., 1058
Hubermann, Leo, 324
Huitrón, Jacinto, 1011
Huizer, Gerrit, 401
Humphreys, Robert A., 124

Ianni, Octavio, 1182
Iduarte, Andrés, 1085
Iglesia, Ramón, 212
Iguíniz, Juan Bautista, 15
Iturriaga de la Fuente, José, 254, 1127
Iturribarría, Jorge Fernando, 754

Jacobs, Ian, 351
Jacques, Leo M., 488
Jamail, Milton H., 169
Javier Arenas, Francisco, 642
Jiménez, Luz, 564-66
Johnson, Charles W., 16
Johnson, William Weber, 279
Jones, Cecil Knight, 3
Joseph, Gilbert M., 190, 351, 489-90
Juárez, Nicandro F., 1166

Kane, N. Stephen, 1109-11
Karsen, Sonja P., 643
Katz, Friedrich, 266, 313, 337, 351, 419, 755-57, 854, 954-56, 1012-14
Kautsky, John H., 344
Keesing, Donald B., 402
Kelly, James R., 758
Kerig, Dorothy Pierson, 957
Kirchner, Louisa D., 1059
Kitchens, John W., 759
Knaster, Meri, 174-75
Knight, Alan S., 351, 958
Knowlton, Robert J., 760
Knudson, Jerry W., 855, 1060
Koslow, Lawrence E., 97
Kossok, Manfred, 345
Koster, C.J., 124
Krauze, Enrique, 278, 644, 1061

269

Wilkie, James W., 183, 207–208,
    245, 248–49, 311–12, 327–28,
    453, 545, 585, 1033, 1157,
    1198
Wilkie, Richard W., 426
William, John B., 507
Wionczek, Miguel S., 427
Woldenberg, José, 150
Wolf, Donna M., 428
Wolf, Eric R., 429–30, 808
Wolfskill, George, 313, 823, 854,
    887, 1078, 1211
Womack, John, Jr., 183, 207–208,
    250–52, 337, 339, 402, 419,
    422, 821, 1040–43
Woods, Richard D., 165

Yáñez, Agustín, 340, 1077
Yeager, Gene, 809
Young, Desmond, 704

Zamora, José H., 314
Zantwijk, R.A.M. van, 463
Zavala, Silvio, 212
Zavala Echavarría, Iván, 1227
Zayas Enríquez, Rafael de, 810
Zea, Leopoldo, 811
Zeuske, Max, 345
Zevada, Ricardo J., 705
Zilinskas, Raymond, 990
Zimmerman, Irene, 32
Zonn, Leo E., 812
Zorrilla, Luis G., 384
Zubatsky, David S., 134
Zuno, Jose G., 508